BY THE SAME AUTHOR

War of Words: Memoir of a South African Journalist

Nelson Mandela

Drawing Fire: Investigating the Accusations of Apartheid in Israel

Robert Mangaliso Sobukwe: New Reflections (editor)

Shared Histories: A Palestine-Israel Dialogue (co-editor)

Southern African Muckraking; 300 Years of Journalism that has Shaped the Region (part-author)

1938: Why We Must Pay Close Attention Today (part-author)

Registered

R ROBBENEILAND
ROBBEN ISLAND
No 2860

Mr Benjamin Pogrund
P.O. Box 1138,
Johannesburg

Robben Island Gaol,
Robben Island.
8th January, 1969.

Dear Pogrund,

Dearest Bengie,

Thank you for your letter
of 18th December. I am thankful to
to learn that you are all right. You
have been through a great deal, Bengie,
and it shows an extremely high standard of
consideration on your part - in light
of my interests, the

HOW CAN MAN DIE BETTER

THE LIFE OF ROBERT SOBUKWE

Benjamin Pogrund

JONATHAN BALL PUBLISHERS
JOHANNESBURG & CAPE TOWN

For
Miliswa, Dalindyebo, Dedanizizwe, Dinilesizwe,
Jennifer, Amanda, Daniel, Gideon

All rights reserved.
No part of this publication may be reproduced or transmitted,
in any form or by any means, without prior permission
from the publisher or copyright holder.

© Benjamin Pogrund, 1990

Originally published in 1990 by
Peter Halban Publishers, London &
Rutgers University Press, New Brunswick, New Jersey, in 1991

First South African edition published in 1990 in hard cover by
JONATHAN BALL PUBLISHERS (PTY) LTD

Reprinted by Jonathan Ball Publishers in paperback in
1997, 2003, 2005, 2006, 2008, 2009 and 2011

This edition published in 2025 by
JONATHAN BALL PUBLISHERS
A division of Media24 Limited
PO Box 33977
Jeppestown
2043

ISBN 978-1-77619-511-4
ebook ISBN 978-1-86842-682-9

jonathanball.co.za
facebook.com/JonathanBallPublishers
x.com/JonathanBallPub

Cover photos by Universal History Archive and Bettmann

Introduction

This book was born in anger. I wrote it in London, after forced emigration from apartheid South Africa. I was deputy editor of the *Rand Daily Mail* in Johannesburg. We paid the price for being too successful in exposing and opposing the evils of apartheid: our owners, the Anglo American Corporation, which dominated the country's economy, closed us down in cooperation with the Afrikaner Nationalist government. After 26 years on the *Mail*, I was so closely identified with it that I could not get another job. I was rejected by other newspapers and by many in the ruling white community. I was grateful to Britain for giving me sanctuary, but I was angry.[1]

I moved to London to become foreign editor of *Today*, a new venture in journalism: a serious daily newspaper in tabloid form. It did not last, and I was made redundant. With a generous payoff, I decided to stay home for a few months and write a book about my friend, Robert Mangaliso Sobukwe.

I sat at my desk, looking through the window at the London sky, often blue, often grey, and thought back to South Africa. I read through the piles of documents and newspaper reports accumulated over the years, and my anger grew hotter: I thought about the cruelty imposed on Robert Sobukwe because of his singular leadership in seeking to end apartheid; that white authority had feared him so much that he was kept in one or other form of imprisonment for the last 18 years of his life, with six years in solitary confinement; and how his early death could have been avoided. I thought about my friend, who endured so much giving service to his people, always with dignity and courage.

My anger spilt into words. Then I came across Primo Levi, an Italian Jewish chemist who was a member of the anti-fascist resistance. He was arrested and in February 1944 was consigned to the Nazi extermination camp, Auschwitz, in Poland. Hundreds of thousands,

---

1 The story is told in *War of Words: Memoir of a South African Journalist* by Benjamin Pogrund, foreword by Sir Harold Evans, published by Seven Stories Press, New York and London, 2000; and M&G Books, Johannesburg, 2000.

mainly Jews, were murdered there and their bodies incinerated. Levi survived until the camp was liberated on 27 January 1945. His first book, *If This Is a Man*, was published in 1947.

I spent days reading. It was like no other book I had ever read, and I often stopped to reflect on Levi's descriptions of his experiences and how he survived. He was driven by a will to live so that he could tell the world what he had seen. I was astonished how he wrote about humanity in the midst of inhumanity. I sometimes found myself laughing out loud—humour in a death camp!

Primo Levi taught me: speak quietly when you describe evil and suffering. I had already written about a quarter of my planned text about Sobukwe. I went back to it, starting on page one, and went line by line, crossing out adjectives. I was still intensely angry, but I lowered my voice.

Apartheid still ruled in South Africa, so I had to disguise some of my sources to save them from possible persecution. I wasn't sure that a book about Sobukwe could be legally published in South Africa, so I wrote for a British readership, wondering all the time how much detail I could give to people who had limited knowledge and interest.

I didn't have a publisher. I got lucky. My wife, Anne, was (and is) an artist and was drawing covers for Peter Halban Publishers, who specialised in books of Jewish interest. The movie *Cry Freedom*, about Steve Biko and Donald Woods, was running in London. Peter saw it and was stirred into wanting to publish a book about South Africa. He asked Anne: did she perhaps know anyone writing a book?

Peter published and so did Rutgers University Press in the US. Jonathan Ball, founder of the publishing firm that bears his name, read the book. My fears were groundless: he was enthusiastic, published the book and went on backing it with repeated editions and printings. So did publishing director Jeremy Boraine (whose father, Alex, a Methodist and political leader, had prayed with Sobukwe). Equally warm support and encouragement has come from current publishing director Annie Olivier.

In 2019, Jonathan Ball Publishers issued a follow-up book, *Robert Mangaliso Sobukwe: New Reflections*, my edited collection of 19 essays by talented thinkers who assessed Sobukwe's legacy.

It is 35 years since *How Can Man Die Better* first appeared. The original text remains the same. An expanding Epilogue has updated the story from time to time. There are 40 photographs. This book is not, and was never intended to be, a treatise about Pan-Africanism. It is a personal book about an extraordinary man and about our unusual, intertwined lives.

Unfortunately, a jarring note needs to be publicised: the ignorance and misinformation that tarnish Sobukwe's memory. Among the worst is a claim that on Robben Island they 'fed him pieces of broken glass mixed with his food, poisoned him in secret, and when he developed traces of lung cancer they banished him to Galeshewe township in Kimberley.' There is not a single word of truth in this; the broken-glass detail seems to be a twisted version of an episode I describe in the following pages, and the rest is equally rubbish. Another claim derives from the fact that no recordings of Sobukwe's voice are available; this, some darkly say, is the result of a conspiracy – by whom it is not clear—to silence him. This too is nonsense. In the late 1950s, tape recorders were not in everyday use; from 21 March 1960 onwards, and for the next 18 years until his death, Sobukwe was in prison or under severe personal restrictions and recording was not possible. It would have been a serious offence to record him. No one did it. I dared not do it because both of us were under constant Security Police surveillance.

The memory of Robert Sobukwe remains strong and I am more grateful than ever to all those who have helped to keep it so by sharing their experiences and views about this 'parfit gentle' man. Zondeni Veronica 'Zodwa' Sobukwe and I were friends for many years; she gave support in the writing of this book and read the original text. Her life of sacrifice and devotion to her husband and their children ended at the age of 91 on 15 August 2018. She was followed by the death of Dini on 5 June 2019, and Dedani on 21 August 2022.

As I said in the original edition, I owe particular thanks to the late Randolph Vigne, who read the original text and offered a host of informed and constructive comments; to the late Hamilton Zolile Keke, who was always cheerfully willing to share his knowledge; and to the late Dennis Siwisa, who read the text and was a source of invaluable information. Simon Richardson was an authoritative and cooperative editor and his imprint remains on the text.

I thank Humphrey Tyler for permission to publish his report on the Sharpeville shooting; Jan Tystad for allowing reproduction of his report in *Dagbladet*, Oslo; *The Times*, London, for permission to publish excerpts from a column by Nicholas Ashford, an admired friend who died young; and *The New York Times* in regard to a column by the late Anthony Lewis.

For later editions I gained much from hours of discussion with Dr Derek Hook of Duquesne University, in Pittsburgh. His quality is seen in his perceptive comments, which provide a fitting end to the Epilogue. He has given great service to the world with two books, both published by Wits University Press: *Lie on Your Wounds* (2019), Sobukwe's prison correspondence: and *Darkest Before Dawn* (2024), writings, testimonies and correspondence from Sobukwe's life.

Despite the help and goodwill of so many people, I bear full responsibility for all information and views.

Finally, appreciation for my daughter, Jennifer Solange Pogrund, for whom 'Uncle Bob' was an everyday although distant presence throughout childhood. And my deepest gratitude to Anne for sharing so much with me and Bob, and for lovingly sharing with me the adventures of life, the joys and the burdens, in the years since then.

BENJAMIN POGRUND
January 2025

Preface

> Then out spake brave Horatius,
> The Captain of the Gate;
> 'To every man upon this earth
> Death cometh soon or late.
> And how can man die better
> Than facing fearful odds,
> For the ashes of his fathers,
> And the temples of the Gods?'
>
> Thomas Babington Macaulay:
> *Lays of Ancient Rome, Horatius*

As the sky began to lighten on a late summer's morning in South Africa, Robert Mangaliso Sobukwe left his home in Soweto to walk to the nearest police station. He was going to demand that he be arrested.

Six other men were with him. Three more joined them during their walk of 4.5 kilometres. All were blacks.* Each newcomer received a salute, right hand raised, the palm open, and a sonorous greeting *'iAfrika'* – Zulu and Xhosa for 'O Africa!' Each responded with the same salute and the cry, *'Izwe Lethu'* – 'Our Country'.

*Unfortunately, it is not yet possible to write about South Africa without constant references to racial groups. That is what apartheid has been about, and to avoid references would be both confusing and require a distortion of reality.

There is no universal agreement about the terms to be used and usage in any event changes from time to time. The words I generally use are: Asians, blacks, coloureds and whites.

Benjamin Pogrund

Workers on their way to trains and buses to get to jobs in the city of Johannesburg looked at them with curiosity; some greeted them, others hurried to be away from them.

An hour later, by 7.30 a.m., Sobukwe and the small group were at the Orlando police station, a single-storeyed building, the walls and roof made of corrugated iron. They halted outside the high wire-mesh fence and waited for others to arrive. They were uncertain about how many might come. Eventually, about 200 men gathered there, with a cluster of women to wish them well.

It was Monday, 21 March 1960. For Sobukwe, it was the day that South Africa was to be transformed by what he had termed 'positive action' against the pass laws.

Until abolished in July 1986, these laws were the basic method used by white authority to control the country's black majority. The laws determined where blacks could live and work, and even what work they could do. Every black adult, both men and women, had to carry an identity document—the 'pass'. Officially, it was known as a reference book. Blacks, however, called it the *dompas*—Afrikaans for 'stupid pass'.

The pass had to be carried at all times, to be instantly produced when demanded by a policeman. Failure to have the pass available courted instant arrest, prosecution and a fine or jailing. Even more important, the pass contained details of a black person's status: whether he was allowed to be in a particular area or city. A person found where his pass did not specify he was allowed to be was also subject to immediate arrest.

In 1958, the number of convictions of blacks under the various control laws—considerably less than the number of arrests—was 396,836. This was an average of 1,087 on each day of the year, weekends included, in a total black population of less than eleven million. The pass laws were responsible for about one-third of the criminal convictions of black people.

The pass laws were hated as the tangible evidence of black subjugation, and for their ravaging effects on the lives of millions upon millions of people.

Sobukwe had called on blacks to end the pass laws by making the system inoperable through mass arrests, thus clogging the courts and the prisons by weight of numbers. On 21 March he was giving the lead and doing precisely what he had asked others to do: to leave their passes at home and to go to police stations to demand arrest. It was the first major public campaign of his organisation, the Pan-Africanist Congress, formed a bare eighteen months earlier in a breakaway from the old-established African National Congress.

The 200 or so men who offered themselves for arrest at the Orlando police station represented not much more than a couple of days' work for a Bantu Commissioner's court where a magistrate usually disposed of a pass case in a few minutes. Taking the plea, hearing evidence and passing sentence was done in sausage-machine style.

It was a deceptively small start to a day which was to transform South Africa.

1

Robert Mangaliso Sobukwe was born in Graaff-Reinet, known as The Gem of the Karoo, in the south-east of South Africa. The Karoo is a vast semi-arid stretch in the centre of the country, but Graaff-Reinet, on its eastern edge, has the blessing of water from the Sundays River, so it is green and fertile. The town was founded in 1786, when the Cape was under the control of Holland, and was named after the governor of the time, Cornelius Jakob Van de Graaff, and his wife, Reinet.

The early history of the town was associated with dissent. At the turn of the eighteenth century, Dutch frontiersmen rebelled against the colonial government in Cape Town, a long 680 kilometres away, apparently because they wanted a more aggressive military policy against the indigenous Xhosa blacks. This led to a shortlived republic. But, with this in the past, the town settled into a rural tranquillity. As it grew it followed the normal South African pattern of a 'white' town with a separate 'location' a distance away for the 'non-whites', in this case a mixture of blacks and mixed-race coloureds. At the start of the 1920s, the official population count was 10,717: 5,139 whites, 3,677 coloureds, 1,883 blacks, and 18 Asians.

Throughout, the town's whites have been predominantly Afrikaners. They are fiercely and proudly so, judging from the view of a retired Security policeman: in March 1984, Lieutenant Hendrik Cornelius Jakobus Pitout, testifying in a civil action brought against him and others by a detainee alleging torture told the judge: 'I come from Graaff-Reinet where even the dogs bark in Afrikaans.'

The 'white' town lies in a hollow and has become renowned for its restoration and preservation of old buildings in the attractive Cape Dutch style. Prosperity once came from ostrich feathers but this has been replaced by income from the district's sheep and fruit.

Driving on the road that leads to Johannesburg the other half of Graaff-Reinet is just outside the town, on a hill on the right-hand side. An effort has been made to prettify it and, from the road, the pinks, blues and yellows of the small houses look charming. Close up, however, the location is as ramshackle, deprived and smelling of bucket latrines as other such places in South Africa, and it has no doubt always been so.

Sobukwe was born in a house near the top of the hill on 5 December 1924. His birth was not registered with the authorities, a common omission among blacks until recent times. His father was Hubert Sobukwe, whose father in turn had come from what was then Basutoland, and is now Lesotho. The family left Basutoland sometime before the Anglo-Boer War of 1899–1902, the war between Britain and the Afrikaners of South Africa. But only after the war did they come south and settle in Graaff-Reinet. Sobukwe's mother, Angelina, was a Pondo of the Xhosa tribe. She grew up in Graaff-Reinet, where she and Hubert met, married and spent their lives. They had seven children, six boys and a girl, but three of the boys died at early ages.

Sobukwe was the youngest child. As was normal at the time, he was given an 'English' name, Robert, as well as a Xhosa name, Mangaliso—meaning 'It is wonderful'. His brothers who survived were Ernest, born in 1914, and Charles, born in 1922; his sister was Eleanor.

The brick building in which Sobukwe grew up at first had earth floors, but later wooden floors were laid. The windows were small but had glass panes. There was no electricity. A sewerage system was provided by an outhouse and a town-run bucket service. Water had to be brought from the open street furrows in the town about half a mile away; later, a tap was installed outside the house.

In the custom of the time, few blacks bought what was called 'European' furniture. Instead, tables, chairs and cupboards were put together by 'bush carpenters'. An old iron bed served for Hubert and Angelina while, for years, the children slept on the floor on mattresses of jute bags once used for packing wool.

Hubert first worked for the local municipality, keeping open the furrows that supplied the town's water. Then he worked in a store sorting wool and labelling the bags. He also had a part-time occupation and income as a woodcutter, buying wood at the market in the town, taking it home and chopping it up to sell as firewood in the location. The children helped take turns at getting up at about 3 a.m. to make coffee and to sort out the logs for Hubert to chop up when he returned at the end of the day from his job at the store. Angelina, as well as looking after the house, worked for a number of years as a cook at the town hospital and then did domestic work for a white family. Together they earned enough to make sure that the family did not go short of food. The children were given new clothes as Christmas gifts, to be used as Sunday best, and the previous Sunday best was brought into everyday school use.

Thus far it is a picture of a hard and simple life which could be repeated ten thousandfold throughout South Africa. An extra ingredient, however, was the emphasis placed in the home on education. Angelina had never been to school and her thumbprint served as her signature. Hubert had completed seven years of schooling. He had wanted to continue, but his mother was dead and a sister who was bringing him up refused to send him to high school: she feared that, if he was educated, he would ignore her and the family. Hubert's disappointment lived with him, and it drove him to encourage his children. According to his son Ernest he had made a vow: should God give him children, he would educate them all. He determinedly fulfilled that pledge.

When Eleanor passed her eighth year of schooling she did not want to continue and went out to work. But Ernest completed his schooling, qualified as a teacher, went on to train as a minister, and eventually was ordained a bishop in the Anglican Church. Charles also qualified as a teacher. So too did Robert, who in due course went on to complete several university degrees.

The initial stimulus came from books in the house. Angelina brought books given by the young son and daughter of the family for whom she worked, and Hubert brought books discarded by the town's library. Hubert read the books and passed them on to his children.

In addition to the stress on reading, there was a strong religious spirit in the Sobukwe house. The family was Methodist and Hubert was a highly respected member of the location's congregation—so much so that, during his lifetime, the street in which he lived was named after him. It is still Sobukwe Street. Regular church attendance on Sunday was obligatory for the children. After the service, each child was required to repeat the text and outline the sermon. 'If you didn't know it, Daddy gave it to you,' according to Ernest—

meaning that there was an immediate infliction of Hubert's *sjambok* (rawhide whip) on the backside—'He was a loving but stern father.' Angelina, on the other hand, was a quieter person who merely scolded the children; only when they were older did she, if necessary, give them a clout.

Formal schooling was provided by a Methodist mission in the location, at the foot of the hill on the main road—actually the church in which the Sunday services were conducted. The pews were used as desks. About 100 children, divided into four classes, were taught at the same time. Reflecting the location's racial mix, the children were blacks and coloureds. The Methodist school went only as far as the sixth year of education. By then the odds were that many children would have dropped out because of the poverty of their parents. Those who were still persevering switched, for the next two years, to the Anglican school in the town where there were proper classrooms and desks. Sobukwe, aged 11, was clearly a suitable candidate for the Anglican school even though, as he said many years later, his standard of English was 'not good'. Sobukwe and his brother Charles went into the same class and were the only ones to pass out of thirteen pupils.

This was the limit of the education provided in Graaff-Reinet for blacks and coloureds. Any further schooling that was wanted had to be sought elsewhere. But the groundwork for a pattern of study had been laid: 'Daddy's law was that before you go and play outside, do your homework,' according to Ernest. 'The homework had to be done while there was sunlight. In the evening we could read using the light from paraffin lamps.'

Then a serious setback occurred: there wasn't enough money to enable Sobukwe and his brother to continue at school. Primary schooling was free, but fees were needed for the next stage of high school. So he and Charles remained at home for the next two years. Sobukwe repeated the Standard 6 level.

During his teens he also had to undergo the rite of passage from boyhood into manhood. His father adhered to traditional beliefs in this respect. For the tribal initiation ceremonies, Sobukwe went with other youngsters into the bush for two to three weeks, smearing his body with ochre-coloured clay. He and his companions were kept in a hut isolated from others, and especially from women, and given instruction in the ways of the tribe. An elder of the tribe circumcised them. That ordeal over, Sobukwe changed the clay on his body to white. A feast marked the end of the ceremonies, with cows provided by the parents for slaughter, and much beer to be drunk. The initiation custom was strongly maintained then; over the years it has weakened, and nowadays, although many young men still go into the bush, often they first have the circumcision done by a doctor.

Sobukwe's chance to continue his schooling, in company with his brother, came in 1940 when he was 15. The mere fact that he was stepping up into the secondary school level put him into the élite: in that year only 5,808 black children—1.25 per cent of the total enrolment, which was in turn only part of those of schoolgoing age because there was no compulsory education for blacks—were in secondary schools. The figure for white children was 16.4 per cent.

The Sobukwe family's Methodist adherence made it natural for him to be sent to Healdtown, even though it was some 225 kilometres from home. Healdtown was then a major institution in black education, one of several schools in the Eastern Cape established by British missionaries in the nineteenth century. They provided a Christian and a liberal arts education founded on English grammar and literature which profoundly influenced generations of students. 'In general, native secondary education tends to be very bookish and academic in nature largely because of financial considerations,' an educationist, P.A.W. Cook, wrote in 1949. Afrikaner Nationalists applied the derisory and angry tag of 'black Englishmen' to the products of this education. After coming to power in 1948, the Afrikaner government rapidly enforced its own views of what black education should be about and set out to destroy all that had gone before.

But that was still to come when, in January 1940, Sobukwe arrived at Healdtown for the start of the new academic year. It was still in the 'great days' of black education, as the Reverend Stanley Pitts, who was Principal from 1950, puts it.

Healdtown was a co-educational academic institution sited on a hill looking out over a large and fertile valley. It embraced a wide range of schooling, starting with the beginners in lower primary and extending to the end-of-schooling matriculation. It also provided teacher training, specialist physical education training and courses in domestic science. It was, in its time, the biggest Methodist educational centre in South Africa, with 1,400 students, most of whom—like Sobukwe—were boarders. The majority of the staff came from Britain and were not ministers but trained teachers. Traditionally, teaching staff were whites, but, by the 1940s, Healdtown was beginning to employ blacks. Already in 1936 a black Methodist minister, the Reverend Seth Mokitimi, had been appointed housemaster and chaplain. By the 1950s a 50–50 racial proportion was reached among the staff. Pupils, however, were always blacks only.

The Sobukwe family's shortage of money, apart from the two-year delay it had caused, meant also that career aspirations were limited: Sobukwe enrolled for the NPL, the 'Native Primary Lower', a three-year course which would enable him to qualify as a primary schoolteacher. 'Native' was then the word used for blacks and, as the name indicates, the course was designed to prepare blacks to teach in black schools.

As a newcomer, Sobukwe went into a wooden-floored dormitory of forty beds, twenty lined up along each side and with a small locker in between each one. He kept his clothes in a suitcase stored in a nearby boxroom. He could have access every morning, but he kept his jacket on a hanger on the wall. Greater privacy came with succeeding years: a ten-bed dormitory in the second year, and sharing with four or five others in the third year, until he finally attained the status of a single room. Like other students he was provided with a bed frame and a brightly coloured mattress cover which he filled with straw. He brought his own sheets and blankets from home.

It was at the start of Sobukwe's second year that one of the enduring friendships of his life began—with Dennis Siwisa, who also trained as a teacher, later becoming a journalist. Siwisa recalls many of the details to do with black schooling and Sobukwe's existence in Healdtown . . .

First bell in the morning was at 6 a.m. But Sobukwe usually slept through it, waking for the second bell at 6.30 a.m. He would wash his face and, at the third bell at 6.40, go to the dining hall for breakfast, to sit on a wooden bench without a back at a long wooden table. On the wood-panelled walls were photographs of past Healdtown teachers and of George VI, the then reigning King of England, and of South Africa.

It could hardly have been a plainer meal: a mug of hot to lukewarm water and sugar, plus a big dry piece of bread called *umgqenya* in Xhosa. Anyone who wanted butter and who had money could buy it and store it. After breakfast Sobukwe went back to the dormitory to wash properly. There was no hot water, except for the occasional bucket he was able to wheedle from the 'aunts' who worked in the kitchen. Otherwise in the cold of winter, showers were usually confined to one or two a week after playing sport. 'It was a tough life, but we enjoyed it,' Siwisa remembers.

The spartan routine was at least partly attributable to the poverty-stricken nature of missionary education. The church was responsible for erecting the buildings, with occasional government help. A government capitation grant enabled schooling to be free, but pupils paid for their boarding. Sobukwe had a bursary from Healdtown —whether for his entire studies or only part of it is uncertain—and he was also helped by Ernest.

School began at 8.30 a.m. but was preceded by 'observation'—the custom for the boys to stand outside and watch the girls come from their separated dormitories. Classes went through until 12.45 p.m., with a short break in between, and then it was back to the dining hall for lunch. Tuesdays, Thursdays and Sundays were the days for meat, beans and samp—porridge made from coarsely ground maize (corn); on other days, only samp and beans. Fruit was unknown but occasionally there were vegetables, grown in the gardens. At 2 p.m., Sobukwe resumed classes for another three hours, with either lessons or teaching practice. Then an hour's relaxation—playing tennis or basking in the sun, or walking to the nearby ravine—before supper which was a repetition of breakfast: bread and sugar-water. From 7 p.m. there were two hours of study in his dormitory, with lights out at 9.30 p.m.—electricity had been installed in 1930—but with an extension allowed for examination study.

It wasn't unrelieved academic toil. Wednesday afternoons were set aside for sport and Sobukwe made full use of this. He was a good tennis player, having learnt the game in Graaff-Reinet. He played rugby, at fullback, for his Healdtown house team—Hornabrook, named after an early governor of the institution—and is said to have been a good tackler. Friday afternoons were free and were usually used for relaxing. Saturdays meant competitive sport against other schools, with teams visiting, or Healdtown teams travelling to away games on the back of an open truck.

If not involved in sport, Saturday was the one day on which Sobukwe could ask for permission to walk the 11 kilometres to the village of Fort Beaufort. The attractions and facilities there were extremely limited, and consisting in the main of Cooper's grocery-cum-drapery store and fish and chips shop. But this was the chance to supplement Healdtown's sparse diet and the few sweets available at the small shop in the institution, by buying fish or returning with fruit or the great luxury of tea. Once a month, Saturday night was also 'bioscope' (movie) night, and occasionally a local music troupe came to give a concert. These events were held in the boys' dining hall. The girls were also admitted and this was the chance for couples to sit together, as Sobukwe did when at one time he had a girlfriend.

Saturday was also the day to catch up on chores such as washing shirts, at least for those who had more than the regulation khaki and white, which were the only ones which the laundry accepted. Sobukwe was already set on his lifelong pattern of dressing neatly and quietly. He did not care much for clothing and would say that he was not a 'snob'. At this stage he favoured long khaki trousers for everyday wear when no uniform was required. Sunday was the day for smart and obligatory wear: grey trousers, white shirt, Healdtown's red and yellow striped tie and a blazer complete with badge on the pocket—an eagle with the Latin motto *Alis velut aquilarum surgent* (They shall rise with wings as of eagles).

Sunday, naturally, was a day of rest—but with a compulsory church service and a Scripture class in the morning and communion once a month. Indeed Healdtown's Christian basis was constantly evident: prayers were said before supper each day and the chaplain read from Scripture; grace was said before all meals. Sobukwe was a willing churchgoer: he was religious but not a zealot.

Siwisa's overriding memory of Sobukwe in those Healdtown days is of a 'a happy, contented person'. He was not given to speaking about his future hopes. He spoke to his friends about sport and girls. He was known to his fellow students for 'his brilliance and for his command of the English language'. He invariably carried a library book with him and went through two or three novels a week. His early Healdtown addictions were the Scarlet Pimpernel novels by Baroness Orczy, and The Saint stories by Leslie Charteris. He devoured all he could find until his tastes widened.

Many years later, Sobukwe himself would say: 'I was introduced to English literature at a very early age by my eldest brothers who had a good library. I was also fortunate in the teachers I had. But especially at Healdtown, there was a Mrs Scott who encouraged my reading. It was a love for literature, especially poetry and drama.'

Sobukwe's academic excellence was drawing increasing interest from his teachers: not only Mrs Scott, but also from Hamish Noble, a carpentry teacher who was an assistant boarding school headmaster, and the Principal and his wife, George and Helen Caley.

Once Sobukwe had completed his three-year teacher training at the end of 1942 he was encouraged by the staff not to go off and start earning a living, such as it would be, as a teacher, but to continue his schooling. So promising was he that he was allowed to prepare for the Junior Certificate public examination—the halfway stage towards completing high school—in one year instead of the two, sometimes three, normally required. The permission of the educational authorities was necessary for this. But as the Caleys explained, 'he was such a clever boy'.

In the June 1943 mid-year internal examinations Sobukwe topped the class. But in August, some four months before the final examination, he began to cough up blood. He was found to have the widespread and dreaded disease tuberculosis. His father came to Healdtown to fetch him. 'We had difficulty persuading him not to take Robert home to die, but that he should go to hospital,' say the Caleys. It was, however, not easy to get him a hospital bed. Facilities were limited, especially for blacks. Mr Caley took up the matter and succeeded in getting Sobukwe admitted to what was then the McVicar Hospital for tuberculosis in the nearby small town of Alice.

The next year, early in 1944, Sobukwe had recovered from the TB and repeated his classes. The Caleys, however, say that he did not write the examinations and was promoted to the next class despite this. Mr Caley says he wrote to the Department of Education that this was 'an exceptional case'. Late in the year, only nine months after leaving hospital, Sobukwe was so well recovered that he was able to win the Eastern Province single championships for blacks.

Now, with two years of schooling still to go, he was assured of the bursaries which Healdtown gave to outstanding students. In addition, the Caleys sponsored him, giving him books and pocket money, taking him to the station at Fort Beaufort so that he could go home in the June and December long holidays, and sometimes buying a rail ticket for him. In the aftermath of his TB, they paid for patent medicines: cod liver oil, Metatone tonic and Angiers emulsion to be rubbed on his chest.

He was a 'group captain'—a senior prefect—and in his last year was appointed head boy. He was zealous in his duties. Siwisa recalls that the toilets were outside, about 10 metres from the dormitories, and that the boys would sometimes not bother to go all the way but would urinate in the open. This was viewed as a serious offence in Healdtown's disciplinary system. Some boys were punished for it and one of them accused Sobukwe of lying on a roof to catch them in the act. The accusation was carried over at least a year later to university when he was called a 'sell-out' because of it. He stoutly defended himself, saying he would act in the same way again if he had to track down offenders.

But his academic prowess remained the dominant fact about him. His reputation was so strongly established that the Reverend Stanley Pitts, who became Healdtown's Governor four years after Sobukwe had left, notes that he was 'the brightest student we had'. The Caleys, speaking in 1981 when they were old and frail, still spoke of him with glowing admiration: Mr Caley's constant phrase was that 'he was so clever'; Mrs Caley said 'his command of English was exceptional'. Together, they remembered the farewell end-of-year speech he gave as Healdtown's head boy: 'It was a most remarkable speech, it was a wonderful speech, it was all about co-operation between whites and blacks.'

As expected, he obtained a first-class pass entitling him to go on to university, when he wrote his finals at the end of 1946 at the age of 22. His subjects were English Higher, Physiology and Hygiene, Zoology, Geography, History and Xhosa Higher.

There is a sad postscript to Healdtown. When the Afrikaner Nationalist government moved in on black education during the mid-1950s, the Methodist Church refused to hand over the school buildings. Only part of Healdtown continued as a school; mostly it was abandoned. Over the years, as decay spread, the roofs of the fine buildings fell in and the gardens were no more.

When Sobukwe left for the next stage of his education, he found that most of the country's universities were closed to blacks. Only the universities of Cape Town and the Witwatersrand gave limited access to handfuls of black students. The premier institution for blacks was near Alice—the South African Native College at Fort Hare.

How Can Man Die Better

The college, founded in 1916, was originally intended for blacks, as the title indicated, but also had a small number of white students. Later, there were no white students, but there were coloureds and Asians. The year before Sobukwe enrolled, the college had 324 students: 260 blacks, 29 Asians and 35 coloureds. Only thirty-one of the students were women; fourteen students came from Basutoland and eighteen from other parts of Africa. The teaching staff was overwhelmingly white.

In its time, the college nurtured many blacks who later rose to leadership. Seretse Khama, first President of independent Botswana, was there in 1946. Robert Mugabe, who led the struggle against white rule in Rhodesia and became first Prime Minister of Zimbabwe, graduated in 1941, as did Oliver Tambo, later the President in exile of the African National Congress. And a year before him, Nelson Mandela.

Sobukwe went into the Wesley House hostel. Theoretically, it was supposed to be only for Methodists like him but, in practice, it drew and accepted students of whatever denomination who hailed from the Eastern Cape, just as Methodists and Anglicans from Johannesburg preferred to go to the Anglican Beda Hall. The Presbyterian Iona Hall tended to be for the 'undetermined' like the Basotho.

The undergraduate rivalry was intense: the Wesley students would, with all due arrogance, say of their residence: 'The only House amidst hostels (Iona) and halls (Beda).' Beda students, in turn, boasted their residence held all the 'bright boys'; they referred to the Wesleyans as 'barbarians'. The women students were apart from all this: they had their separate residence, Elukhanyeswini.

Physical conditions at Wesley were considerably better than at Healdtown: as a first-year student Sobukwe was in a wooden-floored dormitory of sixteen beds, with lockers and cupboards. The wake-up bell was at 6 a.m. and breakfast at 7.45 a.m. Hot water was available for showers and baths. Meals were eaten at tables, eight students to a side sitting on chairs. Breakfast was mealie-meal (corn meal) porridge, milk, bread and butter. A private supply of eggs could be left with the usual kitchen 'aunts' for daily frying or boiling. Lunch was samp. It was soul food for Sobukwe and others raised in the Eastern Cape region. Lights out was at 11 p.m., but those who wanted to could stay out until later.

As at Healdtown, Sobukwe did not have much money to spend.

Now and again he received £1 or £2 from his parents or his brother Ernest, apart from money the Caleys sent. But he did not care. He used the money he had to buy tobacco for the pipe he had taken to smoking, or occasionally to buy cigarettes. It does not appear that he had enough money to join one of the 'syndicates' which flourished among students. Carrying strange titles—such as Mandown, because a member had once knocked down another man—the syndicates enabled students to pool slender resources for a once-a-week treat of a meal from Alice's solitary hotel, the Amatola. As it was a 'white' hotel, and in a country village at that, it was inconceivable that black students could use the front door, let alone the dining-room. Instead they went to the kitchen door at the back carrying their own plates and pots, placed their orders—grilled steak was the favourite dish—and returned to their hostel room where primus stoves reheated the food.

Sobukwe's college fees were £55 a year. During each of his three years of study, he received a £20 loan bursary from the Native Trust Fund, which administered income derived from taxation from blacks, and £20 as a Cape Merit Bursary from the provincial Department of Education. Not only did Mr Caley recommend the bursaries, but he and his wife went on giving substantial help: during each of the three years Sobukwe was at Fort Hare, they paid the £15 balance of his tuition fees, and he could buy whatever books he needed at the Lovedale bookshop and send the accounts to the Caleys. They also paid for his examinations—each subject required a fee—and they met his open account at the pharmacy in Alice.

2

Now began a process of fundamental change in Robert Sobukwe. He had just turned 23 when he started at Fort Hare. This would have been a late age for white youngsters going to university. But it was by no means unusual for blacks, who often started their initial primary school several years later than their white counterparts and then dropped out as they waited for vacancies in succeeding levels of the educational system or, as had occurred with Sobukwe, until money was available.

In December 1946, while awaiting the matriculation examination results, Sobukwe still had no interest in issues outside school and sport—as Dennis Siwisa found on a visit. Siwisa was politically active and wanted to share the growing excitement of emerging African Nationalism, with its heady ideas about democracy generated by the Second World War. Siwisa planned to spend a weekend with Sobukwe but was so disappointed in his response that he returned home 'in disgust'.

But even if Sobukwe wasn't at this stage interested in politics, he had pronounced views and soon landed in trouble. His fellow-students chose him to speak at the 'freshers' social'—a social function for new students—at Wesley House. He launched, in his own words, 'a venomous attack' on parochialism and the frivolous attitude of students in the hostel. 'B.A.' (Bachelor of Arts) stood for 'Blinking Ass', he said, because invariably the students were nothing but asses. The 'senior and saner' students, as they referred to themselves, in the conservative Wesley House were incensed at this insulting brashness from a newcomer. A house meeting voted that no one should speak to him for a month.

In 1948, his second year saw the start of his political consciousness. Three influences were at work . . .

First, he decided to do 'Native Administration', as the study of laws controlling blacks was called. In this course he confronted the details of the means whereby blacks were oppressed. It caused him vast shock. Suddenly he became aware of his situation and that of his fellow-blacks in a way that he had never before considered. During his school years he had, of course, like all other pupils, whether black or white, been fed the standard version of South African history which portrayed white settlers engaged on a civilising mission and bravely facing up to marauding black savages. As part of his history studies he had had to deal with the 'Kaffir Wars' of the Eastern Cape frontier during the nineteenth century.

In the 1940s—and today too—'kaffir' was a highly derogatory racial term for blacks: in conversation many years later, Sobukwe said: 'We used the word at school because we had to. We used it—and made sure that we passed our history examinations.'

In everyday life, Sobukwe was subject with all other blacks to the inferiority imposed on those who were not white. This meant not only racial segregation, already established as a tradition in South Africa, but the poverty which went with it. It is astonishing that Sobukwe became conscious of the racial discrimination of which he was a victim only when he was close to his mid-twenties. Could it really be possible for someone to experience the humiliating effects of discrimination in his everyday existence and yet be as unthinking about it as Sobukwe was? It is difficult to credit, given the testimony from teachers and peers about his intelligence and his perceptions. Yet it was so. Obviously he had knowledge because of his own life. But he lacked insight. As he later described his outlook, 'It was just a matter of accepting things as they were.'

There was nothing exceptional about his passivity and indifference. It was the rule among blacks, and was to stretch into the future. The fact of it helps to explain why white minority rule has endured for so long.

If the study of Native Administration opened Sobukwe's eyes and his mind, his developing views were shaped by a second major influence: his relationship with Cecil Ntloko, his lecturer in Native Administration.

Ntloko had matriculated at Healdtown some years ahead of Sobukwe. He taught for a year, studied at Fort Hare and went to the University of Cape Town where he completed a Bachelor of Arts degree. He studied Native Administration, and continued these studies, as well as law, through correspondence courses at the University of South Africa. He went to Fort Hare in 1947 to teach Native Administration, and remained until 1958.

Ntloko had a strong political commitment to the All-African Convention (AAC), the organisation which came into being in 1935 to co-ordinate resistance to the government's current assaults on black rights. The country's economic plight at the start of the 1930s, caused by the world-wide Great Depression, brought together a wide cross-section of whites in a coalition government. They then formed the mainstream United Party led by Prime Minister J.B.M. Hertzog.

Hertzog wanted to create a fundamental and, he hoped, permanent divide between colour groups. He spoke of his fears in February 1936 in terms which remain central to the outlook of whites up to today: 'If there are two things which have caused constant anxiety to the white people of South Africa, they are the danger of being overwhelmed by the natives, and the danger of mixed blood. Since the time when the Europeans first came in contact with the natives, they have realised the danger of their small numerical strength against the vast numbers of the natives.'

White unity made possible the two-thirds parliamentary majority needed to change the constitution. The result was the Representation of Natives Act of 1936, which ended the limited access by blacks to voting which had begun in the previous century; instead, blacks in the Cape Province were allowed only to vote for three white representatives in Parliament; blacks throughout the rest of the country were restricted to indirect elections for four whites in the Senate, the upper review body of Parliament. As a sop for this derisory level of representation, a Natives' Representative Council (NRC) was created, consisting of elected blacks, nominated blacks and white officials. Further segregation was ensured through a second law, the Native Land and Trust Act: this perpetuated and strengthened the containment of blacks to the 'reserves'; the intention was to limit, in perpetuity, land ownership by blacks to a maximum of some fourteen per cent of the country.

The scale of the deprivation was seared into black political consciousness. Out of the experience came the concept of non-collaboration: although imperfectly and unsuccessfully applied by the AAC, it was to be enthusiastically propounded by the next generation of young black leaders, Sobukwe among them, with consequences which would be played out during the next decade. As developed from the events of 1935–36, non-collaboration meant that blacks, as well as coloureds and Asians, should not take part or assist in their own oppression and should therefore refuse to participate in bodies such as the Natives' Representative Council created especially for them by the government.

Ntloko first met Sobukwe at the freshers' social when Sobukwe's speech created such a stir among students. He was impressed by the newcomer but saw little of him that year. The following year Sobukwe became one of his students. He recalls Sobukwe as a 'good student—very intelligent, a scholar in every respect, a hard worker, with originality'. But the real contact and stimulation came outside the classroom: in Ntloko's twelve years at Fort Hare there were no students with whom he spent more time than Sobukwe and his two close friends, Siwisa and Galaza Stampa (who went on to become a teacher, and then a schools inspector). They were known as the 'Three S's'.

Fort Hare's smallness and isolation helped to create a pressure-cooker environment. Friendships were immediate and close, and direct personal contact was possible with lecturers, especially those who were black. Discussions which began in Ntloko's Native Administration course during the day continued as free-wheeling debates—often heated arguments—at his house at night, sometimes until 3 a.m. Years later, Sobukwe often spoke of his indebtedness to Ntloko for having done more than any other single person to open his mind to the society around him.

In everyday existence, the college was relatively regimented: each morning, students had to attend prayers with the Principal standing at the door to check that everyone was present; on Sunday evenings, students were obliged to attend the church service. But there was a great redeeming feature. As with the stress on learning with which Sobukwe's parents had infused his earlier years, now he could revel in an exceptional quality which Fort Hare provided: 'There was free debate and students could read what they wanted,' says Ntloko.

He began with the main books for his course—*An African Survey* by Lord Hailey, the British expert on colonial policy; *The History of Native Policy in South Africa* by Edgar Brookes, the South African liberal historian; and *Native Administration in the Union of South Africa* by Howard Rogers—a practical everyday guide to administering black lives by a government official. This was also the year in which Edward Roux's *Time Longer than Rope* was published—a vibrant history of black struggle in South Africa. The Fort Hare library had one copy and a long list of people waiting for it. The 'Three S's' booked it out overnight. They were given the book at 5 p.m. and flung themselves into it. They missed supper and went through the night taking turns to read the book aloud to each other.

Sobukwe also launched himself into reading anything he could find on Africa—an unusual interest in those days when only a few South Africans of any colour wanted to know what was happening further north in the continent. He subscribed to the *West African Pilot*, the newspaper founded by Dr Nnamdi 'Zik' Azikiwe, the early campaigner for Nigerian independence, and read newspapers from the Gold Coast, later to become Ghana and the leader of Africa's rush to independence.

Local news was followed as avidly as circumstances allowed. Students didn't have the money to subscribe to the *Daily Dispatch*, the morning newpaper published in East London, the nearest town of any size. But several lecturers and the library received the newspaper, so it was available. Radio news was followed where possible: one or two students in the residences owned radios.

He was also enthralled, in his English 2 studies, by the play *Strife*, by John Galsworthy, first produced in London in 1909 (and there was a BBC television production in 1988). It had an electric effect on him. The story is about a struggle between Labour and Capital, with the two leaders holding to their beliefs to the last without counting the cost. Each, according to his own lights, is finally brought down by lesser men. Sobukwe identified totally with the strikers' leader, David Roberts, even trying to sound like Roberts declaiming in the play.

The events of the time provided the third impelling influence on the 'maturing and growing' Sobukwe, as Ntloko describes him.

Getting to grips with 'Native Administration' in 1948 was peculiarly appropriate, for this was to be a fulcrum year for South Africa. On 26 May, against all expectations, the Afrikaner Nationalist Party was elected to government. The voters, overwhelmingly, were whites, although coloured men in the Cape Province and Natal, and Asian men in Natal, could vote; blacks were confined to indirect representation through white members of parliament. Whatever the colour of voters, only whites could be elected as members of parliament.

The Nationalists who now took over under Prime Minister D.F.

Malan were committed to 'apartheid'—the word that was henceforth to achieve international notoriety.

Up to May 1948 the possibility existed that segregation and discrimination, built into the fabric of South Africa ever since European settlement began in 1652, could be diminished and even perhaps be made to dwindle away gradually. Despite the formal and informal barriers, racial mixing was not unknown, especially in the Cape Town area in the south of the country where European settlement had begun and colour contacts had the longest history. In a number of suburbs there, whites and coloureds lived as neighbours; there was no segregation on buses and local trains, and coloureds had the municipal franchise.

Not, however, that the pre-1948 government of the United Party, headed by Prime Minister Jan Smuts, was all that liberal. It is mainly in retrospect, in comparison with what came after, that it appears benign. Smuts was a visionary on the world stage and was influential in the formulation of the aims of the United Nations; but at home, he relapsed into the white supremacy of his fellows. The Nationalists had a coherent dogma. What they campaigned for, and what apartheid promised, was the purposeful and drastic extension of segregation so as to encase in law what might previously have been partly legal enactment and partly customary practice. Even as whites voted for their new order, so too among blacks was there a flow of new ideas evidenced in the re-invigoration of the African National Congress.

The ANC was already a long-standing political organisation. It had come into being in 1912, two years after the creation of the Union of South Africa from the four separate white-controlled entities which then became provinces. The scheme of arrangement for the Union, approved by Britain as the colonial overlord, allowed for the limited franchise of blacks in the Cape Province to continue but excluded the far greater number of blacks elsewhere. The ANC wanted elementary rights for blacks. It began by asking—begging, really—the British government and the British King for protection from the whites. The ANC was spurned, but its pattern of supplication continued for nearly thirty years.

In the 1940s, the ANC began to break away from mere pleading. With a new President-General, Dr A.B. Xuma, it took on the form and activities of a modern political movement. It was given impetus by the war years—the accelerated industrialisation which drew blacks from the rural areas to become workers in city factories, and the ideas of democracy which were in vogue. Drawing on the inspiration of the Atlantic Charter, the document setting out Allied post-war aspirations for democracy, Xuma invited black leaders to prepare a local charter. They did so in *African Claims in South Africa*, which was adopted by the ANC in December 1945 as a definitive statement of its aims.

'We ... urgently demand the granting of full citizenship rights such as are enjoyed by all Europeans in South Africa,' it said. It demanded abolition of political discrimination based on race, called for the right to equal justice, including nomination to juries and appointment as judges and magistrates, the repeal of laws restricting freedom of residence and movement, the recognition of the inviolability of the home and prohibition of police raids on homes for tax or liquor, the right to own and buy land and to engage in all trades and occupations, the right of every child to free and compulsory education, and equality of treatment in social services.

Even while *African Claims* was being prepared there were other stirrings inside the ANC which would, before the end of the decade, profoundly affect the organisation and South Africa as a whole ... and, too, the life of Sobukwe, then still a scholar at Healdtown.

Young people—they were mainly in their twenties—were intent on transforming the ANC and with it the nature of the challenge to white rule. In December 1942 the ANC's annual conference agreed to the formation of a Youth League. The initial core group was headed by Anton Lembede, who was to become revered before, and after, his early death. The two dozen or so involved with him included Nelson Mandela, Oliver Tambo, Walter Sisulu, Robert Resha, Jordan Ngubane and A.P. Mda—all of whom would feature increasingly in the future. Within two years a Congress Youth League (CYL) manifesto was prepared and approved by Xuma. Five years after he did so, the Youth Leaguers had triumphed, their policy adopted by the ANC, and Xuma removed from the presidency.

A coherent philosophy was being developed for the new African Nationalism. A perceptive commentary by Leo Kuper, a South African-born scholar, in the *Oxford History of South Africa*, says:

> [The Youth League] emphasised the exclusive basis of African solidarity, as a race and as a nation. It argued that, since white

Benjamin Pogrund

South Africans viewed South African race problems through the perspective of race, it was imperative that Africans should do the same. Rejecting interpretations of African oppression in terms of social class, which would have provided a basis for inter-racial solidarity, the Youth League declared that Africans were oppressed as a nation, and under different conditions from those which applied to Indians [Asians] and coloureds.

It described itself as opposed to any form of racism and of discrimination against minorities, and stated it was willing to co-operate with other non-European groups on common issues but, it declared, the only force which could achieve freedom was that of African Nationalism organised in a national liberation movement led by Africans themselves; Africans could co-operate with others only as an organised self-conscious unit, that is to say, when they themselves had achieved unity.

As to relations with Europeans, Africans would be wasting their time and deflecting their forces if they looked to them for inspiration or help in their political struggle.

[At the supra-national level, the CYL was pan-Africanist,] asserting the inalienable right of the African to Africa ... and seeking to galvanise Africans throughout the continent into one homogeneous nation.

In its stance on non-blacks, the Youth League was out of step with its mother body: early in the 1940s, Xuma had begun to forge links with the South African Indian Congress (SAIC). A 1943 campaign against the 'passes' had Xuma as Chairman and Dr Yusuf Dadoo, President of the SAIC, as Vice-Chairman. In 1946, Xuma acted as a spokesman for the Asian community on a trip abroad.

The great divide in black politics at this time revolved around the conflict between 'non-collaboration' and 'collaboration': the argument, carried over from the mid-1930s and the resistance to Hertzog's segregation laws, as to whether blacks should take any part in institutions created for them by the government. The Natives' Representative Council was at the centre of the argument. Its assigned role was to advise the government about black interests; however, the advice did not have to be taken and indeed very seldom was. The government's Secretary for Native Affairs served as the Council's Chairman, with five white official members, four nominated blacks and twelve elected blacks. At a lower level, locations had elected Advisory Boards: the title defined the function.

The controversies were inevitable: To what extent should the oppressed make their oppression possible? Could the system be changed from within? Could co-operation perhaps prove to be but the first step, leading eventually to full participation? Didn't both principle and strategy make it preferable to refuse to co-operate and rather to hold out for more meaningful rights?

It is a reflection of the slowness of movement in South Africa that, forty years later, precisely the same issues were as furiously debated, this time in regard to the two segregated parliaments created for coloureds and Asians.

The ANC had an ambivalent attitude towards non-collaboration. It did not like the system of Native Representatives in Parliament but it backed at least some white individuals in elections and invited some representatives to attend its annual conferences. Some of the representatives achieved considerable reputations for their doughty fight against racial injustice, and especially after the Nationalists began to drive ahead with apartheid. The ANC went along with the Natives' Representative Council in the hope of bringing about desired change. Several leaders—notably Xuma, Matthews, R.V. Selope Thema and W.P.G. Champion—were members. But they were totally ineffective in halting official repressive measures against blacks. In 1946, the NRC voted to adjourn *sine die* in protest against being ignored by the government. Membership continued but the body languished until the Nationalists finally swept it into oblivion.

The Congress Youth League had no doubts on any of these matters. It scorned the parliamentary representatives as much as it did the NRC. The Native Representatives were at best irrelevant and tainted by an insulting paternalism, the CYL argued; at worst they were direct participants in the oppressive system. The ANC had no business allowing any of its leaders to sit on the Natives' Representative Council.

Communism was another divisive issue among blacks. The Communist Party of South Africa (CPSA) had been formed in 1921, and was totally subservient to the Soviet Union. The party slavishly followed whatever orders it received from Moscow and was subject to whatever winds were blowing in the Soviet leadership. Thus it was caught up in Stalin's purges of the 1930s: several leading members were summoned to Moscow, never to be seen again.

Benjamin Pogrund

Having to abide by changing Soviet priorities and outlooks led the party into some bizarre situations, notably its adherence for a time in the early 1930s to a thoroughly racial notion of South Africa as a black republic. Otherwise the CPSA was non-racial in its approach, membership and leadership and its contribution to preserving inter-racial co-operation in South Africa is beyond estimation.

The CPSA's philosophy and its role as the agent of a foreign power made it the object of deep suspicion not only among the ruling whites but also among blacks. Xuma's correspondence with his lieutenants is littered with expressions of hostile mistrust about the communists. This concern was wholly shared, and indeed was eclipsed, by the Youth League which tried to meet the problem of allegiance to the Communist Party by specifying that, while it was acceptable for people to belong to two organisations, once anyone joined the CYL this had to have his foremost loyalty otherwise he had to quit.

3

By 1948, the Congress Youth League had grown into an aggressive force within the African National Congress. But there was no branch at Fort Hare, even though so many of the leaders had studied there. Now this was to change. The Afrikaner Nationalist electoral victory on 26 May contributed to it by sharpening political consciousness.

Some blacks had no illusions about what lay in store for them. A few days after the election, on 2 June 1948, a weekly black newspaper, *Inkundla ya Bantu* (Bantu Forum), said sombrely: 'Our whole race is in a grave crisis . . . The results of the elections have brought us as a community to the parting of the ways. We must now say once and for all time whether we shall remain serfs or free men. A considerable section of the European population has voted openly for a policy of oppression of the African. And now we must turn to ourselves and decide now what we shall do.'

At Fort Hare, 'there was great sadness mixed with anger and apprehension and we believed blacks were in for a real tough time,' recalls Nthato Motlana, who studied science there from 1946 to 1948 and went on to study medicine at the University of the Witwatersrand. Some two decades later, in the aftermath of the 1976 'children's revolt' in Soweto, he became Chairman of the Committee of Ten which articulated anti-apartheid protests.

He provides a dramatic view of life in parts of the country through the eyes of a young black man: 'In the 1940s, the attitude of white South Africans was monstrous, appalling. They were boors, animals. We lived a life of subservience, obsequiousness, fear, of obeisance to the white man in a way that nobody can really understand. When you saw a white man you saw God Almighty and you had to get out of his way. He could kick you, he could kill you and get away with it.' In Pretoria, it was rumoured—rightly or wrongly—'that if you ever walked onto the campus of the University of Pretoria [a wholly white institution for Afrikaners] the students would literally kill you; it was a white man's preserve, and no black could ever walk on the hallowed ground of that university'.

Among Fort Hare students there was already movement towards the ideas represented by the Youth League. A particular role was being played by Sobukwe, together with Siwisa and Stampa. The three friends prepared a daily commentary on political issues, called *Beware*. They wrote it by hand at night and put it on college notice-boards. Their favourite topic was non-collaboration, with fierce attacks on the Natives' Representative Council and advisory boards.

The practical step of starting a CYL branch was taken by Godfrey Pitje, a lecturer in the Department of African Studies. He graduated from Fort Hare in 1945 and later returned to do field work in anthropology. He heard then about Sobukwe—'this brilliant young man' who had come from Healdtown—but did not have any substantial contact with him. Pitje began teaching at Fort Hare in 1948—and was imbued with the spirit of politicising students. His friends were active in the Congress Youth League and he was in contact with them. He was also spurred by the result of the general election. Looking back, Pitje sees the significant changes taking place at that time in the minds of blacks he knew—'from the tribal way of thinking to join the mainstream of Western civilisation; from a feeling of acceptance of the status quo to a complete rejection of what the status quo stood for; from an uncomplaining *"ja baas"* ("yes, boss") to the feeling that every white man is a bastard.' It meant a change in attitude towards the older men who were the leaders of the ANC: until then, they had been looked at with admiration; now those like Pitje looked at them 'as people who were playing up to whites'.

It was in these circumstances that Pitje went to Professor Z.K. Matthews, whom he much admired, to seek his advice about starting a CYL branch at Fort Hare. Matthews approved and Pitje wrote to the League's President, A.P. Mda. An encouraging reply was forthcoming: 'Fort Hare is just the place to start a Youth League,' wrote Mda. 'The young people there are the intellectual leaders-to-be.' Pitje says he was acutely aware that the CYL could never be strong at the college 'if it didn't include articulate chaps like

Sobukwe'. On a Sunday afternoon in August, Pitje called a meeting to discuss forming a CYL branch. About fifty students and staff members attended the meeting in the anthropology lecture room. There was no problem from the college authorities about the meeting; apart from Matthews, they probably did not even know it was being held.

Sobukwe and others asked a number of critical questions, clearly showing that they were not yet quite certain about entering the African National Congress. 'Sobukwe was more under the influence of the AAC than under the ANC,' recalls Pitje. 'The AAC appeared to the youth to be much more advanced in thought. They were questioning the advisory boards and the Natives' Representative Council while at that time leaders in the ANC were involved in these bodies. So an attack on the NRC and advisory boards seemed to be an attack on the ANC's leaders.' Pitje had to convince them about the policy of the ANC and the desirability of starting a branch. He succeeded and, by the end of the day, a formal resolution was adopted to form a Youth League branch. Pitje was elected Chairman. College staff members included Samson Guma, later Rector of the University of Swaziland. From the students, members included Rosett Nziba, a highly politicised and articulate product of Orlando High School in Soweto who was to become among Sobukwe's close followers, Nthato Motlana, Joe Matthews (son of Z.K.) and Peter Tsele, who was to go on to study medicine at the University of the Witwatersrand and to become the first black elected to the Students' Representative Council there. From outside South Africa, names that were to become well known in their own countries in succeeding years were Herbert Chitepo from Rhodesia; Orton Chirwa from Nyasaland; and Ntsu Mokhehle from Basutoland.

A specific task assigned by the branch to Sobukwe, with Joe Matthews and P.V. Mbatha, was to act as a 'research group'. They had to read whatever literature was available with a bearing on the South African political scene or on black politics generally, and report back on it.

'By the end of 1948 we were a very closely knit group,' says Pitje. 'But Sobukwe was towering over us, even those of us on the staff, intellectually, from whatever angle. We readily recognised that he was an exceptional chap. If we had a statement to be released by the group, ten to one Robert would be asked to draft it because we felt he had a better command of the language. He could express himself much better than any of us.'

Mda also was quick to recognise Sobukwe's qualities, and went on to become another powerful influence in his life. 'I remember very clearly that I first heard of him between 1946 and 1947 when he was still a student at Healdtown,' says Mda. 'I heard it from a young fellow in Herschel: he was saying to me that there was a final-year matriculation student who was showing a quality of leadership which had attracted the attention of young people and the minister there, the Reverend Seth Mokitimi. Next I heard of him in 1948, after the Nationalists had come into power and a Youth League branch was started at Fort Hare.'

Mda began to correspond with Sobukwe, setting out his thinking and inviting the younger man to study South Africa in depth 'so that he would have a scientific, concrete basis to his outlook apart from emotion—although emotion is important. In the course of our studies and correspondence we began to understand each other really clearly and began to agree on almost every point. At this time he was already very well advanced politically because he had rubbed shoulders with the intellectuals of the Trotsky group. He was a brilliant boy.'

Mda was even then becoming a legendary African Nationalist figure, and the interest he showed in Sobukwe, the new recruit to the cause, must have had incalculable effects. After helping to found the Youth League in 1944, Mda was, at the age of 32 and then a high school teacher, elected President in January 1948, after the death of Lembede. Although in poor health himself, he held the position through the historically formative months, for South Africa and the ANC, up to December 1949. Thereafter he continued teaching in the town of Herschel until the government took over black education; he turned to law, and eventually, after police harassment, he settled in Lesotho and practised law there. His enduring reputation comes from his development of the ideology presented by the Youth League. He continued, for Sobukwe, as a fountain head of knowledge and strategy.

He describes Sobukwe as an apt and eager pupil who rapidly matured—and even outstripped his master. For, in regard to African Nationalist philosophy, says Mda, 'he went on to develop our position—mine and Anton Lembede's—to a higher level than that in which we were'.

How Can Man Die Better

In April 1949, Mda visited Fort Hare and, for the first time, came face to face with Sobukwe. Thinking back to the occasion, and perhaps adding a collage of later memories, Mda systematically marshalls his thoughts and speaks with magisterial authority: 'My impressions of him fortified the impressions I had of him during our correspondence. He impressed me as a humble man; he had humility. He was not a chap who tried to impose his ideas on other people, or to play big. One would think he was shy: he stood back and listened to other people.

'Secondly, he impressed me as a man with a deep love for his downtrodden black people, and he appeared to feel that he was one in every way. This was a very striking feature because he was so powerful intellectually, yet he felt that he was one with the peasants, with the workers. At one conference, I remember, the young men came in good suits, to impress everyone. He was in overalls. We were embarrassed. We all whispered, "Look at him. He's a true leader of the people."

'Third, he impressed me as a man who was very clear on the issues of national struggle towards final victory. He had fully and uncompromisingly embraced the position of African Nationalism and saw this as a basis for the complete unity of the African people, and the basis for achievement of national freedom for the African people as a step towards a fully fledged democratic order in South Africa.

'Fourth, I found that he believed that a leader must have total commitment to the struggle of the African people for national emancipation, no matter what the hardships may be, or what the obstacles may be.

'Fifth, he believed that the leaders themselves must be in the forefront of the struggle.

'Sixth, I found him to be totally free from any tinge of racism or anti-whiteism. But he was inflexibly opposed to white domination. He made a distinction in this matter.

'Seventh, he had a capacity to win personal attention to himself. He had an amiable character. He could talk quietly, he could laugh uproariously. He was a fine conversationalist and a good listener.

'Over the years, my impressions were confirmed.'

Sobukwe was a rising star outside the Youth League as well, in everyday student affairs. In September 1948, for the annual 'Completers Social', the students who were to continue their studies the next year chose him to speak on their behalf. The exact text of his speech is not available. But his political outlook was by now emphatic and Dennis Siwisa recalls him urging: 'Your starting-point in your struggle for our liberation is non-collaboration, and the boycott of dummy institutions is the first step on the ladder of non-collaboration.'

Siwisa says that the speech stamped Sobukwe 'as an orator of no mean repute. From then onwards he was always called up to make speeches and no meeting—political, cultural, social or even a mass meeting of students—would be regarded as having ended until or unless Robert had spoken.'

In his physical appearance at that time, Sobukwe looked spare, almost gaunt. But the overriding impression retained by Motlana was about his being 'serious-minded': 'Laughter didn't come to him very easily. He would not join in the usual kind of student jocular talk about booze, women and parties. Maybe those who knew him better might have known his lighter moments. But at meetings where I met Sobukwe I always found him somewhat sombre, serious-minded. He was a very impressive speaker. He spoke very slowly, always gesticulating in that manner of his, raising a finger or hand to emphasise a point.

'I remember Sobukwe as somebody serious. One got the impression that, to Sobukwe, the struggle was something serious.'

The esteem in which he was held by his fellows was demonstrated at the start of the 1949 academic year. He was elected to the Students' Representative Council and also elected as its President. Normally a student would be elected one year and assume high office the next year. Sobukwe, however, became President immediately after being elected. If this was unusual, Sobukwe was 'an unusual man', says Motlana.

Most of his presidency was tranquil. It was disturbed only later in the year, and then by events which occurred off the campus. But those events were to affect his life fundamentally.

The first event was a strike by nurses at the Victoria Hospital in Alice about their conditions. They took this action after writing examinations but still with twenty-one days of their contract to complete. They were expelled from their rooms. They spent two weeks sleeping in the open, on the hospital lawn, holding meetings next to the nearby Tyumie River. Students at Fort Hare responded to their plight and supplied them with blankets. But Sobukwe, according to Siwisa, remained aloof at first. He said he was busy with his studies. His fellow-students tried to persuade him that the nurses were his sisters and he had a duty to help them. But for days he remained with his books. Then he did become involved, and rapidly assumed the position of leader with the nurses coming to him for advice and instructions.

One of the nurses was a 21-year-old from Hlobane in Natal, Veronica Zodwa Mathe. 'I loved him at first sight,' she says. There were feelings on his side too. As the strike dragged on she went to Johannesburg to stay with her mother but corresponded with Sobukwe. Two months later, when the authorities agreed to reinstate the nurses, she returned to the hospital to complete her course. She travelled by train. Fort Hare was on vacation and Sobukwe had been at a Congress Youth League meeting in Queenstown. He was on his way to another meeting in Kingwilliamstown, further south, and fortuitously boarded the same train as Veronica. They would marry four and a half years later.

The second event was on 21 October 1949 and is spoken of as 'a night not to be forgotten' by students who were at Fort Hare. That was the night of the Completers' Social. The event featured large in the college's calendar. Students and staff all came together for it. What distinguished the occasion this particular year was the quality of the speeches, especially that given by Sobukwe as President of the Students' Representative Council.

The music that was usual for the social was dispensed with and, instead, three speakers instead of the normal two were billed. In addition to Sobukwe, Ntsu Mokhehle spoke on behalf of the students who were leaving at the end of the year, and another student, Temba Hleli, represented those continuing their studies. Mokhehle would, within a decade, form the Basutoland Congress Party which was strongly pan-Africanist; eventually he was to go into exile, turning to insurgency warfare after being robbed of his electoral victory by Prime Minister Leabua Jonathan in 1970.

The text of Sobukwe's speech has survived, thanks to Godfrey Pitje. As the first record of a major statement by Sobukwe, it is worth quoting substantial parts of it . . .

> I had occasion last year and also at the beginning of this year to comment on some features of our structure of which I do not approve. It has always been my feeling that, if the intention of

the trustees of this College is to make it an African College or University, as I have been informed it is, then the Department of African Studies must be more highly and more rapidly developed. Fort Hare must become the centre of African Studies to which students in African Studies should come from all over Africa. We should also have a department of Economics and of Sociology. A nation to be a nation needs specialists in these things. Again I would like to know exactly what the College understands by 'Trusteeship'. I understand by 'Trusteeship' the preparation of the African ward for eventual management and leadership of the College. But nothing in the policy of the College points in this direction. After the College has been in existence for thirty years the ratio of European to African staff is four to one. And we are told that in ten years' time we might become an independent university. Are we to understand by that an African University predominantly guided by European thought and strongly influenced by European staff?

I said last year that Fort Hare must be to the African what Stellenbosch [University] is to the Afrikaner. It must be the barometer of African thought. It is interesting to note that the theory of 'Apartheid' which is today the dominating ideology of the State was worked out at Stellenbosch by [Dr W.M.M.] Eiselen and his colleagues. That same Eiselen is Secretary for Native Affairs. But the important thing is that Stellenbosch is not only the expression of Afrikaner thought and feeling but it is also the embodiment of their aspiration. So also must Fort Hare express and lead African thought. The College has remained mute on matters deeply affecting the Africans, because, we learn, it feared to annoy the Nat [Nationalist] government. What the College fails to realise is that rightly or wrongly the Nats believe that the Fort Hare staff is predominantly UP [United Party]. So that whether we remain mute or not the government will continue to be hostile towards us. So much for the College.

Sons and daughters of Africa, harbingers of the new world order. What can I say to you? As you see, for the first time since the practice was started, we do not have the nurses with us on this momentous night—Completers' Social. And the reason? The battle is on. To me the struggle at the hospital is more than a question of indiscipline in inverted commas. It is a struggle between Africa and Europe, between a twentieth-century desire for self-realisation and a feudal conception of authority. I know, of course, that because I express these sentiments I will be accused of indecency and will be branded an agitator. That was the reaction to my speech last year. People do not like to see the even tenor of their lives disturbed. They do not like to be made to feel guilty. They do not like to be told that what they have always believed was right is wrong. And above all they resent encroachment on what they regard as their special province. But I make no apologies. It is meet that we speak the truth before we die.

I said last year that our whole life in South Africa is politics, and that contention was severely criticised. But the truth of that statement has been proved in the course of this year. From the pulpit in the CU [Christian Union hall] we have heard responsible and respectable preachers deplore the deterioration of race relations in this country and suggest co-operation as a solution. Dr Bruce Gardner and Reverend Mokitimi are but two of a large number. Professor Macmillan and a number of speakers in our Wednesday assembly, have condemned this 'naughty spirit of Nationalism and non-cooperation' and have told us of the wonderful things that have been done for us, forgetting, of course, that what they say has been done for the Africans the Africans have achieved for themselves in spite of the South African government. The point I am trying to make is that that was politics, whether we loved it or not. So that we can no longer pretend that there is a proper place and a proper occasion for politics. During the war it was clearly demonstrated that in South Africa at least, politics does not stop this side of the grave. A number of African soldiers were buried in the same trench as European soldiers. A few days afterwards word came from the high command that the bodies of the Africans should be removed and buried in another trench. 'Apartheid' must be maintained even on the road to eternity.

The trouble at the hospital, then, I say, should be viewed as part of a broad struggle and not as an isolated incident. I said last year that we should not fear victimisation. I still say so today. We must fight for freedom—for the right to call our souls our own. And we must pay the price.

Benjamin Pogrund

The nurses have paid the price. I am truly grieved that the careers of so many of our women should have been ruined in this fashion. But the price of freedom is blood, toil and tears. This consolation I have, however, that Africa never forgets. And these martyrs of freedom, these young and budding women, will be remembered and honoured when Africa comes into her own.

A word to those who are remaining behind. You have seen by now what education means to us: the identification of ourselves with the masses. Education to us means service to Africa. You have a mission; we all have a mission. A nation to build we have, a God to glorify, a contribution clear to make towards the blessing of mankind. We must be the embodiment of our people's aspirations. And all we are required to do is to show the light and the masses will find the way. Watch our movements keenly and if you see any signs of 'broadmindedness' or 'reasonableness' in us, or if you hear us talk of practical experience as a modifier of man's views, denounce us as traitors to Africa.

We will watch you too. We have been reminded time and again that fellows who, while at College, were radicals, as soon as they got outside became the spineless stooges and screeching megaphones of 'White Herrenvolkism' or else became disgruntled and disillusioned objects of pity. My contention is: those fellows never were radicals. They were anti-white. And as Marcus Garvey says: 'You cannot grow beyond your thoughts. If your thoughts are those of a slave, you will remain a slave. If your thoughts go skin-deep, your mental development will remain skin-deep.' Moreover a doctrine of hate can never take people anywhere. It is too exacting. It warps the mind. That is why we preach the doctrine of love, love for Africa. We can never do enough for Africa, nor can we love her enough. The more we do for her, the more we wish to do. And I am sure that I am speaking for the whole of young Africa when I say that we are prepared to work with any man who is fighting for the liberation of Africa WITHIN OUR LIFETIME.

To the completers among whom I number myself, my exaltation is: REMEMBER AFRICA!

I thought last year that the position was bad. I realise it is worse this year . . . We are witnesses today of cold and calculated brutality and bestiality, the desperate attempts of a dying generation to stay in power. We see also a new spirit of determination, a quiet confidence, the determination of a people to be free whatever the cost. We are seeing within our own day the second rape of Africa; a determined effort by imperialist powers to dig their claws still deeper into the flesh of the squirming victim. But this time the imperialism we see is not the naked brutal mercantile imperialism of the seventeenth and eighteenth centuries. It is a more subtle one—financial and economic imperialism under the guise of a tempting slogan, 'the development of backward areas and peoples'. At the same time we see the rise of uncompromising 'Nationalism' in India, Malaya, Indonesia, Burma, and Africa! The old order is changing ushering in a new order. The great revolution has started and Africa is the field of operation . . .

We have made our choice. And we have chosen African Nationalism because of its deep human significance; because of its inevitability and necessity to world progress. World civilisation will not be complete until the African has made his full contribution. And even as the dying so-called Roman civilisation received new life from the barbarians, so also will the decaying so-called Western civilisation find a new and purer life from Africa.

I wish to make it clear again that we are anti-nobody. We are pro-Africa. We breathe, we dream, we live Africa; because Africa and humanity are inseparable. It is only doing the same that the minorities in this land, the European, coloured and Indian, can secure mental and spiritual freedom. On the liberation of the African depends the liberation of the whole world. The future of the world lies with the oppressed and the Africans are the most oppressed people on earth. Not only in the continent of Africa but also in America and the West Indies. We have been accused of bloodthirstiness because we preach 'non-collaboration'. I wish to state here tonight that that is the only course open to us. History has taught us that a group in power has never voluntarily relinquished its position. It has always been forced to do so. And we do not expect miracles to happen in Africa. It is necessary for human progress that Africa be fully developed and only the African can do so.

We want to build a new Africa, and only we can build it.

The opponents of African Nationalism, therefore, are hampering the progress and development not only of Africa, but of the whole world. Talks of co-operation are not new to us. Every time our people have shown signs of uniting against oppression, their 'friends' have come along and broken that unity. In the very earliest days it was the Missionary (we owe the bitter feelings between Fingoes and Xhosas to the Christian ideals of the Reverend Shaw). Between 1900 and 1946 it has been the professional Liberal. Today it is again the Missionary who fulfills this role. After maintaining an unbroken and monastic silence for years while Smuts was starving the people out of the reserves, the Missionaries suddenly discovered, when the Africans unite, that the Africans have not had a fair deal. In the same stride, so to speak, they form a 'Union-wide Association of Heads of Native Institutions' for the purpose of regimenting the thoughts of the students. A Missionary Hospital closes even though the people are dying in its neighbourhood, and there is a dearth of nurses throughout the country. I am afraid these gentlemen are dealing with a new generation which cannot be bamboozled . . .

Let me plead with you, lovers of my Africa, to carry with you into the world the vision of a new Africa, an Africa reborn, an Africa rejuvenated, an Africa re-created, young AFRICA. We are the first glimmers of a new dawn. And if we are persecuted for our views, we should remember, as the African saying goes, that it is darkest before dawn, and that the dying beast kicks most violently when it is giving up the ghost, so to speak. The fellows who clamped Nehru in jail are today his servants. And we have it from the Bible that those who crucified Christ will appear before Him on the judgement day. We are what we are because the God of Africa made us so. We dare not compromise, nor dare we use moderate language in the course of our freedom.

As Zik [Nigeria's Nnamdi Azikiwe] puts it: 'Tell a man whose house is on fire to give a moderate alarm; tell a man moderately to rescue his wife from the arms of a ravisher; tell a mother to extricate gradually her babe from the fire into which it has fallen; but do not ask me to use moderation in a cause like the present.'

These things shall be, says the Psalmist: Africa will be free.

The wheel of progress revolves relentlessly. And all the nations of the world take their turn at the field-glass of human destiny. Africa will not retreat! Africa will not compromise! Africa will not relent! Africa will not equivocate! And she will be heard! REMEMBER AFRICA!

With rousing calls and ringing denunciations of this order, no wonder that Cecil Ntloko's recollection of the speech is: 'It was too hot!' And no wonder that the assembled students gave Sobukwe a standing ovation. Many staff members, however, were stunned. In a Memoir about Prof. Matthews, Monica Wilson later noted that the speech 'received a mixed reception from the Fort Hare staff but, according to Mrs Frieda Matthews [Z.K.'s wife], "it was quoted for years by students". No one could doubt Sobukwe's ability and dedication, or that he was a born leader.'

Sobukwe's speech, coming within less than two years of his awakened consciousness, is remarkable for its strength and range of thinking. He had come far very quickly. Nor, with all the emotional rhetoric, is the content mere sloganising: there is a passion and direction in the words which come from an understanding of the concepts. This was a confident man speaking to a theme in which he believed and which he was intent on communicating to others.

The speech also contains much of what was to be Sobukwe's later political philosophy: the rejection of any trace of white paternalism; the stress on black self-regard and on an African continental approach to the world; the emphasis on service, and with it, sacrifice; the rejection of colonialism and the reaching out to socialism. And there is the firm declaration: 'We are anti-nobody', followed by his then still-tentative call to whites, coloureds and Asians to establish their security and freedom by committing themselves to Africa.

The reactions to this speech, and to the transformation in his outlook, went beyond Fort Hare. His brother Ernest remonstrated with him: 'We have not sent you [to college] for politics but to study for your degree.'

Reports were also reaching his mentors at Healdtown. They were desperately unhappy.

There is some confusion about the exact sequence of events at this stage of Sobukwe's life. In later years he frequently referred in thankful terms to the whites who had helped him to continue his education, both at school and university. He specifically mentioned the Caleys, and Mrs Scott too in regard to developing his interest in English literature. Mr and Mrs Caley, speaking about the help they gave, said: 'It was a struggle for us to do this,'—and it must surely have been so for a couple whose income came from a missionary institution. The Caleys appear to have been the mainstay in supporting Sobukwe; Ernest contributed. Hamish Noble, the Healdtown teacher, also played a role.

A sense of mission motivated the Caleys. They wanted to help Healdtown to obtain better qualified teachers and they wanted to see more 'educated leaders', as they put it, among blacks. They also liked Sobukwe and respected his intellectual abilities. But they had little understanding of his thinking processes, or of the forces at work in South Africa and the effect these were having on him. It could hardly be expected to have been otherwise in light of their cloistered existence in a secluded institution, their lives dedicated to the institution in furthering the education and Christian well-being of the teenagers and young adults in their care. In their own words, they had their 'own little society', cut off from the world in an era when there were few cars and travel outside the institution was difficult and seldom undertaken.

They were utterly bewildered by the new and emerging Robert Sobukwe. He was beyond their comprehension. Finally, they were left feeling disillusioned, rejected and hurt.

As Sobukwe said in his Completers' Social speech, at the start of the year and the year before he had commented on 'some features' of Fort Hare's structure of which he did not approve. This stemmed from the belief that black teaching staff suffered discrimination both in terms of restricted numbers and the level to which they were appointed.

Thus already in 1948 the ruffling of official feathers had begun. Later, probably early in 1949, Sobukwe set off an even greater storm, directly determining his own future, through his treatment of the Reverend C.W. Grant, who was no less than the Governor of Healdtown and also the person responsible for making recommendations to the Department of Education about the teachers who were to be employed at Healdtown.

According to Matthew Nkoana, a well-known journalist and a member of the Pan-Africanist Congress, in a May 1959 article in

Drum magazine, the Principal [*sic*] of Healdtown made a speech at Fort Hare about the brotherhood of man, suggesting it could be fostered between white and black by personal contact in homes and in informal meetings without changing the state's laws. Sobukwe addressed him: 'The moment I step out of your home, sir, after a show of the brotherhood of man, the police will pick me up for a pass offence.'

'But that won't be my fault,' replied Grant. 'It will be,' protested Sobukwe. 'You are part and parcel of the set-up in this country. The church cannot absolve itself from this. The Methodist Church itself is pursuing a segregationist policy: it has different stipends for its white and black ministers.'

Grant said this was because African congregations could not afford to pay more. 'Then why is it that white ministers who administer to African congregations get more than their African colleagues?' went on Sobukwe remorselessly.

In that environment, at that time, and among those people, it must have had the same shock effect as a bomb exploding in their midst. Sobukwe punctured missionary paternalism by pointing up the discrimination suffered by blacks. But blacks were not supposed to address whites in this way; young black men were not supposed to challenge their white teachers like this.

Grant returned to Healdtown and told the Caleys that 'on no account could he appoint Robert to the staff'. The scandalised clergyman said: 'He's a trouble-maker. We can't have him here. We don't want him here.'

The cherished dream of the Caleys was crumbling. They had been looking forward eagerly to Sobukwe completing his degree at Fort Hare and serenely returning to Healdtown as a teacher. This is what their struggles had been for. And Sobukwe had the same goal: he had gone to Fort Hare to prepare himself for teaching at Healdtown. 'It was all arranged,' said the Caleys.

Mr Caley remembered that this was 'the first adverse criticism of Robert and I went hot-foot to see him'. He found Sobukwe coming out of the library and they stood and talked for the next one and half hours.

Siwisa says Sobukwe told him afterwards about the discussion: Caley said he had been told that Sobukwe was now anti-white; that he wasn't the Robert he had known at Healdtown because he now spoke badly of whites and insulted them; he wanted Sobukwe to confirm or deny the complaint. No, Sobukwe replied, he was not anti-white but he was anti-white supremacy. But why this change, Caley asked. At Healdtown he had been an example of a good chap, and even at Fort Hare he was said to have been very good up to the previous year. What had happened this year? Sobukwe replied that it was the books he had read, and the impact of his lectures.

Mr Caley's recollection of the conversation fits in with this account in its main respects: he said he asked Sobukwe about his 'rudeness' towards Grant . . .

Sobukwe: 'You wouldn't like me to be a hypocrite, sir.'

Caley: 'No, I wouldn't like that, but I don't understand why you have changed.'

Sobukwe: 'Have you read Smuts' Native policy?'

Caley: 'No, I'm a teacher and I'm not supposed to take any part in politics. I know nothing of this.'

Nor did he apparently know what to say when Sobukwe made the point that they couldn't even go to a café together to have a cup of tea because of the segregation which, pre-dating the Afrikaner Nationalists, was the norm of the place and the time.

Seen through Caley's eyes that day, Sobukwe had turned into something strange and frightening. 'His hair was long, he was very unshaved, his eyes were staring, he wasn't his quiet self at all,' was the way he described his encounter to Mrs Caley when he returned home. 'He looks different, he behaves differently and he feels differently.'

Sadly, the Caleys never did understand. Talking about it more than three decades later, the 'dreadful shock' it had been was still evident even while they spoke about the 'native children' they had known—the mere use of the phrase betraying their place in a bygone era. 'Robert was like a member of the family until then,' they said.

It seems that Mr Caley also presented Sobukwe with an ultimatum: that he return to being what he had been or lose the financial assistance he was getting. Sobukwe rejected this. Mr Caley offered him time to think it over but Sobukwe insisted that he knew his mind. Later, however, after consideration, the Caleys dropped the ultimatum. They thought: 'If we help him perhaps he will change his outlook. We will show him that not all whites are against blacks.' The threat of withdrawal of finance got around, however, and Hamish Noble was reported on the Fort Hare campus as saying that if Sobukwe lost his scholarships he would personally replace the money.

There is another, inexplicable, side to the story. The Caleys said that they helped Sobukwe financially at Fort Hare 'on the understanding that it would be paid back'. Sobukwe was in fact the third student whom they helped: the others were Present N. Tshaka, who was to become a lecturer at the University of Transkei, and W. Kgware, who later became Rector of the University of the North. 'Robert wrote to us to say he was going teaching, and when he got a permanent job he would start paying back,' said the Caleys. 'But we never heard from him again and he never sent us a penny. We wanted to help, not to get trouble-makers but to get educated leaders. Robert was a very big disappointment to us. We never sent anyone else to Fort Hare. We felt that if we hadn't sent him to Fort Hare he wouldn't have become like this.'

On his side, however, and as far as can be established, Sobukwe never spoke about being financially indebted to the Caleys. In later years, whenever he referred to them he did so in warm terms, with no hint of any lingering tension.

As a result of his conflicts with the Healdtown authorities, uncertainty continued about whether he would go there. Some friends also opposed his going to Healdtown, but for different reasons. A letter to Godfrey Pitje from a Congress League leader, Tsepo Letlaka, written on 4 August 1949, said: 'I am very keen about Mangaliso ... I cannot imagine him going to rust and rot in Healdtown next year. We must be cautious how we disperse our forces about the country.' Letlaka, incidentally, a decade later became one of Sobukwe's most devoted followers. He eventually went into exile, but was able to return by agreeing to settle in 'independent' Transkei, the first black tribal state created by the South African government. He went on to hold Cabinet rank there, as Minister of Police.

With Sobukwe's stay at Fort Hare coming to an end, the Principal, Clifford P. Dent, gave him a 'To whom it may concern' testimonial which seems to have been written with the aim of saying the barest minimum in the coolest possible way. Dated 2 November 1949, it read: 'He is now studying for his final examinations in English 3 and Xhosa 3, with Native Administration 2 as an additional subject. His marks show ability and progress considerably above the average. He is a man of influence among his fellows and has this year been Chairman of the Students' Representative Council.'

Sobukwe sent a telegram to Siwisa to announce his end-of-year examination results: Passed but no distinction. There was, in fact, more to it than that. For, as Prof. Matthews was later to write to a colleague, he had 'proved himself to be a student of outstanding ability both inside and outside the classroom. I happen to know that his professors were disappointed that he did not manage to obtain distinctions in his major subjects in his final year. This we attributed to the fact that he did three major courses instead of the usual two, all of which he passed creditably. In fact, as far as Native Administration is concerned, I know for a fact that he qualified for a distinction in that subject but he was not awarded the distinction because he had listed English and Xhosa as his major subjects, and Native Administration II as a minor.'

In his last year at Fort Hare, Sobukwe appeared to be considering law as a career: if he wished to do it he would need Latin so, together with a few others, he studied the language for a few months on a very part-time basis in the afternoons or evenings or on Sundays. Sigcau Thamsana, a senior student in classical studies, gave free lessons.

Neither law nor the quietness which a teaching career at Healdtown would have meant came to pass, however. Nor did a job come easily. It took several months before he was offered a position as a teacher at the Jandrell Secondary School in Standerton. The offer came from the Principal, W.S. M'Cwabeni, who had studied at Fort Hare in 1946 and 1947. He had met Sobukwe while visiting Healdtown in 1946 and then again at Fort Hare the following year.

First, however, there was the pride of graduation. Most of his family was with him for the occasion and a rare group photograph shows his father looking stern and dour; his mother, too, has a set appearance about her; they are people whose struggles to get to this day are seen on their faces as they pose for the unaccustomed camera. Sobukwe is a graceful young man: he is tall but slightly built, with a delicacy to him. His face is open and innocent. He fits the description of fellow-students as a young man who took life seriously.

4

Even while job-hunting, Sobukwe was engaged in the Congress Youth League whose activities were to climax at the December 1949 annual conference of the mother body.

By early that year the new Youth League branch at Fort Hare had begun to attract attention from outside. Letters were arriving from black leaders giving encouragement and expressing the thought that Fort Hare was the right place for a branch. A praising letter even came from Dr A.C. Jordan, a highly regarded lecturer in Bantu Languages at the University of Cape Town, who was not an ANC man but a known supporter of the All-African Convention.

The reason for the enthusiastic interest can be attributed not only to the intensity which the Fort Hare students and staff members put into their politics, but also to their particular way of dealing with the split in black national politics. 'The general view of the students was: we are not going to be parochial, we don't close our minds. If the AAC people have something to teach us or tell us we will accept it,' explains Godfrey Pitje. 'The fact that we were a baby of the ANC did not make us believe the ANC was some infallible body. Indeed we went out of our way to criticise them.'

He notes that 'the little group at Fort Hare was unique because, generally in black politics, if you expressed misgivings or criticised, you were either howled down or accused of being quisling or something. But this particular group didn't encourage that type of thing. When somebody attacked or raised questions, if you dared try to howl him down or label him, you were yourself attacked. The feeling was: look, give him an answer if you've got one; don't antagonise him, don't write him off, it might be that he does not know and it is your duty to inform him.'

In April 1949, the President of the Congress Youth League, Mda, visited Fort Hare to marshal forces in shaping the ANC's policy at the end-of-year conference. A leader had to be elected according to policy, he said, and there was to be a definite policy to which any aspiring leader had to commit himself. The Cape provincial annual conference in June provided a trial run. Sobukwe played a leading role in clarifying the issues, judging by the lengthy conference reports in *Inkundla ya Bantu*. He emerged as a major standard-bearer for African Nationalism. The principal success of the CYL came in the conference's endorsement of what was becoming known as the Programme of Action—a set of aims and strategies to achieve liberation. Sobukwe wrote an early version which was approved by the Fort Hare Youth League. But it was Mda who wrote the Programme which was discussed by the youth and then approved by the conference. Mda recalls that Sobukwe was 'the most articulate' of the youth who took part in the debate.

Attention now focused on the ANC's national conference to be held in the Magasa Hall in the location outside Bloemfontein, a city which was, and is, an Afrikaner citadel. The date was 16 December—a public holiday called Dingaan's Day and observed by whites in remembrance of the Boer defeat of Zulus led by their king at Blood River the previous century.

CYL members lobbied hard among conference delegates as a whole for the Programme of Action. They allocated groups of two from among themselves to call on prospective candidates for the ANC's presidency to ask if they would commit themselves to the programme. Xuma brushed them aside and Prof. Matthews refused to be tied to anything. Dr James Moroka agreed and so became President-General. A CYL leader, Walter Sisulu, was elected Secretary-General.

In the Youth League's own election, a surprised Godfrey Pitje was voted in as President. By his own later admission, he did not view himself 'as a leader in the ordinary sense but rather as a member of a team'. He promptly nominated Sobukwe as National Secretary and this was accepted by the conference.

The Programme of Action became crucial to much that occurred thereafter, either because of those who propounded it or those who moved away from it. The mere title became a call to arms for the African Nationalists who judged political action by whether or not it deviated from the programme's contents.

The Programme set the goal of 'freedom from white domination and the attainment of political independence'. Specifically, it called for direct representation in all the governing bodies of the country, and abolition of all differential institutions for blacks such as representative councils and existing parliamentary representation. The Programme suggested a national fund to finance the struggle for liberation and appointment of a Council of Action; wide press dissemination of ideas to raise political consciousness; boycott of differential institutions, together with strikes, civil disobedience and non-cooperation; a national one-day stoppage of work; establishment of urban and rural organisations to improve the workers' standard of living; creation of educational and cultural bodies for training, to improve black awareness and to unite the cultural with the educational and national struggle.

Sobukwe's direct participation in these stirring events was not to last long, however. With a teaching job in Standerton available, he was now to land up a far distance from his Eastern Cape home area. He went north and entered the Transvaal province for the first time. His new life was starting, 160 kilometres to the east of Johannesburg.

The town of Standerton, where Sobukwe arrived early in 1950, serves a countryside made rich from maize-growing and cattle. But it has little else to distinguish it. The town owes its start to the discovery in 1886 of gold in Johannesburg: it was sited on the Upper Vaal River as a stopping place for diggers travelling from the east coast. It was, and is, a typical South African town with total division between white and black residential areas, and with the area for blacks some distance away from that for whites—in this case, about 1.5 kilometres. When Sobukwe was there, the total population was nearly 11,600: 6,200 blacks, 4,700 whites, 480 Asians and 200 coloureds.

Blacks are present in the white town, with its wide paved streets and substantial commercial buildings and houses, because their labour is needed; they are also more than welcome to spend their money in the white-owned shops. It would be catastrophic for the town if this were not so. But it is also made clear that the black presence must be limited. Nowhere is this more apparent than in the municipal building which houses a Carnegie Library: this is a heritage of the 1930s when the Carnegie Corporation of New York sponsored a study of a major social problem in South Africa at that time: the plight of unskilled whites who had left the land and were destitute. One result was the funding of libraries in a number of country towns. In Standerton's case, the library did not keep up with the liberal spirit of the Carnegie Corporation. Well into the 1980s (and perhaps later still), there was an additional signboard over the Carnegie Library's entrance: 'Whites Only', repeated in Afrikaans: *'Blankes Alleen'*.

In the location for blacks, only the main roads are paved. The rest are rutted, some so badly that driving a car is difficult. The houses are the usual tiny products of mass, low-cost housing for blacks. The few shops bear no comparison in appearance and range of goods with the town's business centre. Piles of rubbish lie in heaps. The night is made bright by high masts carrying powerful lighting, intended as a deterrent to crime. Dilapidated as the place looks, there is yet a vitality to it, especially at weekends as people stroll around and visit friends. The hum of voices fills the air, radios are kept at full blast, and a game on the sand soccer field is sure to draw a crowd.

However rudimentary the location now, it was more so when Sobukwe lived there, although at the time it was newly built. Toilet needs were served by buckets. There was no electricity. Few houses had piped water; instead there were communal taps: the closest one for Sobukwe was on the street corner about fifty metres from where he lived. The semi-detached municipal houses of two rooms and a kitchen had flat cement slabs for the roofs. A few more substantial owner-built dwellings were dotted among them. Motor cars hardly existed for the people of the location. Standerton's railway station offered the link with the outside world and a four-wheeled cart pulled by two horses was the means of getting to and from the station. Two trains from Durban *en route* to Johannesburg arrived each day in the afternoon and late at night, and two trains from Johannesburg to Durban in the afternoon and evening. Johannesburg was four hours away—enough to place it beyond the reach and experience of most of the black people in the district.

It was a quiet place and, unlike today, crime was rare. People could walk around without fear of being molested. Nor were the police a bother. But the control was incessant. Whites would rarely enter except for official purposes and would in any event normally need an authorising permit. Black visitors entering the location had to report to the municipality's office at the entrance and advise the number of the house they were going to and for how long they would be there. If the authorities got word that a visitor had not reported, a black policeman—and sometimes whites also—would go along to check.

The Jandrell Secondary School, where Sobukwe taught, is now the Madi Higher Primary School and Jandrell has moved to new premises elsewhere in the location. But the appearance of the original building is hardly changed. Erected by the municipality in 1945, it was named after a Dutch Reformed Church missionary, the Reverend J.D. Jandrell. It is a U-shaped, single-storeyed brick building standing on top of a hill, on the edge of the location and overlooking the river. The school grounds have a few bushes, a couple of poplar trees and a few flowers, but even grass cannot do much in the grey, flinty ground. The classroom floors are bare cement. Each classroom has a small coal stove in a corner: on winter days, with sub-zero temperatures, the stove does little to warm up the room. The teacher usually gets as close to it as possible. There are no frills: merely desks and a blackboard. There is no library or hall. The school was built as a minimum-standard component of segregated education, and it has remained that way.

Sobukwe's duties, from 8 a.m. to 2 p.m., five days a week, were to teach history to pupils in Standard 6 and Forms 1 and 2, English to Standard 6 and Form 2, and Scripture to the forms. Displaying an entirely new talent, he took on the training of the school's senior choir, which went on to win prizes.

More than thirty years later, M'Cwabeni's admiration for Sobukwe remained unbounded: 'He was loved by all who came into contact with him. He was loved by the young and by the old. He became a leading member of the staff and they all accepted him as such. The pupils worshipped him and they were none the worse for it.'

The serious-minded Sobukwe of Fort Hare seems to have loosened up, for another colleague, Butana Eleazor Nodada, who retired in 1982 after teaching at Jandrell for thirty-six years, remembered him as 'ever-smiling'. He is viewed with veneration in the location, to the extent of diffidence in speaking of him: 'When a person becomes an eagle it is difficult to talk about him,' said Martin Vilakazi, a shop clerk.

Sobukwe was supposed to live with the M'Cwabenis. But they had a large family and, as one house was insufficient, M'Cwabeni obtained a second one across the street. Sobukwe had a room in this second house, took his meals with the M'Cwabenis and spent his evenings with them. They were his audience for 'political lectures', as Mr M'Cwabeni described it. He was a conscientious teacher, always completing the marking of schoolwork before going to bed. Over weekends he went to sports functions. His interest in tennis again showed itself and he organised a club among teachers in the location, playing three times a week, summer and winter. He also put together a teachers' team to play soccer against the older boys.

At the same time, Sobukwe and Veronica kept in as close contact as they could. Now qualified as a nurse, she went to work in Durban, first at Springfield Hospital and then at McCord Hospital; then she moved to Ladysmith, a town halfway between Durban and Johannesburg. She and Sobukwe wrote to each other. Occasionally she travelled to her home in Johannesburg, allowing them a few minutes together on Standerton station; occasionally, too, she came to stay with him.

Although Sobukwe was still National Secretary of the Youth League, his connection with the African National Congress had weakened, principally because the Youth League under Godfrey Pitje had gone into a state of decline. Pitje felt that he was the wrong person for the job of President: he was over-awed by the people he met in Johannesburg who, he felt, knew far more than he did about African Nationalism. He had left Fort Hare and was doing teacher training at the Wilberforce Institution at the small town of Evaton, about forty kilometres south of Johannesburg. He called no meetings of the Youth League executive and attended no ANC meetings. He never contacted his National Secretary, and never heard from him. But at least, the following year, he knew that Sobukwe was engaged in political activity because some young men who had studied under Sobukwe at Standerton came to Wilberforce to continue their education and told him Sobukwe had brought them into the ANC. In fact, Sobukwe was the Secretary of an ANC branch in Standerton. He was also still maintaining his contacts with African Nationalism through Mda and was writing occasional unsigned articles in the publication of the Bureau of African Nationalism in East London.

Thus passed two uneventful years for Sobukwe. But for the country at large these were fast-moving, turbulent times. The Nationalists were embarked upon their programme of enforcing apartheid in every possible nook and cranny of South African existence. The laws tumbled out: 1950 alone saw enactment of the Population Registration Act, the most basic of all apartheid laws, intended to classify every single South African into a defined racial category; the Group Areas Act, which began the process of dividing the entire country into separate residential and business areas for different racial groups, as the prelude to ordering people into their 'correct' group area; the Immorality Act, which extended prohibitions on inter-racial sex; and the Mixed Marriages Act, which debarred inter-racial marriage.

In addition, Parliament passed the Suppression of Communism Act: it provided for the proscription of the Communist Party of South Africa, and also gave the government the power to ban by administrative decree other organisations deemed to be furthering the—widely defined—aims of communism. The same arbitrary action could be taken against people, publications and meetings. Here was the start of the long succession of assaults on personal liberty.

The Communist Party voted itself out of existence shortly before the banning law was enacted (three years later, it was re-started underground). Before quitting, however, the CPSA attempted to mobilise anti-government forces against the planned banning law. It called for a mass strike on 1 May, May Day. But black feelings were mixed about the communists and inside the ANC there were open disagreements whether to support or ignore the call. Leading members of the Youth League went to meetings in black ghettos such as Orlando and Alexandra and urged people to ignore the strike and to go to work as usual.

In the event, the protest was held and degenerated into violence. Eighteen blacks died, some from police gunfire, others when strikers attacked non-strikers. The deaths brought about the unity which the communists had been seeking: a day of protest and mourning was called for 26 June and this time the African National Congress joined in without reservation. The observance of this day became a significant annual event.

Black, coloured and Asian political leaders began discussing how best to oppose discriminatory legislation. They took inter-racial unity further in reaction to the government's intention to remove the lingering remnants of common roll voting rights of coloured men in the Cape and Natal and Asian men in the Cape. The ANC sent a letter to Prime Minister Malan calling for direct representation by blacks in government and for the repeal by 29 February 1952 of the pass laws, the Group Areas Act, the Separate Representation of Voters Act (which terminated coloured and Asian common roll representation), and the ending of cattle-culling in black rural 'reserves'. It threatened mass action in defiance of laws and regulations.

Malan rejected the demand. On 26 June the Defiance Campaign was launched. By the end of the year just over 8,000 volunteers had been arrested for breaking the law: blacks and Asians, for example, went and sat on railway station benches marked 'whites only', or entered post office entrances assigned to whites.

By early the following year the government had given itself a new law with which to curb protest: no longer was it a mere technicality punishable only by light fines or imprisonment to contravene a racial law; now, if the contravention was done by way of protest against the law it became a vastly more serious offence. Thus using the 'wrong' railway station bench, if intended as a protest against apartheid, could mean a heavy fine, or three years in jail, or ten lashes—a whipping—or a combination of any two of these. Those who 'incited' others to break the law by way of protest faced an even heavier fine, or up to five years in jail, or ten lashes, or any two of these. A second conviction made whipping or jailing compulsory. The leaders called off the Defiance Campaign.

The campaign did not have unanimous support inside the ANC because of the gathering dismay among some about what they believed to be the perversion of the organisation. The specific charge was that white and Asian communists, together with black communists, had moved in on the ANC and were exercising an undue and increasing influence behind the scenes. Those who felt this way were scattered through the ANC, but the chief anxiety lay among some people who had come through the Youth League. There was still little that was organised about them, but those who held these views were beginning to be known as 'Nationalists'. Sobukwe was one of them: he spoke in later years about his uneasy feeling that the campaign was a 'communist stunt'.

At this stage the Nationalists had a sense of particular betrayal about the Programme of Action of 1949. They were alarmed because they believed that the programme which the CYL had striven so hard to bring about had been pushed aside, and with it their control of the ANC's direction. More and more, the Programme of Action became their rallying point. They saw it not only as a statement of desired action but as a declaration of philosophy.

Nor did all of them accept that the Defiance Campaign deserved support just because it was predicated on a form of non-collaboration and therefore fitted in with the aims of the Programme of Action. They were suspicious: as far as they were concerned, they had not had a hand in planning it and the decision-making was not theirs.

An additional factor was the ANC's increasing co-operation with other colour groups. This, of course, had begun in the early 1940s with Xuma's link-up with the South African Indian Congress, but it accelerated after 1950 as the ANC acquired other alliances: the South African Coloured People's Organisation (SACPO) was set up for coloureds and, in 1952, whites formed the Congress of Democrats (COD).

The COD was viewed by the ANC's Nationalists as the front organisation for white communists and was hence a special focus for hostility. They were not alone in this. The COD's founding conference in Johannesburg drew a crowd of interested, anti-apartheid and left-wing whites. But many of them were so appalled at what they saw as stage-management on the part of the extreme left that they refused to get involved in the new organisation. Instead, they went off and joined other anti-apartheid whites to form the Liberal Association which, during the next year, became the Liberal Party with a non-racial membership.

Standerton was not a centre of Congress activity, or of any kind of black political activity, and the closest that the town came to the Defiance Campaign was a meeting in the location addressed by Nthato Motlana. He was there because Sobukwe arranged the meeting and asked the ANC in Johannesburg to send a speaker. Sobukwe did not become a defier. His explanation, in personal conversations in later years, was that he had been told by the ANC in Johannesburg to stand by and await a call to action; the call did not come. No, says Motlana, that explanation for not defying was over-modest; indeed the opposite applied because it was 'incredibly brave' of Sobukwe simply to organise the meeting. Teachers were generally not called upon to defy because the ANC realised that any teacher who did so was bound to lose his job, he says.

Motlana says his recollection is that he did not go to Standerton to ask people to defy: 'That wasn't the way we operated. We asked people to volunteer to defy but it would have been out of character to do that in a small country town like Standerton where the laws are so vicious and people's tenancy of their township houses and their jobs is so tenuous. To ask such people to defy the laws would not have been on. I would probably just have spoken about the general political situation.' Speaking at the meeting, incidentally, had its own dangers for Motlana: it no doubt added to the Security Police dossier against him and later in the year a banning order was imposed on him.

Mrs M'Cwabeni feared Sobukwe's involvement in the meeting. She had no idea that he was actually responsible for it. All she knew was that he intended going to it and this worried her: she asked him not to say anything at the meeting. In fact, he went all the way and got up and addressed the crowd which gathered for the rare event—'The only political meeting to be held in the township in all its history,' says Motlana—held in the open on an empty, rocky piece of ground. There to observe, to listen and to report was the white location superintendent.

At an investigation instigated by the local inspector for black schools, Sobukwe was found guilty of unprofessional conduct in that he had addressed a political meeting against the government. He was told not to report back for work in the next school year, in January. This led to members of the Jandrell school committee going to Pretoria to call on the Transvaal Director of Native Schools. 'They wanted to know why Sobukwe had been warned,' says M'Cwabeni. 'They did not want to lose a good and reliable teacher. They pointed out that to them the ANC was not a political party. It was just a watchdog looking after the interests of black people and only spoke when it had to.' Clergymen formed the majority of the members of the school committee. After they had conveyed their views—from the innocent standpoint of country people, it seems—the Transvaal Director agreed that Sobukwe could continue as a teacher. The Director wrote to Sobukwe demanding written assurance that he would not take part in politics. To which Sobukwe replied that he had 'never brought politics into the classroom and did not intend doing so'. There the matter rested, and Sobukwe resumed teaching.

But he had learnt from the Defiance Campaign and was to apply the lessons in the future.

5

Once past the trouble over the meeting, quietness returned to Sobukwe's life, marred by the death of his father in November 1952. But, in 1954, there were two major events in his life: marriage and a change of career.

He and Veronica were married on 6 June at St Paul's Anglican Church at Jabavu in Soweto. Following traditional custom, he paid *lobola* (bride price) to Veronica's mother in the considerable amount for those times of £100. His monthly salary in Standerton, when he had begun teaching there, was £22. The Saturday ceremony was attended by a small number of relatives and friends. The next day, Sobukwe returned to Standerton to wind up his job there, for he had been appointed to a position at the University of the Witwatersrand and was to move to Johannesburg.

The university, known as Wits, is in the front rank in South Africa in terms both of size and quality. It is English-language and has a liberal tradition. Until 1960, when the government's Extension of University Education Act forced it to comply with apartheid and reduce the number of black students, the university admitted blacks on merit. It practised what was known as 'academic non-segregation', although blacks were excluded from most student sports and social activities. The academic staff consisted entirely of whites except for a handful of 'language assistants' in the Department of Bantu Languages (since renamed Department of African Languages)—one of the posts given to Sobukwe.

Although a language assistant was a lesser status than a lecturer, appointment to the university's academic staff was an exceptional and signal event for a black person. His salary was £550 a year, rising by £50 a year to the top notch of £750. By white standards it was a modest income, but it put him into the upper bracket as far as blacks were concerned. He had social security protection, also rare among blacks, through compulsory membership of the university's pension and medical aid funds. His duties were to give practical classes to beginners in Zulu, even though he was Xhosa-speaking and from the Eastern Cape, the home area for the Xhosa. The languages are related to each other.

Sobukwe's formal application for the post was in response to an advertisement in *The Bantu World* newspaper and offered two names as referees—Professor Matthews and G.I. Mzamane, lecturer in Bantu Languages at Fort Hare. He also sent a testimonial from M'Cwabeni at Jandrell school. All three gave him enthusiastic support.

Matthews, in addition to describing Sobukwe's academic strengths and that he had 'exhibited gifts as a leader of men' while President of the Students' Representative Council, went on to say: 'I always found him painstaking in his work, courteous in his demeanour and frank and open in the expression of his views.' Mzamane went even further about academic distinction: 'One is justified, I think, in placing Mr Sobukwe in the category of being one of the most brilliant students of Bantu Languages that have passed through Fort Hare. His outstanding ability goes along with sound scholarship and intensive reading ... Great contribution to Bantu Literature and Linguistics can be expected from his pen in the future.' M'Cwabeni wrote of his pleasure in writing a testimonial but his pain at losing Sobukwe: one of the 'pillars' of Jandrell and 'a born African gentleman, cultured and with all the qualities that one would expect of one who has attained his standard of education ... His influence over the students and pupils has at all times been very good and this may be attributed to his Christian character which is above all else, I think, a credit to his parents.'

Returning to Johannesburg in June, Sobukwe and his bride moved into her mother's house at 1526 B, White City, Jabavu. There was an acute shortage of accommodation for blacks and they could not get their own house immediately.

'White City' was the nickname, passing into general usage, for the Jabavu area because of the white-painted roofs and walls of the domed concrete houses. Township side streets are seldom referred to by name, and instead people find their way around according to zones and house numbers.

The entire house they shared—one bedroom, lounge/diningroom and kitchen—would fit easily into many British or American living-rooms. Veronica's mother and step-father had the bedroom. The lounge/dining-room was given over to the new married couple. The front door opened into this room so a rod holding a curtain was put up to create a 'passage' from the front door to the kitchen. They had no furniture of their own but Veronica's mother lent them a studio couch.

After nine months they were allocated their own municipal house: 684 Mofolo. It was a standard house, officially designated a '51/6-type'. They could not buy it, even if they had wanted to, because government policy did not allow this. The policy of the time, founded in apartheid, was that blacks had no right to a permanent existence in the urban areas but were there as 'temporary sojourners', as the official phrase had it, while their labour was needed. Hence they were debarred from owning land or buildings.

The Sobukwes now enjoyed the luxury of a bedroom, a sitting-room, a dining-room and a kitchen—all tiny rooms, it is true, but it seemed like a good deal of space to them. The main bedroom measured 8 ft 11 ins by 9 ft 3 ins, and there wasn't much of it left after a bed had been put in. The only furniture they could afford to buy was a bedroom suite. Veronica's mother lent them a kitchen table. So two rooms were empty at first.

The house did not have electricity—that was to come to Soweto only about twenty years later—and they used candles in the bedroom and paraffin wick lamps in the other rooms for lighting. Cooking was done on a spirit stove. Later they bought a coal stove for the kitchen and this also provided the only heating in the house in the winter. There was one cold water tap, in the backyard, six paces from the kitchen door. The lavatory was in the backyard and had waterborne sewage. The house fronted onto a sand road, like most in Soweto. It was a few minutes' walk to a tarred road and then to a grocer's store, owned by Tshabalala, well stocked by ghetto standards but a far cry from what was available in stores in the city.

Housing for Soweto was provided on a mass scale at the lowest possible cost. A new house, such as theirs, was handed over with rough-finished walls, no interior doors, no ceilings below the asbestos roof, and bare earth for the floors except for cement in the kitchen. The cost of building a house was £200—that is, twice the amount of Veronica's *lobola* and less than half Sobukwe's annual university salary. The Sobukwes hired and paid workers to plaster the walls, put down wooden floors, put in interior doors and put plastic tiles on the kitchen floor.

Their first child, a daughter, Miliswa (meaning To plant deep), was born shortly before they moved into the new house. Then came a son, Dinilesizwe (Sacrifice to the nation), and finally twin boys, Dalindyebo (To make riches) and Dedanizizwe (Give way, nations). The house shrank quickly. At first, Miliswa shared a bed with her parents and Dinilesizwe (Dini) had a pram; then Miliswa and Dini slept in the sitting-room on a couch which opened up at night, and the parents shared their bed with the twins.

The job at the university began in the second half of the academic year, on 1 August. Each day Sobukwe left home at about 7 a.m., after a solid breakfast of porridge, eggs, bread and tea. He was usually late and ran the mile to Dube station for a train to the city. Most days he was home by 5.30 p.m. The house had a small garden and he spent as much time as he could in working it, evenings and over weekends: he grew flowers, and was proud of his tomatoes, pumpkins, cabbages and potatoes.

Veronica resumed work in between having the children, doing general district nursing in Soweto, and says: 'It was a happy family life. He often arrived home with a paper-carrier of food he had bought. He loved being with the children. He spent a lot of time with them. He told them a lot of stories, Xhosa stories.'

When the children had gone to bed he prepared for his classes and studied for another degree. At the start of 1955, the University of the Witwatersrand accepted him for the degree of Bachelor of Arts with Honours. But he first had to complete some background undergraduate courses: during the next two years he studied Phonetics, Southern Sotho 2, Social Anthropology and Comparative Bantu Language—'doing very well in most of these,' according to the university. He went on to collect and analyse Xhosa riddles for an Honours thesis. An Honours degree, with a second-class pass, was conferred on him at a graduation ceremony on 22 March 1958.

The event was a milestone for him and for education—because he proved to be the last black student allowed to do an Honours degree in the Department of Bantu Languages; a year later the government restricted the entrance of blacks to the 'white' universities. This particular bit of apartheid was to remain in force for the next nineteen years.

Settling still further into academia, Sobukwe was nominated by the university in 1959 as its observer at an inter-church conference on African Writers. He spoke in terms which went against the creeping censorship which was now well advanced in South Africa, urging the use of language which truthfully reflected the subject, even sexually explicit language. During the same year he acted as a reader of language manuscripts for the Oxford University Press.

But the enjoyment of domestic and university existence, even working towards fulfilment of the promise of a brilliant career in African languages, was not enough. He was too conscious of the emotions stirred in him through his studies and discussions at Fort Hare; he was too mindful of his own words of farewell and commitment to his fellow-students of less than a decade before: 'Let me plead with you, lovers of my Africa, to carry with you into the world the vision of a new Africa, an Africa reborn, an Africa rejuvenated, an Africa re-created, young Africa. We are the first glimmers of a new dawn ...'

So he again became directly involved in politics, which meant the African National Congress. He joined his local Mofolo branch and meetings were regularly held at his home, with Veronica making tea for more than twenty people packing into the dining-room. The number of visitors calling on him at night and over weekends began to rise.

The hibernation of Standerton was over. He was picking up the threads of the debates of his student days, and the motivating force was the Youth League's Programme of Action. He began to link up with others of similar mind, and this led to contact with the Nationalists within the ANC.

The anxieties of the Nationalists were heightened by the events which followed the ending of the Defiance Campaign. After an hiatus, the ANC in 1953 took the first steps towards a new campaign: it deplored the deterioration in race relations in the country caused by the enforcement of apartheid and, enunciating a call that was to become a familiar one down the years, said that only a national convention representative of all races could improve the situation. The following March, executive members of the ANC, the South African Indian Congress, the South African Coloured People's Organisation and the Congress of Democrats met and announced their intention to organise a Congress of the people to prepare a 'freedom charter'.

Some form of anti-apartheid political activity was sorely needed.

Benjamin Pogrund

A contemporaneous account by Muriel Horrell of the South African Institute of Race Relations testifies to that—and also provides an illuminating picture of how the government's grip on the country was gradually tightening. Summarising the events of 1954–55 she said: 'The past year has been an intensely demoralising and confusing one for the non-white people. There was a great upsurge of feeling amongst them in 1952 when the Defiance Campaign was embarked upon ... Considerable fervour and willingness for self-sacrifice were revealed.' But the legislation containing extremely severe penalties had been enacted, she noted, the campaign had been suspended and many of the leaders were proscribed: 'Since then the official policy of "control" has continued—the police have raided the homes of leaders and have taken notes at meetings, passports have been refused to those who have made "political speeches", teachers who associated themselves with school boycotts have lost their jobs, the presence of "informers" in the townships is suspected. Political leaders of the ANC, the SAIC and SACPO continue to work together for the implementation of a Freedom Charter and on other projects, but their following has dwindled.'

It was during this period, in an attempt to regain a political initiative, that the Congress of the People was held: about 3,000 delegates met on an open lot of ground called Freedom Square at Kliptown, Johannesburg, on 25 and 26 June 1955. The uninvited guests were the 200 armed white and black policemen who cordoned off the area and searched everyone, authorised by a warrant which said they were investigating a charge of treason and looking for 'inflammatory or subversive' literature. Despite this, by the end of the two-day meeting, the Freedom Charter was adopted by those present.

The Charter said that South Africa belonged to all those who lived in it, and that only a democratic state based on the will of all the people could secure to all their birthright without distinction of colour, race, sex or belief. It said there should be universal franchise, and the repeal of all laws which discriminated on grounds of race, colour or belief. The preaching of discrimination on such grounds should be made a punishable offence. Banks, mines and monopoly industries should be nationalised and the land re-divided among those who worked it. Police raiding of private dwellings should be abolished, no one should be imprisoned, deported or restricted without a fair trial. There should be equality of economic opportunity, and no child labour or workers kept in compounds. There should be freedom of speech, movement and association. People should be free to live where they wished, slums should be abolished, education should be free, compulsory and equal for all. Free medical care and hospitalisation should be made available to all.

The Charter concluded with a flourish of words: 'Let all who love their country and their people now say, as we say here: These freedoms we will fight for, side by side throughout our lives, till we have won our liberty.'

The government's response was eighteen months in the making. Then, at dawn on 5 December 1956 the police arrested 156 people of all colours throughout the country and brought them before court on charges of High Treason, a capital offence. The Freedom Charter was at the core of the prosecution: the government alleged it was a communist document. The trial dragged on with charges withdrawn against various batches of the accused until finally, in March 1961, the last remaining thirty were found not guilty.

The prolonged proceedings placed a severe burden on the ANC and others in the Congress Alliance, as indeed they were intended to do. When leaders were not actually in jail they were pinned down in a courtroom or having to take part in the continuing process of consulting with lawyers and helping to prepare their defence. Leaders also had to be circumspect in the nature of their ongoing political activity, lest they created more opportunities for the government to harass them.

These factors apart, the Freedom Charter had a divisive effect inside the ANC in furthering the alienation of those, like Sobukwe, who were already uneasy. By this stage, the Nationalists were an identifiable group who called themselves 'Africanists'. They had begun their own newsletter at the end of 1954. Many of the contributors wrote under pseudonyms, usually because they were teachers and to be identified would have meant being fired. With a drawing of an African warrior in traditional dress on the front, the cyclostyled newsletter varied in describing itself as issued by 'African Nationalists—ANC' or the 'Africanist Movement' or the 'Orlando ANCYL'. The address it gave, however, was consistently the home of P.K. Leballo. Sobukwe wrote for it. The message the newsletter propounded was one of simple, unswerving adherence to the Programme of Action—the text of which was repeatedly published—

and scathing indictment of anything which could be held to be a deviation from a pure African Nationalist ideology.

The Africanists in the ANC were scattered around the country and maintained informal contact with each other. Z.B. Molete was one of them. He came to Johannesburg as a teacher in 1956 after serving, three years before, as Secretary of the Students' Representative Council and the Congress Youth League at Fort Hare. When he allied himself with the Africanists early in 1956 he says there were perhaps one hundred of them: 'a loose association of people who shared the same ideas'. Leballo was the Chairman and meetings, lasting up to three hours, were held regularly on Sunday mornings.

Sobukwe's involvement in politics was, however, kept separate from his teaching duties at the university. In that milieu, his dominant interest was language. A friendship developed between him and a white student, Merton Dagutt, then seventeen and excited and impressionable in his first year at university. Dagutt, later to become a prominent banker in Johannesburg, studied Zulu 1.

Dagutt would go to Sobukwe's office for a chat, or they sat on the grass outside. 'When I first met him he seemed to be wholly interested in the artistic side of life,' says Dagutt. 'He was writing a Zulu translation of Macbeth. One of his ambitions, he told me, was that he wanted to translate all of Shakespeare into Zulu—to demonstrate the power and the beauty of the Zulu language, and because of the power of the original English, which was why he was using Shakespeare.'

On many days they strolled together through Braamfontein, the suburb adjoining the university then in the process of being transformed from a residential into an office block area. 'He used to bring sandwiches and eat in his office and then we would go for a walk. There was a lot of construction under way and there were many black workers lounging on the pavements during lunch breaks. As we came past, many of them would stand up and give the Zulu royal salute—an upraised hand and a cry of *"Bayete"*. Sobukwe responded shyly and would gently say hello to them. There was this instant acknowledgement of the man as a leader. This tribute in the streets happened quite often.'

Dagutt remembers his first impression of Sobukwe as a 'strange' one because it was the first time that, as a white South African, he had to learn from a black South African. But that psychological hump was surmounted and he remembers: 'We all responded extremely well to him as a teacher. He spoke quietly to us, and very gently. I remember feeling that he wasn't teaching down to us, but that he was trying to understand our struggles with a new language.'

A memory that endures for him is of Sobukwe as a neat dresser, always wearing a tweed jacket and grey trousers. In an era of mass poverty among blacks, that alone made him stand out and was perhaps part of the reason for the recognition given to him by those construction workers.

One of the issues openly discussed in Sobukwe's class was how he felt about being a black teacher at Wits. 'He said he felt economically satisfied that he had been able to achieve more than he ever thought he could. He had a good income and was doing the work he wanted to do while having the time to write and to meet people. The only difficulty, he said, was that travelling in on the train in the mornings there were lots of insults from *tsotsis* (young ghetto gangsters), who mocked him for being a black 'white man' and for carrying a briefcase and for being dressed as he was.'

What Dagutt did not know was that it was a self-inflicted difficulty: as a matter of choice, Sobukwe rode in the packed third-class carriages instead of the more comfortable and far less crowded second-class because he wanted to be close to the people of the ghetto.

This was a time of heightened political feelings at the university because of the government's incessant threats to academic freedom, part of its attacks on personal liberty in the country as a whole. One way in which the feelings manifested themselves was that there was a good deal of recruitment to the causes and factions which sprang into being. But Sobukwe remained aloof. Dagutt asked him why he did not join the liberals because he seemed so close to them; he replied that all he wanted to do was to write poetry and he did not want to get involved in politics.

One morning—the Zulu class was held at the start of the day—Sobukwe came in slightly late. This was unusual because he was always punctual. 'He was ashen grey,' says Dagutt. 'He was sort of the same colour as his trousers. I have forgotten how he began. He must have begun by apologising for being late. Then he said that he found it very difficult to talk that morning. He told us: "As I came out of my house this morning there were about seven dead bodies just lying outside. They had killed each other in a faction fight [the term for inter-tribal violence]. I had heard the noise in the night, but one doesn't go out. When I saw the bodies I asked myself, why did they kill each other in a faction fight and the answer was that some of them were Zulus and some of them Basotho. I asked myself why they killed each other outside my house, and the answer was that my house was on the boundary between different tribal areas in Soweto. And I asked myself why my house was there, and the answer was that I was a Xhosa and my wife was Zulu and so the government didn't know where to put us, and put us in between."

'Then he said he was sorry but he was too upset and he could not carry on the class and he walked out. About a fortnight later I was at one of the many academic freedom meetings which were being held. There was a crowd of staff and students in a small seminar room arguing over what action to take. From the floor—he was sitting where I couldn't easily see him—suddenly came those familiar warm, round tones of Sobukwe's voice. He made a political speech. It was along the lines that we were going about it the wrong way, that we had to see the academic freedom issue as part of a broader social and political struggle. The news got round that Sobukwe had entered the political field.'

For Sobukwe, the brief speech was a conscious step across the dividing line between his Soweto existence and the protected environment at the university which he entered for a few hours each weekday.

It was at this point that we first met. In mid-1957 I had moved to Johannesburg from Cape Town. I was working for an industrial company and outside office hours was active in the Liberal Party, as a member of the Transvaal Provincial committee and in helping to run a branch in a black area, Sophiatown. I also wrote for *Contact*, the liberal magazine owned and edited by Patrick Duncan—a man of intense sincerity and moral commitment to non-racialism, all the more astonishing in the light of his background as a former British colonial administrator in Basutoland and son of a Governor-General of South Africa. He was white and had been a defier in the Defiance Campaign of 1952.

I was engaged and my fiancée, Astrid, was a student at the University of the Witwatersrand. Zulu 1 was one of her subjects and she used to tell me about Mr Sobukwe, who took practical classes in the language and who was much admired by his students for his teaching ability and his courtesy towards them. I knew the name: my black political friends were speaking about him as an impressive member of the Africanist group. With the unceasing ferment in the ANC because of the clashes with the Africanists and other dissident groups, that made Sobukwe a person of interest.

We first met accidentally: I had to fetch Astrid, went into the lecture room, Sobukwe happened to be there and Astrid introduced us.

I knew him as Bob, and that's the name I always used. Others addressed him as Robert or Mangie or Robbie. As he grew in academic stature he acquired the nickname Prof.—which became popular among his supporters.

We began to see each other from time to time: during lunch hours and for a Saturday afternoon in his office. We talked and talked, going over the issues which interested us both. These principally concerned developments inside the ANC and the searching for a means to achieve liberation for South Africa's black people. My initial impressions of him were more negative than anything else. I thought he was too academic and too timid. I was struck by his reaction to the invitation I conveyed to him late in April to write an article for *Contact*. He agreed willingly but said he would have to write under a pseudonym as, firstly, he thought the communists might try to dispossess him of his university post if he came out too openly against them. The danger seemed far-fetched to me and I was never certain to what extent it was a well-founded fear; but it did indicate the depth of anxiety among those in the ANC who were opposed to communists. Secondly, he said he lectured to white students and he felt it unwise to express publicly views of an obviously nationalistic character.

My view of Sobukwe was confirmed by Peter Tsele, the former Youth League leader at Fort Hare who was now a medical doctor in the Pretoria district. He said that, while Sobukwe was a good person, he was not prepared to do active work but preferred to remain behind the scenes. When Sobukwe gave me the article for *Contact* I considered it rather school-boyish in its approach and lacking in clear political thinking.

A few days later, a Saturday afternoon spent with Sobukwe in his office at the university again left me unimpressed. I thought his timidity showed in the several statements he made about his rather academic role in the Africanist Movement; that he was supposed to be editor of *The Africanist* but being at the university he found it difficult to get in touch with people and thus he did not do much on the paper; and his several but vague references to wanting to go into business so that he could take part more freely in politics.

On the other hand he was strong and clear in expressing Africanist ideology; in analysing the divisions among blacks along tribal lines which had been accentuated by white settlers, and expressly the British and missionaries, in the nineteenth century; in describing the fathering of modern African Nationalism in South Africa by Anton Lembede, the role of A.P. Mda, the formation of the ANC Youth League, and the adoption of the Programme of Action. He spoke with force in detailing the Africanist belief that for blacks to develop an effective political organisation they first had to develop a national consciousness. This was the only way to unite blacks, he said, and the only means of achieving it was by building up black nationalism. According to the Africanist concept of the future South African society, it would be one in which all would have equality of opportunity and all would be Africans, irrespective of race, by virtue of the fact that they were born in Africa or had made their home in Africa.

I thought his thinking was patchy, becoming naïve and insufficiently considered in looking into the future consequences of his policy. I was also dubious about him as a practical tactician.

I asked him whether he wasn't being contradictory in speaking of a non-racial society while at the same time pushing the idea of black nationalism.

It was only a partial contradiction, said Sobukwe, as once the new South Africa was created there would be no more racialism. Meanwhile, however, black consciousness must be fostered, and much as he did not like the prospect he had no alternative but to accept the inevitability of armed conflict between white and black. Whites would not freely and unwillingly relinquish their position. The history of oppression throughout the world showed that no ruling class ever willingly and of its own accord conceded rights to the oppressed. When the stage was reached that blacks were prepared to offer total opposition then a process of education would start. After the revolution, there would be no anti-white feeling. China was an example: as the Red Army conquered an area, the political educators had moved in and established an ideological basis.

How Can Man Die Better

I questioned his reasoning, pointing out that people's emotions could not be turned on and off like a tap. To obtain total opposition from blacks it would be essential to get them to hate whites with every bit of their being: how could this be changed overnight after victory? In addition, South Africa was a twentieth-century complex industrial state, and if large numbers of whites were ever indiscriminately killed, who would administer the country, industries, commerce and farms? By the time a revolution came about, if ever that is, blacks would in all likelihood not yet have been allowed by whites to acquire skills on a mass scale.

But, said Sobukwe, a substantial number of whites would be prepared to remain in South Africa, in order to help run the country. In addition, people would almost certainly be prepared to come in from abroad.

Did he really, I asked, think that, in a situation where a great number of people had been killed merely because of the colour of their skins, others of the same colour would be willing to stay around?

He supposed not, but he returned to his original point that the only way to build up the black political movement was to push the idea of black nationalism.

We liked each other, enjoyed our debates and so our contact continued. Either we met alone or together with others in the Africanist Movement: principally P.K. Leballo, Zephaniah ('Zeph') Mothopeng, who had been fired as a teacher by the government after the introduction of Bantu Education—a quiet thoughtful man, who would over many years undergo one jailing after another; and Peter Raboroko, a teacher who was given to high-flown philosophising and who was ranked, by Africanists, as their leading theoretician.

Several meetings were held at Leballo's home in Dube. I always had difficulty in understanding him: words came out of him as a series of explosions of sound and much of it was rambling and disconnected. An anti-white racism often seemed to be lurking just under the surface, on occasion breaking into actual words. But, almost as a contradiction, there was always personal politeness towards me and a readiness to listen to my views.

It was not long before I went into total reverse on my original very critical assessment of Sobukwe. After yet another evening's encounter and discussion, I wrote in mid-June to a friend: 'Sobukwe was magnificent, clear, reasonable and eminently sensible. The more I see him, the more I like him and am impressed by him . . . a great fellow this.'

What I had initially viewed as timidity was, rather, I was starting to realise, the hesitation and doubts of an honest man who was struggling to decide what he should do; who was trying to reconcile the conflict between the exceptional economic and social status he enjoyed as a black man, allied with his contented family life, with his emotional and intellectual commitment to gaining freedom for blacks.

I was now more alive to his integrity and his willingness to consider, and to debate, opposing viewpoints. I was also responding to the personal warmth and the good humour that suffused his personality and which showed itself in the smile which would so often light up his face. He always spoke quietly, his deep voice making a sonorous sound of the words. He had the habit in conversation of emphasising a point by jabbing the air with his right index finger and exclaiming: 'Thaaat's right!'

His opposition to communism was absolute. He rejected it as a creed, believing it to bear its own oppression. And more particularly, he had the Africanist angry belief that communists had subverted the African National Congress and the black nationalist struggle.

Where his economic thinking could be defined, he described himself as probably more of a 'Fabian socialist' than anything else.

With all this I remained unconvinced about his argument that, overnight, blacks could be turned from hating to loving whites. This issue repeatedly arose and was combed over in detail in years to come with neither of us giving way.

Physically, we lived in entirely separated worlds. We could visit each other but it was becoming more and more unusual in South Africa among blacks and whites. If I wanted to go into Soweto I needed an official permit giving me permission to do so.

In mid-1958, my own life changed and this had a bearing on my relationship with Sobukwe. I joined the *Rand Daily Mail,* Johannesburg's English-language morning newspaper, as a reporter. Because of my new job I resigned from the Liberal Party. My lack of training in journalism led to my being sent to report the magistrates' courts in Johannesburg for three months. But my chief interest was in black politics: I had an implicit belief that change would emanate from this area of society, even though almost all whites ignored or despised it. I spent much of my own time, especially over weekends, talking to people involved in the left and attending meetings which I then reported for the *Mail*. By late in the year this became my full-time work on the newspaper.

One result was that Sobukwe and I saw each other more than before, and our friendship grew. He was a primary figure in the hectic events inside the ANC so we were constantly in touch. Apart from the *Rand Daily Mail*, I was also doing much of the reporting from the Johannesburg area for *Contact*. I needed to keep this separate from my full-time work so I looked for a pseudonym: Sobukwe came up with a rough translation into Zulu of my surname's apparent meaning, 'On or over the ground': *Umhlabeni*.

Up to this time, blacks had generally featured in the white establishment Press only during time of rioting, or as the subject of reports about criminals and court cases. Although the 'native problem' was fundamental to everything that was happening in South Africa, the argument on what to do about it raged among whites exclusively. The natives themselves seldom came into the picture. Their views were not wanted.

Fortunately, Laurence Gandar had become editor of the *Rand Daily Mail* earlier in 1958. Under his editorship, the *Mail* broke new ground not so much through its reporting on the racial situation— important as this was—but principally because of the quality of Gandar's political analysis in which he assailed apartheid and called for a more equitable society. The government and many whites came to hate the paper with a quite frightening intensity; conversely, among blacks and anti-apartheid whites, the *Mail* became a beacon of hope.

Gandar was receptive to the *Mail* reporting on black politics in a serious and consistent way. It meant going to meetings in the black ghetto areas and spending hour after hour, day after day, sitting at conferences which often started three, four or five hours late and which staggered on into the early hours of the morning. Repeatedly, the pattern was that at the start of a conference several journalists would be present, both whites and blacks. By the end of the first day I would be the only white person around, with a few black journalists with me. By the end of the third day, the chances were that I was the only journalist still sitting patiently waiting for the story to break. The *Mail* began to publish news about black political developments, and went on to give news about the everyday lives of black people, whether their troubles with passes or the state of roads in ghettos.

The *Mail* became the pacesetter in South African journalism in this as much as in other spheres of reporting and comment.

6

The *Rand Daily Mail*'s willingness to report in the neglected area of black lives was tied in with developments in the country whereby entirely new patterns were being created which would profoundly affect the future. The Afrikaner Nationalists had now been in office for a full ten years and were firmly in control.

A general election they called in April 1958, the second since 1948, saw their majority again increase, so that they now held two-thirds of the seats in the all-white Parliament. The Liberal Party's policy of non-racialism was put forward by three candidates: all lost heavily. Only whites voted in the election; the Nationalists had just won a six-year battle to expel coloureds and Asians from the common voters' roll. Whites automatically had the right to vote, but coloureds and Asians had had to meet educational or property qualifications. Two weeks before the whites-only election, a coloureds-only election was held for three Members of Parliament, all of whom had to be whites; not much more than an eighth of the potential coloured voting population took part. Blacks remained completely excluded from voting. Conversely, more whites were given the franchise: the voting age for them was dropped from 21 to 18.

A 'national workers' conference'—the African National Congress was behind it—had met and called on blacks to stay at home from two days before the 16 April election 'until such time as the people's demands have been met'. The pre-election strike drew little support. In countering the protest, the government imposed a ban on gatherings of more than ten blacks in major urban areas—and this remained in effect until it was lifted at the end of August.

Clearly, growing numbers of whites were in favour of more apartheid and the government was feeding their prejudices. The major racial laws introduced by the Nationalists were in place and were being relentlessly applied and extended. A vast amount of government energy was going into imposing apartheid, reaching into every conceivable detail of the lives of the 3 million whites, 9.6 million blacks, 1.3 million coloureds and 440,000 Asians.

A society was being created in which racial discrimination against blacks was entrenched on a scale unknown in the world.

That year, yet another amendment to the Group Areas Act tidied up a few more loose ends in the process, begun in 1950, to segregate people of different colours into their own residential and business areas. It said that 'disqualified persons' could buy refreshments in restaurants or tea rooms as long as it was not necessary for them to sit down and consume the refreshments purchased. What this meant in practice was that those who were not white were being given a concession: they could enter a restaurant or tea room in suburbs and city centres designated for whites and could buy food and drink—on condition they did not try to sit down and eat on the premises. The concession would, of course, help ensure that white-owned businesses did not lose customers.

The Group Areas pattern went on as before: overwhelmingly, desirable areas in which coloureds and Asians lived and traded were designated for white occupation, whereas only handfuls of whites ever found they were in the racially 'wrong' area. The official machinery for seizing the property of coloureds and Asians was working smoothly, which meant it was a time of heartbreak for the owners of expropriated homes and shops. Government valuators decided how much compensation was to be paid, and kept the amounts low. Owners and tenants were evicted and ordered to move to group areas assigned to their racial group, at lengthy or inconvenient distances away. Whites took over their property at bargain basement prices.

For blacks, enforced removal—under other laws—was also under way. Johannesburg's Sophiatown, a suburb known for its liveliness as much as for its crime, and where blacks enjoyed freehold rights of land tenure, had already been zoned for whites and the clearing out of blacks was being pushed forward. A vast new ghetto was growing up on farm land to the south-west of Johannesburg, with low-cost city council and government houses being built *en masse* for those moved from elsewhere in the city. The new area did not yet have a name but later a public competition yielded Soweto, an acronym for 'South West townships'.

How Can Man Die Better

Not everyone was being given housing, however: in Sophiatown, only those who had registered their names as residents in 1954 were accepted. Large numbers of people who had defied the government at the time, or who were there without official permission, or who had entered since then, were facing a desperate future. Meanwhile, life was made miserable for them, and everyone else in Sophiatown and its neighbourhood, by incessant police raids in the early hours of the morning. As always, people were defenceless against the roughness of police behaviour.

There were also forced removals in the rural areas, a prelude to the huge re-locations to come in later years. The pattern was well established for ordering blacks to quit land wanted by whites. Victims were ordered to go somewhere else, and the slightest sign of resistance led to armed police moving in and burning down huts. Rural unrest flared up intermittently: that year, there were troubles of one sort or another in Tembuland, Transkei, Sekhukhuneland and the Western Transvaal. The African National Congress was barred from several of these areas.

The notion of reconstructing the tribalism which had been on the wane was propounded by the Minister of Native Affairs, Dr Hendrik Verwoerd. He and his senior officials travelled tirelessly to attend the installation of officially recognised chiefs. Those chiefs who did not collaborate were summarily deposed. Several of them and other dissidents were served with arbitrary 'removal' orders, forcing them into exile in faraway, lonely places where they eked out a wretched existence. But, by September, 298 tribal authorities —the basic ground-level administrative unit—were established, plus twenty-six district authorities and eight regional authorities. One territorial authority—the top of the bureaucratic heap—also existed, in the Transkei.

Black workers in the cities were equally at the mercy of their employers and the state, and full advantage was taken of them. Strikes were prohibited and transgressors faced criminal charges— after, on occasion, the police got through breaking heads outside factories. Unions for blacks were not recognised in law, although individual employers could agree to treat with them (only a handful were actually thought to do so). A country-wide network of government labour bureaux was now established: employers had to hire all their black workers through the bureaux, except for workers returning to the same employer within twelve months. This mechanism was meant to control the number of blacks going to work in the cities, allowing in from the rural 'reserves'—the land reserved for blacks and which acted as reservoirs of labour—only as many as were needed by employers. The bureaux also directed black workers to the white farms, where vile conditions did not easily draw willing recruits. Farmers were in any event demanding workers because the labour pattern was being disrupted through action to get rid of 'squatters' and tenants who had traditionally been given the use of small plots on white farms in return for the labour of the entire family, children included. And the bureaux played the additional role of making it easier to blacklist workers, such as those who went on strike in the cities and were ordered back to the reserves—which often meant dooming them and their families to starvation. The threat of what could befall them was a potent weapon to ensure that blacks with jobs did not step out of line.

Worker unity was under continuing attack, with government insistence that those trade unions which were racially mixed had to be segregated. The effects were showing in the growth of racially divided, and conflicting, trade union federations. Tensions among workers were also fed by 'job reservation'—allocating specified jobs to people of a particular colour, with the aim of protecting whites. In May, for example, the work of driving trucks to cart rubbish, refuse and nightsoil in the city of Durban was reserved for whites only. In August, fifteen categories of work in the section of the iron, steel, engineering and metallurgical industry which was concerned with the manufacture of windows, louvres and doors, were reserved for whites. The government's tribunal recommended that, in Cape Town, the work of ambulance drivers and attendants, firemen and traffic policemen above the rank of constable be reserved for whites. It said that no further coloureds should be recruited as traffic constables and those already employed should be transferred to non-white areas. In a related step, from 1 July, coloured traffic constables were not allowed to arrest white offenders. The tribunal also recommended that 84 per cent of drivers and conductors of passenger buses in the Cape Town area had to be whites. Still other investigations were under way so that large numbers of black, coloured and Asian workers lived under threat of loss of their jobs.

Government wage boards fixed minimum wages for black unskilled workers. The system was so cumbersome and neglectful of workers' interests that a number of major municipalities still paid minimum wages of about £103 a year—as fixed sixteen years before, with only a small allowance for the rise in the cost of living. In industry, blacks earned about £156 a year, compared with the £820 of whites. In contrast, the Poverty Datum Level, a sociological measure indicating the amount needed for mere survival, stood at £282 a year; 87 per cent of black families in Johannesburg were estimated to be living below the bread line. Yet incomes were even lower in gold mining while, in farming, cash wages were as low as £48 a year with in kind payments, of maize and use of land, estimated at a further £50 a year.

A new trend was also pushing down wages: the government was encouraging white businessmen to set up factories in 'border' areas—on the edges of the reserves. Later this decentralisation policy was to become a major plank of apartheid, with attempts to turn back the tide of blacks streaming into the cities. Now, in its early stages, it was a licence for white businessmen to make money: they were able to start border factories free of any legal requirements about levels of pay and free of any trade union action, thus getting away with paying only a third of the already low wages of black workers in the cities. Employers in the cities also had their methods of getting cheaper than cheap labour: by taking on blacks whose passes were not in order, they were able to pay them a pittance; any worker who protested, or who objected to poor working conditions, knew he would be tossed out, to haunt the streets in search of a job while risking arrest, or to face return to rural poverty.

Apartheid permeated all education, with segregated schools and teacher colleges for each colour group. The ideology behind it was Christian National Education, conceived by Afrikaner Nationalists during the 1930s. The 'Christian' in the title was Afrikaner Calvinism, and 'National' meant apartheid and love of one's own. The numbers of black school pupils and teachers again increased steeply during the year, helping to make up for the deficiencies of the past. But the quality of education was plunging, reflecting the ideological view of the debased place of blacks in society and because the allocation of government money remained low. The amount was fixed, and was to remain unchanged for years to come, with the decree that additional funding could come only from taxes paid by blacks. The pay of white teachers was increased during the year; that of blacks was not. The black teachers in any event earned substantially less than their white counterparts, even those few who had equal academic qualifications. The same, incidentally, was true for black nurses and any black doctor in government service. Facilities in black schools were universally poor, and looked even worse when compared with white schools. About £54 was spent that year on educating each white child, and less than £8 on each black child.

The gap in education was also reflected in the numbers in the four senior school classes: for whites, 20.2 per cent of the total enrolment; for blacks, 1.1 per cent. The government was also winding down the amount of money it provided for school feeding; never very great, it was now only a twelfth of what it had been two years before when parents had been given the cruel choice of having money spent on meals for their children or on extending educational facilities.

This was also the first year that government subsidies to private schools were totally abandoned: it affected hundreds of Roman Catholic and Anglican schools that had refused to be swallowed up when the government took over all black education five years earlier. The schools had to apply for registration as private institutions; those situated in areas zoned for whites under the Group Areas Act were turned down. At least forty Catholic schools were to close at the end of the year. During the year, a number of teachers—the exact total was uncertain—were dismissed without being given any reasons or any hearing; it served as a continuing warning not to be outspoken. At the post-school level, the Extension of University Education Bill came before Parliament in August but was postponed to the next year. Its title was misleading because in fact it cut down access to so-called white universities; these English-language universities lost the right to admit blacks, coloureds and Asians unless a special permit was issued, for each person, by the government department which handled the racial group involved. At the same time, buildings were being erected for special apartheid colleges for blacks, derisively dubbed 'tribal' or 'bush' colleges. Once-flourishing night schools for black adults, which promoted literacy classes, were in sharp decline because of official obstruction.

Although denied the vote, every black male had to pay a head tax each year. It was recorded in the pass, and failure to pay could mean instant arrest, prosecution and, often, jailing. The law had already been amended to increase taxes from the end of the year, making them even more discriminatory: not only did the head tax still have to be paid, but taxation for blacks began at eighteen, as against twenty one for other colour groups, and the level of income at which general taxation was started was set at a lower level of income than that for other colour groups. So the most poorly paid South Africans were made to carry a heavier tax load—and again, unlike anyone else, a criminal sanction attached to non-payment. Blacks also had to pay special tribal levies, plus a monthly levy for the education of their children, as well as paying for school books, stationery and the cost of cleaning and maintaining school buildings. In the face of the poverty of so many, the government was ending assisted sub-economic house rents for those at the lowest end of the scale; instead, rents were to be fixed at economic levels to recover what was being spent on building houses.

Despite the lack of government charity and concern about the needy, the great myth was being propagated, and continued as a mainstay of official propaganda, of the white man's burden in carrying blacks financially.

Apartheid already existed on all trains and was now being extended to all buses. Durban had been ordered to have totally separate buses for whites and people of other colours by the first day of that year. In January, the new Nursing Council sent out forms for all nurses to complete so that a register could be compiled. The Council had been created the previous year as a statutory body to control the nursing profession. Only whites could sit on it. Nurses had to be formed into racially separate branches; coloureds and blacks had their own advisory boards and could, separately, each elect one representative—white—to the Council. The Council's registration set off troubles during the year because it also served as a means of forcing black women to apply for passes: they had to give the Council an identity number, which could only be obtained by registering with the Native Affairs Department. The infant death rate for whites was 28 per 1,000; for blacks, inasmuch as it was known because black births and deaths were often not recorded, it was nearly 400 per 1,000 in some city ghettos. The old-age pension for whites was a maximum of £126 a year. Blacks got less than £21 a year.

On the international scene, July saw the government return to full participation in the United Nations in New York, after having earlier walked out because of criticisms of its domestic racial policy. India told the UN that, acting on the previous year's General Assembly appeal to South Africa to negotiate with India and Pakistan about the treatment of Asians—an issue which had first been raised in 1947—it had written to South Africa, but had not received any reply. Britain, the United States and Brazil constituted a 'good offices' commission to seek agreement with South Africa to accord international status to South West Africa, the territory over which South Africa had exercised a League of Nations mandate since after the First World War.

In Africa, Ghana had achieved independence the year before and, under Kwame Nkrumah, was the beacon of freedom for the entire continent. The rush to independence was on.

At home, racially mixed marriages were not legally possible, and had not been since 1949. The Immorality Act barred inter-racial sex, and there were hundreds of prosecutions of transgressors, mainly white men and black women. The Act affected not only casual sex: several racially mixed couples who lived together and had children were hauled into court and jailed, although the publicity they received did lead to early ending of their imprisonment.

As a recurring theme, there was tougher enforcement of Section 10 of the Native (Urban Areas) Consolidation Act—which meant greater strictness in the pass laws, for Section 10 was the vital clause which defined the criteria which blacks had to fulfil to gain the right to live and work in city areas. On 16 October, teams of officials began issuing passes to women in Johannesburg. This was already causing anguish in other parts of the country for what now lay ahead was that women would be as susceptible as their menfolk to being stopped by any policeman and dragged off to jail. Protests erupted in Johannesburg, and nearly 2,000 women were arrested, to appear in mass criminal trials.

Black men arrested for contravening the pass laws—it was a criminal offence to be in any of the cities or towns for more than seventy-two hours without permission—were, it turned out, often spending three months as labourers on white-owned farms. It was cloaked as a form of parole. Considerable publicity was given to the way in which men disappeared after being sentenced, and to the cruel conditions which some suffered on the farms. Alongside this system, farmers could buy the services of prisoners, and there was publicity too for the savagery of their behaviour.

Bureaucrats were also hard at work on the system that made enforcement of apartheid possible—Population Registration. The law, initially introduced in 1950, was to ensure that every single

How Can Man Die Better

South African was put into a defined racial pigeonhole. Each person was given an identity number, part of which was a racial classification: thus 00 meant a white South African, 01 a coloured, 02 a Malay, 04 a Chinese, 05 an Asian, down to an 09 for a Nama of South West Africa. Two sections, 06 for 'Other Asian' and 07 for 'Other coloured', provided for those who could not be fitted in elsewhere, a sort of miscellaneous of the human race.

Those vital two digits were intended to, and did, affect life from birth to death, with every detail specified and fixed by law: in which hospital you could be born; in which suburb you could live; which house you could buy; which farm you could buy; which nursery school and school you could attend and which university or technical college; which cinemas and theatres you could go to; which buses, train compartments and taxis you could travel in; which bus stops, railway pedestrian bridges and platforms you could use; which beach you could swim from; which municipal swimming pool you could use; from which library you could get books; which park bench you could sit on; in which restaurants you could eat; which lavatories you could use; in which hotels you could stay; whether you were allowed to enter a municipal hall; which jobs you could hold and how much you would earn; how much liquor you could buy and possess; who you could legally have sex with and who you could marry; how easily you could get a passport for travel abroad; how much your old age pension, disability or war veteran's pension would be; which sportsfields you could use, and the quality of the facilities available to you; whether you could vote; which hospital you could go to if you fell ill and which doctors and nurses would attend to you; which hearse you would be carried in when you died; and in which graveyard you would be buried.

By September 1958, the government was able to announce that 95 per cent of the Central Population Register was up to date. 'Race classification boards' had disposed of a total of 45,024 'borderline' cases: many people had undergone such racial 'tests' as having a pencil pushed through their hair to check the crinkliness, or having their fingernails examined because the moons were supposed to indicate something about racial origin. In pursuing the goal of racial purity, the requirements for classification were changed from time to time, with different weight given to family background, physical appearance and social acceptance. Families could be, and were, split with some members trying successfully for white status and the privileges that went with it, and others being classified as coloured. As a spin-off, malicious people had a field day as neighbours and enemies informed on people who were 'trying for white', as it was known.

A slight tinge of moral discomfort was beginning to reveal itself among some Afrikaner Nationalists—not many of them—about the *baasskap* (literally 'boss-ship', and meaning white supremacy) of apartheid. They were beginning to feel uncomfortable that their naked white domination was viewed with distaste by the world outside. Even within the Afrikaner group, a few lonely but notable voices were asking pointed questions about the morality of apartheid. Of greater significance, an Afrikaner think-tank, the South African Bureau of Racial Affairs (Sabra), was studying ways of making apartheid respectable by giving it an intellectual foundation.

Out of this came the concept of 'separate development'. There were fierce disputes among Afrikaners about evolving a racial policy, with the conflict at this point centred on whether only the government should be in contact with black leaders. While the tussling was going on, Verwoerd became Prime Minister. He took over in August, after the death of J.G. Strijdom, in his prime a racist fire-eater known as the 'Lion of the North', who had in turn succeeded Malan.

Verwoerd insisted that contact with blacks had to be confined to whites in government. He broke the opposition he faced by taking over Sabra's emerging policy as his own. That policy was an extension of the tribalism which was already a centrepiece of Nationalist ideology, aimed as it eventually evolved at nothing less than the Balkanisation of South Africa, with division of the country into one state for whites (with coloureds and Asians included), and nine or ten states for blacks, one for each tribal group. These became known as Bantustans, following the government's new term, 'Bantu', derived from the word 'people', as used in linguistics. The word was resented by many blacks as much as was native. African was the desired term. Which word was used usually reflected political consciousness: blacks who worked in government institutions, and many ordinary people too, followed the official nomenclature; blacks in anti-apartheid circles, as well as liberal whites, spoke of Africans.

The confidence trick at the core of the policy was that whites, who then made up 20 per cent of the population, abrogated for themselves some 86 per cent of South Africa, with the Bantustans occupying the remaining 14 per cent. The land for the tribal mini-states derived from the 'reserves' which had been created in 1913, and extended in size in 1936, as areas set aside for exclusively black ownership, and used in practice as reservoirs from which to draw black labour when and as needed for the white-owned mines, factories, homes and farms. Blacks were not to enjoy any rights in the new white state; they could live there only for as long as their labour was needed—and even stricter controls were to bring about a reduction in their numbers. As they would be 'foreign workers', ran the Nationalist argument, much like the Turks who were 'guest workers' in West Germany, who could complain if they were not accorded any of the benefits of citizenship? 'The National Party supports the policy that the white man wants to retain his domination over his part of the country,' Verwoerd told Parliament in March 1959 in support of the Promotion of Bantu Self-Government Act which created the legal framework for what was to come. He added, however, that the Bantustans could develop into full independence—which, in time, came to result in the creation of tribal mini-states, with blacks willy-nilly becoming citizens at the cost of their South African citizenship.

Separate development spelt a grim reality for blacks. It meant, in the first place, that they were to lose even the reduced rights conferred on them by their second-class citizenship and were to become strangers in the land of their birth; it meant that the dispossession and enforced removal, often at gunpoint, would become more ferocious; in particular, the targets now would be the old, the ill, the women and young children who could not provide labour. And it meant intensification of the pass laws, to root out those blacks deemed to be in the cities illegally—that is, again, people whose labour was not needed and who therefore did not have permission to be there.

The white opposition United Party sought for a policy which it could offer as an alternative to the Bantustans. More and more, however, it was becoming a pale shadow of the Nationalists, weakly trying to match their racist appeal to white voters. The issue of the amount of land to be added to the reserves brought the internal dissension to a head and resulted in a breakaway by twelve Members of Parliament, who went on to set up the Progressive Party, later called the Progressive Federal Party, and pursuing a rather more determined anti-apartheid policy.

As the government colossus embarked on this awesome social engineering, it encountered growing resistance from blacks. The long-term impact of separate development was still only dimly perceived and understood, if only because the policy was still being evolved; but every black person was beginning to suffer its immediate effects.

Through most of 1958, the African National Congress was engaged on two fronts: externally, trying to offer some opposition to the government; internally, racked by conflicts. Some of the conflicts were ideological in origin, centring on the Africanist Movement, while others had to do with unrest among members because of poor administration and handling of finances. In the Cape Town area, the ANC was split into two different sections, each claiming authority. Disunity was rife in other parts of the country too, but the Transvaal province was worst of all.

The Transvaal troubles had broken into the open in the middle of 1957 when several branches began to campaign for a new provincial executive. The basis of the call was dissatisfaction with the way the province was run. But the branches were told that because of the government's attacks on the ANC—bannings were increasing and the Treason Trial was under way—the leadership should be supported. The 'We stand by our leaders' call created a serious dilemma for Sobukwe and others who were unhappy on ideological grounds about events inside the ANC. For there was certainly much merit in the argument that leaders under attack should be given unquestioning support; not to do so would play into the government's hands in its efforts to cripple the ANC by emasculating the leadership through arbitrary administrative decrees. On the other hand, the alternative was to give the leaders *carte blanche* to do almost as they pleased without having to account for their actions. It also meant that the leadership perpetuated itself in office with banned people remaining on executive committees and operating behind the scenes, again without being accountable to the membership.

It was the last set of factors which bothered the Africanists. They were alarmed that not only was an unrepresentative leadership being created, but its existence in the shadows could make it even more subject to communist influence.

The ANC national executive intervened to put the province's affairs in shape, and promised a conference for a new executive as soon as it could be held. But the internal conflict did not abate; instead it was transformed into a full-fledged ideological battle. The former Transvaal leadership was no longer the primary target of criticism. The policies and outlook of the national leadership were the targets. Who was to control the ANC, and what the organisation should do, were the issues at stake.

An early skirmish had occurred in May with the expulsion from the ANC of Leballo and Josias Madzunya on the grounds of anti-Congress activities. Madzunya was leader of the ANC's branch at Alexandra, outside Johannesburg; although a black ghetto it was an area where blacks had the right to freehold tenure—almost the last urban one left in South Africa. It ranked among the worst slums in the country, gangsters terrorised the inhabitants, and the politics were fierce. Madzunya was a familiar and striking figure: dark-faced, he had a large black beard and wore a long black overcoat throughout the year, even on the hottest days, and always buttoned up. He earned a living by buying and selling boxes and operated from a street corner on the edge of Johannesburg's central business district. He had a long record as an African Nationalist. He would also acquire a reputation in due course of backing away from campaigning at the last moment.

Madzunya and Leballo had the same strange mesmerising characteristics: when either of them addressed a public meeting the words poured out in torrential waves, rapidly building up to the point where there was no discernible coherence but only a scream of disconnected words. Each of them could get a crowd jumping hysterically within minutes.

Leballo did not accept his expulsion. Instead, from his position as Chairman of the Orlando branch, he promptly expelled the official who had sent him the expulsion notice—Duma Nokwe, then Assistant National Secretary-General and also a member of the Orlando branch.

The much-awaited Transvaal conference was set for Saturday and Sunday, 1 and 2 November, at the Communal Hall in Orlando, a favoured site for Congress meetings in the Johannesburg area. It was to be a combined annual and special conference.

Benjamin Pogrund

A report I wrote in *Contact* on 1 November summed up the opposing policies and views of the two sides. On the one hand, the ANC's policy was one of universal suffrage and the equitable distribution of the wealth of the country among all persons, irrespective of colour or race. Indeed, co-operation with other racial groups was an essential part of the ANC's policy. On the other hand, the Africanists argued that the ANC had not adhered to its 1949 Programme of Action and was so influenced by the communists that it perceived the struggle as one of class rather than of African Nationalism, resulting in too great a degree of co-operation with other races and insufficient attention to forging the African people into a united group.

The organising activity leading up to the conference was intense. Claims, assertions and rumour abounded, with each side declaring its confidence in victory. Six weeks beforehand it was already clear that the decisive issue would be the selection of delegates. Fierce jockeying was under way and a number of branches were said to be so split that no agreement was possible on delegates. Both the leadership and the Africanists were busy arranging to have 'volunteers' present. The intentions were plain. On the leadership's side the volunteers were to maintain order and discipline; there was no doubt that this would include any strong-arm action required to enforce decisions about who was, and who wasn't, an acceptable delegate. Leballo and Madzunya were looming as particular problems: they were determined to get into the conference, come what may.

Their attitude was shared by other Africanists. They did not intend to allow the leadership to disqualify any of their delegations or members. Their plan was to get inside the hall and to move an immediate vote of no-confidence in the Chairman, whoever he might be, and then to elect a 'neutral' Chairman—in fact, one of their own, Zeph Mothopeng. The Chairman would then move immediately to elections, with the Africanists sweeping the board. That, at least, was the theory.

To get to this end-point, the Africanists agreed there had to be violence. They reached this conclusion at a meeting from which Sobukwe was absent. However, he was present at a subsequent meeting and spoke against the notion of going in regardless of the consequences. But his was the only dissenting voice in the group of about twenty.

How Can Man Die Better

That Sobukwe did not command unswerving, blind support was also revealed in private statements by Leballo about Africanist tactics. He said Madzunya was to be put in as President of the Transvaal ANC. Leballo himself and Sobukwe were to be held back and would go for the ANC's national leadership at the annual conference in December, he as President-General and Sobukwe as Secretary-General.

Amid these swirling currents, there wasn't total unanimity about how best to pursue African Nationalism within and through the ANC. Nthato Motlana was a known Africanist sympathiser but he was a notable opponent of any split. He was now practising as a medical doctor in Soweto, and his consulting rooms were the venue for many of the Africanist caucus meetings. 'These were my buddies,' he says. 'We all resented the role the Communist Party was playing in the mother organisation and wondering what to do about it. But I opposed the breakaway. I've always felt that you must meet problems and differences and that our struggles, in Zimbabwe and elsewhere, were held back by breakaways. The CP was very influential but very small. It never attracted a large African clientele. I think it's a great pity the Africanists broke away. It led to a lot of strife.'

But other Africanists who were fixed in regarding the conference as a last-ditch stand included some who were determined on the desperate stratagem of kidnapping members of the top leadership of the ANC the night before the conference. The victims were to include Chief Albert Luthuli, the ANC's President-General, Oliver Tambo, the national Vice-President, and Nelson Mandela, at that stage a former executive member who had been banned for several years but who was active in secret. The idea behind the kidnapping was to remove the leaders from the scene because Africanists believed that, during the last Transvaal conference, these ANC leaders had gathered at a house nearby and had sent messages on how the meeting should be run.

The kidnapping was seriously intended and awaited only the approval of a wider group of African Nationalists at a meeting scheduled for 28 September. This wider group comprised others in the ANC who shared the Africanists' criticisms of the leadership and their anxiety about communist influence but saw themselves as more moderate and less prepared to stage a make or break showdown, especially if it involved violence. In the event, the kidnapping did not happen, presumably because the wilder people in the Africanist camp were talked out of it.

Sobukwe was deeply worried about what was likely to occur at the conference. He was certain there was going to be bloodshed. He was sure there would be a lot of knifing and also shooting, as he said he knew that both sides intended being armed with guns. As only a handful of blacks could legally obtain firearms it meant that guns would be coming from the criminal underworld.

My assessment prior to the conference was that the leadership was going to win. Sobukwe agreed—in a private conversation between us, that is. He believed that whatever happened at the conference two 'ANCs' would emerge; neither side would accept the other's leadership and one or the other would break away to start its own movement.

Sobukwe's sober analysis apart, the euphoric expectations of the Africanists went unfulfilled at the conference. It turned out that they had entirely misread the willingness of the bulk of ANC members to tolerate precipitation of violence inside the organisation, and they had totally underestimated both the popular strength and the tactical skill of the leadership. The one person in particular who outplayed and outmanoeuvred them was Tambo, who was the Chairman of the conference. Luthuli was present and sat next to Tambo throughout the meeting. He gave an opening speech but the Africanists accorded him scant respect.

At an early stage on the first day of the conference—as usual for Congress meetings it began more than two hours late—it became evident that the Africanists had a hard-core group of about 100 in the crowd of 600. Everyone who wanted to attend was allowed in without hindrance, including Leballo and Madzunya. The group, many of them carrying long sticks, were at the back of the audience and they gave concerted shouts of support, with foot-stamping and cries of *'Afrika!'* to any Africanist speaker. After Luthuli's opening address, one after the other they were given every opportunity to express themselves, from Mothopeng: 'People in this country are divided into two groups, oppressed and oppressor; there can be no co-operation between them because their interests are clashing'; to Madzunya screaming: 'You can't ask me when I am struggling, to co-operate with elements of the oppressor.' In between, Sobukwe spoke, entirely in Sesotho with interpretation into English. He attacked white domination and defended black nationalism.

How Can Man Die Better

The afternoon of speeches gave way to an evening of wrangling over the election of a credentials committee which would have the task of checking on who was actually an official delegate. The Africanists grew angrier with Madzunya warning against 'monkey tricks'; Tambo continued to be placatory, but calmly pushed ahead with getting a credentials committee elected. Late in the night, with voting taking place, he called on Sobukwe to help count the show of hands. Sobukwe was taken by surprise and complied—and aroused Madzunya's ire. In a moment there was wild disorder and Sobukwe was surrounded by a seething crowd of Africanists. He and a few others went outside, saying the atmosphere in the hall was 'too tense'. I went also, but whereas they returned I did not: one of the Africanists rushed up to me with the warning: 'Go peacefully now. We do not want to hurt you.' Tambo also sent me a message that he had heard I was to be attacked. I was conspicuous as the only white person in the hall, so I left.

The next morning, Tambo's strategy was revealed. He had spent Saturday assessing the Africanists' strength. On Sunday he simply made sure that he had more thugs than they did. The Africanists arrived outside the hall in the same numbers as the day before; but Tambo had about 130 men carrying pieces of wood, sticks, lengths of iron and truncheons—apart from the 400 to 450 ordinary delegates and others. It was rumoured that guns were hidden in a small room at the back. With everyone outside the hall, only the delegates who had passed screening by the credentials committee were allowed inside—about 200 of them from 80 branches.

And that was the end of it. Tambo stood at the door. The Africanists moved off and about fourteen of them spent two hours in the garden of Leballo's house a few minutes' walk away debating their situation. At 5 p.m., they approached the hall and two of them went up to the door to hand over a letter addressed to the conference chairman. The letter was seized from them and they were chased away. The letter was later read to the conference, which was still proceeding with its business of tidying up the Transvaal's affairs, and it was noted.

Although signed by Selby Ngendane, as Secretary of the Africanist group, it was drafted by Sobukwe. It stated the nub of the Africanist view: 'We have consistently advocated African Nationalism and whenever we have stepped onto a political platform we have expounded that doctrine. In 1949 we got the African people to accept the nation-building programme of that year. We have stuck honestly and consistently to that programme. In 1955, the Kliptown Charter ... [was adopted]. We thought it was in irreconcilable conflict with the 1949 programme, and for that reason, opposed it.'

The letter went on to say the Africanists had put their case 'logically and peacefully' at numerous conferences—'It has, however, come to our notice that armed thugs have come to the conference today at the invitation of the leadership for the sole purpose of murdering certain Africanists who are thought to be the leading personalities in the movement. Ours is a political battle, aimed against white domination. We are not a para-military clique engaged in the murder of fellow-Africans.' Therefore, 'We have come to the parting of the ways ... We are launching out on our own as the custodians of ANC policy as formulated in 1912, and pursued up to the time of the Congress Alliance.'

Sobukwe went home. There was an air about him of accepting the inevitable. He told me he believed the three Africanists allegedly targeted for shooting were Leballo, Madzunya and Peter 'Molotsi, and that three killers had been assigned to each of them. Later that evening, Tambo replied to the accusations about arms-carrying supporters by telling me tersely: 'I have no such information.' Among the ANC leadership, there was almost a sense of relief that the crunch had finally come, mixed with relief that they had won the day. Luthuli told me, with a dismissive wave of his hand, 'Let them go.' Tambo said: 'I think the future is hopeful.'

At the end of the weekend, I wondered what the future held for the Africanists; whether, having been beaten so soundly after mobilising all their resources, they were now a spent force. But they had no such doubts.

7

Imbued with their belief in themselves and in their message, the Africanists set about the practicalities of creating a new political organisation. The working committee set up with Selby Ngendane as Secretary planned a launching conference for January 1959 but then postponed it to April. Work began on preparing a draft constitution. A target membership of 100,000 was set for 30 June 1959.

In early December, Sobukwe told me that the Africanists were 'meeting with great success'. They had just begun to send people on recruiting drives and were excited about the response. A paid-up membership—at two and sixpence a year—of 'over 5,000, mainly from the youth', was claimed by Ngendane. In the Free State province, it was said, seven branches, each with twenty to thirty members, had been started in areas where the ANC had never been able to get going; money was being collected and many promises of cash had been received from black businessmen.

The breakaway had been a Transvaal event and Africanists in other parts of the country were now calling for instructions. At first it was thought a good idea for them to try for a substantial attendance at the ANC's annual conference in Durban in December 1958. This was dropped, although a few local Africanists sought entry to the conference as ANC branch members. The credentials committee turned them away.

By mid-March, the Africanists were claiming to have not less than fifteen branches in the Cape Town area, each with at least fifteen members. The same sort of success was reported in the Eastern Cape with a whole series of branches being created. This was Sobukwe's personal doing: he went there late in January and said he found that it wasn't the Africanists' point of view he had to sell, but rather the wisdom of leaving the ANC.

Amidst these heady political times an acute personal dilemma was building up for Sobukwe. He had received an offer of a job in the Department of Bantu Studies at Rhodes University. This university, at Grahamstown in the Eastern Cape, was all-white although it maintained some links with Fort Hare, an hour and half's drive away. Named after Cecil John Rhodes, the nineteenth-century magnate who founded his fortune on diamonds and became a British Empire-builder, the university drew many Rhodesians as students, and was usually politically conservative. The job offer to Sobukwe was as a full-ranking lecturer, and was hence a significant improvement on his position at the University of the Witwatersrand.

The letter which Sobukwe now received from Rhodes, he told me, tactfully asked him for an assurance that he would not take too active a part in politics. In his reply he told the university he could not give that assurance. Meanwhile, as a result of the high public profile which the Africanists were experiencing—and the allegations in some newspapers of anti-whiteism—Sobukwe said he was having 'some trouble' at Wits concerning his political involvement and he did not think he could continue in his job there for much longer. He was trying to decide on some other way of earning a livelihood so that he could devote more time to politics. He was thinking of working full-time in politics and living off what the Africanist Movement could pay him.

But these worries were put aside for the moment as the Africanists went into their first national conference—their launching conference. It was held from 4 to 6 April at the Orlando Communal Hall, the same venue where the breakaway from the ANC had occurred five months before.

A sense of purposefulness was evident right from the start. It was no accident that the conference opened three minutes ahead of the scheduled 3 p.m: Sobukwe had said beforehand that he regarded timekeeping as an important element in creating a disciplined and ordered movement, and he was strongly critical of the ANC's habitual one- to three-hour late starting of meetings. (The timekeeping momentum, incidentally, was generally maintained during the conference, but within a matter of months the new organisation was tending to fall into the ways of the old.) The singing of the national anthem was at a faster pace than was usual, with the Chairman—Mothopeng—beating time with his hands. Wandering about by delegates was discouraged. Even the soft drinks habitually sold at political gatherings were for once refreshingly chilled: someone had had the sense to order a refrigerator.

The pan-African theme was marked. It was seen in the slogans on placards on the walls and stage, such as 'Africa for Africans. Cape to Cairo, Morocco to Madagascar', 'Forward to the United States of Africa' and 'Free Banda—Kaunda—Kenyatta'—all of whom, at that time, were in British colonial jails. The continental theme was maintained in the reading of messages received—which also gave the Africanists a notable propaganda coup—for there were cables of good wishes from Sekou Touré, Supreme President of the Republic of Guinea, and another from the father of Africa's twentieth-century independence, Ghana's Kwame Nkrumah. He wished the meeting 'every success in uniting Africans in non-violent constitutional struggle against colonialism and racialism for human rights and self-determination'.

First Banda, then Kaunda, had been invited to open the conference. But neither was free to come—and even if they had been, they would never have been given visas to enter the country.

The formal opening was by Sobukwe. It was public confirmation of what was known behind the scenes: he had become the leader of the Africanists. He was a changed man from what he had been only a year previously. In fighting within himself and finally reaching the decision that he could not forsake what he regarded as his duty, to establish and to lead this new movement, he had gained in strength and stature. It showed in his opening speech: he was scholarly as always, but there was now also a fluency and passion which put it among the finest oratory I had heard. It deservedly drew tumultuous applause. Away from the public platform, Sobukwe was still essentially a retiring person, with the innate kindness and gentleness which, then and in later years, caused so many people to respond to him after only brief acquaintance.

The simple fact was that, both intellectually and personally, he stood head and shoulders above the other Africanist leaders. That does not mean the others were people of no consequence. Far from it. There were among them men of ability and dedication. But Sobukwe was a man in his own class. With him at the helm, with him insisting on discipline and hard work, and with him largely directing policy, the prospects for the emerging organisation had to be given more weight than would otherwise have been the case.

Benjamin Pogrund

Sobukwe's exposition of Africanism was the most thorough yet attempted. In the broad canvas he covered he began with the international scene: the world was split into two large hostile blocs, the capitalist and socialist represented by America and Russia, he said. Each was armed with terrible weapons of destruction and they behaved as though they did not believe that co-existence was possible. There was again a struggle for Africa, with both blocs trying to woo the continent at a time when the entire continent was suffering a new birth.

In South Africa it was a time when 'the naked forces of savage *Herrenvolkism* are running riot'. He spoke of a determined effort being made 'to annihilate the African people through systematic starvation'; of the attempts to 'retard, dwarf and stunt the mental development of a whole people through organised mis-education'; of the thousands who roamed the streets in search of work and were being told 'by the foreign ruler to go back to a "home" which he had assigned him whether that means the break-up of his family or not'; and of the 'distinctive badge of slavery and humiliation'—the pass—being extended 'from the African male dog to the African female bitch'.

On race, he said: '. . . there is only one race to which we all belong and that is the Human Race. In our vocabulary, therefore, the word race, as applied to man, has no plural form. We do, however, admit the existence of observable physical differences between various groups of people. But these differences are the result of a number of factors, chief of which has been geographical isolation.' The existence of 'national groups' was recognised: they were the result of geographical origin within a certain area, as well as a shared historical experience. The Europeans were a 'foreign minority group' which had exclusive control, and was the dominant and exploiting group responsible for 'the pernicious doctrine of white supremacy which has resulted in the humiliation and degradation of the indigenous African people'.

On Asians, Sobukwe described them as a foreign minority group which was oppressed, but some of them, the merchant class in particular, had become 'tainted with the virus of cultural supremacy and national arrogance' and they identified themselves with the oppressors. The downtrodden Asians who alone could identify themselves with the indigenous black majority had not yet produced their leadership—'We hope they will do so soon'.

How Can Man Die Better

True democracy could only be established when white supremacy had been destroyed. The African people could be organised only under the banner of African Nationalism in an all-African organisation 'when they will by themselves formulate policies and programmes and decide on the methods of struggle without interference from either so-called left-wing or right-wing groups of the minorities who arrogantly appropriate to themselves the right to plan and think for the Africans'.

In the same context, multi-racialism was opposed because 'the history of South Africa has fostered group prejudices and antagonisms and if we have to maintain the same group-exclusiveness, parading under the term of multi-racialism, we shall be transporting to the new Africa these very antagonisms and conflicts'. It was a method of safeguarding white interests, implying proportional representation which, because it was irrespective of population figures, was a complete negation of democracy.

Sobukwe listed three major aims: firstly, politically, 'the government of the Africans, by the Africans, for the Africans, with everybody who owes his only loyalty to Africa and who is prepared to accept the democratic rule of an African majority being regarded as an African. We guarantee no minority rights because we think in terms of individuals not groups.' Secondly, 'economically we aim at the rapid extension of industrial development in order to alleviate pressure on the land which is what progress means in terms of modern society. We stand committed to a policy guaranteeing the most equitable distribution of wealth.' Thirdly, 'socially we aim at the full development of the human personality and the ruthless outlawing of all forms of manifestations of the racial myth'.

Further clarification came the next morning when delegates put questions to him. One said: 'I am not sure whether he is more inclined to socialism or communism,' and was told by Sobukwe that it was not necessary 'to give names to things. We do not have to follow particular ideologies if we do not accept them completely ... we borrow from East and West—political democracy from the West and planned economy from the East. And this planned economy has no meaning unless it means finally, equality.' Asked about redistribution of wealth, he said he would not stand for any differentiation of wages, whether for a plumber or a doctor—and 'if you want to confiscate the property of those who have it now, that will be a decision for the people. It could be acquired by payment of compensation. But if it is not a totalitarian state it will be a decision for the people.'

He was asked, too, about the Africanist stand on education, whether or not to boycott schools—the issue which a quarter of a century later was to be an equally agonising problem for black parents and children. 'We condemn Bantu Education outright,' said Sobukwe. 'But because of the conditions in this country we have not been able to put up our schools to give our children the education we would like to give them.' The choice was to keep the children out of school and have them roam the streets, or send them to school 'to acquire the three R's as well as Dr Verwoerd's indoctrination. But all of us here did not learn about the pass laws or about politics in the classrooms. If we want our children to have any education at all we are compelled to send them to schools but our duty is to counteract what they are taught. If the child can read, we can educate him. If Verwoerd can teach him about Bantu Authorities we can teach him about the liberation movement. I want to be practical about this: it is easy to condemn Bantu Education but you want to know about sending your children to school.' Loud applause greeted his statement.

Discussion ended and the conference moved briskly through its agenda. It adopted a series of founding documents: a manifesto, a constitution and a statement of policy, each of which was really an extension of what Sobukwe had said in his inaugural address.

The proposal in the draft constitution that the organisation be called the Africanist Liberation Congress was dropped in favour of stressing the continental concept through the name, the Pan-Africanist Congress. The official colours were to be green, black and gold—the same as the ANC with similar symbolism: green to represent the 'youth and vitality of the continent', black 'the colour of its people', and gold 'wealth actual and potential'.

Five aims were adopted: '(a) to unite and rally the African people into one national front on the basis of African Nationalism; (b) to fight for the overthrow of white domination, and for the implementation and maintenance of the right of self-determination for the African people; (c) to work and strive for the establishment and maintenance of an Africanist Socialist democracy recognising the primacy of the material and spiritual interests of the human personality; (d) to promote the educational, cultural and economic advancement of the African people; (e) to propagate and promote the concept of the Federation of Southern Africa, and Pan Africanism by promoting unity among peoples of Africa.'

There was a concealed sting in (d), again illustrative of the Africanists' still-developing attitude on race. During the conference, Sobukwe and others had made their emphatic rejections of any racial concepts and their stress instead on the 'human race'. On the other hand, there was not only the denunciation of white supremacy but also an accompanying refusal to co-operate with non-Africans, especially whites. These opposing standpoints were reconciled by adding the qualification that anyone who accepted Africa as his home was accepted as an African. It was thus possible, even if only in theory, to distinguish between those whites (and Asians) who were oppressors and those who were not.

In its draft form, the constitution acknowledged the distinction by referring in (d) to people 'of African descent', thus clearly encompassing black Africans, white Africans, and Asian Africans. The alteration in the final document to 'African people' was subtle but the meaning was inescapable. It could in a sense be said to be in line with the non-racial concept because 'African people' could include all those who had accepted Africa as their home. In practice, however, the intention was certainly to restrict the possibility of non-Africans becoming members of the PAC. As events were to show this was, however, by no means the end of the road in Sobukwe's thinking on this issue.

There was also a 'Disciplinary Code' which I thought was probably a throwback to the disciplined times of missionary schooling: it was a strange jumble of ideas ranging from Democratic Centralism and practical details about running a national movement, to exhortations to members to 'refrain from tale-bearing, back-biting, gossiping, rumour-mongering and spreading lies and distortions of truth', 'develop healthy and sound personal habits' and 'maintain an exemplary standard of cleanliness'.

The elections saw Sobukwe unopposed as President and elected by acclamation. Madzunya had viewed himself as a candidate but fell back in the face of the obviously overwhelming support for Sobukwe. Leballo was opposed as National Secretary, but won. The 'inner circle' of the Africanists had decided who they wanted for the executive and the various 'cabinet' posts and this was mostly the way it went.

One last-minute switch in the executive was important: Jacob

Dumdum Nyaose, the leader of the three black trade unions which had rejected the ANC's anti-election strike, was at the conference and urged the formation of a PAC labour wing. The Africanists were wary about going in for bloc representation from workers; Sobukwe was worried that Nyaose would use his leadership of workers as a bargaining hand inside the organisation. Instead, the Africanists wanted people to join as individuals, and members who were workers in turn to join trade unions. Nyaose was unknown to most of the leadership and Sobukwe indeed met him for the first time at the conference. Nyaose's argument was so persuasive, however, that he was rapidly taken on to the executive and put in charge of labour. In due course, in October that year, Nyaose created a new Federation of Free African Trade Unions (Fofatusa), which was intended to be the labour extension of the political body.

Exactly who, and how many, the delegates represented was difficult to say. On the whole they were better-dressed than the people who usually attended ANC meetings and this perhaps indicated that they came from better-educated and hence better-paid sectors of the community. There were few women and they were a much smaller proportion of the crowd than at ANC gatherings. As for the numbers present, not only was no figure given for total membership but the official claim that 634 delegates were at the conference was patently wrong: the true figure was closer to 300.

This notwithstanding, the conference participants, Sobukwe among them, ended the three days in a state of exultation. They were on their way.

So it was a masterful Sobukwe who met with the Press when the conference closed. On Bantustans, he said: 'We reject them *in toto*. We grant to nobody the right to Balkanise us.' On the extension of passes to black women and intensification of police pass raids: 'We condemn them.' On whether violent or non-violent methods would be used: 'We have not yet discussed methods of struggle.' This last reply, although brief, was pregnant with meaning for what it revealed was that not only was the PAC keeping open its options but, unlike the ANC, it was not dedicating itself to non-violence as the morally correct policy to follow.

Everything went fine until the matter of co-operation with other organisations was raised by the two reporters from the left-wing weekly newspaper *New Age*, one of whom was Robert Resha, a member of the ANC's national executive. First, Peter Raboroko of the PAC executive, in charge of education, replied that there would not be any co-operation; then Sobukwe qualified this by saying there could be co-operation with the ANC. Challenged further about the Liberal Party, there was shilly-shallying. Then Sobukwe said they would 'co-operate with the issue and not with the organisation concerned'. With Resha still pressing away, the Press conference ended with no one able to gauge exactly what the Africanists' attitude really was.

Anyone interested in semantics would have had an instructive time in the racial ways of South Africa in looking at the next day's white Press. The *Rand Daily Mail* published a report written by me which began: 'Nearly 300 Africans meeting in Orlando, decided yesterday to form a new political organisation pledged "to overthrow white domination". It will be called the Pan-Africanist Congress ...' That might seem straightforward enough. But most whites shrank from the word 'African', and to use it, as the *Rand Daily Mail* did, was the mark of a liberal or worse. So other South African (and Rhodesian) newspapers which carried my conference report— distributed by the national news agency—changed 'Africans' to 'non-whites'.

Afrikaans newspapers were driven to more extreme contortions because to translate 'African' into Afrikaans was to come perilously close to 'Afrikaner'. This they could not stomach. Hence their references to the banner displayed at the conference, 'Africa for the Africans ...', were translated into Afrikaans as *'Afrika vir die naturelle'* (Africa for the natives) or *'Afrika vir die nie-blankes'* (Africa for the non-whites). Both English and Afrikaans newspapers described the Africanists as the 'extremist rebels' of the African National Congress—ironically so, for these newspapers viewed the ANC as 'extremist' too.

One Afrikaans newspaper, *Die Volksblad* (People's Paper), used a headline which, clearly, was an expression of total and absolute disbelief that anyone could actually have uttered the thought: 'Native looks to the day when Pretoria will have a black premier,' it said.

During the next few days, as journalists visited Sobukwe for interviews, he was described as 'suavely spoken' or 'smooth-speaking', and 'a new and still unknown element in South African politics'. He was also given a more attentive and sympathetic hearing and was reported by *The Star* in Johannesburg as saying: 'No, I would not call myself an extremist. The only whites who have anything to fear from us are those who persist in trying to maintain white *baasskap*.'

8

Relations with people of other colours and with other organisations continued to be a thorny issue for Sobukwe and the PAC. As the task of building up the fledgling organisation got going in earnest, new situations and challenges exposed some fuzziness and contradictions in outlook.

There was nothing surprising in this; it was hardly to be avoided in a society growing more divided and complex by the day as apartheid bit deeper. Anyone wanting to maintain inter-racial contacts faced perplexing problems. How to forge political relationships, or personal friendships, across the white-black colour lines when equality of opportunity and quality of living were so hopelessly one-sided? Among blacks, many feared that the automatic right enjoyed by whites to the best possible education and access to wealth gave them undue advantage and manipulative power over other colour groups when they worked together inside organisations.

For many years, the African National Congress seemed to be immune to these problems. The ANC had been established to express black aspirations so it was natural for membership to be restricted to blacks. But political thinking developed and by the 1950s, even as apartheid was being enforced, the concepts of multi-racialism and non-racialism were gaining credibility in anti-government circles. The ANC's restricted membership began to look increasingly anomalous in an organisation fighting against racial segregation.

Yet black anxieties could not simply be wished away, or ignored. The ANC's way out was to foster parallel organisations for people of like mind but different colours. The Asian community already had its long-established South African Indian Congress, and the creation of other organisations was now encouraged. Hence the

Congress Alliance which came into being, consisting of the black ANC and separate Asian, coloured and white bodies, plus a fifth body, a trade union federation.

While blacks-only was a matter of expediency for the ANC, it was close to being a tenet of faith for the African Nationalists who became the Africanists who became the Pan-Africanist Congress. Black self-pride and self-respect were integral to their existence and they were aggressively insistent on blacks bringing about their own freedom. They also believed intensely that it simply wasn't possible for people of other racial groups to share the struggle honestly with them.

Multi-racialism was a dirty word to them; they saw it as the means whereby minority whites, and Asians, crept into the liberation struggle and took over control. At a level of principle, they saw it as reinforcing racial thinking because, even while it posited the coming together of racial groups, it did so on the basis of the existence of different racial groups, thus perpetuating the notion of racial separateness. Instead, the PAC approach was not to recognise race at all and to speak only of human-beings.

However, there were human-beings and human-beings: you could be fully accepted if you were an African; but who was an African? In theory, the concept was colour-blind. In practice, it wasn't. For the other element created by South African society also played its part—the effects of the poison of white racism. Since the 1940s, when blacks had cast aside pleading and begging for justice and had turned to militant demand, a reactive anti-whiteism had become a discernible factor.

Again, it was no surprise. Whites were the oppressors, so blacks could easily slip into responding to the rejection and viciousness of which they were victims with their own rejection and hatred. The mere declaration of fighting 'white domination' was an implicit statement against whites. A black man publicly humiliated as a black man by a foul-mouthed and racially arrogant white policeman acting in the name of the white system would have to be more than a saint not to be left cursing whites in general. Repeat that experience a thousandfold each and every day and the ground is made ready for anti-white feelings.

Yet, in general, it did not happen that way. As far as the ANC was concerned, elements of feeling against people of other colours did sometimes surface. But the leaders, with only the occasional hint of a dissenting voice, were committed personally and politically to co-operation with other colour groups, and this remains embedded in the ANC up to the present.

The position of black nationalists was rather more complicated. Despite their dedication to non-racialism, in practice the stress on blackness carried a message of anti-whiteism. Even more, anti-whiteism offered strong emotional opportunity for uniting blacks: it was a potent rallying cry which could go beyond tribe and class. And indeed, that the nationalists could play on this appeal contributed towards the ANC's refusal to throw open its doors to all colours: there was nervousness among ANC leaders that their ideological opponents would use it as a weapon and could thereby gain popular support.

For these reasons, by the time the PAC was formed, the black nationalists had acquired a widespread reputation for anti-white attitudes. My own newspaper helped to further the image: my report about the breakaway by Africanists from the ANC was the main story in the next day's *Rand Daily Mail* under the headline: 'Big-Scale ANC Split'. A large sub-headline said: 'Powerful splinter group proclaims "anti-white" policy'—although there were no references in the text which conveyed anything of the sort. The headline had been approved, if not written, by an Assistant Editor, Ivor Benson—partly, no doubt, because he shared the widespread white prejudice and ignorance about the nature of African Nationalism, and partly perhaps because (as emerged later) he was a rabid white right-winger who was an admirer and friend of the British fascist Sir Oswald Mosley. As my name was on the report, and as newspaper readers often do not realise that reporters are seldom accountable for headlines, the misinterpretation not only stuck to the Africanists but dogged me personally into the future.

The public image of the Africanists was also distorted by the occasional intervention of influential white political commentators. They lived in the world of white politics and were invariably uninformed about black politics, such as a columnist on the country's largest circulation newspaper, the *Sunday Times*, whose glib summation was: 'Who are the "Africanists"? To put it bluntly—they are Africans who are anti-white . . .'

It was never as straightforward as that. Among the Africanists there were certainly people who could be described as having intense animosity for whites. While Leballo, for example, was always polite to me personally, on public platforms he often declaimed in violent racial terms against whites. Sobukwe was always defensive about Leballo, saying that he had had searing racial experiences as a volunteer in the South African army in the Second World War, and was actually a good fellow. But I thought there were others like Leballo: in attending PAC meetings—often as the only white person present—I invariably felt nervously conscious of my skin colour in a way that did not occur at meetings of other organisations.

But to dub all the Africanists or the movement as anti-white was crude. Sobukwe, for example, was already a friend of mine, and our relationship was to grow a lot closer with the years. There was not a vestige of racial feeling in him. He simply accepted people as people, both then and always. Although I did not have the same closeness with other Africanists, there were people like Zeph Mothopeng, Z.B. Molete, A.B. Ngcobo and Jacob Nyaose of the PAC's national executive, and Raphael Tshabalala of the Witwatersrand regional committee, with whom discussion and friendship could come easily, irrespective of difference in skin colour and background.

Political views apart, making friends was difficult because of the impediments created by the government. Personal relations were complicated by the sheer physical difficulty of spending time together; even travelling in company from one city suburb to another required ownership of a car because of the apartheid on buses, trains and taxis. And the sight of whites and blacks travelling in the same car, unless a black person was clearly the chauffeur, could bring police suspicion and questioning—made almost certain, because of the law against inter-racial sex, if it was a white man sharing a car with a black woman, or even more perhaps, a white woman with a black man. None of us could go and have a cup of tea together or go to a restaurant for a meal.

In regard to Sobukwe, it was difficult at first to get to his home as I needed official permission to enter the black townships; but I did visit him a few times and avoided being halted by police patrols. Once I started specialising in reporting about black lives I was able to get an unusual facility: a permit issued by the Johannesburg City Council giving me the right to enter the townships twenty-four hours a day, throughout the year. Sobukwe in his turn could visit me at my apartment in a whites-only suburb in Johannesburg: it was legal—provided he did not stay overnight—but was anti-social in white terms. The government and the white community frowned on blacks and whites becoming friends. Few whites invited blacks as guests to their homes, and to do so in a rented apartment or house could endanger occupation as leases barred any behaviour classed as a 'nuisance' to neighbours.

The restrictions were on the white side. Most blacks did not have inhibitions in regard to contacts across the colour-line.

And therein lies the ultimate conclusion about the Africanists, for at no time did any of their feelings against whites come remotely close to resembling the harsh attitudes of whites towards blacks. There was even a sense akin to embarrassment among them about being hostile towards whites or Asians: anyone in the PAC leadership was always open to being challenged on the issue and would, for example, treat with the utmost seriousness questions which I flung at them asking why they shouldn't be derided as mirror-images of the white nationalists.

When all was said and done, black nationalists simply had too much responsibility towards the broader long-term interests of South Africa for them to play the racial game to the full. They realised the irreparable damage which could be done to a society made up of people of different colours who would have to go on living together into the future. Not only that—and without wanting to drift into metaphysical debate—the ethos among blacks in South Africa did not permit of gross racist attitudes, let alone action. The patience of blacks, and for so long their non-violence, has been a South African miracle.

There is a final point to be made on this subject: Sobukwe could not conceivably have been at the head of an organisation which was racist.

It was against this messy and often inconsistent and irrational background that Sobukwe and his colleagues set out to clarify their policy, sometimes by way of response to situations which did not fit into the established body of African Nationalist thinking. One of their first public rows, however, was of their own making: at a meeting in May held in Mofolo in Soweto, Sobukwe delivered a biting attack on liberals, thereby venting the deep-seated anger in some black circles about the historical role of whites in general in the black struggle.

So-called friends of blacks, he said, they were the only people who could split blacks. He named three of them in particular: the

Benjamin Pogrund

Right Rev Ambrose Reeves, Anglican Bishop of Johannesburg; Father Trevor Huddleston, the Anglican priest, later Archbishop, renowned for his anti-apartheid fight in Sophiatown until removed by his church in 1956, and for his superb book, *Naught For Your Comfort*, published that same year; and Patrick Duncan, of the Liberal Party and owner/editor of *Contact* newspaper.

Every time the ANC had embarked on a campaign, such as its anti-pass and defiance campaigns, the liberals had come 'with the big hand of friendship', said Sobukwe. But during the Defiance Campaign it was the black who went to jail. Only a handful of Asians went to jail and one liberal, Duncan, had gone in during the last stages of the campaign: Duncan had then wanted to be elected to the Senate in Parliament as a representative of blacks. When the ANC grew in strength yet another ally had offered itself—the (white) Congress of Democrats. The COD now wanted to set up one congress for all. Sobukwe said blacks had started building a nation when they set up the ANC in 1912, but the liberals had kept creeping in. 'The PAC says there will be no compromise with anybody who is not an African,' he said.

A tactful but still stinging reply came swiftly from Patrick van Rensburg, the Liberal Party's secretary. He described Sobukwe's attack as 'unfortunate' and appealed for those opposed to *baasskap* and discriminatory laws and practices not to fight among themselves. And, he said: 'I will not stop fighting because Mr Sobukwe does not like the colour of my skin. The sooner people in this country stop thinking about skin colour, the better.'

Sobukwe continued his attack in a lengthy article in *Contact* on 30 May. It was the most significant statement yet of the PAC view of co-operation with others and was a big step forward from the confusion during the Press questioning at the end of the previous month's inaugural conference. That Sobukwe was willing to write for the liberal paper in the midst of the PAC distancing itself so vehemently from liberals was due partly to the inherent contradictions of the time and place, and partly to my persuading him that he needed to explain where he stood.

'For a long time,' he wrote, 'the impression has persisted in the minds of many people in this country and probably abroad, that the Africanists are a wild "cowboy" crew, undisciplined and confused. The South African Press has created this picture in most cases, out of sheer malice. The Press set about creating an effigy that it christened

"African Nationalism" or "Africanist" and then systematically and methodically destroyed that effigy. Needless to say that at no time did the Press criticise either African Nationalism or the Africanists.'

Having delivered that broadside, he went on to explain the Africanist adherence to non-collaboration and, internationally, its support for Nkrumah's policy of 'positive neutrality'.

On co-operation with other groups, he said: 'Our contention is that the Africans are the only people who, because of their material position, can be interested in the complete overhaul of the present structure of society. We have admitted that there are Europeans who are intellectually converts to the African's cause, but, because they benefit materially from the present set-up, they cannot completely identify themselves with that cause.

'Thus it is, as South African history so ably illustrates, that whenever Europeans "co-operate" with African movements, they keep on demanding checks and counter-checks, guarantees and the like, with the result that they stultify and retard the movement of the Africans. The reason is, of course, that they are consciously or unconsciously protecting their sectional interests...

'Of the Indian minority we say that they are an oppressed national group. But among them has emerged a merchant class which has become tainted with the virus of national arrogance and cultural supremacy. The leadership of the Indian people, unfortunately, is drawn from this class, which, like the "sympathetic" whites, is concerned with protecting its own sectional interests.

'The only Indians who can, because of their material position, be interested in the complete overthrow of white domination and the establishment of a genuine Africanist democracy, are the poor "coolies" of the sugar plantations of Natal. But they have not yet produced the leadership of their own. What we wish of them is that they should reject this opportunist leadership and produce their own leadership...

'Politically we stand for government of the Africans for the Africans by the Africans with everybody who owes his only loyalty to Africa and accepts the democratic rule of an African majority, being regarded as an African.

'We guarantee no minority rights because we are fighting precisely that group-exclusiveness which those who plead for minority rights would like to perpetuate. It is our view that if we have guaranteed individual liberties we have given the highest guarantee necessary and possible. I have said before, and I still say so now, that I see no reason why, in a free, democratic Africa, a predominantly black electorate should not return a white man to parliament, for colour will count for nothing in a free Africa.'

The absence of any specific reference to coloureds was no accident: there had been a significant switch in policy inside the organisation and Sobukwe was to make it public that weekend, on 31 May, when a regional organisation for the Witwatersrand was set up. The 200 people at the meeting at the Orlando Communal Hall were said by the PAC to represent 9,086 members in 33 branches. It seemed a reasonable claim to me, given the intensive recruiting which had been going on. Privately, leaders said membership was not increasing rapidly, but was growing slowly and steadily. They were not having the great rush of popular enthusiasm they had anticipated but found they had to go from door to door and speak to people individually. Once this was done, they said, the proportion of recruitment was high.

In his keynote speech, Sobukwe dealt with membership by coloureds as though it had always been straightforward: PAC ideology logically included coloureds, he said. In fact, fierce argument lay behind the decision. Coloureds had been a problem for the PAC: some in the organisation pointed to them as indigenous to the continent and as fellow-victims of white oppression; others noted that coloureds generally craved acceptance by whites and turned their backs on blacks. There was no doubt that racial feelings were part of the argument: many coloureds looked down on blacks as inferiors, while many blacks scorned coloureds because of their racially mixed parentage.

The issue of membership had been precipitated by the action of a coloured man in Cape Town who, immediately after the PAC's founding conference, had written to Sobukwe pledging full support and asking for assistance in setting up a branch there. The writer was John Gomas: he had been a member of the Central Committee of the Communist Party of South Africa when it dissolved itself in 1950. When the party was re-created underground in 1953, Gomas was excluded.

Whatever the party's view of Gomas, for his part he had turned against the communists and now saw a political home in the African Nationalism of the PAC. His history of struggle made him a legendary figure and Sobukwe considered it unthinkable to reject him. However, Sobukwe had a hard job persuading the entire PAC national executive of this, and once the executive had agreed more hard work had to be put into getting the branches to accept the change. They did, and Sobukwe was therefore able to speak as though the PAC had always intended to include coloureds.

The decision about coloureds provided an immediate focus for debate at an afternoon get-together between Sobukwe and Mothopeng and three white left-wingers which I had coincidentally arranged. Sobukwe's acceptance of coloureds as indigenous people, like blacks, who had their roots in the country and continent, led to one of the whites demanding: 'Why not their fathers as well?'

It was a torrid few hours of confrontation for the PAC leaders. Questions were thrown at them: If they opened membership to all colours, wouldn't only a handful of whites and Asians want to join? Did they suffer from such an inferiority complex that they were unable to face the prospect of a small number of people of other colours being in their organisation without these people taking control? Surely there were tasks for which whites could offer expert knowledge? By way of example, one of the whites pointed out that, if it came to armed struggle, his experience in driving a tank during his Second World War military service could be of assistance to blacks. As left-wingers, he added, they were treated as outcasts from their own white group, so why should the Africanists reject them?

The discussion left everyone dissatisfied. The whites felt the Africanists had not justified the refusal to accept them. Sobukwe and Mothopeng were uncomfortable because they were unable fully to validate the exclusion of all whites. They promised to look again at their policy on relations with whites and Asians.

Although whites were in general uncaring about black politics, the debates about PAC policy were followed with keen interest in some circles. The rise of the Africanists had excited Afrikaner academics in their South African Bureau for Racial Affairs. Some of them viewed black nationalism as a parallel force to Afrikaner Nationalism; it was something they believed they could understand and sympathise with; they thought it fitted into their racial dream, just then emerging in the 'separate development' scheme, whereby blacks would be sent off into their separate tribal 'homelands'. There was similar interest among the Security Police: inasmuch as their attitude could be gauged, they seemed almost to welcome the new movement, no doubt because of its anti-communist stance and its conflict with the African National Congress.

But such honeymoon as there was—and it was purely in the minds of the Afrikaners, with not the slightest trace of it among the Africanists—did not last long. Reality soon intruded. The hopes of Sabra members had come out of *naiveté* and sheer inability to understand that African Nationalism was not merely the counter-face of Afrikaner Nationalism, but in its struggle to free blacks and to turn South Africa inside out, was the deadly enemy of the white Afrikaner rulers. By the time Sabra woke up to this its own leadership was in any event on the way out, defeated in its conflict with Prime Minister Verwoerd on the immediate issue of his insistence that contact with blacks had to be confined to officials of the government.

By mid-1959, the Security Police were taking their first obvious steps against the PAC, in the form of fake leaflets which sought to stir up antagonisms with the ANC. Using the PAC's address, these criticised a boycott campaign being waged by the ANC against products of Afrikaner Nationalist-controlled companies. Sobukwe phoned me with a quick disclaimer for publication in the *Rand Daily Mail*: 'We have stated time and again that we are not fighting the ANC. Our battle is against white domination.' The leaflet apart, the police were evidently not yet sufficiently alarmed about the PAC and it did not suffer the draconian action of which the ANC was regularly victim, in the banning of leaders and meetings. But as with the ANC, Security Policemen, mainly whites but including a few blacks, were always present at PAC meetings, spending long hours sitting in their cars outside halls or on the fringes of open-air meetings. No doubt they had their informers inside also; it was a reality of all radical opposition to the government.

The PAC went on organising. Inexperience and lack of money had their effect, however, and on National Heroes' Day on 2 August—a new all-black anniversary proclaimed by the PAC—Leballo admitted that the ambitious target of 100,000 paid-up members by 31 July had not been met. He said membership totalled nearly 25,000 in 101 branches throughout the country. The 100,000 figure was set again for 16 December when the Africanists planned their first national congress.

Heroes' Day—the date marked the twelfth anniversary of the death of Anton Lembede, the founder of the ANC Youth

League—gave Sobukwe the opportunity to announce the PAC's first political drive. This was to be a 'status campaign' aimed at obtaining courteous treatment for blacks in shops and in their everyday lives. 'This is an unfolding and expanding campaign involving the political, economic, and the social status of the African,' he said. 'We are reminding our people that acceptance of any indignity, any insult, any humiliation, is acceptance of inferiority. They must first think of themselves as men and women before they can demand to be treated as such. The campaign will free the mind of the African—and once the mind is free the body will soon be free.'

Sobukwe and I had discussed the idea of a status campaign. It perfectly suited the PAC: the clear need for it was summed up in Sobukwe's passionate few words; it would serve to encourage black self-respect; it meant mobilising black spending power; and it offered more than enough to engender popular enthusiasm.

Some work towards getting better treatment for blacks was already in progress: Bob Bodley, a ship's captain turned small-time publisher in Johannesburg, had, on his own initiative, come up with a 'People of Africa Pledge Courtesy' campaign whereby the city's stores were to be persuaded to put colourful stickers on their doors to show that blacks were welcome as customers and assured of polite attention. Bodley, who was white, both believed in the concept and stood to make money out of publishing directories listing the names and advertisements of participating stores. Several leading department stores took part, but even Captain Bodley's enthusiasm could not spread it through the city, let alone the mining towns and the rural towns where blacks had perforce to stand back respectfully for white customers or risk being thrown into the street. Several years later, however, when the campaign was long forgotten, the distinctive stickers bearing a map of Africa were still to be seen on the doors of Stuttafords, the most prominent of the department stores catering for wealthy whites.

The PAC's status campaign was never able to prove itself. Thought was already being given to a different and even more significant target, the pass laws.

9

To denounce the pass laws was easy enough: every conference of blacks did so vehemently, the loathing and the resentment pouring out, all the greater now that women were also being driven into the web of control. But how actually to attack the laws? As early as August 1959, Sobukwe was having secret discussions inside the PAC about a plan for outright defiance, to be undertaken early the next year. The underlying thinking came straight out of the 1949 Programme of Action: positive action and non-collaboration with the oppressor.

At this stage, Sobukwe envisaged a campaign in which black trade unions would play a major role—a notion intended both to take advantage of, and to foster, developments in the labour field. Most black workers were unorganised but the government was alive to the danger, to itself, if this were to change. So while enacting job reservation laws to keep blacks out of skilled occupations, the government had also, in 1954, changed the Industrial Conciliation Act, which regulated labour affairs, to deepen racial divisions among workers and to block the organisation of blacks. That was backed by Security Police hounding of those who still tried to organise blacks.

The Act stipulated that no new racially mixed unions could be formed; those which already existed—chiefly with white, coloured and Asian members—were forced to divide themselves into segregated racial branches and only whites could sit on the executives. Black workers were excluded from the Act: this meant that unions for blacks could not obtain official registration, which in turn meant they could not form part of bargaining procedures; the only way that black workers could negotiate for themselves was if employers decided to go counter to the government's wishes and agreed to deal directly with a black union.

How Can Man Die Better

Most white workers were happy enough to fall in with the government's dictates. Yet although black workers were cast into the wilderness, they still sought to co-operate with other racial groups, through the South African Congress of Trade Unions, (Sactu). Not all were of the same mind, however: political splits were carried over into the worker sphere and eight unions, representing a total of 14,000 to 17,000 black workers principally in the garment, baking and laundry industries, went their own way. Strong Africanist sentiment existed among several of these union officials and they rejected Sactu because of its multi-racialism, its partnership in the Congress Alliance and its emphasis on political struggle as against specific worker issues.

The labour scene, always one of shifting currents, grew still more complex with the entry of the American-dominated International Confederation of Free Trade Unions. A delegation visited South Africa in 1957 and found Sactu wedded to the rival Eastern bloc's World Federation of Trade Unions. So it encouraged the white-run Trade Union Council of South Africa (Tucsa) to help promote black unionisation. Out of this, in October 1958, came the formation of the blacks-only Federation of Free African Trade Unions, (Fofatusa). The President of the new body was Jacob Nyaose, Secretary of one of the dissident unions and who had been elected Labour Secretary on the PAC's national executive at the founding conference. Sobukwe and his colleagues had high hopes that Fofatusa's strength would snowball, giving the PAC a separate but closely connected labour movement.

It was as part of this process that Sobukwe began to plan the campaign: workers were to be urged to leave their passes at home and report to the nearest police station on their way to work. They would, he anticipated, be arrested and prosecuted for not carrying a pass; this would have the twin effect of putting pressure on the government through clogging police stations, courts and jails, and on employers to intervene because they would be without labour. He planned also to send letters in advance to employers asking them to help their workers by protesting against passes. But he saw this as a formality for he did not believe he would receive any replies: the overwhelming bulk of white employers were uncaring about the way the lives of workers were ravaged by the pass laws.

Sobukwe discussed the plan with members of his executive at a meeting over the weekend of 5 to 7 September 1959. They endorsed it and agreed that the details would be finalised at the first annual conference scheduled for December. The starting-date was to be kept secret for as long as possible, to reduce the danger from government counter-preparations.

At the two-day December conference, the plan was taken forward in a formal resolution by the 271 delegates from 153 branches, said to represent about 32,000 members. The conference did not take place without incident: seventy-five delegates travelling by road from the Eastern Cape were halted by the police for an alleged traffic offence and missed the first day. It was the usual sort of tactic used to harass blacks going to political gatherings.

As with the founding conference, strict timekeeping was a feature of the meeting. There was a crispness, too, in the wording and thrust of resolutions, again leaving the impression that this was a serious organisation intent on bringing a new style to black politics. Sobukwe's personal stamp was evident, and he was the public star too: as he rose to give his presidential address, delegates cheered and sang some of the new songs which had come into being with the PAC: 'We are unfortunate because all the nations are riding on us', and 'We Africans are crying for our land which has been taken by the whites. Let the whites leave our land alone.' Liberation songs, usually the instant product of a campaign or event, were as strong in the PAC as they were in the ANC: they sound a lot better sung melodiously in an African language than they do in English translation.

Sobukwe spoke for nearly two hours, in English with an interpreter translating passage by passage into a vernacular. There was no trace of the reserved, almost timid, person I had met two years before. Now he was strong and fluent, scholarly and scornful, as he lambasted apartheid and white rule. At this time, his inner strength and resolve could be seen to be growing almost by the day.

All his formative student years were revealed too as he spoke passionately about the PAC's belief in the goal of a United States of Africa—a commitment underlined during the conference in the reading of cables from Kwame Nkrumah, President of Ghana, and Sekou Touré, President of Guinea. 'Africa marches on undauntedly to its cherished goal of independence and unity,' said Nkrumah in his message, while Touré pledged fraternity to the PAC 'for the unconditional re-conquest of your most legitimate human rights, the recovering of your national soil and of your property and the respect of your dignity'.

The applause for Sobukwe at the end of his speech was uproarious, although a national executive attempt to offer him the tribute of an old-fashioned tribal-style orator loudly declaiming his history and virtues went awry and was called off after ten minutes because the orator was so poor. Sobukwe's popularity was obvious and his re-election as President never in doubt.

For the first time, the anti-pass campaign emerged into the open with the passing of a resolution, after debate behind closed doors, instructing the executive: to call on the nation to take decisive and final positive action against the pass laws; to embark immediately on a campaign of intensive organisation in order to get the nation ready for this action at the very earliest time; to institute an immediate tax on PAC members in order to establish a national fund to finance the campaign, paying £1 2s. 6d. (it should be noted that black workers were calling then for a minimum wage of £30 a month, an amount which probably only a few were earning); and, whatever form of action the national executive committee might decide on, to adhere strictly to the slogan of 'no bail, no defence, no fine'. The conference also agreed the status campaign should be implemented, but that action against the passes should receive top priority.

Anyone could have been forgiven for believing that this was merely another wordy and worthy decision. Here was a new organisation, whose claim to 32,000 members was doubtful, giving vent to the general black rage against the passes. But what substance lay in its protest?

Only twelve months before, the African National Congress, at its annual conference, had once more condemned the passes and decided on a series of regional conferences, culminating in a mass conference, to lead up to 26 June 1959 as 'a day of mighty demonstrations against the passes'. Little of it had happened; but the ANC had run a boycott of potatoes, in protest against slave labour conditions on farms, followed by an economic boycott of products of Nationalist-owned businesses.

The ANC again assailed the pass laws at its annual conference in December 1959, a week before the PAC met. It designated 31 March as 'Anti-Pass Day' when deputations would call upon local authorities and government officials in charge of black affairs throughout the country to urge abolition of the pass laws. This was among several campaigns planned for the year: 15 April was to be

Africa Freedom Day and public meetings were to be arranged to plan mass demonstrations to coincide with the government's intended celebration, in May, of fifty years of the Union of South Africa; 26 June, now fixed on the protest calendar, was also to be marked by demonstrations.

Within less than three months, all this would be eclipsed. Circumstances were gradually coming together which would elevate the PAC's decision to attack the passes into one of the most significant events in South African history.

The first and most direct factor was the oppressive weight of the pass system. The suffering was so enormous, and the cries of protest from blacks themselves and from whites opposed to apartheid so loud, that even the government and Parliament finally gave attention to reducing the number of 'petty offenders'—as they were called—going to jail. By 1958, the number of annual convictions was nearly 397,000—from the 143,000 of five years before.

In a bid to cut down on arrests, a new law in 1959 allowed a policeman to issue a spot summons if he thought a suspect might, if taken to court, get a low fine. The Commissioner of Police issued an order in June instructing his men to give 'better treatment' to blacks who had passes and to avoid arresting them for minor offences. But whatever good might have been intended was rendered largely meaningless because the Commissioner also left no doubt that black men remained subject to instant arrest if they could not produce a pass proving they had permission to be in a city, and that the same rules applied to black women. That led the South African Institute of Race Relations to conclude in a report written in May 1960: 'It is very doubtful whether, as a result of this order, arrests for pass laws offences were reduced in number to any significant extent.'

So the protests against the passes continued, from the PAC and ANC, and in February 1960 from the newly formed Consultative Committee of fourteen organisations established by the Anglican Bishop of Johannesburg, the Right Reverend Ambrose Reeves. The Committee distributed a pamphlet condemning passes and members joined with the ANC in a silent demonstration on the steps of Johannesburg's City Hall, traditionally a place for staging public protest. The ANC handed a city council representative a memorandum urging that Johannesburg tell the government that the influx control system should be abolished. The Liberal Party, the

How Can Man Die Better

Progressive Party, the white women's anti-government organisation the Black Sash and the Natives' Representatives in Parliament were all pushing away at the pass laws.

Virtually everyone—black as much as white, coloured and Asian—did so in the belief that the changes they sought were possible. Despite the increasing Nationalist majority in Parliament and the grinding down of opposition during the 1950s, both in Parliament and outside, hope continued that whites could be persuaded—or at worst, nudged with a minimum of force—into agreeing to extend rights to the voteless majority. It was seen largely as a matter of how best to present the case for change so as to have it accepted. The adherence to non-violence by the PAC, the ANC and all other opposition groups was not only a mixture of moral principle and a pragmatic attempt to minimise inter-racial violence, but most basically of all was pursued because it was judged capable of success. Demonstrations by protesters holding placards, public meetings, memorandums submitted to government and local authorities, calls for non-violent strikes, and the new tactic of economic boycotts, were still basic to black political dissent.

As a second factor, Africa's sweep to freedom contributed massively to the sense of what was possible. Nine independent states already existed and four more, including the continent's giant, Nigeria, were due to go on the same road that year. A bloody revolt in the Belgian Congo had already led to a lessening of European control; the French Cameroons, Nyasaland, Northern and Southern Rhodesia, Tanganyika, Uganda, Kenya, Guinea, Algeria, Angola and Mozambique were each in different stages of demanding the end of colonial rule. There was every reason to wonder how long South Africa's whites, forming less than 20 per cent of the population, could hold out.

That is why, on 4 January 1960, the *Rand Daily Mail* could editorialise: 'The Sixties opens in an atmosphere of expectations, a heightened awareness of pending change.' Referring to Africa, the newspaper said: 'In a few years' time Africans will be governing the greater part of this continent ... This will be a decade of great change for the world and for Africa. Can we in South Africa hope to escape the implications?'

The expectation of imminent change was reinforced on 3 February when Harold Macmillan, Britain's Prime Minister, gave his historic address to the South African Parliament in which he spoke of the 'wind of change' blowing through the African continent. Dealing with South Africa, he said that Britain had always given its support and encouragement, 'but there are some aspects of your policies which make it impossible for us to do this without being false to our own deep convictions about the political doctrines of free men'.

His words created a sensation. It was not only his memorably phrased projection of what was occurring, and would occur, in the continent, but his notice to South Africa's whites, so politely given, that they could no longer count on Britain's uncritical support. It was a speech adding to hope among blacks of change to come. But to the Nationalists it was a provocation: Prime Minister Hendrik Verwoerd spoke in a voice shaking with suppressed anger as he responded to Macmillan, formally thanking him while saying that 'there must not only be justice to the black man in Africa, but also to the white man'.

An ominous third factor was making its appearance: violent death. At the best of times, black lives were cheap in white eyes and nowhere more so than in the mines where black workers earning a pittance formed the bulk of the work-force, with skills jealously guarded by the small number of highly paid white miners. Accidents occurred repeatedly in the country's huge gold and coal mining industry. But a new level of tragedy was reached on 21 January with a major collapse at the Clydesdale colliery at Coalbrook, near the town of Vereeniging: 429 blacks and 6 whites were entombed.

Three days later, on a hot Sunday afternoon, even while the fruitless rescue efforts were still frantically under way at Coalbrook, political violence erupted in the Cato Manor black slum outside Durban, on the east coast. A raiding party of eight white and eighteen black policemen was searching for illicit liquor and arrested several dozen people. A black policeman apparently stepped on a woman's foot, she began shouting, a crowd gathered and threw stones, and the police opened fire. Up to that point, it was what had happened on scores of occasions: time and again black unrest was quelled by police gunfire and the killing of a few people. But this time the pent-up frustrations of the victims overflowed and the slumdwellers struck back: their stones, knives and pangas killed nine policemen—four whites and five blacks. It had never happened before on such a scale, and even the mass raids and arrests which followed could not entirely restore police nerve. A reaction was soon to be seen.

And finally, another factor was coming into play: the commitment by Sobukwe and his colleagues to submit themselves for arrest, not to ask for bail, not to have lawyers defend them in court, and not to pay any fines. It was summed up in their slogan: 'No bail, no defence, no fine.' What might once have been a tactic had become an issue of principle and was bound up with the split from the ANC. The Africanists were scornful of the ANC's decision to end its 1952 Defiance Campaign after the government put through legislation vastly increasing the penalties for anyone who contravened a law as a means of protest against the law, providing for compulsory flogging for a repeated offence, and singling out those who encouraged or incited others to break the law. In addition, the Africanists believed that the ANC was influenced by white and Asian communists hidden in the shadows. All the more reason, therefore, to insist that an organisation's leaders be up front and visible to all.

For Sobukwe, it also had to do with personal pride: he would not ask others to do what he was not himself willing to do, he constantly repeated in personal conversations. He believed, with pure and absolute faith, that his role as a leader was to go ahead of his people, to show them the way so that they could follow. But, I was asking him, wasn't this unwise? Wasn't this an unnecessary sacrifice of the leaders who should be doing the planning and directing? No, he did not agree; leaders had to prove that they were going to share the burden with their people; members could not be expected to adhere to the PAC's slogan, 'Service, Sacrifice, Suffering', unless they saw the leaders living it themselves.

His pride and belief drove him to make a fierce declaration when visiting Cape Town at the start of the year. He believed that his commitment, more than that of any other PAC leader, was doubted by the ANC: whether he would give up his job and luxuries to go to jail. Questioned about it at a public meeting by an apparent ANC supporter, Sobukwe replied: 'I have a wife and four children, at 684 Mofolo, of whom I am very fond. If I don't launch, you can go and burn them down in the house.'

With the benefit of information about his Fort Hare years, is the effect of Galsworthy's play, *Strife*, discernible? This is the way David Roberts led his striking workers, enduring privation, for himself and his family, for the cause to which he had given himself. Is it over-fanciful to see the influence of the play on Sobukwe the student carried over into the outlook of Sobukwe the political strategist?

Once the ANC, at its December conference, had decided to take action against the passes on 31 March the odds were that the PAC would have to launch action before then. Sobukwe firmly insisted that he was not competing with the ANC but, on the other hand, he could not fail to be aware of the pressure from his own supporters for vigorous action that would both fulfil their sense of mission and show up all that they claimed was defective about the ANC.

The PAC's internal organisation was assisted by its access to duplicating facilities: Leballo was employed at the United States Information Service, USIS, in Johannesburg and used the office facilities to produce leaflets. That was in addition to his own duplicating machine at his home. Leballo's job at USIS was probably the basis for later rumours that he had been employed by the US Central Intelligence Agency and, from this, that the CIA played a role in directing the PAC. There is no reason to believe that any of the rumours were true: there was never any suggestion that the USIS local director, David Dubois, was anything more or less than a capable information official with much sympathy for black interests in general. Anyone who knew Dubois knew that he would have made a job available because Leballo was badly in need of employment. It is possible, but not certain, that Dubois was aware of what Leballo was doing for the PAC on the side and that he chose to ignore it.

During February, Sobukwe went by car to parts of the Cape Province on a recruiting drive and to check on the PAC's state of readiness. Leballo and a few other leaders were with him. In the Port Elizabeth area, they found there had been hardly any headway: support for the ANC was strong and entrenched. Despite this, a local newspaper, the *Evening Post*, reported that he spoke at 'a well-attended meeting which was held in secret in a house in Port Elizabeth'. In Cape Town, on the other hand, several thousand came to listen to him: not only was the ANC there riven by argument, but the local people were largely migrants who suffered especially cruelly from the influx control laws and thirsted for a chance to express themselves. Sobukwe gave them a public message: get ready for the call to leave your passes at home.

How Can Man Die Better

He also had far-reaching influence on people who came to listen to him, such as Mxolisi 'Ace' Mgxashe, aged 16 and in the second year of high school in the Langa ghetto outside Cape Town. 'We had been hearing rumours about this new organisation, and how outspoken its leaders were,' he remembers. 'So I went with friends to a meeting. I was convinced on that very day. I had not been involved in any politics but Sobukwe opened me up to the kind of situation in which we were living as an oppressed people. I was also impressed by his command of the language: he spoke a pure Xhosa, untouched by township lingo, as one normally got from the peasants. Even the migrant labourers were very impressed because, at that time, leaders were considered as being from the élite and usually spoke in English, or as the saying went, "they spoke English through their noses". But in Sobukwe, people felt they could identify with him.'

Mgxashe promptly joined the PAC. Eventually he was jailed for two years, served his time and then went abroad to work for the PAC.

Much the same reaction was experienced by another young man who was a university student. He also saw and heard Sobukwe for the first time that day, and was so stirred that the course of his life was altered. 'Sobukwe was a powerful speaker, honest and sincere,' he says. 'I think he made a tremendous impression, particularly on young people in Cape Town.' He explains he was at the meeting more by accident than design; the Sunday afternoon meeting was held on an open space known as Bunga Square in Langa and many people passed by because the football fields were nearby. He saw a crowd on the square, stopped to listen and became interested. 'The challenge to take part in anti-pass demonstrations appealed to me,' he says. 'And what impressed people most was the fact that the leadership was going in front.'

He too joined the PAC, and later was jailed for three years.

Sobukwe returned to Johannesburg from his tour excited by the reception he had received and convinced that a campaign would succeed. Members of the national executive agreed with him. They shared Sobukwe's belief, as described by Z.B. Molete, who held the Publicity and Information portfolio on the national executive: 'We knew that if we were to survive and move forward as a political organisation, we would have to attack the pass laws and use a different method from anything the ANC had tried in the past. We knew also that the people understood the problems brought about by the pass laws, therefore there was no need to go and preach to them, to teach them about the problems they encountered. All that was needed was the determination of the leadership itself and perhaps new methods of struggle. Principally, it was the African who had to bear the burden of the struggle because he was the one concerned and other racial groups were not.'

Molete had additional confidence because he was a key leader in the industrial complex surrounding the town of Vereeniging: a tradition of militant action already existed there, and Molete was sure that PAC organisation was solid. Other leaders, such as Lennox Mlonzi of the Witwatersrand regional executive, were less certain. He lived in the same Mofolo area as did Sobukwe and was concerned about the PAC's lack of penetration. But Mlonzi had the same belief in historical purpose as his colleagues—and he and they were also persuaded by Sobukwe, and the others who had gone on the Cape visit, that the country was ready and waiting for them to give the lead.

There was crucial support also from A.P. Mda, who was still the *éminence grise* behind the scenes in black nationalist thinking. His recollection of events reflects the grave issues which were being confronted. 'The PAC was ready,' he says. He stresses this even while acknowledging what the PAC was not able to accomplish: 'It could not be expected to carry us right to the shores of freedom. In the nature of things the PAC could not. Because the ruling white group had all the cards on its side: it had the political power, it had the state machine under its control, it had an all-white army to sustain the state power, it had the police force, the weapons of destruction, and social, cultural, economic and political solidarity as the group in power. As against that, we had the peaceful freedom-lovers, the volunteers throwing away their passes, unarmed. The armed military group could drown the whole campaign in blood.'

Sobukwe was not blind to the problems. He had reservations about the state of readiness of the PAC, although he accepted Fofatusa's assessment that many thousands of workers, especially in the towns of the Witwatersrand, would come out in support of the campaign. He knew, too, that the actual number of PAC adherents was considerably less than the 30,000 to 35,000 publicly claimed. The figure in March 1960 of those who had signed membership forms—which he gave me some ten years later—was just over

20,000 people. This, however, did not necessarily mean 20,000 regular dues-paying members and indeed those who paid dues could be counted only in hundreds. The PAC national office thought itself fortunate if monthly income was more than £40. The Western Cape region around Cape Town had the biggest number of supporters: about 8,000. Next was the Vaal industrial triangle, including less than 1,000 in the ghettos of Johannesburg. Natal had about 500 supporters, and there were more than 1,000 in the Eastern Cape. By way of comparison, I estimated the ANC's membership tally at that time at 27,000–28,000.

Although membership figures are important, they are not always the full story—and this was especially true of both the PAC and the ANC at the time. Difficulties of organisation, which included police and other official harassment, worked against regular branch meetings and collection of subscriptions. Both movements clearly had pools of sympathy and support which went beyond simple membership numbers. But how big were the pools? How many people were out there waiting to respond to a call to action?

However ready, or not ready, the PAC was, Sobukwe believed it could not afford to wait any longer. Sobukwe expected the ANC's anti-pass campaign, which had by now been postponed to 31 May, to fizzle out—which would have the result of creating disillusionment among blacks, who would, therefore, not respond to any later calls issued by the PAC for action against the passes. Hence he believed the PAC had to get in ahead of the ANC. There could be no delay.

It was in these circumstances that Sobukwe took his decision about a launch date. 'It was left to him to decide,' says Molete. 'He was very impatient. With the time approaching to launch the campaign you could see the change in him. We didn't know the date but we could see its approach through his impatience. But nobody questioned him.'

In the first week of March, Sobukwe sent circulars to PAC branches throughout the country ordering them to get ready.

On the morning of Friday, 18 March he went fully public. He called a Press conference and a handful of journalists, myself among them, sat with him in a small bare office rented by a black trade union in Mylur House, a building in Bree Street on the edge of Johannesburg's city centre. Sobukwe announced that a campaign to end the pass laws would be launched on Monday. He outlined the details: PAC members were being urged to leave their passes at home and to surrender themselves for arrest at the nearest police station. They were being told that, if the police refused to arrest them, they should go home and return to the police station later in the day. 'No bail, no defence, no fine' would be strictly adhered to, he said. After serving the expected jail sentences, PAC members would again offer themselves for arrest. Some PAC men were being kept out of the campaign so that they could ensure continuity.

Members were being instructed to conduct the campaign in a spirit of non-violence. If ordered by the police to disperse, they were being told they should do so quietly and in an orderly manner. They would gather in small groups because they did not want to give the police the chance to baton charge them. Sobukwe passed round copies of the letter he had written to the Commissioner of Police.

The campaign, Sobukwe noted, 'will last until our demands are met'. It was the first step in the PAC's aim to achieve 'freedom and independence' for blacks by 1963.

He said the PAC believed that the only correct line against the pass laws was that which they were taking, and he revealed that, two weeks before, he had written to Chief Albert Luthuli inviting the ANC to come into the campaign on the basis of the 'no bail, no defence, no fine' slogan, and with the leadership in front. No reply had yet been received. (In fact, the ANC wrote to reject participation: 'We must avoid sensational actions which might not succeed, because we realise that it is treacherous to the liberation movement to embark on a campaign which has not been properly prepared for and which has no reasonable prospect of success,' it said.) He had also written to the Liberal Party: because it had black members the party would willy-nilly be involved in the campaign and he had offered it 'the opportunity to create history with us'. The Liberals had told him they would discuss it. (As later transpired, Nana Mahomo also carried a specific message from Sobukwe to Liberals in Cape Town asking for their support.)

The journalists questioned him about his motivation: his voice grew resonant as he spoke about the instant arrest to which black men were subject through the pass laws—and with the extension of this system to our womenfolk it might happen to my mother, my wife, my daughter. It's a situation we cannot tolerate any longer. The white man behaves as though he were an occupation power. He regards the Africans as a subject people. In order to entrench their privileges the whites have surrounded themselves with oppressive laws. We have no obligation to obey these laws. Our people have obeyed them in the past because they were frightened of not obeying. We are no longer frightened.'

His familiar 'Thaaat's right', with right forefinger stabbing the air to emphasise his thoughts, came frequently as he went on: 'The things we fight for are accepted as normal in every other society. We want a non-racial society. In a free Africa, the only difference between black and white will be colour—which we cannot help. We do not regard South Africa as an exception: she is an integral part of the continent and whatever solution we find for South Africa must be concerned with the solution for the rest of the continent. We have stated in the past, and shall continue to do so, that we believe in only one race on earth, the human race. National groups, like Africans, coloureds, Asians and whites, exist as a result of geographical origin and shared historical experience. So long as any government caters for group interest we cannot have peace in South Africa. What counts is the individual; if we guarantee the rights of the individual no other guarantee about minority rights is needed.'

He said that, two days earlier, he had written to the Commissioner of the South African Police, Major-General C. I. Rademeyer. It must have enraged the Commissioner to have a black man write a personal letter to him in such accusatory terms. More, it is a haunting document in the light of what actually happened . . .

> Sir: My organisation, the Pan-Africanist Congress, will be starting a sustained, disciplined, non-violent campaign against the pass laws on Monday, 21 March 1960. I have also given strict instructions, not only to members of my organisation but also to the African people in general, that they should not allow themselves to be provoked into violent action by anyone. In a Press statement I am releasing soon, I repeat that appeal and make one to the Police too.
>
> I am now writing to you to ask you to instruct the Police to refrain from actions that may lead to violence. It is unfortunately true that many white policemen, brought up in the racist hothouse of South Africa, regard themselves as champions of white supremacy and not as law officers. In the African they see an enemy, a threat, not to 'law and order' but to their privileges as whites.

Benjamin Pogrund

I, therefore, appeal to you to instruct your men not to give impossible demands to my people. The usual mumbling by a police officer of an order requiring the people to disperse within three minutes, and almost immediately ordering a baton charge, deceives nobody and shows the police up as sadistic bullies. I sincerely hope that such actions will not occur this time. If the police are interested in maintaining 'law and order', they will have no difficulty at all. We will surrender ourselves to the police for arrest. If told to disperse, we will. But we cannot be expected to run helter-skelter because a trigger-happy, African-hating young white police officer has given thousands or even hundreds of people three minutes within which to remove their bodies from his immediate environment.

Hoping you will co-operate to try and make this a most peaceful and disciplined campaign.

When the other journalists left I stayed behind. I jotted down some basic biographical details about Sobukwe—date of birth, family background, education—which I thought I should record in case I had to write reports about him, and we chatted for a while about the prospects for the campaign. He was calm and controlled. He was at peace with himself. He had come to terms with what he wanted to do with his life: it was to be a life of political commitment, and he was resigning from the university.

In my own mind I had doubts about the likely support for Monday and I was worried about my friend. But I kept those dismal thoughts to myself. In advance of Sobukwe taking and announcing his decision, I had written a report for that week's issue of *Contact* saying the campaign would begin within weeks. 'It is impossible to estimate what hope of success the campaign has,' my report went on. 'The Africanists claim a membership of about 34,000. If a substantial number of these are willing to go to jail for defying the pass laws ... the political situation in the Union could change dramatically. It is possible that, with large numbers of PAC members offering themselves for arrest, other Africans will follow suit. The Africanists would start a snowball rolling in setting off general African resentment against the passes.'

Now, on the eve of the launch, I still believed the PAC had incalculable potential for drawing support from blacks, chiefly because of the emotionalism inherent in its African Nationalist creed and because of black resentments of the time. And, of course, I knew Sobukwe's integrity and his leadership gift in attracting people. But I was less certain about the extent to which the PAC had thus far been able to develop an organisational base from which its message could be conveyed. I was concerned too about the risk of violence: Sobukwe's letter to Rademeyer had been well-put; if the demonstrations were on any scale, the danger of police violence would grow. That's the way it was, and is, in South Africa.

There was also a not unexpected event. On the Friday night I was at my desk in the *Rand Daily Mail*'s newsroom, writing my report on the Press conference, when I sensed the door opening at the far end. As I looked up, a dark, black-bearded face showed itself, and when the eyes had found me, the body in its long overcoat followed. It was Josias Madzunya. I sat back and laughed, guessing what was on. I was right. Madzunya had come to give me a statement dissociating himself from the campaign. The reason he gave was that there had not been enough preparation. He was a maverick as always.

21 March had not been Sobukwe's original choice. He had fixed on Monday, 7 March. But campaign leaflets had not been produced. Jordan Ngubane, formerly editor of *Inkundla* newspaper and now a PAC member whose parallel membership of the Liberal Party had caused some early difficulties, had promised to arrange for four sets of leaflets of 100,000 copies each. These were to be distributed at fortnightly intervals as a major prelude to the campaign. The PAC had no money but Ngubane said he would arrange the financing and would have the work done cheaply by a printer in Natal. But Sobukwe was shocked to discover that Ngubane had not done anything and, on about 5 March, he postponed the launch date by a fortnight, hoping that printed leaflets would still materialise. But none did. Sobukwe decided to go ahead and the PAC hurriedly duplicated as many leaflets as could be managed for distribution over the pre-21 March weekend.

The extent to which the campaign was negatively affected because the planned publicity material was not available can only be guessed at, but clearly it must have been considerable. The duplicated leaflets were not remotely adequate and there were not enough copies for mass distribution. There was no chance for the call to defy the pass laws to percolate widely or deeply. Ngubane sent Sobukwe a three-page letter—it reached him on Saturday, 19 March—urging that the campaign be delayed. But Sobukwe chose to go ahead.

The weekend was quiet. The PAC held a few meetings: the one I decided to cover, in a Pretoria ghetto, did not draw much of a crowd and this added to my doubts about what was about to happen. So did a lifeless conference held by Fofatusa in Johannesburg. On a more upbeat note, a PAC member who worked at the state-run South African Broadcasting Corporation's apartheid radio station for blacks spent Sunday, unknown to his bosses of course, putting stirring traditional war songs on the air.

And Sobukwe's final instructions were read out wherever a PAC meeting was held. It was an eloquent plea for non-violence and a stirring dedication to freedom; it was brave and it rang true with sincerity of purpose. As with the letter to the police, it has a special poignancy in view of what happened only a few hours later . . .

Sons and daughters of the Soil, Remember Africa!

Very soon, now, we shall be launching. The step we are taking is historical, pregnant with untold possibilities. We must, therefore, appreciate our role. We must appreciate our responsibility. The African people have entrusted their whole future to us. And we have sworn that we are leading them, not to death, but to life abundant.

My instructions, therefore, are that our people must be taught NOW and CONTINUOUSLY THAT IN THIS CAMPAIGN we are going to observe ABSOLUTE NON-VIOLENCE.

There are those in our own ranks who will be speaking irresponsibly of bloodshed and violence. They must be firmly told what our stand is.

Results of violence: Let us consider, for a moment, what violence will achieve. I say quite POSITIVELY, without fear of contradiction, that the only people who will benefit from violence are the government and the police. Immediately violence breaks out we will be taken up with it and give vent to our pent-up emotions and feel that by throwing a stone at a

How Can Man Die Better

Saracen or burning a particular building we are small revolutionaries engaged in revolutionary warfare. But after a few days, when we have buried our dead and made moving graveside speeches and our emotions have settled again, the police will round up a few people and the rest will go back to the passes, having forgotten what our goal had been initially. Incidentally, in the process we shall have alienated the masses who will feel that we have made cannon fodder of them, for no significant purpose except for spectacular newspaper headlines.

This is not a game. We are not gambling. We are taking our first step in the march to African independence and the United States of Africa. And we are not leading corpses to the new Africa. We are leading the vital, breathing and dynamic youth of our land. We are leading that youth, NOT TO DEATH, BUT TO LIFE ABUNDANT. Let us get that clear.

The government, knowing that they stand to gain by an outbreak of violence, may most probably stoop down to the level of employing certain African renegades, political [sic] or by throwing a stone at the police from a distance. Our Task Force will, therefore, have to move on either side of every batch and to make sure they deal with saboteurs. Anybody who agitates for violence or starts violence whether he belongs to PAC or not, we will regard as a paid agent of the government. Let the masses know that NOW.

The principal aim of our campaign is to get ourselves arrested, get our women remaining at home. This means that nobody will be going to work. Industry will come to a standstill and the government will be forced to accept our terms. And once we score that victory, there will be nothing else we will not be able to tackle. But we must know quite clearly, NOW, that our struggle is an unfolding one, one campaign leading on to another in a NEVER-ENDING STREAM— until independence is won.

This is not a game. The white rulers are going to be extremely ruthless. But we must meet their hysterical brutality with calm, iron determination. We are fighting for the noblest cause on earth, the liberation of mankind. They are fighting to retrench an outworn, anachronistic, vile system of oppression. WE represent progress. They represent decadence. We represent the fresh fragrance of flowers in bloom; they represent the rancid smell of decaying vegetation. We have the whole continent on our side. We have history on our side. WE WILL WIN!

The government will be ruthless. They will probably try to cut us off from one another, censor the Press, use their propaganda machinery to malign the leaders, mislead the people and spread falsehood about the campaign. Let nobody depend on either the Press or radio. I, myself, MANGALISO SOBUKWE, or one of the PAC leaders, acting on my behalf, will call off the struggle, after our demands have been fully met.

FORWARD THEN, TO INDEPENDENCE NOW, TOMORROW THE UNITED STATES OF AFRICA!

Yours for emergent Africa,
Mangaliso R. Sobukwe
President, Pan-Africanist Congress.

10

On Monday, Sobukwe woke up before 5 a.m., a bit earlier than usual. But once out of bed it was the normal daily routine: after Veronica had heated a kettle of water on the spirit stove he bathed in a tub in the kitchen. With sunrise more than an hour away, he dressed by candle-light in the bedroom, putting on a white shirt, dark trousers, a jersey to ward off the early-morning chill, and his comfortable sports jacket. He ate his usual breakfast of porridge, eggs, bread and tea.

The children weren't in the house: the previous evening a friend had come with a car so that the Sobukwes could take them to the house of Veronica's mother, in another part of Soweto. They were being cared for there by the young girl who had been hired to help with the children when Veronica, after having the twins, had started work again. When Sobukwe and Veronica returned home they had prayed together before going to bed: for a successful campaign and for the welfare of everyone taking part.

By 6.30 a.m., Sobukwe was ready to leave. By then I had already been there to wish him well: I had driven into Soweto an hour before to cover whatever the day's events might bring. I found Sobukwe as composed as he had been on Friday. We shook hands and, with the sun on the horizon, I went off to continue my 'dawn patrol' around Soweto. Even though it was too early to be certain about the day as a whole, at that stage workers seemed to be going to trains and buses in their usual numbers, and only occasionally did I come across small groups of PAC people.

The signal that it was time for Sobukwe to go came with the arrival of six PAC men who lived nearby in Mofolo, among them Lennox Mlonzi. Sobukwe greeted them with a big smile and the cry of '*iAfrika*', and they responded, '*Izwe Lethu*'. Sobukwe and Veronica said little to each other as they parted. He kissed her. She said a prayer to herself that everything would go as well as he expected.

He went off carrying a favourite curved pipe. The only visible sign that this was a day different from others was the small piece of paper pinned to his jacket lapel with the printed slogan: 'Africa for Africans. PAC.' The others had the same. The group walked the short distance down the unpaved street to the main tarred road, turned right and went to the local corner landmark, the grocery store owned by Tshabalala. About ten to fifteen men were there. They were still there a short while later when Veronica walked past on her way to her day's district nursing. She stopped for a few minutes, and went on.

'We were quiet and very serious,' says Mlonzi. 'There was no discussion between us. We could see people streaming up to Dube station from Mofolo, all on their way to work despite our call. We just looked at them.' At the store they bought newspapers, the *Rand Daily Mail* and *The Bantu World*. They read the front-page reports—in the *Mail* it was under a double-column headline: 'Saracens used in Rand "show of strength".' Sobukwe turned to the others and said: 'Boys, we are making history.' Despite the disappointment about their small numbers, his comment got to the heart of what each man was feeling and thinking.

The main news of the day they read in the *Rand Daily Mail* was that a ban on atomic bombs was closer because the Soviet Union had made a surprise offer of co-operation on checking underground tests. In Georgia, USA, the Ku Klux Klan was trying to persuade shopkeepers to display pro-segregation labels. At home, the chief political news was to do with the recent announcement by Prime Minister Verwoerd of a referendum—with only whites voting—to decide whether South Africa should become a republic, breaking its links with the British Crown. As a reminder that this was a God-fearing country, a news item revealed that three men were being charged in Johannesburg with breaking the 64-year-old Sunday Observance Act: they had been involved with a game of cricket played between whites and others who were not whites. And a new finding was reported, that the incomes of between 50 and 75 per cent of Johannesburg's black families were insufficient to meet minimum standards of health and decency. The newspaper's editorial dealt with an electricity breakdown in the city caused by a power shortage.

How Can Man Die Better

At Tshabalala's, no more men arrived so the group set off again. They walked up the long hill towards Dube station and turned right to head for Soweto's main police station in Orlando. A few others joined them on the way. I drove past once or twice, and saw this small knot of men walking silently and determinedly, picking their way through the people hurrying to work and the peak-hour buses and taxis. The police left them alone, except for the Security policemen who drove past now and again. An hour later they reached the police station, 4.5 kilometres away, and their spirits lifted as they found scores already there, standing outside the wire fence. There were smiles, right hands raised in salute and cheerful shouts of '*Izwe Lethu*'. The black policemen on duty, only a few of whom were allowed at that time by their masters to carry sidearms, stood silently. The real menace lay in the plain-clothed white Security policemen inside the station yard, and the large number of uniformed white policemen, many of them carrying rifles.

PAC women from nearby houses brought coffee. Eventually, by 8.20 a.m., when a crowd of 150 to 200 had gathered, Sobukwe, Leballo and a few others walked through the gates. They went to the room of the officer in charge and Sobukwe knocked on the door. The white officer, Captain J.J. de Wet Steyn, later testified that he asked the 'adult Bantu man', as he put it, what he wanted. 'I am Sobukwe. We have no passes and we want the police to arrest us.' Steyn replied: 'I'm busy and you must wait a bit.' He was annoyed at being interrupted and told Sobukwe to wait outside the police station. Later, Steyn went outside and warned the crowd to stop making a noise or he would 'take steps'—which is a South African police way of threatening official mayhem. Although a policeman for thirty-one years and in charge of a major police station in Soweto, Steyn did not know that the PAC and ANC had different salutes, and indeed he even testified that the crowd outside gave the (ANC's) thumb-up salute; he thought the PAC's palm-up salute was the 'Hitler salute' from the 1930s. But there was no mistaking his heavy-handed approach as he warned the PAC people: 'If there is any interference with the execution of police work there is going to be trouble.'

So the PAC men spent the first half of the morning lazing in the sun, sitting on the grassy slope outside the police station, or under the shade of nearby tall bluegum trees. There was not a cloud in the sky and by mid-morning it was hot enough for jackets to be discarded. It was obvious that the police were confused and did not know what to do.

During the morning, Harold Sacks, The *Rand Daily Mail*'s Crime Reporter, arrived and brought me the news that large crowds had gathered in several black townships about 50 kilometres away, and that the police had opened fire at a place called Bophelong, killing at least two people. I went and told Sobukwe: he was visibly upset. We again said goodbye because I decided to go to see what was happening. I left him, still waiting for the police to act.

In fact, the area around Vereeniging – on the other side of the town from the ill-fated Coalbrook colliery – was the centre of major demonstrations. In two ghettos, Bophelong and Boipatong, 4,000 had come together and marched on the police station in the steelworks town of Vanderbijlpark. When the crowd did not disperse, the police opened fire: one man died, in the first death of the day. Shortly after, the police killed another man in Bophelong. Sabre jet fighters flew low, Harvard propeller planes roared across at near-telephone pole height. Saracens drove around threateningly and armed policemen threw teargas and used batons to break up demonstrations. In Evaton, 10,000 people demanded to be arrested, but scattered when the Air Force planes flew low over them.

At Bophelong, when I arrived, the Harvards were coming in again just above the telephone poles, but people had grown used to them and roared defiance and shook their fists. Then I learnt that the police were moving in strength to deal with even bigger crowds in a Vereeniging ghetto called Sharpeville. I had never heard of the place. Together with a *Rand Daily Mail* photographer, Jan Hoek, I went there. Journalists were ordered to get out, but we drove back in again, as did another two journalists in their car, Humphrey Tyler of *Drum* magazine and photographer Ian Berry. That, of course, meant we had to avoid the police as we now courted arrest for being in the township without permission.

Early in the morning, 5,000 to 7,000 blacks had marched to the municipal offices at the entrance to Sharpeville. The police used teargas and a baton charge to disperse them. During the morning, people went to the police station in the centre of the township. At various times, leaders went inside the wire fence surrounding the building and told police officers that the people had left their passes at home and wanted to be arrested; the police said they could not lock up so many people. By 1.30 p.m., the crowd was certainly in the thousands: the numbers later became a matter of dispute as the police, wishing to stress how much danger they said there had been, gave the figure as 20,000; other estimates put the crowd at about 5,000. Police reinforcements arrived until there were 300 of them, with Saracen armoured cars.

There are conflicting versions of what then happened but it seems that another demonstrator was arrested – several had already been seized – the crowd pushed against the fence, one, or perhaps two, policemen opened fire and then there was a full volley from revolvers, rifles and Sten-guns. No order to fire was given. The shooting went on for at least forty seconds. Several policemen, including Sten-gunners reloaded and fired again and some also used revolvers. It was a slaughter.

The police account stressed the hostility of the crowd. At a later inquiry, for example, a police officer said he saw a small grey car being swallowed up by the crowd and thought the people in the car were being attacked. He said he had no time to do anything about it. But in fact, that was my car and the demonstrators were completely friendly. Once they knew I was from the *Rand Daily Mail*, they wanted to tell me about the hardships they suffered from apartheid. I spent some time sitting on the kerb listening to them. Then we drove around the edge of the crowd, until suddenly there was a fusillade of shots. As I turned the car towards the shooting, people were running towards us. Some shouted, 'Watch out, watch out, they'll shoot you!' In the silence which followed we saw the nightmare scene of the field strewn with bodies. Then a crowd, transformed into a mob by what had just happened, attacked us, and I frantically drove the car through a barrage of stones and sticks. The car was badly damaged and, shaken and frightened, we were lucky to get away with our lives.

The story of the shooting came from Tyler, and Berry took the extraordinary photographs of people being mowed down. Contrary to what the police claimed, they too had found people in the crowd friendly and wanting to tell them why they were there, and that they were demonstrating peacefully. Tyler's vivid account in *Contact* on 2 April tells of hearing a single sound like a shot, and while he was still wondering what it was,

> ... the shooting started. A gun opened up toc-toc-toc and another and another. The shots had a deep sound ... The first

rush [of people] was upon us, and then past. There were hundreds of women. Some of these people were laughing, probably thinking the police were firing blanks. But they were not.

Bodies were falling behind them and among them. One woman was hit about ten yards from our car. Her companion, a young man, went back when she fell. He thought she had stumbled. He turned her over in the grass. Then he saw that her chest was shot away. He looked at his hand. There was blood on it. He said: 'My God, she's gone.'

There were hundreds of kids running too. One had on an old black coat and he held it behind his head as he ran, to save his head from bullets, I suppose. Some of the children were leaping like rabbits, hardly as tall as the grass. Some of them were hit too.

Still there was shooting. One policeman was standing on the top of a Saracen and it looked as if he was firing his Sten-gun into the fleeing crowd. He was moving slowly from side to side. It looked as if he was panning a movie camera—from the hip. Two other policemen were on the Saracen with him. It looked as if they were firing pistols, but I could not hear pistol shots separately from the toc-toc-toc of the automatic guns.

Most of the bodies were strewn in the road which runs alongside the field we were in. I saw one man who had been lying still get up, dazed, and walk a few paces. Then he fell in a heap. A woman sat with her head cupped in her hands.

One by one the guns stopped shooting. There was nobody moving in our field except Berry. The rest were wounded or dead. There was no crowd any more. It was very quiet.

The toll was 68 dead and 186 injured (the precise number of deaths is uncertain, and has been variously also stated as 67, 69 or 72). The injured included 40 women and 8 children. Medical evidence revealed that more than 70 per cent of the victims were clearly shot from the back; at the most, only 15 per cent of wounds could be identified as inflicted from the front. Three policemen were said to have been slightly injured by stones.

That afternoon's *Star* newspaper in Johannesburg carried the headlines, evidently based on a police account of events: 'Police open fire under hail of stones—Many casualties in Vereeniging location

—Doctors called to hospital.' It was wrong then, and was perpetuated twenty-seven years later when *The Star* published a book to celebrate its hundredth anniversary and reproduced its Sharpeville headline as fact.

Parliament happened to be in session in Cape Town. During the afternoon, Prime Minister Verwoerd was on his feet with a statement: blacks had been instigated to try the impossible and challenge the authority of the State; the PAC was an extremist group which was against whites. He went on to give a lurid, and highly fictionalised, version which again obviously came from the police: the police had had to force their way through a crowd of 20,000 surrounding the police station, he said. Their vehicles were attacked with stones and sticks and attempts were made to get at the men on the vehicles. Stones rained on the police and the mob advanced on them. As the police were told to load, three shots were fired at them from within the crowd. The shouting crowd advanced on the police who fired a volley without an order having been given. The crowd immediately fell back and fled.

An even cruder reaction to the initial news of the shooting—when the full dimensions were not yet known—came from Dr Carel de Wet, a medical doctor who was the Nationalist Member of Parliament for the Vereeniging area: 'It is a matter of concern to me that only one person was killed,' he told Parliament. A good deal about the government's attitudes is revealed by de Wet's later career: the reward for his bloodlust was a job in the Cabinet and then a posting to London as South Africa's Ambassador. As far as is known, Britain did not object to his appointment.

In mid-week a yet wilder version was given by the government *Vaderland* newspaper: it spoke of 'a bloodthirsty mob of more than 25,000, each armed with a stone and a *kierie* (stick)', and of insistent appeals to the crowd—'if they were asked once they were asked ten times'—to halt their attack on the police. But all to no avail, said the newspaper.

At the end of the week, even when a fuller sense of what had happened was becoming known, the government still tried to sell a monumental lie to the world. Its High Commissioner in London issued a statement: 'According to factual information now available, the disturbances at Sharpeville resulted from a planned demonstration of about 20,000 Natives in which demonstrators attacked the police with assorted weapons including firearms. The demonstrators shot first, and the police were forced to fire in self-defence and avoid even more tragic results . . .'

A subsequent judicial inquiry did not blame anyone. That the judge was not able to issue a report whitewashing the police can in part be attributed to the swift response to the shooting by Bishop Ambrose Reeves. He arranged for lawyers to rush to the hospitals where the wounded were being kept under guard and to take statements from them; this testimony played an important part in the judicial inquiry.

The entirely one-sided death and injury made Sharpeville a massacre, and a direct result of apartheid. A prime reason for the shooting can be attributed to the notorious lack of discipline and restraint among white policemen, allied with the encouragement given to them to treat blacks as inferiors. On this occasion, perhaps as an additional factor, the policemen were especially on edge because of the killings at Cato Manor two months earlier.

The 705 bullets fired by the police that day changed South Africa, and nothing was ever to be the same again.

For Sobukwe, the day had already brought the arrest he wanted. At about 11 a.m. three Security policemen arrived. They went into the police station and came out soon afterwards. They stood inside the station grounds, and one of them—Ngcai, a black policeman—read out a list of names from a piece of paper: Robert Sobukwe was the first. Ten names were called out . . . P.K. Leballo, Selby Ngendane, Lennox Mlonzi, Rosett Nziba, J.D. Nyaose—the PAC leadership. 'Will you all come in,' said Ngcai. Sobukwe led them into the charge office, to be told they were under arrest. Armed white policemen stood by. 'What's the charge?' he asked. 'Incitement.' 'We have left our passes at home. We want to be arrested,' he said.

Later, there was a hubbub outside because the police told the remaining PAC members to go home. They refused and insisted they wanted to be with their leaders, saying: 'We have come to be arrested.' Finally, a police officer shouted: *'Sluit hulle toe'* ('Lock them up'), and they were also arrested, but kept apart. There were similar scenes at other police stations in the area where PAC men had gathered for arrest, at Moroka, Pimville and Newlands.

The Security Police drove Sobukwe to the clinic where Veronica was working to fetch the keys to the house and took him to his home: they asked him for his pass and he gave it to them. They produced a search warrant and after going through the house seized

How Can Man Die Better

documents such as copies of *The Africanist*, a magazine—*Science and Freedom No 14*—and a report on an All-African People's Conference. It was the sort of material which the police usually seized, somehow apparently believing it was subversive. They took Sobukwe to his office at the university and there again seized the same range of published material such as *Liberation*, a discussion journal published by the Congress Alliance. At 1 p.m., Sobukwe signed a receipt for the batch of documents taken from his office, and was driven to Marshall Square, the central police station in Johannesburg. The same was done with the other PAC leaders: Security Police went to the homes of each one for searches before taking them to Marshall Square.

In the immediate aftermath of the Sharpeville killings, truckloads of armed soldiers were rushed into the area; I saw them as I drove back to Johannesburg with Hoek in our shattered car, using back roads wherever possible to avoid questioning by the police.

During the day, information trickled through to Sobukwe and his followers about the large crowds of demonstrators in Evaton, Sharpeville and Cape Town. Then news reached them about the police shooting at Sharpeville. The details were not known, nor was there exact information about the number shot, but agitation and anxiety ran through the group of PAC people at Marshall Square. Sobukwe put out a calming message, reminding them they had to expect that anything might happen. A journalist, Stanley Motjuwadi, who visited him that week, wrote in later years: 'He was depressed and almost at the point of tears—the Sharpeville tragedy had hit him really hard.' The next morning they were able to get hold of the *Rand Daily Mail*, with its fuller accounts of what had happened. Ngendane was with Sobukwe and says: 'He was very upset. He had done his best to ensure a very orderly and peaceful campaign. How could so many die for saying they will no longer carry the symbol of slavery?'

Sobukwe and his fellows helped to keep up their spirit with political songs. A favourite was one, sung slowly and heavily, which went back to Youth League days: '*Thina sizwe esintsundu/ Sikhalela Izwe Lethu/ Elathathwa ngaba Mhlope/ Mabawuyeke umhlaba wethu*' —Xhosa for 'We the black nation/ Are crying for our country/ Which was stolen by whites/ They must leave our country alone.'

In Cape Town, meanwhile, on the morning of 21 March, hundreds of people gathered at three police stations. More than 1,000 were arrested at Wynberg, the government said. As *Contact* reported, the PAC 'scored a major success ... when a nearly total stay-at-home strike combined with a pass resistance campaign was achieved in the three principal African townships of Langa, Nyanga and Nyanga West'. A march by 5,000 people on the Langa police station was dispersed by their young leader, Philip Kgosana, because he feared that violence might follow. Kgosana, a boyish-looking 21-year-old University of Cape Town student from the Transvaal, was the PAC Regional Secretary for the Cape. He was to emerge as a charismatic leader who played an astonishing role in the days to come.

Meeting Sobukwe during his visit to Cape Town in February had strongly influenced Kgosana. Not only did he throw himself into working for the PAC but, as Randolph Vigne, then of the Liberal Party in Cape Town, says, 'At this stage, Kgosana's every action, every inflection of his voice, every gesture, pretty well, was an aping of Sobukwe. He was absolutely infatuated with Sobukwe and his manner, and he simply repeated Sobukwe's ways and views.'

That evening, 10,000 people gathered at the Langa police station, apparently in the belief that the authorities were to give them an answer to their complaints about the passes. But a magistrate banned meetings in the area, the police arrived in strength and, after only the barest of notice, baton charged the crowd. Stones were thrown at the police, and they opened fire. The peaceful, praying crowd became a mob, setting shops and government buildings alight, stoning cars and buses and killing a black driver who worked for a newspaper. The police shot and killed either two or four men—the number is uncertain—and injured scores. Army and police reinforcements went in during the night.

In the country as a whole, a great tide of anger was building up. The day after Sharpeville, the PAC issued a defiant statement, which was given a few inches of space in newspapers: 'Our plans are to be arrested in great numbers until industry is affected by a labour shortage. We shall not stop until passes have been abolished. We call on the government to halt forthwith the continued display of military strength by the police against an unarmed people. Ours is a non-violent struggle.' Thousands of blacks stayed away from work all week in Vereeniging. The Security Police carried out dawn raids hunting for documents—what sort was unclear—and the government banned public meetings in many parts of the country. But on the same day that it did so, on Thursday, 24 March, several hundred blacks offered themselves for arrest in Cape Town and were locked up. The next day, Kgosana led another 2,000 in a march to the main police station in the city and they asked to be arrested; after discussion—such negotiations between police and black demonstrators were virtually unheard of until then—the police promised that no one in Cape Town would be asked to produce his pass until conditions returned to normal, and the crowd dispersed at Kgosana's request.

Now came another dramatic response: ANC President Luthuli issued a call for a Day of Mourning—a stayaway from work the next Monday, 28 March. It so happened that, during that same week, Luthuli was giving evidence for the defence in the still-ongoing Treason Trial in Pretoria and he summed up the hopes of the ANC (the argument could apply equally to the PAC) about the use of protest to bring about peaceful change: one stay-at-home would not lead to the realisation of black ambitions, but he believed that a series of them would force the white public, out of sheer self-interest, to persuade the government to enter into negotiations with blacks to see if their demands could be accommodated; alternatively, the white electorate would be influenced to change the government.

The government frantically sought ways to defuse the crisis. On Friday, 25 March came the announcement that it intended bringing a law before Parliament on Monday to ban the PAC and ANC if the need arose. The next day, Saturday, Commissioner of Police Rademeyer issued a startling statement to the Press: 'In view of the fact that Bantus, as a result of intimidation, are so gripped by fear to carry reference books and are even afraid to carry any money, I have decided to relieve this tremendous tension and to prevent innocent and law-abiding Bantus from landing in trouble.'

This unusual concern for the welfare of blacks was the attempt at a face-saving cover for what was in fact one of the most significant retreats ever made by the white rulers. For the commissioner went on to say: 'I have instructed that no Bantu male or female is to be asked for his or her reference book or any other documents. No Bantu will be taken into custody because he is not in possession of his reference book. Bantus must not be arrested or detained for all sorts of petty offences. They must be warned or summonsed to appear.'

It was not a wholehearted capitulation. The Minister of Justice, Frans Erasmus, immediately spoke about pass law enforcement 'when the situation returns to normal'. But despite this qualification, it was a retreat. The PAC had won. The pass laws were suspended.

Events were moving rapidly, however, and there was no opportunity to savour the triumph. Nor did the PAC even wish to. It had declared war on the pass laws and mere suspension was rejected. An immediate statement said: 'It does not change our plans. We want the total repeal of the pass laws. We shall continue and intensify the struggle until the pass laws are totally abolished. And the government must negotiate with the arrested leaders.' In any event, the commissioner's statement could not diminish the sense of outrage so intensely felt by blacks. It was that feeling to which Luthuli responded on the same day as the statement. He took a new giant step forward with an act of outright defiance of white authority: he urged blacks to burn their passes. A photograph of him burning his own pass appeared in a Sunday newspaper.

But the ANC initiative upset the PAC. Faulty planning by the PAC was now evident because, with almost all the leadership either in jail or sent out of the country, there was no certainty about the chain of command. Sobukwe was in jail and was receiving visitors. He was receiving reports and sending out instructions. On the day after Sharpeville, Mothopeng was caught by the police reading a note smuggled in by a visitor: '1. Monies first problem. 2. Organisation revived throughout Wits [Witwatersrand]. 3. Propaganda bulletins coming out. 4. Planning next immediate intensive surrendering campaigns. 5. Everything OK. Good luck.'

Encouraging as that news must have been, it wasn't a satisfactory way to run a national campaign and the impetus became more and more difficult to sustain. The one national executive member still free and in the country was Z.B. Molete and on 24 March he phoned me with a statement that the PAC was still pushing away: 'We call upon the African people to intensify the pass campaign and to dedicate themselves to the complete overthrow of the pass laws for every African in this country forthwith as a result of the brutal murders of the Africans at Vanderbijlpark, Sharpeville and Langa.'

There was another spokesman, William Jolobe. He was a shy man who spoke in a hesitant, roundabout way; he had been doing typing and some office work for the PAC and the day after Sharpeville he came to see me to say he was in charge and acting for Sobukwe.

PAC leaders have subsequently confirmed that Jolobe, junior as he was, was indeed Acting President for the next two years. On 24 March he too phoned me with a message: 'We are telling people to stay at home and go to jail. They must return to their homes—stay there until we hear from Mr Sobukwe. There must be no work—so that the employers must feel the pinch. Then bring pressure on the government.'

After Luthuli's announcements, Jolobe phoned to tell me he had visited Sobukwe in jail and was conveying a statement from him. He read it to me and I accepted it as the authentic voice of Sobukwe. These were emotional days and the statement assailed the ANC:

> If evidence of ANC rank opportunism was still required, their call for a day of mourning on 28 March instead of their previously announced coffin-carrying, placard-bearing pass demonstrations of 31 March, provides that evidence.
>
> The ANC opposed our campaign. It called it sensational, ill-defined and ill-planned. We showed them and their bosses that we could plan and run the campaign on our own without the advice of sections of the oppressor class.
>
> The ANC is now trying to bask in the sunshine of PAC's successes. Luthuli now has the courage which he has lacked for over twelve years to burn his reference book after passes had been suspended. Supported and boosted by the white Press, he has been making one foolish statement after the other, pretending that he has a following in the country.
>
> The position is quite clear: the African people will take their instructions from the leadership of the PAC which has led them so far on the road to freedom and independence. They will treat with contempt and scorn the opportunists who hope to reap where they have not sown.
>
> Our advice and warning to the ANC and its liberal friends is: Hands off our campaign. We do not need your interference. Go on with your coffin-carrying and other childish pastimes but leave the African people to fight their struggle without you. Tell your bosses you cannot sell the African people because you do not control them.

Because of the reduced nature of PAC communications, it is unlikely that this statement received any wide circulation. That apart, Sobukwe had certainly misjudged the mood of huge numbers of black people, including those in PAC strongholds. For the Monday, 28 March protest proved the biggest in the country's history. In Cape Town, an estimated 95 per cent of black workers did not go to work; in Johannesburg, 85 to 90 per cent; in Port Elizabeth, 85 to 95 per cent; in Durban, 20 to 25 per cent; in Pietermaritzburg and other smaller cities there were also sizeable strikes.

But trouble broke out in Johannesburg's ghettos at the end of the day: people who had ignored the strike call were assaulted as they returned home; their passes were seized and burnt; the police took tough action. As rioting and arson raged into the night, a black policeman was killed. In Cape Town, nearly all the city's 60,000 blacks stayed home and refused to return to work. Coal, milk and newspaper deliveries were disrupted, bread and meat were short, hotels and garages struggled with few staff, ships lay idle in the harbour, and major building projects were halted.

The nightmare fears of whites were coming true: they were facing a rising tide of black resistance. An alarmed government rushed to impose its will. On the Monday, the threatened legislation to ban the Pan-Africanist Congress and the African National Congress was introduced in Parliament. On Wednesday, with the Bill still on its way through the parliamentary process, the government declared a State of Emergency in many parts of the country: it took on sweeping powers to detain people without trial and to ban meetings; 'subversive statements'—such as inciting anyone to oppose the government—were made a serious offence.

Hundreds of people were arrested in the early hours of the morning—even before the emergency regulations were promulgated. That led, later in the day, to a flurry of habeas corpus applications before courts. Some of those detained were released by court order, and promptly re-arrested; some managed to escape and flee the country, including Oliver Tambo, the ANC's deputy president. People of all colours and political persuasion were detained. Among them was Z.B. Molete: he was kept in jail for about five months.

As word spread in Cape Town's black ghettos that leaders had been arrested, crowds gathered. Their emotions were heightened by the other events of the night: '. . . early in the morning of Wednesday, the police raided Langa with immense brutality, breaking down doors, pulling people out of bed, beating them up, throwing them into the streets.' Then a procession set off: '... the men from Langa walked, in peaceful informal formation, unarmed and unarrogant, towards Cape Town,' *Contact* reported in its next issue, on 16 April. 'They came to tell their troubles, trusting and still friendly, believing that non-violence could not provoke violence, and that they would be heard.' They formed a 1.5 kilometre-long column, 30,000-strong, walking quietly through white suburban streets, their ranks opening to let cars, buses and even police vans pass through without hindrance. Kgosana was still free and he was at the head of the march, in blue running shorts and a frayed brown jacket: no shouting, no violence of any kind, he told them. 'The atmosphere was warm, hopeful—there was a belief that at last one of their leaders could tell the government of their difficulties and ask for a new system: no passes and a fixed minimum wage—everywhere,' said *Contact*.

Kgosana halted the crowd at the edge of the city, only a few blocks from the Parliament buildings which were by then ringed by armed policemen and soldiers in armoured cars. After an argument with a Security policeman, Kgosana agreed not to attempt to lead his supporters to Parliament. Instead, he told them to wait for him and he walked down the street to Caledon Square police station to say he wanted a meeting with Justice Minister Erasmus. Cape Town, and South Africa itself, stood on the brink. Anything could happen. The police had never before had to deal with such a huge number of demonstrating black people in the heart of a white city. Kgosana spoke to Colonel Ignatius Terblanche, the policeman in charge of the district. Terblanche in turn phoned Erasmus, who gave him harsh instructions—the actual detail has never been disclosed—about how to deal with the crowd. Many years later, Terblanche recounted his protest: 'I said to the Minister, "Please sir, I'm in full control," and he said, "Carry out my order".' Terblanche said he put down the phone and bowed his head in prayer: 'Dear Lord, I'm not capable of handling this situation. I'm handing it over to You.' With that inspiration, he went outside and promised Kgosana an interview with the Minister.

Kgosana, on his side, also recalled the events many years later: 'Terblanche came back and told me he had fixed up an appointment with Erasmus. He said I must tell our people to disperse and then come back for the meeting with Erasmus. Our orders from PAC

President Mangaliso Sobukwe were very clear. We were to disperse when ordered to do so by the police. There was to be no violence on our part ... I kept my side of the bargain and asked the people to disperse peacefully. They went away, and I later came to meet Erasmus. His side of the bargain was not kept. I was promptly locked up and spent the next nine months behind bars without trial.'

At the time, it was not entirely clear what had happened to Kgosana, except that he had disappeared. The emergency regulations forbade identifying detainees. A week after the arrest, Erasmus refused to tell Parliament whether he was in jail.

Terblanche's refusal to carry out Erasmus' orders lost him any chance of promotion. It also revealed official attitudes: 'I was blamed for not using force. I was an outcast, even among my colleagues,' he remembered. 'But, if I had used force, it would have been a massacre.'

Terblanche admitted to being disturbed by the arrest of Kgosana: 'I was hurt because it stamped me as breaking my promise.'

More than twenty-seven years later, Terblanche was given belated promotion: at the age of 84, and long retired, he was made an honorary brigadier. The government said it was because of his work after his retirement. But Terblanche thought differently: 'I feel a wrong has been set right,' he said. He was seemingly referring to his lack of promotion rather than the betrayal of Kgosana and the black people of Cape Town.

The night after Kgosana's arrest, heavily armed police, soldiers and sailors began putting rings of steel around Cape Town's three ghettos for blacks—starting with Langa and then, later, Nyanga East and Nyanga West. They stood at 30-metre intervals, with bren guns placed at many points. Water and electricity were cut off to the ghettos and no one was allowed to enter or leave. Two parents taking their baby to hospital were shot at, and the baby killed. Day and night, police went from house to house, arresting hundreds, kicking down doors, beating up men and women in their homes and in the streets and ordering them to return to work. It took a week for the government forces to break the popular resistance.

That was a long time for people whose financial position did not enable them to stockpile food. They were helped in their resistance by white liberals—from the Liberal Party and the women's anti-apartheid organisation, the Black Sash, who swiftly raised some £1,000 and bought maize meal, beans and other staples, and succeeded in getting truckloads of food through the cordons. The food was given to PAC committees for distribution.

The liberal role had begun before the anti-pass campaign because Liberal Party leaders such as the Cape Chairman, Peter Hjul, and Patrick Duncan and Randolph Vigne, were in personal contact with local PAC leaders. There was another link because Kgosana, struggling to survive as a student, was a part-time *Contact* seller.

These relationships assumed critical importance as the campaign began. But unlike other times in South African history when whites of various degrees of liberalism had helped blacks in political campaigns but extracted a price for doing so through exerting influence on the course of events, on this occasion aid was given unstintingly and without strings. The Cape Town liberals offered their assistance in whichever way it might be needed, whether making *Contact*'s offices in the city centre available for meetings and phone calls, or putting Kgosana in touch with the white establishment press, and later with foreign journalists, so that he could explain the nature of the campaign. There was also a day when Duncan played a central part in avoiding the possibility of bloodshed when he landed up as an intermediary between a crowd of demonstrators and the police.

It was not an entirely unruffled relationship, and Kgosana for instance was irritated by an attempt by Duncan to discourage him from going to a meeting with a leading local communist, Brian Bunting. On the other hand, Duncan gave inestimable help simply by refusing to acknowledge the existence of the State of Emergency and publishing copious details about events in each week's issue of *Contact*; the newspaper's sellers showed the same courage in standing up to harassment by the police. Duncan was later prosecuted.

It was, on the whole, a working relationship of mutual respect, and local PAC leaders viewed it as such at the time.

At the public level, the state's violence grew worse. An amendment to the emergency regulations giving the police the power to use force in maintaining public order set off an orgy of indiscriminate assaults even outside the ghettos: in the name of clearing Cape Town's streets of 'agitators', policemen beat up any blacks and coloureds they happened to encounter. Complaints elicited a bland statement by the Minister of Justice that reports of the use of undue force were unsubstantiated.

The entire Citizen Force and army reserve—all whites-only—were on standby and units were mobilised to deal with the protests which had now spread far and wide through South Africa to small country towns where black violence on any scale was previously unknown ... Stellenbosch, Worcester, Hermanus, Paarl, Beaufort West and Ermelo. Many stayed away from work and crowds were dispersed by police using teargas and batons. In Durban, the Cato Manor slum was a focus of unrest with 10,000 people attempting to march on the city. Sporadic clashes occurred between black groups and the police in the city's white suburbs, with blacks beaten back by gunfire. Johannesburg, Germiston, Port Elizabeth, East London, Cradock and Bloemfontein all saw unrest, arson, the burning of passes and unbridled police crackdowns.

It is unlikely that the full scale of what happened, and the vengeance wreaked by the authorities, will ever be known: the mechanisms for recording and reporting, through newspapers and concerned organisations, were not up to the task.

In the fevered climate of the time, there was a widespread expectation that anything was possible when Verwoerd came to Johannesburg on Saturday, 9 April to open the annual agricultural and industrial show, that year known as the Union Exposition to mark the fiftieth anniversary of the Union of South Africa. Verwoerd gave his speech and sat down—and soon after was shot by a white farmer, David Pratt. Two bullets hit Verwoerd in the ear and cheek, but he survived. A court later found that Pratt was mentally disordered.

But 9 April, much as it was a frightening shock to Afrikaners, also turned out to be the turning point: on that day the government's rule was visibly back in place. The law proscribing the PAC and the ANC was promulgated by 8 April and by then both organisations had closed their public operations. White authority had been shaken and rattled and had faltered, but—as it was again to prove in the 1970s and in the 1980s—its capacity for ruthlessness and its determination to survive were greater than its opponents credited.

What if Sobukwe had not carefully ordered his followers to be non-violent? What if Kgosana had not held on so tightly to that enormous throng in Cape Town? What if the thousands of black marchers in Cape Town had wreaked violence on the city centre and in white suburbs? If any of this had happened, the police and army would have killed *en masse*: there cannot be the slightest doubt about that. But what further black rage would that have set off, with what wildfire consequences throughout South Africa?

Speculation apart, the actual toll of lives, inasmuch as it could be assessed, was heavy: in addition to the Sharpeville deaths, 83 civilians, probably all blacks, were killed and 365 injured. Among the police, 3 blacks were killed and 59 of all races injured.

On 10 April, the police announced that blacks without passes again faced immediate arrest.

11

After two nights and a day in the Marshall Square police cells, Sobukwe and his colleagues were driven the few blocks to the Johannesburg magistrates' courts. From the basement cells there, they were taken upstairs for a brief appearance in court, to be remanded in custody for a few days. Armed policemen stood at the doors of the courtroom. Sobukwe and his colleagues still wore their 'Africa for Africans' paper lapel badges. Speaking in a calm voice, he said: 'On behalf of my colleagues, I request that we be allowed to attend the funeral of the people shot at Vereeniging.' Could that be arranged? the magistrate asked the prosecutor. No, bail could not be allowed, replied the prosecutor, drawing Sobukwe's response: 'We don't ask for bail.' But that was it: the magistrate said he could not make an order allowing them to attend the funeral.

Then they were transferred to The Fort, built in 1898 by the Boer government of the Transvaal Republic to defend Johannesburg against the British, and the city's main prison until early in the 1980s. It was at the top of Hospital Hill, a ten-minute drive from the courts. The main section for blacks—for like all South African jails, strict apartheid existed between whites and those of other colours—was known as 'No 4'. It was notorious for the treatment meted out to blacks. As an awaiting-trial prisoner, Sobukwe was able to wear his own clothing, have food sent in to supplement the jail rations, have newspapers and books and receive visitors regularly.

Although Madzunya had dissociated himself from the anti-pass campaign, that did not save him and two of his supporters in Alexandra township. They were arrested and put together with the PAC leaders. But Sobukwe made his feelings evident: 'When Sobukwe and I first met in No 4 he looked at me as if I am not there,' according to Madzunya. 'He just walked past me, he ignored me.' Once the trial began, however, Sobukwe softened and accepted Madzunya as a co-accused.

The contact with visitors made the passing of messages possible, and Sobukwe succeeded in smuggling out a note which was sent on to Ghana, for President Nkrumah. Read later in the month to a conference of African states it bravely said the PAC leaders 'are not afraid to face the consequences of our action ... we are convinced that we shall be free by 1963, and towards that end we shall continue to struggle'.

Sobukwe was no longer on the staff of the University of the Witwatersrand. A letter from him dated 21 March was received by the Registrar the next day. In Sobukwe's neat handwriting, it revealed that, even while taking his own momentous decisions, he had been mindful of how his actions might be used to damage the university. So, courteous as ever, he removed himself ...

> I hereby wish to tender my resignation from the position of Junior Language Assistant in the Department of Bantu Languages.
>
> Circumstances have arisen which make it necessary, in the interests of the university, that I resign and that my resignation take effect from the earliest date the university may decide.
>
> I wish to thank you for the attitude you adopted in refusing, in the face of terrific pressure, to interest yourself and the university in my political life.

Exactly what pressure he was referring to is unknown. Perhaps it was a reference to the university ignoring the government's threat when he was elected President of the PAC in April the previous year. Whatever it might have been, the university now posted a formal acceptance of the resignation to Sobukwe's home, saying it would take effect from 31 March.

As he had anticipated, an attempt was made to use his academic position: late in April, a question was asked in Parliament as to whether any university staff had been connected with the PAC or ANC. The office of the Minister of Education circulated the question to universities and was blandly advised by Wits in a short letter that it had learnt about Sobukwe's leadership of the PAC in April 1959, that he had carried out the normal duties attached to his academic position until 21 February, when he told his department head in writing that he was ill, and that he was now no longer on the staff.

As the serenity and security of the university job receded into the past, Sobukwe lived with the reality of being black and in custody. At the end of the week of the Sharpeville massacre he and his colleagues were brought back to court for another remand—with Sobukwe charging that some of his men had been assaulted, 'both within and outside the Johannesburg Fort'. But the magistrate would not allow the complaints to be taken further: they had to be reported to the jail or police authorities, he said.

Sobukwe became accused No 1, described as a 'Lecturer, 35 years, Msutu, male'. He and twenty-two others were formally charged in that, said the State, between 1 September 1959 and 22 March 1960 they did 'wrongfully and unlawfully ... advise, encourage, incite, command, aid or procure natives in general or some of them ...' to commit the offence of being without a pass by way of protest against a law. In other words, the charge was framed under the Criminal Law Amendment Act introduced in 1952 to break the ANC's Defiance Campaign. It transformed the minor offence of contravening the pass laws into a much more serious crime of incitement. The penalty Sobukwe faced was a fine of up to £500 and/or jailing for up to five years.

Normal apartheid applied in the court: the public gallery at the back of the room was split down the middle by a waist-high wooden partition with a 'whites' notice on one side, and 'non-whites' on the other. But one witness box served witnesses of all colours, and so did the dock, no doubt to the annoyance of Afrikaner Nationalist purists. The 'non-whites' gallery was packed as the magistrate, J. de K. du Plessis, drew a blank in calling on the accused to answer to the charge. He made the entry in the trial record: 'All the accused refused to plead.'

Sobukwe, as spokesman for the group, then told him (at least in the breathless form transcribed by a typist from the court recording): 'Without impugning your personal integrity and honour, Your Worship, we refuse to plead, because our contention is that the law under which we are charged is a law made exclusively by the white man, specifically for the oppression and suppression of the blacks, and the officers who administer that law are themselves white, and in this whole drama only the accused is black and we don't feel that justice can be done under the circumstances and we therefore refuse to plead.'

'Without impugning your personal integrity . . . '? That seems a strange way of speaking by someone trying to overthrow the entire system, especially when followed by a blunt rejection of the law and the officials administering it. Yet it did not strike any false note. Sobukwe was giving expression to his innate regard for the functioning of law and was again, quite unconsciously, reflecting the belief among blacks that a reasoned approach could persuade whites to end apartheid. He was observing the tenet of South African justice whereby the personal integrity of a magistrate or judge is unassailable, and to question it is to commit the criminal act of contempt of court. That magistrates or judges in political trials, especially at that time, could invariably—but, to complicate the issue, not always—be relied upon to bring in verdicts which suited the government, did not detract from the force of the principle.

Another factor was that Sobukwe always spoke to everyone with the utmost politeness. Poor men, rich men, servants, bosses, black, white, men, women, policemen, friends, enemies, clerks, labourers . . . he treated them all in exactly the same way, speaking pleasantly and with a grave courtesy. The effect on whites, and government officials and policemen in particular, could be electric when faced by this black man—a supposed inferior—speaking with assurance and total politeness and without a hint of either hostility or obsequiousness. They were stopped in their tracks, and might even respond with courtesy. So it was natural for him to address the magistrate in this way, even though he could have no illusions that blacks accused of challenging white authority stood little chance at the hands of a white civil servant.

The magistrate dealt briskly with Sobukwe's refusal to plead by noting, as was usual in such cases, a plea of not guilty for all the accused and calling the first witness to come forward—a black Security policeman who testified about attending PAC meetings. His name was Solomon Mdunga.

That he was a policeman serving the interests of the white government did not increase his status in the eyes of the white prosecutor, who still addressed him as Solomon—the first-name way in which whites usually spoke to blacks.

That apart, Mdunga did not please his masters. Cross-examined by Sobukwe—'What would you say the African opinion about the pass laws is, would you say they like the pass laws, or they hate them?'—he replied: 'Definitely they hate them, they don't like them ...' A succession of other policemen read from their notes of meetings where speakers had attacked the passes, and were questioned. But there was a limit to which magistrate du Plessis allowed that sort of cross-examination. When Sobukwe asked a constable whether the government which made the laws was black or white, du Plessis broke in: 'That is of no concern in this case. This court is not concerned with the political aspect, but purely with the legal aspect of this matter ...'

Sobukwe had some fun with another witness who quoted him as having said at a PAC meeting: 'Passes, permits, there is their waterpipe. It's Parliament. Close the waterpipe, we want to fight, act, once for all.' It was 'gibberish', said Sobukwe. But there was no escaping the magistrate: 'Are you satisfied that these notes are the gist of what was said by the speakers?' 'Yes, Your Worship,' said the grateful policeman.

Leballo questioned another black constable: 'Do you carry a pass?'— 'Yes. It is the law of the country, made by the government.' 'Is it a government of a white minority or a black majority?' Du Plessis: 'Do not answer that question.' And to Leballo: 'I am not prepared to allow questions of a political nature. They do not assist the court.'

Behind the scenes there was strong debate among the PAC men about how to conduct their case. Their slogan, 'no bail, no defence, no fine', meant that no lawyers would be briefed. But how far should they go in fighting the government case? The prosecution was going for a conviction on the grounds that the PAC had incited all blacks to break the law. There was agreement among the accused that the government case should not be left unchallenged, and therefore that witnesses should be cross-examined so as to refute the charge of incitement. There was also agreement that they should seek to narrow the charges against them by arguing that members of a particular political organisation, the Pan-Africanist Congress, had taken a resolution to oppose the pass laws and in obedience to their own resolution, members of the organisation surrendered themselves for arrest.

Some pressed also for Sobukwe to go into the witness box to put forward the Africanist standpoint and this view prevailed: Sobukwe duly gave evidence, outlining the history and purpose of the PAC. Cross-examined, he took a scornful crack at the notoriously poor taking of notes by Security policemen at political meetings. When the prosecutor read a portion of a speech and asked him if he had made it, he said: 'I don't talk such nonsense.' 'Pardon?' said the surprised prosecutor. 'I don't think I'll be capable of talking such nonsense,' said Sobukwe.

When Sobukwe later came to sum up the defence case in the court he spoke scathingly about black leaders: while blacks went to jail during political campaigns, their leaders spent a lot of money on bail and lawyers, he said, and because of this the PAC decided to carry out its campaign according to 'no bail, no defence, no fine'. And: 'I am happy to say that we have kept that promise so far.' But the words masked division which had crept into the PAC's ranks: he had wanted to speak in even tougher terms, but some of his fellow-accused insisted on him 'toning down' because they were growing worried about the length of the sentences they might get.

On 4 May, du Plessis gave his verdict: Sobukwe and eighteen others were guilty of inciting people to commit an offence as a protest against the laws. Four were acquitted.

Sobukwe spoke before sentence: It would be remembered that the accused refused to plead to the charge, he said. 'They felt they had no moral obligation to obey the laws made by a white minority. I do not wish to impugn the personal honour and integrity of the magistrate but an unjust law cannot be applied justly.' The accused believed in the human race; the history of the human race had been a struggle for the removal of mental, moral and spiritual oppression; they would have failed in their duty had they not made some contribution to the struggle. 'If we are sent to jail there will always be others to take our place. We are not afraid to face the consequences of our action, and it is not our intention to plead for mercy.'

The magistrate's no-politics stance disappeared. The accused, said du Plessis, had used 'every conceivable device and argument' to prove to blacks 'how they were suffering'; they had dangled under their noses 'the utopia of freedom' from influx control, from arrest and raids and of increased wages. 'Not only was it your object to fill the jails with the impressionable masses of the native people, but in that manner you intended to paralyse trade and industry and so undermine the economy of the country, in order to compel the government to change its laws,' he said. 'Whether a law is unjust or is considered unjust or not, the law of the land must be obeyed. The harm done by you, both politically and economically, is difficult of assessment. This court must accordingly impose adequate sentences, not only as a punishment to you but as a deterrent to others who may be similarly minded.'

As far as Sobukwe was concerned, he went on, he would take into account that no-one but he could have called off the campaign, and this did not appear to have been done. People were exhorted to fight the pass laws and join the PAC campaign. Pamphlets were also distributed indiscriminately in the townships. Sobukwe had said quite unequivocally that the PAC had as its object the ending of what was called white domination in South Africa, and the establishment of a non-racial democracy. The abolition of the pass laws was the first step towards this aim. There was no doubt, said du Plessis, that blacks generally had been incited.

The sentences: Three years' jail for Sobukwe; two years each for Leballo and three others; eighteen months each for the remaining fourteen, including Madzunya.

While Sobukwe fought the issues of his campaign in the courtroom, the government was struggling to keep control of the country. Sobukwe and his colleagues were jubilant. 'We are creating history' was the phrase on every one of their lips.

The first wave of State of Emergency detentions scooped up about 1,800 men and women in what gave every appearance of being a panicky and confused selection process. The dozen or so white men at The Fort were a microcosm of the process: former communists who had not been politically active for years, current communists, and liberals who were anti-communist, were locked up together. The one-time communists surmised they were in jail because their names were still on 'Spengler's old list', Spengler being the colonel in charge of the Security Police in Johannesburg.

The detentions led to an unusual meeting. One day in April, Sobukwe was in a line of black men waiting to see the jail doctor; in a separate queue alongside were white men detainees, including Monty Berman, a former communist who knew Sobukwe, and Joe Slovo, a well-known communist who was later to go into exile and become Chief of Staff of the combined ANC-CP military command and, later still, General Secretary of the South African Communist Party. Even in 1960 he would, more than most, have personified for Sobukwe the communist enemy opposed so implacably by African Nationalism.

But here they were, black nationalist and white communist in jail together although separated inside the jail by apartheid, enemies who were prisoners of a shared enemy. Berman, with a sense of the drollness of the situation, said to them: 'You two don't know each other. Allow me to introduce you. Mr Sobukwe, Mr Slovo, Mr Slovo, Mr Sobukwe.' He remembers that they greeted each other cordially. Sobukwe himself retained a pleasant memory of the encounter: he was testifying in court at that time and he remembered Slovo congratulating him with the word, 'Brilliant'.

In addition to these arrests, over the next few months the police and army raided large numbers of ghettos. They often repeated the Cape Town pattern with soldiers sealing off a township and patrolling the streets while the police carried out house-to-house searches. Many thousands were arrested for a variety of alleged offences, whether participation in rioting, or possession of dangerous weapons, or 'vagrancy', or failing to have a pass, or being in arrear with taxes. Contradictory official statistics make the exact extent of arrests uncertain, but the government did acknowledge that, by the first week of May, 18,011 blacks were seized. They were either released without being charged, or were rushed through courts—often in secret sessions inside prisons—and jailed, or were syphoned off to work virtually as slaves on white-owned farms. Nor did release from jail necessarily mean the end: some men returned home to find they had lost their jobs and were therefore 'endorsed out'—ordered out of the city into rural poverty.

Many of those detained, as Muriel Horrell wrote in that year's Survey of Race Relations, 'disappeared suddenly, leaving their families in a state of acute anxiety and, often, financial distress. The prisons officials were frequently unable or unwilling to disclose the whereabouts of the arrested persons ... particularly in the Cape Town area, numbers of juveniles were arrested, taken home in custody to collect their clothes, and then sent off by train, handcuffed in pairs, to an unknown destination.' The youngsters were rescued only after the parents brought urgent court applications.

Prisons were seriously overcrowded—and this, combined with authoritarian callousness, led to new tragedy: poor conditions and poor food at Modder B, an old gold-mine barracks for blacks near Johannesburg converted into a jail, brought on scores of cases of pneumonia with many deaths among non-political black prisoners.

It was also a turning point in my life because it sparked my interest in jail conditions, with far-reaching consequences a few years later. In a combined operation with Obed Musi, a brave and tenacious reporter on *Golden City Post*, a weekly newspaper aimed at blacks, I investigated what was happening inside Modder B prison. Apart from the stringent restrictions of the State of Emergency regulations we had the hazards of the Prisons Act enacted the previous year: the key stipulation for the Press was Section 44 (f) making it a criminal offence to publish any information about prisons or prisoners 'knowing the same to be false, or without taking reasonable steps to verify such information . . . '.

The purpose was to seal off the jails from public view. Apart from occasional breaches, that's exactly what was achieved. But Musi and I managed to get together enough information about Modder B to expose what was happening there. The Prisons Department confirmed eighteen deaths to us, which was sensation in itself; a few months later, it became known that the toll had actually been forty-two.

Meanwhile, trials arising out of the March disturbances and involving both PAC members and others went on and on as white authority set about the task of reminding blacks who was boss. The 142 ordinary PAC members who had also offered themselves for arrest at Orlando police station on 21 March were sentenced to fines of £300 or three years' jail. Like Sobukwe, they refused to plead because they said they had no hand in making the laws, had not been consulted about them, and therefore had no moral obligation to obey. Among them was the 16-year-old Aubrey Mokoape; the magistrate did not question his age but gave him the same sentence as the adults.

In Cape Town, Philip Kgosana was released from detention after four months and, together with several dozen others, charged with incitement. He fled the country and the charge against the remainder eventually petered out in June the next year.

In Durban, fourteen men were jailed for up to two years for taking part in an unlawful gathering or procession. Hundreds of others around the country, in cities and small towns, were jailed and fined for burning their passes and inciting others to do so, or inciting people not to carry their passes, or for threatening people with violence if they did not hand over their passes. There was also lashing: in Durban, a youth who offered himself for arrest without a pass was sentenced to a beating of three cuts with a cane; in Johannesburg, five young men were given eight to ten cuts. In Evaton, the trial of thirteen men on public violence and incitement finally ended, the next April, with the dropping of charges. And in Sharpeville itself, only in June 1961 were five people jailed for one to three years on charges of public violence and incitement while fourteen were acquitted.

When the State of Emergency was lifted, on 31 August, South Africa gave every appearance of having returned to normal. But it was a different society from what it had been before 21 March.

Among Afrikaners, the shock effects of Sharpeville had, in the early days of the emergency, brought to the surface the worries of some, mainly academics and churchmen, about the morality of naked apartheid. On 19 April, Paul Sauer, the government's chief spokesman in the absence of Verwoerd—still recovering from the assassination attempt—created headlines because he seemed to be articulating those feelings by saying in a public speech: 'The old book of South African history was closed . . . at Sharpeville. For the immediate future, South Africa will have to reconsider in earnest and with honesty her whole approach to the native question.' Although he qualified this by saying that passes had to be retained, his speech was so much out of the ordinary that it aroused enthusiastic hope among many opposed to the government that Afrikaners were finally coming to recognise the need for change. But it was not so. Afrikaner leaders closed ranks and rushed to repudiate Sauer; he fell silent.

A fortnight later, on the same day that Sobukwe was sentenced, the Minister of External Affairs, Eric Louw, set out the government's intentions. During the Second World War, Louw's pro-Nazi propaganda zeal combined with his physical appearance had earned him the nickname of 'South Africa's Goebbels'. Now he was standing in for Verwoerd at a meeting in London of the Commonwealth, of which South Africa was still a member. About one hundred journalists were at a Press conference at South Africa House, the then High Commission in Trafalgar Square, to hear Louw say that whites were not prepared to abdicate in favour of a probable 'Bantu dictatorship'. He said Verwoerd saw no reason for a change in the basic policy of separate development. He rubbed in the message by noting that South Africa's domestic policies were its own affair and not the concern of Commonwealth members. As he left the building he was booed by a large crowd standing outside. Some shouted 'murder, murder'.

In case anyone still had any doubts about the government, a statement by Verwoerd was read to Parliament later that month: separate development remained; steps would be taken to prevent incitement from continuing; the government would do more to supervise the administration of blacks in cities; influx control would continue. He promised a concession: the pass which blacks had to carry would be reduced in size.

Thus the Afrikaner response. From now on, apartheid was applied more rigidly and sternly than ever. South Africa went into its hard, unyielding 'granite' years. Separate development was driven forward with total dedication. No opposition was brooked. Rural communities were given no choice but involvement in the system of tribal authorities. More money was also put into buying blacks: the pay of tribal chiefs and headmen was increased. In the cities, municipalities were ordered to carry out to the letter government instructions in tightening control of every aspect of the lives of blacks.

The jailing of PAC members created a new group of prisoners—large numbers sentenced to long terms for political offences. As the numbers of PAC prisoners rose, and they were joined by members of the ANC and others, the creating of special security sections in prisons became a growth industry.

The bannings of the Pan-Africanist Congress and the African National Congress remained. That did not mean the organisations disappeared; although badly damaged, they went underground and tried to regroup. To be caught furthering 'the aims and activities' of the organisations could now draw up to ten years' imprisonment. Fierce penalties introduced in response to the unrest also remained in force, such as the tenfold increase in punishment—from six months to five years, with compulsory whipping or jailing for a second offence—for intimidating people from going to work, or even jeering at them.

Non-violent black protest was again stamped upon the following year, when a National Action Council dominated by members of the African National Congress and led by Nelson Mandela called a strike: it had a mixed response, but government repression brought the ANC finally to end its non-violent tradition. The Communist

Party, illegal since 1950, regrouped and combined with the ANC to form a military wing, *Umkhonto weSizwe* (Spear of the Nation). Umkhonto mounted its first political sabotage on 16 December 1961 by blowing up electricity pylons. The PAC had its own offshoot, *Poqo,* which wanted to kill as many whites as possible. More about Poqo later.

The spiral of repression, protest and greater repression spawned ever-tougher laws: 12-day detention without trial became 90-day detention which became 180-day detention which became indefinite detention. Locked away in the secrecy of police cells, torture became rampant; the number grew of detainees who died in mysterious circumstances—although, more often than not, police murder was obvious. Personal rights were steadily whittled down, whether in ending the traditional right to hold meetings on the steps of the Johannesburg City Hall and on Cape Town's Grand Parade—a large open space in the city centre—or arbitrary bannings on a wholesale scale.

At first, immediately after Sharpeville, there was a flurry of activity in the business community. Memorandums were prepared and delegations called on the Prime Minister and other ministers about the 'serious ill effects on South Africa's economy', as the Cape Chamber of Industries put it. For some businessmen, the chief anxiety was to provide safeguards for blacks who, they said, wished to work but were threatened by intimidators. Others said the 'wave of lawlessness' had a genuine basis of grievance which 'agitators' had been able to exploit, and they urged the government to consult with leaders acceptable to city blacks. But there was a limit to business liberalism: a joint delegation from industry and commerce supported controls on the influx of blacks to the cities.

Millions of pounds were wiped off the value of shares on the Johannesburg Stock Exchange, and the Exchange's president warned: 'Confidence in the future of South Africa is ebbing.' Industrial leaders worried in public that overseas investors had lost faith in the country, and that it would grow more difficult to draw investment and attract skilled immigrants.

But as the government proved its determination, and capacity, to ignore criticisms and to push ahead with its ideological schemes, the business community settled into reaping the financial benefits of having a captive labour force at its disposal. In the years to come, a few well-known business leaders regularly made speeches protesting against apartheid, but in their corporate operations did little or nothing to end the poverty pay of their own black workers or to extend training for skills.

There were significant repercussions too among the Christian churches: all churches practised apartheid to greater or lesser degrees, the Afrikaans churches openly so by having segregated churches and allowing only whites in the 'mother' church; the English churches, on the other hand, generally pronounced against apartheid—but everyday practices were often racially discriminatory. Now the Anglican Archbishop of Cape Town, Joost de Blank, said that the events of 21 March had confronted the Church in South Africa with the gravest crisis in its history. On that day, he said, blacks turned not only against those whom they considered to be their white oppressors, but also against the Christian Church as being identified with them.

The religious agonising led a group of Afrikaans theologians to publish a milestone book, *Delayed Action*, challenging support for apartheid, and to the World Council of Churches organising an inter-church gathering in South Africa. Named the Cottesloe Consultation after the Witwatersrand University residence where it was held, it was a momentous meeting in clarifying and sharpening international church attitudes towards South Africa. The consultation denounced racial segregation—and the Afrikaans churches quit the world body.

It was one more step in the withdrawal of Afrikaners into their laager. The process was intensified by the wide range of other international forces precipitated by Sharpeville. The UN Security Council deplored the loss of life and blamed the country's racial policies; the government furiously rejected this 'interference' in its domestic affairs.

Calls for a boycott of South African goods had been made at a conference in November 1959 of the newly formed All-Africa Trade Union Federation. During 1960, as governments throughout the world protested against what was happening in South Africa, the boycott began to roll forward. In Britain, the Labour and Liberal parties had coincidentally backed a boycott in March of forty products, including tinned foods, cigarettes, wines and fruit—a modest start to what came later. The boycott had not been a success, reported a London correspondent of *The Star*, but Sharpeville had suddenly brought it into focus: 'It seemed to confirm the propaganda of the past months. The allegations so continuously levelled [about the evils of apartheid] were held to be proved.' The prevailing public mood was expressed by Sir Laurence Dunne, Chief Metropolitan Magistrate in London, when he told twenty-nine anti-apartheid demonstrators that their opinions were shared by many in Britain. 'I don't suppose there is anybody in this country who does not view with great pain what has happened elsewhere,' he said—before finding them guilty, and imposing fines, for acts of disturbance in making their protests. The boycott committee was transformed into a permanent anti-apartheid committee, and this became the Anti-Apartheid Movement which was to do so much in the years to come to foster an anti-apartheid consciousness.

In due course, boycotts were imposed by Ethiopia, Nigeria, Sierra Leone, Liberia, India, Ghana, Malaya and Barbados in an ever-widening circle—even though in some cases trading continued behind the scenes.

South Africa was still a member of the International Olympic Committee, but what was to become a far-ranging sports boycott was gathering momentum. The whites who controlled sport in South Africa were arrogantly blind to the forces building up against them: at a meeting in January 1961 they insisted that the only way in which blacks, coloureds and Asians could gain selection for the Olympics was for their representative bodies to affiliate to the white controlling bodies—and to be represented by white delegates; they also had to take part in racially separate trials. No one seemed to blush when it was pointed out that weightlifter Precious McKenzie, a coloured man, had lifted more than anyone else during trials—but had been passed over in favour of a white man for Games selection. McKenzie, incidentally, emigrated to Britain and went on to represent his adopted country with honour.

The international boycotts were helped by an infusion of exiles from South Africa. During the State of Emergency several score political figures escaped, to the derision of the government. But the number of exiles swelled: within three years, at least 400 leaders and active supporters of the ANC and PAC were out of the country. They set up the PAC and ANC in exile, and became a potent and influential anti-apartheid lobby abroad—ultimately to the great dismay of the South African government.

At home, Afrikaner Nationalist adherence to domination and segregation, fixed more firmly in place after Sharpeville, went together with poverty wages, loss of homes, inadequate housing, starvation, overcrowded transport, stunted education, harsh rule, inferior status and denial of expression. These were the ingredients for a time-bomb for the future.

12

Many of the developments in South Africa were to pass Sobukwe by because he was now a convicted prisoner. Immediately after being sentenced he was taken back to The Fort: he was no longer awaiting trial, with the accompanying rights and privileges. Instead, he was subject to the harsh conditions which applied to black prisoners, and the brutality and hostility which was the everyday way in which warders treated them. Behind the high walls, apartheid kept black and white prisoners in separate sections; some jails were for blacks only. White warders were in charge, but the sections of jails for blacks usually also had black warders.

Aubrey Mokoape, although in a different group from Sobukwe, was also at The Fort and he describes the aggression of the warders when the truck bringing him and other convicted PAC members from the courts backed up to the jail's main gate. 'As we ran inside the warders were shouting, "four, four, two, two", which means stand in fours or in twos. They had a lovely way of confusing you: They shout, "four, four", and just as you try to stand in fours they shout "two, two". And while we were doing this they were hitting us with batons and hands, and they were clouting and kicking us, and swearing at us.'

When Sobukwe arrived he handed over his clothes and was given prison uniform which, for blacks, consisted of moleskin trousers ending above the knee, known as 'shorties' or '*tsotsi* pants' (tsotsi—young gangsters), a khaki or red shirt, and a jersey. For the first few days they walked uncomfortably barefoot—it was early winter—on the stone floors. Then they were given rubber slip-on sandals, but no socks. Sobukwe also underwent another jail routine: he had his head shaved—not with clippers, but with an open razor blade wielded by a convict using a little water and soap, and often leaving the scraped head cut and bleeding.

Benjamin Pogrund

The convict was one of the *bandiete*—Afrikaans for bandits—the long-term prisoners. Some had a silver star on their shirt to show they were monitors. They played a major role in running prisons because they did the day-to-day work for the warders. At first the black *bandiete* at The Fort showed as much animosity as the warders towards Sobukwe and his colleagues, cursing and assaulting them. But the PAC men set about politicising them, using every opportunity to explain why they were in jail and pointing out that the *bandiete* were doing the warders' dirty work. Sobukwe had particular success in educating a thug called Maxie, who was a member of Johannesburg's most notorious gang, the Msomis. Maxie came round to declaring that he was sorry he had begun his life of crime before he met Sobukwe, and his endorsement did much to change the attitude of the *bandiete*. After a few days they became friendly and helpful, for example in letting in newspapers, or in allowing visits to go well beyond the official times. As a sentenced prisoner, Sobukwe was now entitled to one visit of thirty minutes every three months for the first two years, and then one visit a month.

Without access to government records, the sequence of the next three years is not always certain. But it seems that, shortly after being sentenced, Sobukwe and Leballo were removed from their fellows and taken to Pretoria Central Prison. This was because other PAC accused in Pretoria wanted them to testify in their case.

Pretoria Central is one of the chief jails for long-term prisoners; it has special significance because it also houses the gallows for executions. No one who has done time in Central forgets it: for days before an execution—and during most of the last decade South Africa has hanged an average of ten people a month, most of them blacks—melodious, mournful singing rises from the condemned section; in the silence of an execution morning, the thud of the trap doors opening reverberates through much of the huge building. Alongside Central is Pretoria Local which, increasingly during the 1960s, came to be used for political prisoners.

While in Pretoria, Sobukwe apparently did not undergo what was officially called 'Observation'. If so, he was fortunate. Other PAC men were, however, subject to it.

The theory of Observation was that sentenced prisoners were to undergo psychological examination so that the best means of rehabilitation could be devised for them. Basic to this was that they had to remain in their cells to ponder upon their crimes and repent of their deeds. No visitors were allowed. In practice, the prison warders who were described as psychologists were not equipped for the job, and prisoners were often not even aware that they were undergoing an assessment programme. Instead, Observation was one of the most feared aspects of prison existence and was often viewed as worse than almost any punishment. It was applied both to black and white prisoners.

As PAC men describe it, ten to fifteen of them were in a cell, locked in morning, noon and night. They had a bucket to use as a toilet but no toilet paper. Each morning and afternoon the cell door was unlocked and two of them took turns to carry the bucket down the passage, empty it and wash it. They had another bucket, for water, which was refilled twice a day. They were each given a thin sisal mat and old, thin, dirty blankets. There were no pillows. They slept on the cement floor. Each morning they had to fold up the mats and blankets and put them in the passage. They spent the day inside the bare cell, sitting or standing. They had no books or newspapers; not even the Bible, which was usually given to prisoners.

Food was served three times a day: metal plates were skimmed along the floor through an opening at the bottom of the door. The meals were the standard fare for black prisoners: breakfast was soft porridge—known as 'pap' in South Africa—with a smidgen of brown sugar and a mug of strange-tasting liquid that was supposed to be coffee. Lunch, at 11 to 12 o'clock, was boiled maize, occasionally with a carrot or beetroot in it. Supper, at about 3 p.m., was pap or boiled maize, with one or two pieces of meat added three times a week. The maize often looked and tasted rotten, and worms were regularly found in the porridge. Fruit and milk were unknown.

The only washing they could do was to take turns using a mug of water from the cell's supply to wet hands and face. The only clothing for each man was a shirt, jersey and *tsotsi* pants; all were barefoot. It was the only clothing they had and they never took off anything. The cold—and it was mid-winter, with below-freezing temperatures—could barely be endured.

Somehow, jail officials sincerely believed that they were doing something good for the souls of the prisoners in their care. But prisoners viewed it differently. 'It was like hell. That's when you really felt these people are cruel,' says Joe Moabi. He was among those who had surrendered for arrest at Orlando; later he became a member of the PAC national executive in exile.

After three to four weeks had passed—and by then they were dirty and stinking—they were allowed out for their first exercise and a quick shower, a *bandiet* putting a blob of liquid soap on each man's head. They were given a change of clothing and it was back to the cells for another three weeks.

It was grim, but at least they had the solace of being together in a group. Other prisoners, both political and criminal, often had to endure Observation on their own in a small cell.

Security was tight. Most of the warders were whites, and there was only fleeting contact with the *bandiete*, making it difficult to break down their hostility.

But what sustained the PAC men was their self-discipline. Neither here nor at any time later was there any trace of the homosexuality, liquor or *dagga*—the South African version of marijuana—common among prisoners. Instead, beginning at The Fort and carried through into each jail, they organised themselves into groups which assigned study subjects and organised daily debates.

In June, Sobukwe and Leballo were transferred—by truck under armed guard—to Stoneyard, the nickname for the jail in Boksburg, a gold-mining town less than an hour's drive to the east of Johannesburg. They were now together with a group of some 160 PAC men.

The communal cells at Stoneyard were larger than Pretoria and each took about twenty-five men. The basic conditions were much the same as Pretoria: a toilet bucket, although a larger one, thin sisal mats on concrete floors, inadequate blankets and wormy food. Nor was any reading material allowed. But now everyone had a pair of slip-on sandals: even without socks, that was a great improvement. And, most important of all, unless a capricious warder ordered them to remain in their cells, they could spend most of each weekday in the inner courtyard outside their cells, enjoying the sun. They could also have cold showers, and were even given small pieces of blue soap.

Sobukwe, like everyone else, had his own eating utensil, a metal spoon, usually carried at the waist. Meals were dished out in the courtyard; that was done even if it rained, but he could step into his cell to eat.

Inspection by officers and sick parade took place each morning.

How Can Man Die Better

The parades were a notorious feature of South African prisons. One or two warders from the jail's 'hospital' section went from cell to cell asking if anyone was ill. Unless the condition was considered serious enough to justify removal for a doctor's examination, the same medicine—a liquid mixture—was the usual cure given for headache, stomach-ache and sore eyes.

The jail has left its particular memories. 'The place was infested with bugs,' says Matthew Nkoana. He had given up journalism to defy with Sobukwe and had also been sentenced to three years' imprisonment. 'They gave us dirty blankets. We had to wash them and the cells. But that didn't help us a great deal with the bugs—they were pouring down the walls at night and biting us. The food was bad. We complained constantly about it. There was no improvement. On my first day I had my arms folded. That apparently was offensive. One of the warders slashed me on my arms with his cane but the Officer Commanding rebuked him in my hearing and said, "These are not ordinary prisoners".'

Despite the poor conditions, the discussion groups were extended. Men could move from cell to cell giving lectures because at the end of each day the warders counted heads and did not check names. The presence of black warders and black *bandiete* made smuggling possible: they brought in bits and pieces of newspapers, a whole page sometimes; vitamin tablets were also on the wanted list, to make up for the physical suffering of the Observation period.

The accent was on education and debating and a 'Syllabus committee' decided the issues. People were assigned a subject and presented it for discussion. Sobukwe's speciality was political science, and he led many discussions about the nature of government and the sort of government which PAC wanted for South Africa. Other topics included the reason for the split from the ANC and the nature of communism.

A 'Publicity committee' had the job of getting hold of newspapers and reading out relevant items. A 'Discipline committee' dealt with problems between prisoners: if someone misbehaved he could be brought before the committee and, if necessary, he could be ostracised. An 'Education committee' arranged as much teaching as possible—especially relevant because several school pupils were among the prisoners. A journalist gave lessons in writing, and the committee dealt with world affairs and current affairs, such as the then tension between Israel and Egypt, or East-West relations. The

'Recreation committee' organised the popular *mrabaraba* stones game, and made up draughts boards—which the prison authorities at first confiscated, before letting them be. This committee also moulded a blanket into the shape of a rugby ball and demonstrated the finer points of playing rugby—a sport popular among many South Africans, but the special passion of Afrikaners.

The food was so wretched that two of the PAC men finally protested and threw away their rations. The prison authorities cracked down on them: each was sentenced to seven days' spare diet which meant not only reduced food but also being kept in a special section with only one blanket apiece.

Others wanted to join in the protest, but Sobukwe intervened. 'Chaps, our struggle is not against food,' he told them. 'Those are small things. You must expect those things to happen in jail. We have not come here for food. We must direct our struggle along the straight.'

He remained the undisputed leader. Each morning, PAC prisoners who met him gave him the greeting *'Izwe Lethu'*, and received his smiling *'iAfrika!'* response. 'There was tremendous respect for him. His personality generated respect,' says Mokoape. 'He moved around among us all the time. It was a very close association, a very free spirit among all the people there.' No one ever saw Sobukwe looking depressed or upset; he was always cheerful, imbued with a belief in the Africanist vision and fortifying that outlook in his supporters.

But there was, among the leaders, a worry that they had miscalculated the prison terms they would get. The anti-pass campaign had been based on the notion of being arrested, serving a jail sentence, and promptly repeating the process upon release—a continuous and, hopefully, escalating cycle of non-collaboration in the full spirit of the 1949 Programme of Action. It had been anticipated that the government would use the severe penalties introduced to break the Defiance Campaign, but even then the PAC apparently underestimated the probable jail sentences, believing they would run for a maximum of a year or eighteen months.

Not all the leaders were in jail. Two members of the national executive had been sent abroad on the eve of the campaign, and Z.B. Molete, of Evaton, was told by Sobukwe to stay out of prison for as long as possible and to keep the organisation going. But the original plan to have several layers of leadership available, one taking over from another, was not working in practice because there hadn't been time to develop enough leaders.

So it was with dismay that Sobukwe, in jail, saw the PAC floundering because of the absence of leadership. He still attempted to remain in charge of the organisation: warders were bribed to carry messages in and out, and Molete came on visits to report and receive instructions. But it was an increasingly unsatisfactory situation. Intense debates went on about whether to lodge appeals to the Supreme Court against the severity of their sentences. Additional pressure to do so came from some families outside, and especially from parents of younger prisoners.

At the centre of the argument was whether appeals would run counter to the intentions of the 'no bail, no defence, no fine' pledge. Sobukwe felt that they were a negation of the campaign slogan. Finally, however, he agreed that appeals should be lodged on behalf of his fellows but not for him. But then he was included and, although unhappy, he went along with it. One argument advanced by Leballo was that, if bail could be obtained pending the hearing of appeals, the anti-pass campaign could be re-vitalised. But there was no bail, and the Supreme Court turned down the appeals lodged by the leaders. Some rank and file members were more successful. Mokoape, for example, had his three-year sentence cut in half and was also given the option of a fine. He returned to school, went on to complete a medical degree, became a student leader and was again jailed for anti-apartheid activity. Later, and inexplicably, the leaders sent a message to Joe Slovo in his capacity as a barrister to ask about the possibility of challenging the judgment in the Appeal Court. But it came to nothing.

The argument about appealing set off new lines of thought. The PAC men began to ask each other: Should they be in jail? Some said they should be outside fighting, and perhaps they should not have surrendered themselves. The soul-searching also led them into wondering whether they had been asking too much in expecting to bring down the government simply by surrendering as they had, by purely Gandhian methods.

The act of bringing an appeal never seemed to detract from Sobukwe's public image as the leader who offered himself ahead of everyone else. It appears to have been generally accepted as a necessary tactic in dealing with a tough and powerful enemy and in no way affecting his credibility.

Benjamin Pogrund

One day, suddenly, there was a great fuss inside Stoneyard. The authorities had discovered that Sobukwe was smuggling messages—the orders to PAC members outside—and his cell was searched. Newspapers were found and this led to immediate transfer for him and four other leaders—Leballo, Mothopeng, Nyaose and Ngendane—to another Boksburg prison, Cinderella.

Two to three months later, everyone was brought together again in a new move to Stofberg, not far from Sharpeville. They were the first prisoners in this new farm jail, which had previously been a Dutch Reformed Church theological seminary.

Sobukwe's conditions were improved in some ways. He had a new sisal mat, blankets and clothing. Food was more varied because vegetables were supplied from the prison's gardens. But there were still worms in the porridge. 'It was part of the menu,' jokes a former prisoner. He also now had a spoon with a proper handle; at Boksburg, the handles had been cut short, apparently to prevent their use as weapons.

As a farm prison, Stofberg had a feeling of openness about it, despite the two high wire-mesh fences which surrounded the buildings, with watch towers at the corners and warders with rifles and guard dogs on patrol in the corridor between the fences. The PAC men—there were about 150 of them—occupied their own wing in a building. Sobukwe was again in a communal cell, although a more spacious one than before.

But the big change now was the opportunity to work, building an earth dam. After the months of idleness, many welcomed it; not all, however, for it was rough labour. Breakfast was brought in the mornings by *bandiete* and was eaten in an open yard outside the cells, whether rain was falling or not. The sick parade which followed was as derisory as at Boksburg. Then Sobukwe and the others lined up and, pushing wheelbarrows and carrying picks and shovels, they marched for about fifteen minutes to an adjacent fenced-in area, with its own set of four watchtowers.

They dug up earth, loaded it into coco pans and pushed these along a rail line they had built. Sobukwe wielded a pickaxe and pushed the pans with everyone else. They ate lunch at the dam site and at 4 p.m., at the end of the working day, marched back in 'four fours', carrying their tools.

A fenced-in enclosure stood between the dam and the prison buildings. That's where the daily check for weapons was carried out.

How Can Man Die Better

As with the others, Sobukwe lined up each day to strip naked and to hand his clothing to a warder who searched it and dropped it on the ground. He had to bend over while a warder looked into his rectum. Then he dressed and went through. Sometimes warders ordered the *tausa*, an undignified leap into the air, with arms and legs splayed wide, so that warders could peer into body crevices.

At one stage, cement was poured at the dam. The PAC men took the opportunity to pay their respects. They wrote into the wet cement: Sobukwe Dam.

Stofberg had black warders, but only whites dealt with the PAC: that was intended as part of the maximum security to which they were subject and made smuggling more difficult. The warders were hostile. They all seemed to be Afrikaners and they plainly viewed the PAC men as their enemies who had to be disciplined. Especially at the dam site, assaults were part of the day, with a warder deciding that a prisoner was not working fast enough and giving him a clout with any convenient length of wood. The prisoners lodged complaints, but the commanding officer was as openly hostile as his men and no action was ever taken that anyone was aware of. The officer had a habit of standing and watching them work, swagger stick under his arm and a glaring scowl on his face. They dubbed him 'Hitler'.

Now and again the PAC men, especially the younger ones, deliberately pushed coco pans off the rails. It was calculated to bring on a screaming frenzy from the warders and was followed by the *drie maaltye*—three meals—punishment. That was the way used to gain a rest from work.

Although the harassment was continual, Sobukwe was never hit. The warders drew back from that; even they must have known what they could have precipitated had they touched him. 'They knew we regarded him with great respect and that we didn't want anything to happen to him,' says Joe Moabi.

'Stofberg will go down in history as hell,' says Ngendane. 'Robben Island in all its savagery was a little better. At Stofberg, we had to uproot trees. We used bare hands most of the time to clear the forest ... Officials were vicious. False charges against prisoners were common. Corporal punishment was carried out in public as a warning. I still have memories of young schoolboys screaming with pain as the heavy cane descended on their bare buttocks.'

The pressure from the warders eventually came to a head when two prisoners refused to push their wheelbarrows any faster than they were doing. They could walk, but not run as the warders kept telling them to do. The guards berated them, but the men went on at their own pace. Sobukwe backed them. There was an altercation and Sipho Mgomezulu, an ex-boxer, threatened Laff, the warder in charge: 'If you hit me, I hit back.' Laff went away, but in the middle of the day all the PAC men were ordered to leave the dam. As they went into the adjoining fenced-in enclosure, the gates were closed, penning them in. There was a shout, *'Slaan hulle'* (Hit them). The next moment, a horde of warders rushed in and set upon the prisoners with pickaxe handles, batons, sticks and whips. It was a 'carry-on', in jail language.

Victims of the assault have only a confused memory of pandemonium, of trying to escape the avalanche of blows, of shouts of abuse from warders, of screams of pain by prisoners, and of the sight of bloodied heads. 'It was anarchy,' says Lennox Mlonzi. 'You couldn't know what was being done to what person. You had to cover yourself, that's all.' Sobukwe was not hit, but struggled to intervene, to tell the warders to stop.

Mgomezulu was singled out for attack and landed up in the jail hospital for several days. Then he was sentenced to a term of solitary confinement for fighting. Moabi and several others were given eleven days' solitary for fighting.

It has gone down in PAC history as 'The Battle of the Pickaxes'.

Nursing their bruises and wounds, the PAC men were ordered to get back immediately to work at the dam. At the end of the day, Sobukwe spoke to them, again giving the message that they had to remember why they were there: 'We all agreed that we are creating history. You must understand that when you create history you must take the good and the bitter. We are in the process of doing that. I am sorry about what has happened but it is part of the struggle.' He told them to return to work and to continue at the same pace as before—'and if they mean to beat us to death they can do so'.

They went on working, but now the warders left them alone. They did not complete the dam because they were again transferred—as always, under strong armed escort—to jail at Witbank, 130 kilometres east of Johannesburg. The town is surrounded by vast earth dumps, the debris from underground coal-mining. It also often has an evil-smelling fog hanging over it, from the chemical plants in the district. But the jail proved to be the best Sobukwe had been in so far. The officer in charge was fair—he told them briskly that he would carry out his duties without caring what government was in power—the food was better, and the clothing for winter included a jersey, socks and shoes and long trousers for everyone. Even more, to his delight, Sobukwe could pursue a favourite hobby because he was put to work in the gardens, digging and planting vegetables. He wrote to his wife: 'We are in open country once more, and for that am thankful. One can see far into the distance.'

He had a short break from jail routine when PAC members, still on trial for public violence arising out of the 21 March demonstration at Sharpeville, were able to arrange for him to testify for them. At this stage, the PAC aim was to avoid going to jail, or at least to keep down the length of it, so some of the accused had engaged Jack Unterhalter, a Johannesburg barrister, who was white. Unterhalter was a leader in the Liberal Party and had met Sobukwe in pre-Sharpeville times. Now he saw him shuffle into the court in Vereeniging wearing leg irons. 'The magistrate, O'Brien, was very angry and he ordered the prosecutor to take immediate steps to have him unshackled,' he says. 'I remember so well a white policeman kneeling at the feet of Robert Sobukwe, as he stood in the witness box, removing the shackles.'

Sobukwe's testimony also stuck in Unterhalter's mind: 'My impression of the evidence he gave was that it was completely truthful, that he was not prepared to say anything other than the truth, even though he was the leader of the PAC and these were PAC members standing in the dock. An example I remember is that he identified the PAC flag which had been used by the accused, and ironically this helped to close a gap in the prosecutor's case. I've always thought of it as an outstanding example of a man of probity and principle.'

Yet another move was ordered and, by the second half of 1961, Sobukwe was in Pretoria Local, adjoining Pretoria Central and with the main gate fronting on the road to Johannesburg. Local had by then been converted for the growing numbers of political prisoners, with whites and blacks kept in separate sections.

I had not been in touch with Sobukwe after his arrest. I cannot explain it, but remain ashamed of my behaviour. I was badly shaken by my near-death after the shooting at Sharpeville and, looking back, perhaps unconsciously I linked Sobukwe personally with the episode and therefore stayed away from him. I am not sure. The weekend after the shooting I made an apprehensive return to Sharpeville to report on the help being given to people in a community which was in a state of shocked grief. I went on to become deeply involved in reporting the State of Emergency. The politics of it belonged to my sphere of reporting and close friends were among those locked up without trial.

But only during the next year did I again make contact with Sobukwe. I went to see Veronica Sobukwe and after discovering that Bob was in Pretoria Local, I wrote to him. A reply dated 4 October 1961 came quickly, after passing through the jail censors. It was written on an official prison letter form; he had to state my occupation and he wrote 'Professional' instead of the 'Journalist' which could have drawn suspicious attention. It established the pattern for the years to come: I was in touch with him as a friend, not as a journalist. The government allowed me to keep contact with him as a friend; relations would not have been allowed in my role as a journalist. On the other hand, it also meant that I was severely constrained as a journalist in using information which I acquired as a friend.

That first letter told a story in itself: not only did it reveal details about Sobukwe's conditions, but it showed him as warm and cheerful as ever. He was also charitable about my long silence:

Dear Benjie,

I have about five letters to reply to and yours was the last to arrive. But I have decided to indulge in a bit of favouritism and write your letter first. Thanks indeed for your letter. It was a real pleasure to read it.

Through the kind permission of the prison authorities, I am able to write and receive one letter per week and have one visit per week. I have, therefore, been able to write fairly regularly to my people at Graaff-Reinet and also to see my wife. Unfortunately children are not permitted inside the grounds, so I last saw my kids at Witbank.

Thanks for the news about Jennifer [my daughter had been born in July]. I had not received the glad tidings yet. I am glad to have got the news from the proud father himself. Since both of you are so easy to please I don't think Jennifer's task, to make you happy, should be a difficult one! I am sorry I cannot come and pay my respects in person to the lady, but hope to do so when I have left gaol.

My daughter is in Basutoland, attending school there. I learn that two weeks ago she was taken ill and that my wife has rushed to Basutoland to see her. Haven't heard any more since then.

Glad to learn you have taken up Zulu again—particularly Astrid. I was sorry when she had to give it up because of your interference [a joking reference to my wife who had dropped out of university after our marriage].

Thanks for remembering me, Benjie—and thank you also for your offer of help. As I said earlier, I am allowed a visit per week so that it should be possible to arrange for my wife to skip one week so that I may meet you.

Zeph [Mothopeng] and Jacob [Nyaose] remained behind at Witbank. I am with PK [Leballo]. And we both would be happy to see you. You may perhaps be able to send me some books to read. We are allowed to receive approved literature—that EXCLUDES Westerns.

Give my greetings to Astrid and the kid. I wish them the very best. Remember me to Pat [Duncan] and Dave [Dubois] when you do write to them.

Salani kahle! [Keep well]
Yours very sincerely

Bob

The letter spurred me to action. I contacted Mrs Sobukwe to find out what could be done to help her. I was also able to visit him: we met on each side of a thick wire-netting screen, but I could see enough to know that he was thinner than when we had last been together. His hair was closely cropped. A warder was present so we kept our conversation in check: politics and prison conditions were barred.

On a later visit I asked, in as roundabout a way as I could, about Nelson Mandela, who was also in jail. After organising the May

1961 stay-at-home campaign, and so successfully eluding the police that he earned the title of the Black Pimpernel, Mandela had left the country and travelled abroad. He returned home but was captured and jailed for incitement and leaving the country illegally (only two years later, in 1964, in a second trial, was he charged with seeking to overthrow the government, for which he was sentenced to the life imprisonment which attracted so much world attention two decades later).

Sobukwe told me that he and Mandela were sitting side by side and sewing mailbags—traditional jail labour requiring the repair of dirty and smelly canvas bags. They were talking a lot. I told him rumours were doing the rounds that Mandela had become an Africanist. Sobukwe smiled and said no, it wasn't true.

The sewing of mailbags was normally done in the cells. But Sobukwe and Mandela and a half-dozen other political prisoners, most of them PAC at this stage, were allowed to do the job in the prison yard, sitting on a concrete ledge against a wall, says A.B. Ngcobo, who had been the PAC's National Treasurer and leader of the Natal province. He had offered himself for arrest in Durban on 21 March, together with about fifteen other regional leaders, on the firm principle that the leaders should be seen to go first. It was a hot day and black policemen brought them iced water. They were arrested only after news arrived about the shooting at Sharpeville. Ngcobo served a few months in jail for not carrying his pass. On his release he found a message from Sobukwe, smuggled out of jail, ordering him to go to the Transvaal to organise. He was arrested there and was one of the first to be charged under the Unlawful Organisations Act: two years' imprisonment followed.

The conflict between the PAC and ANC was put aside inside prison, he says. Relations were friendly and people greeted each other by the tribal clan names reserved for close friends and admirers—*Madiba* for Mandela, and *Mfene* (Baboon) or *Hlathi* (Forest) for Sobukwe. They talked about politics, literature, religion and sport, and shared their books. One such discussion was on the issue of who was the greatest English writer, Shakespeare or George Bernard Shaw.

However, the authorities must have been bothered about the contact between Sobukwe and Mandela, and they were separated.

Sobukwe's conditions at Pretoria Local were at least as unpleasant as at the earlier jails. Like his colleagues he had his own cell, measuring about 6 by 7 ft, complete with a toilet bucket. The cold was intense, and sleeping on a thin sisal mat on a cement floor with two thin blankets—dirty, until replaced after a few months—was a terrible ordeal. The food was bad and the discipline strict. Again he wore off-white *tsotsi* shorts, a short-sleeved shirt and a brown bunny jacket; no socks or shoes, but rubber sandals. For washing, there was no towel or even a strip of cloth until they each bought their own small wash rag. They had to buy their own toothbrush and toothpaste. At Christmas, they were allowed to buy sweets. Heads were shaved once a month; they were able to get hold of a pair of clippers and so avoided the razor-scraping routine. The days began with a wake-up siren at 5.30 a.m. and ended with lock-up at about 4 p.m. On Saturdays, lock-up was at 2 p.m., and on Sundays at 11 a.m. Lights-out was at 9 p.m. They tried to lay hands on a copy of the official jail regulations so that they could know their rights, but this was refused them.

At first, no books or newspapers were permitted. Sobukwe relied on smuggled pieces of newspaper: it was in this way that, five weeks after the event, he learnt from a scrap of paper that the US and the USSR had hovered on the brink of war in the Cuban crisis.

Apart from the Bible, in English, he was allowed subscriptions to the *Reader's Digest, English Digest* and an English literary magazine, *John O'London's*. As his letter to me indicated, he was able to receive books.

He gained comfort from a Roman Catholic priest, Father Reg Webber OMI. Webber was an official prison chaplain and thus had access to Pretoria. As Sobukwe was later to tell me, he was also an exceptional human-being who put out his hand to the political prisoners. Ngcobo says of him, simply, 'He was one of the finest persons I've ever known.' Sobukwe remained a Methodist but found a natural human affinity with the priest. Only one of the politicals was a Catholic but all went to Webber's Wednesday church services, held in the open yard. Afterwards he saw each man individually and privately, to discuss their 'personal problems'.

Sobukwe's conditions of imprisonment, then and before, were bad. But they were not as bad as P.K. Leballo tried to tell the world they were. Leballo was released after his two-year sentence, banished to a remote part of the country, and then given permission to move to Basutoland, the British-ruled territory surrounded by South Africa and which is now independent Lesotho. In October 1962,

Leballo was in London, *en route* to the United Nations in New York, when he was interviewed by the *Tribune,* a Labour weekly newspaper. Some details he gave were undoubtedly accurate; but others were exaggerated or untrue, such as describing Sobukwe as 'terribly emaciated . . . in constant pain'.

The South African government was alarmed about the damaging effects of the report and acted to rebut it before it spread any further: Gordon Winter, a reporter with the English-language and ostensibly anti-apartheid newspaper the *Sunday Express* of Johannesburg, was given exclusive access to Sobukwe. His report lacked conviction because it was clearly counter-propaganda. But it had enough substance to blunt Leballo, and the published photographs did show Sobukwe in good health. As Winter was later to say, the arrangement for him to see Sobukwe was actually part of the cover being created for him: he was on his way to becoming a government security agent.

The publicity did at least have a beneficial effect. Sobukwe and his colleagues were allowed more time outside their cells and their food improved; they even got hot food.

Sobukwe knew that he would have to serve every single day of the three years of his sentence. He knew that, as a political prisoner, he was denied the one-third remission for good behaviour allowed as a matter of course to murderers, robbers, rapists, thieves and other criminals. Ironically, even while discriminating in this way, the government refused to acknowledge that there was such a thing as a 'political prisoner'; it spoke only of people who had contravened one law or another.

Early in 1963, as the date for Sobukwe's release—3 May—drew nearer, word began to spread that the government was fearful about seeing him go free. In February, two Security policemen visited Mrs Sobukwe—she was still living at the Mofolo house—and asked questions about her husband's birthplace and family. They did not say why they wanted the information, but a visit of that sort was becoming the prelude to arbitrary government action.

During the first week of March, Members of Parliament were reported as wanting to know what the government intended doing. Leading the pack was Mike Mitchell, a Durban lawyer viewed as the up and coming 'white hope' in the opposition United Party—and trying hard to show himself as more zealous than the Nationalists in defending white interests. He tabled questions in Parliament asking when Sobukwe would be released and whether the government intended taking action to curtail his activities and movements—'if so, what action and if not, why not?' The Minister of Justice, Balthazar Johannes (John) Vorster, duly replied: 'It is not considered in the public interest to furnish the information asked for at this stage.' He did, however, add the obvious—that no remission was being granted 'in view of the nature of the offence committed by him'. A government newspaper, *Dagbreek* (Daybreak), followed up by quoting 'informed circles' that Sobukwe would not be allowed to go free. 'The general opinion is that Sobukwe should not be released because he will be a danger to the State,' it said. He would probably be banished to his birthplace in the Eastern Cape.

The reason for the government's anxiety was later given by Vorster to Parliament in a glowing, but unintended, testimonial to Sobukwe: '... there has been no change of heart in him during the time he has not been in our midst ... we are dealing with a person who has a strong, magnetic personality, a person who can organise, a person who feels that he has a vocation to perform this task [of challenging the security of the State] ...'

Even with Sobukwe locked away in jail and despite the government's growing armoury of repressive laws, black protest had not ceased. The causes and motivations varied, but there had been disturbances in the past months in many rural areas, including Transkei, Sekhukhuneland, Mabieskraal, Peddie, the Northern Transvaal and Zululand. There had been rioting again in ghettos in Cape Town and Port Elizabeth and in the small, out of the mainstream, town of Warmbaths. There was a constant run of strikes by black workers, who often were arrested and fined for doing so because strikes by blacks were illegal. And, as mentioned earlier, *Umkhonto weSizwe* and other groups were bent on sabotage; although the physical damage they were causing was minimal, their activities contributed to a sense of crisis.

But overriding all this in immediate impact and in determining Sobukwe's fate, was an offshoot of the PAC called Poqo. The name had been informally used in the Cape before Sharpeville in speaking of PAC members: the Xhosa phrase was *Ama-Afrika Poqo*—The real owners of Africa. When, late in 1961, the movement sprang up in the ghettos of Cape Town, linked with its growth in the Transkei, the phrase became shortened to Poqo, translated as Our own or Pure. Totally for blacks, Poqo seems, as a specific entity, to have begun among the younger men in Langa and to have swept through Nyanga. It was fuelled by the savagery with which the government had crushed the peaceful anti-pass protests; the betrayal and arrest of Philip Kgosana no doubt added to the despairing mind-set that there was no point to non-violence. The feelings of hatred towards whites were inflamed because many of the men in the Cape Town ghettos were out of work and the authorities had chased wives back to rural starvation. The men were subject to incessant police raids and the abuse and assaults that went with these. Many came from the Transkei and they were bitter about the imposition of tribal authorities there and the collaboration of tribal leaders with the government. In a power struggle inside the PAC, the young men linked up with ghetto thugs and took over through a mixture of appeal and threat. The local PAC leadership fought back but lost.

Poqo spread rapidly, meshing in with existing PAC underground groups. Greater co-ordination came about after August 1962 when Leballo reached Basutoland and put himself in command. He was now acting President of the PAC. But the Poqo movement derived essentially from emotions of hatred and, short of a coherent political strategy, did not lend itself to control. On 22 November, in Paarl, near Cape Town, local grievances—the all too familiar story of abysmal living conditions and cruel and incompetent rule by local authorities—combined with Poqo passions to set off a rampage through the white town and the killing of two whites. In previous months there had already been a run of murders of black policemen and informers. The police claimed to have killed five of the attackers.

An alarmed government appointed a judge to investigate the attack. Even while he was doing so there was a series of Poqo skirmishes with the police, and the killing of policemen and tribal chiefs. On 2 February, Poqo murdered five whites, including two young girls, at a road camp in the Transkei. The judge rushed through an interim report—made public on 21 March, the anniversary of Sharpeville. He described PAC and Poqo as one and the same body, and that it intended to overthrow the government by revolutionary means that year. He urged the government to swift action.

That provided more than enough excuse for the Nationalists to push through another draconian law, strengthening their hold on the country. It was legislation close to the heart of John Vorster: he had been appointed Minister of Justice in August 1961 and was earning the admiration of his fellow Nationalists as an unyielding upholder of white law and order. He came to politics after an undistinguished career as a lawyer, but the clue to his outlook lay in his Second World War activities: he had been interned in Koffiefontein camp for a lengthy time because of his Nazi sympathies. By the beginning of 1963, he had already made his first major attacks on the rule of law by introducing detention without trial for twelve days as well as 'house arrest'—a do-it-yourself imprisonment whereby he could issue arbitrary orders to people requiring them to remain at home at nights and weekends, or on a full 24-hour basis. He had also banned the white Congress of Democrats, bringing to four the number of proscribed organisations. He was now engaged in putting new faces into the police force, which was to have the effect of transforming it into a far more purposeful organisation—and, not at all incidentally, more ideologically committed to white rule.

Vorster was aided in wanting to put his authoritarian instincts into practice by Leballo: for no apparent reason except conceit, Leballo called a Press conference in Basutoland late in March to claim that Poqo had 150,000 members and to threaten dire action. Poqo and PAC were one and the same thing, he said, and the movement 'stands by its pledge to free the African people in 1963'. Asked how this would be achieved he replied: 'By revolution—we are absolutely confident that we will succeed.' For good measure he added that the killing of whites would be an inevitable part of the revolution. He derided the South African police and said that he and other PAC members easily and frequently travelled between Basutoland and South Africa.

The startling headlines achieved by Leballo were a great help to Vorster as he moved for new restrictive laws. Although the details were not spelt out by Leballo, Poqo's aims were frankly murderous. I knew of them because, from an early stage, a member of Poqo provided me with a flow of information, giving me an update after each secret meeting he attended. According to the details I was getting, during the weekend of 7 and 8 April, members were to rise up and set about slaughtering as many whites as possible; the killing was to start in city streets. They were also to attack police stations, seize armouries, blow up power stations and police stations, and set petrol tanks alight (garage attendants were to drop lighted matches into underground petrol tanks; no one seemed to realise that any explosion was likely to prove fatal for them). Domestic servants were to poison the food of their white employers. The hope, and belief, was that other blacks would join in *en masse* once the killing started.

Leballo's intentions were so bloodthirsty that they led to his destruction. Basutoland's colonial government knew about the plans, apparently from an informer, and was apprehensive because of its information that Poqo was also to murder whites inside Basutoland. This plan was entirely Poqo's and had nothing to do with any Basutoland organisation. The number of whites in the country was not large, but the Basutoland police were simply too small in number to handle such a crisis.

When, on 29 March, Leballo sent two women assistants across the border into South Africa, to the town of Ladybrand, to post letters to Poqo branches giving them instructions, the Special Branch secretly tipped off the South African Security Police about them. This was done with the approval of the Resident Commissioner—the British colonial official in charge of the country—and London was advised of it. When the South African police were contacted, it was clear to the Basutoland authorities that they had no idea of the ramifications of Poqo's plans.

The two women were seized: Cynthia Lichaba, aged 18, found with about seventy letters from Leballo in her handbag; and Patricia Thabisa Lethala, aged 19. The letters put South African police inside the Poqo network. Mass arrests followed immediately. Where the police knew the identity of the leader of a cell but not the members, they spread a message calling a meeting—and grabbed everyone who came. Poqo was broken.

For months to come, large numbers were charged: in mid-June, Parliament was told that 3,246 Poqo members had been arrested and 124 of them had already been found guilty of murder and many cases were still proceeding. Other studies showed that scores of death sentences were imposed for murder, and jail sentences of up to life imprisonment for planned attacks on people. Many people were also prosecuted for belonging to the banned PAC and jailed for up to eight years.

The two women couriers were charged with being members of the PAC. Each was jailed for eighteen months.

How Can Man Die Better

In Basutoland, the local police raided Leballo's office on 1 April but he escaped into the mountains. Whether he was tipped off to get out of Maseru is not clear, but once he was in hiding the hunt for him was not pursued with any vigour: his capture would have been an embarrassment to the Basutoland government with likely pressure from South Africa for him to be handed over. This apart, reports circulated—but were never substantiated—of groups of Poqo members trying to get to Basutoland to kill Leballo for what he had done. Whatever the truth of that, he eventually got away from Basutoland—with British assistance—and remained acting President of the PAC in exile based in Tanzania's Dar es Salaam until he was deposed in 1979. He died in 1986.

Clearly, there was often no distinction between PAC and Poqo in the eyes of members. Leballo certainly did not mean there to be a distinction, and other PAC leaders saw Poqo as an extension of what had been before. The South African government believed the one belonged to the other. If all this was truly so, then Sobukwe as President of the PAC was also the leader of Poqo. In several court trials his name was mentioned in connection with Poqo—but no actual evidence was ever put forward about his involvement. That was surely a strange omission at a time when the government was looking for justification for keeping him in jail after his three-year sentence expired: what better than to prosecute him for sending orders to Poqo, for receiving messages from Poqo, or whatever?

It wasn't done because there was no evidence—because Sobukwe was not part of Poqo. Z.B. Molete, then of the PAC National Executive, says: 'I never heard of a message from Sobukwe to Poqo.' Hamilton Zolile Keke, jailed for ten years for membership of Poqo, and who went on to become the PAC representative in London and then in Baghdad, does not believe that Sobukwe knew about Poqo. The movement was too crude and lacking political direction, he says. 'Had Sobukwe known of it he would have vetoed it,' he says. 'Sobukwe would not have sanctioned a situation where people with pangas and stones were given orders to attack well-trained Boers.'

Indeed, by the time Poqo developed there is no indication that Sobukwe was still in control of the PAC. The system of communication from inside prison was proving insufficient for him to be closely in touch and to take key decisions. His movement was in a virtual state of suspense, waiting for his release, and this provided the opportunity for angry young men to make the running, and for Leballo to move in and to steer them as his own, as his means of asserting leadership. Molete also notes: 'Leballo always claimed Poqo as the PAC's military wing but it wasn't formed by the PAC.'

In PAC circles, some have wondered why Leballo chose to go public about Poqo late in March, and to set 8 April as the start of the uprising. He knew as well as anyone else that the government was nervous about releasing Sobukwe and was considering what to do. Was he aiming at provoking the government into clamping down on Sobukwe, so that he could remain leader of PAC? Others discount the notion, and say Leballo wasn't clever enough to carry out such ploys. They believe he was led astray by his own boastfulness and that he simply blundered.

Whatever the truth, Leballo's actions must have been a crucial factor in official decision-taking, especially for a government which had no understanding of the nature of black anger and aspirations, and couldn't have cared less about them anyway. Its political intelligence was crude and its insights even more so; it always viewed restless blacks merely as the pawns of agitators. As far as it was concerned, Sobukwe was Poqo.

Of course Sobukwe was a menace to white South Africa. Vorster had at least learnt enough to be able to assess him as a dangerous enemy who, from the perspective of Afrikaner Nationalist rule, had to be curbed. But in his ignorance, and that of his police and judicial advisers, he damned Sobukwe not for what he was but for what he wasn't.

The outcome was a decision not to use existing powers to banish or ban Sobukwe but to enact an entirely new method of political emasculation: to keep him in jail after his sentence had ended. This was done by providing that anyone convicted under security laws could be imprisoned after his sentence had ended if the Minister of Justice considered he was likely, if released, to further the achievements of any of the objects of communism (as defined by the government). Not for the first, or last, time therefore, the government cynically used its ostensibly anti-communist legislation against a known anti-communist.

The law was put into effect for just over a year, until 30 June 1964, but could then be extended for periods of twelve months by a resolution of Parliament—which made renewal a formality. As will later be seen, that indeed is what was done year after year until the law finally was allowed to expire after six years. It was known as the 'Sobukwe Clause', and he was the only person against whom it was used.

A report on 3 May 1963 in the London magazine *The Spectator*, by Kenneth Mackenzie, said much. Under the blunt headline, 'Barbarism', it began: 'It is difficult to imagine a more refined form of torture than to wait until a man is within days of completing a long prison sentence and then announce that he is not going to be released after all, but will be kept in jail indefinitely.'

Writing in 1971, Professor Anthony Mathews, Dean of the Faculty of Law at the University of Natal, Durban, said this: 'It is fortunate that this provision, which authorised the punishment of a man for what it was thought he might do, has now passed into history. It violated sacred principles of justice by setting at nought the maxim *nulla poena sine crimine* (no punishment without crime). It may be regarded as a close relative of the Bill of Attainder which the American colonists found so hateful that they outlawed it in the Constitution. The fact that the clause was used in only one case in no way diminishes the injustice suffered by that man or the obnoxious nature of the law.'

But no such scruples troubled the government in April 1963. Not only was the Sobukwe Clause rushed into law within ten days but it formed part of a General Law Amendment Act which continued the process of reducing personal liberty by widening police powers of arrest and making it easier for the government to gain convictions in court against those who opposed it. This was also the law which extended incommunicado detention without trial to ninety days, repeatable indefinitely.

The same session of Parliament increased the penalty for the illegal use of explosives and added to the government's powers to use the army to back up the police for domestic unrest, actual or anticipated. And thought control was taken further by streamlining the already heavy censorship of books, magazines and films. Earlier government threats in this direction, with specific warnings to the opposition English-language Press, had coerced the newspaper industry during the previous year into introducing its own Code of Conduct. Over the years government pressure and blackmail were to ensure that the Code was made progressively more restrictive so that less and less news could be published.

The United Party said it objected to the Sobukwe Clause, but voted in favour of the principle of the law as a whole. That schizophrenic behaviour, of opposing but trying to placate white voters by showing it was strong on maintaining 'law and order', had become the party's way of life and was eventually to destroy it. Some appeals to release Sobukwe came from abroad, from Harold Wilson, then in opposition as the leader of Britain's Labour Party, and from Conservative and Liberal MPs there too.

But on 1 May, on the day the law came into effect, Sobukwe was already a prisoner in another jail.

An announcement by Vorster that day said: 'The Cabinet has decided that Robert Mangaliso Sobukwe whose prison sentence expires on 3 May 1963, will be detained under the Suppression of Communism Act of 1950, as amended by the General Law Amendment Bill which has just been passed by Parliament.'

He was in fact already on Robben Island, the maximum security prison in Table Bay, eight kilometres from Cape Town.

From early in April, in Pretoria jail, as the date neared for his release, tension was growing in him, says A.B. Ngcobo. 'He planned to go on organising as soon as he got out. There is no doubt about that. But he was giving me messages that if anything happened, this or that should be done about restructuring the national executive. He had a premonition that something was going to happen, that he would not be allowed out. He was worried about being separated from the people he led.'

It was a normal prison day on 23 April. But at supper-time, in mid-afternoon, 'suddenly warders went into his cell; other warders told us he was being taken away. He called out to us in Xhosa, *"Ngidliwa draft"* ("I'm on draft"—draft was the jail word for transfer). None of us knew where he was going. He walked past carrying a few books. Among them was a book I had lent him, *The Wisdom of Solomon*. We shouted *"Izwe Lethu"* and he responded, *"iAfrika"*. He disappeared. The next morning, warders told us he had been taken to Robben Island.'

He was flown in a military plane to an airfield in the Cape, driven to the harbour in Cape Town and taken by boat to the island. Total silence was maintained until Vorster's announcement.

Only on the night of 1 May did Veronica Sobukwe learn what had happened, when I was able to contact her. She had planned a visit to Pretoria jail the next day. As soon as she heard the news she borrowed a car and set off on the 1,500-kilometre drive to Cape

Town, in the hope of seeing her husband—and to seek an interview with Vorster to ask for his release. She did not get the interview but she did visit Sobukwe.

At the same time as announcing Sobukwe's future, Vorster disclosed the rules for this new type of imprisonment. Evidently to try to blunt criticism and to acknowledge Sobukwe's unique status, he was not to be kept in a cell but in quarters which had been used by coloured warder trainees. 'He will have complete freedom of movement within a large prescribed area,' said Vorster. 'Newspapers can be supplied to him, and he will be able to receive visitors weekly. He will by no means be treated like a prisoner, but receive special treatment in respect of food, movement, using leisure hours, hours of rising and retiring, clothing, etc.'

Journalists and two Members of Parliament were taken to look at him. He was willing to see them. He was dressed in the same grey flannel trousers and sports jacket he had worn on 21 March 1960. Asked what he felt about his new life, one of his first thoughts as he looked at the wooden floor, was: 'No more cement floors.' He was reserved—one reporter thought he was 'ill at ease'—but was his usual polite self as he told them he was not surprised at the action taken against him; it was 'one way in which the white suppressor believes he is safeguarding his privileges'.

But events had moved suddenly for him and he pushed away other questions: 'Forgive me if I get mixed up now and again. My thoughts have not been ironed out. I have been out of contact. For myself I would not mind what type of action they take against me. I am speaking honestly, even if they keep me here for life.'

13

No one has ever been known to escape from Robben Island and live. The strong Atlantic currents sweeping past the island and the cold water make swimming from it impossible, even though the mainland is only about eight kilometres away, except for the highly trained and specially prepared. The rocky shores make access by boats impractical. The only landing place, apart from a small beach, is a concrete quay. A lighthouse, built after many shipwrecks, warns ships to beware.

The island is roughly oval-shaped; it is nearly flat and low-lying, with the highest point only twenty metres above sea-level, and is covered by scrub. It is big enough—about 3.2 by 1.6 kilometres—for its airstrip. The island's name, given by early Dutch arrivals at the Cape, came from the numerous seals—*robben* in Dutch—originally found there. Grey slate is quarried on the island and was used in the late seventeenth century by Dutch settlers to build a large fort in Cape Town: it still stands and is known as the Castle.

The island has a long history of use for banishment. Legend has it that a group of Portuguese convicts were put on it in 1525. Nearly one hundred years later, eight English convicts were put ashore with orders to help provision passing ships; four drowned in trying to escape to the mainland. Early last century a Xhosa leader and prophet, Makana, was interned there after taking part in a rising against white colonists in the Eastern Cape. He tried to escape but, with some companions, drowned in the surf when their boat capsized.

For the next nearly one hundred years, until 1931, the island housed the incurably ill, especially lepers and lunatics. During the Second World War, huge guns were placed on it to guard Cape Town against attack from the sea. In 1960 it became a maximum security jail and was increasingly used for black male political prisoners: by the mid-Sixties about 1,500 were there. In the early years they did much of the arduous work of quarrying the slate for building their own prison.

The island's position in the middle of Table Bay ensures a magnificent view of Table Mountain, the majestic backdrop to the city. But in the winter months, the north-wester wind which drives dark rain clouds across the mountain brings a miserable dampness to the island.

That made it an unpleasant first winter for Sobukwe in his temporary quarters. He did not have much space in which to move around and was locked inside the bungalow at night; the authorities explained this was because of a shortage of guards. In August, as the winter cold was dying away, he was served with a new notice signed by the Minister of Justice ordering his confinement to a different part of the island—to a fenced-in irregular-sized area on which 'buildings Nos. 158, 159 and 160' stood, forming part of the coloured school, and officially measuring 150 ft by 170 ft by 90 ft by 180 ft (45 by 51 by 27 by 54 metres).

That was the size of his world. He had full freedom inside it. He could go to sleep when he wanted and stay in bed for as long as he pleased. He could put on a tie or wear shorts. He could spend the day reading or staring at the mountain. But he was not allowed to move outside the high barbed-wire fence. And, to make sure that he did not do so, a warder was on duty at the entrance gate throughout the day with a sentry box as shelter from the elements; from 4 p.m. onwards, through the night, two warders were on guard. Emphasising the security, all the warders were whites. There were also guard dogs.

Sobukwe's living quarters—a freshly painted white bungalow—had two small rooms. He used one as a bedroom-study: it was simply and cheaply furnished by the authorities with an iron bedstead and coir mattress, cupboard, table and wooden chair, bookcase and floor mat. Sheets and blankets were provided. The other room, painted light blue, served as a kitchen. Some months later, mustard and orange curtains were put up in both rooms. A short distance away, also inside the enclosure, was a small ablution block with hot and cold running water and a shower, and a second, unoccupied, bungalow.

The same conditions served on him in May applied: he was to be treated as a prisoner-plus, with a status unheard of in South African jails. His food was to be of better quality than he had been getting as a black prisoner. In addition to the books and magazines allowed by jail regulations he could receive South African newspapers and could listen to the radio—but only to the state-owned South African Broadcasting Corporation. He could go to bed and get up when he pleased, and was not subject to any lights-out rules. He could submit requests for 'further privileges' to the Minister of Justice.

It was a bleak, solitary life. The only people he was able to speak to were his Afrikaner prison guards. But even they, according to what they told other prisoners, were under orders not to speak to him; some, however, said that they did speak to him. He was allowed to write and to receive two letters a week: these went through the prison censors and each one was invariably held up for weeks. He was allowed few visitors. During the first nine months the Roman Catholic and Methodist clergymen who ministered to prisoners on the island saw him once each. Veronica visited him and so did his elder brother, Ernest, now an Anglican priest.

His only contact with the island's prisoners was a visual one, but it gave him considerable pleasure. The hundreds of PAC and Poqo members who at that stage formed the bulk of the prisoners were keenly aware of his presence and were excited at being in such close proximity to him. They seized their chances to make their feelings of respect known. Sometimes, *en route* to the seashore to collect seaweed for fertiliser, they were marched along a footpath close to the fence of Sobukwe's enclosure. As they went past they always looked at him, removed their round cloth caps and raised their right hands in the PAC salute; ANC members often gave their thumb-up salute. The salutes always enraged the warders who would dash among the prisoners threatening to beat them, and yelling a frenzied mixture of *'Kyk voor'* ('Look forward'), *'Hy's nie julle koning nie'* ('He's not your king')—and eventually, *'Drie maaltye, drie maaltye'* ('Three meals, three meals'). The punishment of a 24-hour fast never deterred anyone.

Sobukwe returned the salutes and if he was outdoors would bend down, pick up a handful of earth, hold it up and let it trickle through his fingers. They knew he was addressing them as 'Sons of the soil of Africa'. He also sometimes gave them a clasped hands greeting, which they took to mean his urging of unity among them. No words were exchanged.

But on one occasion, as they marched past, a PAC man, recalling

How Can Man Die Better

Macaulay's Horatius, spoke in Xhosa loudly enough for everyone to hear: '*Xa kunje siye sikhumbule amazwi ka Horatius: Indoda ingafa kakuhle njanina* . . .'

Which meant: 'When it is like this we remember the words of Horatius':

> And how can man die better
> Than facing fearful odds,
> For the ashes of his fathers,
> And the temples of his Gods?

Sobukwe could hear the words, and called out in Xhosa: '*Ewe*' ('Yes').

The poem was a favourite in PAC circles. It was always declaimed, in English, whenever PAC prisoners observed commemorations on the island, such as a memorial service when one of their fellows died. The story of Horatius was known because it was in books used in black schools so everyone had grown up with it. It is also part of the romanticised, heroic tradition which so many of the Africanist leaders seem to have acquired during their 'English' missionary education.

The man who recited the poem for Sobukwe was Matthew Mokoena, who was serving a sentence of eleven years. He was chairman of a PAC branch near Johannesburg and was a former primary school teacher. On the island, he was chairman of the Disciplinary committee. Years later, in 1979, the government called him as a witness in a case against PAC men. He refused to testify, thus deliberately risking a five-year jailing and, worse perhaps, the wrath of the Security Police; fortunately, he got away with it and was released not long after.

To avoid the encounters with Sobukwe, the warders marched prisoners along a road about a hundred metres away: but it was still hats off and a salute from them for that lonely figure.

For many PAC prisoners, and especially those who had only recently entered political struggle, and prison, through Poqo, this was their first, thrilling, sight of Sobukwe. To someone like the young Hamilton Keke, 'It was a privilege to see the greatest politician in Azania in the flesh.' Once a van carrying Sobukwe—he sat in the cab next to the driver—broke down and a *span* (group) of prisoners was ordered to push it while he remained in it. That 'indicated to us that he was feared by the authorities,' says Keke. For Mxolisi Mgxashe, serving two years for belonging to and furthering the aims of Poqo, 'Each time we saw him it was a great inspiration to us. The fact that he was there with us inspired us. It made us defiant towards the *Boere*. They wouldn't dare beat us in his presence.'

Just how intense the feelings about Sobukwe could be was portrayed by an ex-prisoner writing under the pseudonym of D.M. Zwelonke in *The New African* magazine in London in 1968:

> Every time our *span* of twenty approached that place on our way to work an explicable feeling of joy had filled our hearts: anxiety and worry was banished; suffering and hunger, forgotten; regret and self-pity condemned as traitors to our cause, and pushed into the dungeon of accursed fires. Then our minds would be filled with vision, and we could see a New Africa we so much yearned for, so much suffered for, being just around the corner ... We needed to see the silver lining in the dark clouds of suppression that so dangerously hung over our heads—what we needed was hope. We felt re-vitalised and re-dedicated, because no one occupied that house other than he most loved by his followers, Robert Mangaliso Sobukwe.

There was also a daily reminder of his existence among them. At the entrance to the prison's office block a blackboard displayed the number of prisoners in different sections, and the total number. Each day the changing tally was written in chalk, and was followed by '+ 1'—a clear reference to Sobukwe because his status was different from everyone else. So it would be '1,248 + 1' or '1,386 + 1' or whatever. Each day, the PAC men checked that '+ 1' was still among them.

There was sly fun at the expense of warders: Zwelonke explained that the white warder in charge of his *span* was given the Xhosa nickname *Hodoshe*. The warder knew it but did not know the meaning: it was the Xhosa name for a big green fly which feasts on human faeces.

Sobukwe wore his own civilian clothing and did his own washing and ironing, and kept his quarters clean. Clothes for dry cleaning were sent to Cape Town. He took up the right to listen to the radio: he supplied the money and the authorities bought him a radio capable only of receiving South African domestic broadcasts. In August, he started a garden inside the enclosure, using seeds sent by the Defence and Aid Fund in Cape Town. 'The soil is extremely sandy and is infested with slugs and snails,' he wrote to Veronica. 'I intend to lay out a vegetable garden and a small flower plot.' And indeed he grew cabbages, tomatoes, beans and flowers. It was a reason for early rising: he worked in the garden from 5.30 a.m. until about 9.30 a.m. and again for a couple of hours after 4 p.m.

But after a few months he had to abandon it for a time: a shortage of fresh water on the island led to a ban on water usage except for drinking and washing. With the number of political prisoners rising because of opposition to apartheid, shortage of water was a perennial problem. Fresh water was brought by tanker from the mainland. Attempts by the authorities to make use of water lying close to the surface of the island caused trouble: it was brackish and unpleasant and drove prisoners to protest through hunger strikes when it was used in cooking their food. When later he was able to resume gardening, if only temporarily, he reported to Veronica: 'I have destroyed my pumpkin plants. Like the fig tree in the Bible they produced a plethora of foliage but no fruit. The squashes behaved admirably. They turned a brilliant gold and were a pleasure to behold. So too were the cucumbers.'

The summer brought its own discomfort because of the heat in the bungalow. Outside, shade of a sort was provided by a thin, straggly tree. All the time, morning and night, there was no escape from the sound of the waves on the shore nearby.

But there was also pleasure in the Cape's summer weather, as Sobukwe wrote to Veronica: 'We have been experiencing glorious weather lately. The days are clear and warm and the evenings clear and cool. There is a lovely moon in the sky, quite unlike the moon on which America's Ranger [an unmanned camera expedition of the time] landed. This is a silver moon with no craters and thick dust. And as it shines on the sea it transforms the latter into a wide stretch of polished glass. It is the type of evening in short that reminds me of you because everything beautiful reminds me of you.'

With gardening denied, Sobukwe spent nearly all his time reading and studying, usually doing so in the kitchen. He enrolled for a Bachelor of Economics degree at the University of London. He listened to news broadcasts on the radio and, occasionally, a play in the evening. He tuned in every morning to the religious programme with sermons by clergymen of different Christian denominations.

From 3 May, the day of his changed status, the authorities scrupulously observed the terms of the order that he was to have better food, which meant upgrading his 'Bantu' diet. Now he had maize (corn) porridge, milk and coffee for breakfast; meat every day for lunch with maize porridge and vegetables, and black coffee; for supper, three slices of bread, coffee and milk. Later, maize rice was provided instead of porridge for lunch, and later still Sobukwe asked for the morning porridge to be dropped. The result of the improved diet, and no doubt the lack of physical work, was that his weight went up. In 1960 he had weighed 174 lbs and he was 150 lbs when he was taken to Robben Island. By the end of the year he weighed 162 lbs. He seemed to be in good health, except for pains in his left shoulder joint and in the lower back, apparently the result of the years in cold prisons. He was able to see the prison doctor whenever he wanted to.

We were in touch by letter from soon after his arrival on the island. His basic needs were catered for because he was a prisoner, but much else was needed because he was in large measure in solitary confinement and was not part of any organised activity. I decided that life had to be made as tolerable as possible so that his intellectual vigour could be maintained and his spirit sustained. Those were my goals.

The immediate task, however, was to get in to him whatever the prison authorities would allow. As that wasn't at all certain, it was a step by step process. Then, and always, the official hold-up of letters was maddening. It was made even worse by the arbitrariness of the censorship. I never once received a letter from him with any part blacked out; what the authorities did was to seize letters and not tell either of us that they had done so. It might have been that a single sentence—or a single word?—offended some faceless security official. Whatever it might be, the entire letter disappeared. Because of the delay in forwarding letters it could take several months before it dawned on me that I was not getting Sobukwe's reply on an issue I had raised because the letter hadn't got through to him, or a letter from him had been blocked. As the handling of Sobukwe's affairs widened and became more complex I built up files to keep track of what was what.

How Can Man Die Better

What was allowed through to him, and which excited him, was a set of interviews in the *Rand Daily Mail* in which I questioned South African church leaders from a range of denominations about apartheid. 'I could picture your victims squirming and ah-ah-ing, attempting to put you off with the usual meaningless pious platitudes,' he wrote. 'But you brought them back to the point mercilessly. I felt like the small three-year-old fellow whose mother woke up one night in the midst of a tremendous thunderstorm and hurried to his room fearing that she would find him terrified. But there he was at the window, jumping up and down and shouting with excited joy as each flash of lightning burst across the sky, "bang it again, Lord, bang it again!" I, too, felt like shouting "hold him there, Benjie, hold him there!" Thanks, old chap, it was a kingly banquet.'

I was also sending him new clothes. He was frankly nervous about my taste in clothing, because I had always teased him that he dressed too plainly and needed to have some colour in his clothing. But he was relieved by the first pair of trousers he received: 'I just couldn't have chosen a better shade myself. If that is what you call breaking with conservatism, then you are a first-class gradualist.'

His existing degrees enabled him to register for a Bachelor of Economics degree at the University of London and the Wolsely correspondence school in Oxford, England. He chose five subjects for his first year: Economics, Economic History, British Government, International Law and Social Ethics. He felt he could not enter for the 1964 examinations because it 'would entail high pressure swotting in a field that is absolutely new to me,' he wrote in a letter. His target was 1965. 'But, oh, the amount of reading required ... Were I outside I would be able to borrow most of the books from the library, but being here, I have no option but to buy them.'

I tried to find a library in South Africa which would co-operate, but nothing doing. So there was no choice but to set about raising the money for the books he had to have, and to have them posted to him as quickly as possible. Money was also raised so that he could receive the two daily English-language newspapers in Cape Town, the *Cape Times* and the *Argus*, plus the *Rand Daily Mail* by post from Johannesburg and two Sunday newspapers. After a while he felt he was getting too many newspapers. The feeling was understandable because other subscriptions still included the *English Digest*, *John O'London's* and the *Reader's Digest*. He had a special liking for the *Reader's Digest* and was irritated because for many months the magazine tended to go astray as it was still being sent to him at Pretoria prison. He complained to the colonel in command of Robben Island—who lent him his own copy.

In November, Veronica took leave from work—she was still a midwife in Soweto—to visit him, together with their children. She wrote to Vorster asking for an interview so that she could discuss staying on the island during her visit. She was turned down on both counts. The best she could get was three visits a week. She and the children stayed in Langa, one of the black ghettos. But it meant a long journey to and from the harbour, so on later visits they stayed at an hotel in Cape Town. That sounds simpler than it actually was because at that time the overwhelming majority of hotels did not accept black—or coloured or Indian—guests. But the Tafelberg—Afrikaans for Table Mountain—a modest hotel in a coloured area on the edge of the city centre, was happy to provide accommodation and that became Veronica's base on her visits. To get to the island she and the children used the official ferries which sailed to a regular daily schedule. They paid the usual fares.

The warders were always polite and addressed her as 'Mrs Sobukwe'—an unusual courtesy for a black woman. But each time she went, white wardresses at the harbour strip-searched her and checked her belongings; on the island, only her belongings were again searched. In return for the indignities the family was allowed contact visits, and met Sobukwe in a small interview room.

At least two people were refused visits: Professor Wellington, retired head of the Department of Geography at Witwatersrand University, who had got to know Sobukwe as a colleague and kept up the contact; and Eulalie Stott, a former President of the Black Sash, and then a member of the Cape Town City Council. She was one of the white liberals who had defied the government and taken food through the cordons around the black ghettos in 1960. She was a friend of mine from the days of the Liberal Party and I now turned to her for on-the-spot help in Cape Town. Over the years to come she did whatever was required, raising money, fetching and delivering goods to the ferry boat in the harbour, and looking after the family during their visits. She was superb at overcoming intractable problems. It merely needed a letter or a phone call to her and she would march in, sweeping obstacles out of the way.

Sobukwe knew of Eulalie Stott from my letters. He knew of my close friends, Ernie and Jill Wentzel, who were early mainstays of the support system building up around him; he knew of others too, such as Nana Mahomo, the former PAC executive member, who was sending aid from abroad; and Nell Marquard, widow of a noted liberal, who was becoming a cherished correspondent and friend. Father Webber of the Roman Catholic Church kept up the contact established in Pretoria jail: he sent a Bible as a gift and wrote regularly. Sobukwe's family—his mother, and 'Buti' (brother Ernest) and others—visited him when they were allowed and did everything they could. On 20 November 1963, Sobukwe wrote to me: 'I believe it was God's will that I should come here to realise how much love there is in the world and to get my sense of values right. Above all else I have had a chance to know myself—neither saint nor devil: just a bundle of capabilities in the hands of God.'

Despite the restricted access to Sobukwe I had every hope that I would be able to see him, because of our friendship and continuing contact. A new factor also arose: I was given a year's leave of absence from the *Rand Daily Mail* to research the history of communism on a grant from Stanford University in the United States. I had a pipeline into the inner recesses of the government in Pretoria and I used this to make inquiries about getting permission to interview Sobukwe. My pipeline existed because, in 1961, I had landed in jail for a few days after refusing to tell the police who had given me information for a report I had written for the *Rand Daily Mail*. The CID police officer who questioned me, and who personally escorted me to The Fort in Johannesburg after I was jailed by a magistrate, was Major Hendrik van den Bergh. He was polite to me and I was polite to him. We parted, inside The Fort, with a handshake.

I did not see him again and knew nothing of him—until, eighteen months later, out of the blue, van den Bergh sprang into prominence by being appointed chief of the Security Police. He went on to create and to become the powerful and feared head of the Bureau for State Security, BOSS. He owed his sudden promotion to his friendship with the Justice Minister, Vorster: they had been detained together at Koffiefontein during the Second World War.

Van den Bergh and I had lunch together very occasionally and argued furiously over politics. Even more occasionally—about half a dozen times in fifteen years—I approached him on behalf of friends who were in trouble. On this occasion I phoned him to ask if I could visit Sobukwe and he indicated I could probably get additional interviewing time. I wrote to Sobukwe to ask if he was willing to be interviewed. His reply—'Will be delighted to oblige' —came back in a telegram. A telegram from a prisoner? It seemed crazy. Once the first had been allowed, it became a useful method for swift communication between us, but sparingly used so as not to upset the prison authorities.

Going to the island meant calling in at Security Police headquarters in Cape Town for a permit. They knew all about it and no problems occurred. Two ferry boats ran from the mainland harbour and the trip on a clear summer's day took less than an hour. In winter, when the north-wester was at its peak, the boats might have to follow a triangular course across Table Bay, needing two hours and more for the trip. Those winter sailings were much on my mind as I roamed around the ferry boat: the hold was at the front and a steep, narrow ladder led down to it; in it were rows of ordinary wooden dining-room chairs bolted to the metal deck. Prisoners had to make their way down the ladder handcuffed and leg-ironed in pairs, one man's right hand and leg chained to another man's left hand and leg. There were no prisoners on any of my trips: but I stood there trying to imagine the terror and sickness among the captives being taken to the island, and especially those from the rural interior who had never been to the sea; the ship heaving and rolling, the waves smashing thunderously against the steel hull.

But there was no time for such thoughts on the island: as I was taken to the interview room in a hut near the quay, a van bringing Sobukwe arrived. He was sitting in front next to the driver. Meeting like that, in maximum security conditions, he the country's No 1 prisoner in his grey trousers and tweed sports jacket, me a visitor who had managed to get in to see him, and each of us chaperoned by our friendly Prisons Department escort, was a bizarre event. It was also a happy moment for us as we shook hands and were shown into a small bare room. We were left there alone and undisturbed, sitting at a rough wooden table built onto the wall. That was the first of six day-long visits spread over the next three months. On the first day, I was taken to the Officer Commanding, Colonel C.A. Wessels, who welcomed me to the island. I was also taken to the warders' mess for lunch; thereafter I brought sandwiches and Sobukwe and I spent the days together without interruption.

I was even allowed on one occasion to bring a camera and to take pictures—albeit head and shoulders only—of Sobukwe. That was a considerable extra concession in view of the Prison Act's prohibition of photographs of prisons and prisoners.

I had no illusions about the reasons for being given all these facilities, my contact with van den Bergh notwithstanding. First, reports were continuing to appear abroad alleging that Sobukwe was being starved and beaten. Much of the details were wrong. I was given permission to write about his conditions and his state of health and there was obvious official hope that my reports would put the record straight. The one restriction, to which I agreed and to which Sobukwe agreed when I told him of it—and of the van den Bergh pipeline—was that I was not allowed to seek his views on the law under which he was jailed. That aspect disposed of, it was revealing of his level of personal probity that he insisted on going public to repudiate the allegations of his poor conditions—even though the stories were being spread by PAC leaders in exile.

Second, I believed that the government was extremely anxious to know what Sobukwe was thinking and that I was being used as a convenient way of looking into his mind. He understood the game as well as I did. We worked on the premise that the room was bugged. We thought the microphone was probably in the ceiling above the table. We spoke of personal matters and of our families and friends. We scribbled a few notes to each other when we had especially private details to convey. We went over some of the events since 21 March 1960. I switched on my tape recorder when we discussed historical events.

The days of discussions could not on the whole have pleased whoever had the job of listening for it was only too obvious that he had not the slightest regret about his actions, that he remained dedicated to African Nationalism and pan-Africanism and to gaining freedom for blacks.

But what also rapidly emerged was that he had reached the conclusion that he could no longer serve those aims as a prisoner. He had decided to seek to leave the country. He told me that Veronica was instructing lawyers to prepare an application for an 'exit permit'. This is a special document allowing South Africans who are denied a passport to leave the country; the catch is that the moment such people cross the border, they lose their South African citizenship and face arrest if they ever re-enter the country without permission.

Sobukwe said I could publish his intentions and he gave me a short statement to explain his decision: 'First and foremost, my wife and children have been deprived of full and complete family life for over three years now. And I don't think it's fair to expect them to wait until that day, "this side of eternity", when the Minister of Justice will deem it fit to release me.' [A reference to a mocking statement by Vorster that life imprisonment for political prisoners meant 'this side of eternity'.] 'Secondly, the children, when they were down here, took our parting very badly. And for their sake, I think I should take steps to ensure that we shall be united soon and that I can supervise their upbringing. Thirdly, I cannot pretend that I relish the idea of being fossilised on Robben Island. I want to use whatever talent I have usefully and creatively for the benefit and advancement of mankind.'

He told me too that he was affected by the other prisoners on the island, even if he did see them only at a distance. 'I know I am better off than they are. For example, I can buy extra foods and toilet articles, up to R10 a month [South Africa's currency had by then changed from pounds to Rands (R)], and whatever is left in the way of food I just have to throw away, I can't give it to anybody. And yet I know that these prisoners would be extremely happy to have these things. It affects me because I keep on comparing my conditions with theirs. I am allowed newspapers and a certain number of letters. But as a result, I am in contact with the world while at the same time I am detached from it. That leaves me unsettled and frustrated. I am virtually in solitary confinement, as the only people I see, apart from a very few visitors, are the warders.'

His application to emigrate was lodged, but it took months for a decision to be taken. In August, the government disclosed its rejection. No reason was given but, clearly, there was as much fear of Sobukwe at loose in the world outside as of Sobukwe at loose inside South Africa. Had he been allowed to go abroad he could have been a towering influence in mustering anti-apartheid forces to pressurise South Africa. The government recognised the dangerous probabilities and decided to keep him locked up.

At that time another strand was discernible to me. For the more I saw, during my visits, how the prison authorities were treating

How Can Man Die Better

Sobukwe, the more I became convinced that there was still a lingering hope in government circles of bringing him over to their side. The black 'homelands' were being set up and to have gained Sobukwe's agreement to work in his 'own' Xhosa tribe would have been an inestimable coup. He and I actually discussed it and laughed about it, with him pointing out wryly that, apart from his fundamental opposition in principle to the Bantustans, he was a living denial of Afrikaner Nationalist racial ideology: his mother was a Mosotho, and his father Xhosa; he had married a Zulu woman and had taught Zulu at university; so what was he and what were his children?

Perhaps he should have been more circumspect; perhaps he should have dissembled and lied and told the listeners what they would have liked to hear, of a Robert Sobukwe who was willing to collaborate; perhaps I should have coaxed him towards this as the means of gaining his freedom. But not the slightest suggestion of any of this ever arose: he did not conceal his beliefs. He knew as well as I did what he was doing, and that he was forsaking what chance there might have been for release from jail.

Two officers in particular dealt with Sobukwe, Captain G.J. Visser and Head Warder L.B. Verster. Apart from their irritating habit of addressing him as 'Robert', they were pleasant and friendly and he was equally so towards them. But a reserve was maintained because, as he told me, 'Although most of the officials on the island go out of their way to make my stay bearable, the fact does remain that one is imprisoned and the relations with them can never be completely friendly.'

Yet Visser and Verster did things for his comfort on such a scale that they could only have been acting on orders from the top. On one of my visits Sobukwe and I agreed that it would be a good idea for him to have a record player: he liked classical music and I could send him records. I approached Visser, who obtained permission. So I went round to friends in Cape Town and collected money for a record player. I knew that Sobukwe's kitchen had an electrical power point in a wall but that there wasn't one in his bedroom. To allow for that, and in case too he wanted to listen to music outdoors, I bought a battery-operated set. On my next visit, Visser was on the quay to meet me and as I stepped ashore I held up the cardboard box I was carrying and said, 'I've brought the record player.' His face fell as he pointed to the lettering on the box and said, 'It's a battery set.'

'Yes,' I replied, 'I wasn't sure where Mr Sobukwe might wish to play it.' He broke in, 'But man, when you said you were bringing a record player, I had a power point put in specially in his bedroom so that he could lie in bed and listen to music.' I had no reply to that one. It was also Visser who told me he had had a window built into the wall of Sobukwe's bungalow on the side facing Table Mountain so that he could enjoy the view.

When I first saw Sobukwe on the island he was thin but seemed in reasonably good health, except that he had lost several teeth at the side of his mouth. What did worry me, though, was that his skin looked dry and lustreless. I suggested that he spend time in the sun and that he needed fresh fruit to supplement his prison diet. Approval was forthcoming via Visser. In Cape Town, a deck chair was organised and shipped to the island. For the fruit, Eulalie Stott gave me the names of two of her friends, also Black Sash members, Moira Henderson and Noell Robb. We met, inappropriately, at the Koffiehuis (the Coffee House), the city's leading Afrikaans restaurant and renowned for its *melktert* (milk tart). They willingly agreed to pay for a weekly parcel of fresh fruit: the best way to do it seemed through Stuttafords, the city's leading upmarket department store—very English and very white—which sold excellent-quality fruit. Stuttafords never turned a hair, at least not visibly; an order for a parcel of mixed fresh fruit and a packet of biscuits for Mr Robert Sobukwe was accepted without hesitation, for delivery each week to the Prisons Department Ferry in Cape Town Harbour. After only a few weeks Sobukwe's appearance was transformed, his face refreshed and glowing.

But one strange situation seemed to lead into other odd byways. On my last visit, Head Warder Verster was at the quayside and asked me to have tea with him in the mess before I saw Sobukwe. He told me that Sobukwe had recently found broken glass in his food and that a full investigation had been carried out; the authorities believed it was caused by accidental breakage in the prison kitchen but were not totally sure. Security involving Sobukwe had been stepped up. Verster was deeply worried about the fruit parcel from Stuttafords because someone who saw Sobukwe's name on it could decide to harm him. 'I am examining every bit of fruit in the parcels,' he said. 'I am using a magnifying glass to check every orange, apple and every grape to make sure there are no puncture marks in case some madman tries to poison him.' He begged me not to tell Sobukwe about his fears because it could only alarm him. I agreed and we worked out a new system: I would give money to the island authorities and they would buy fruit of the same quality as supplied by Stuttafords. Later, the arrangement reverted to Stuttafords but the parcels did not carry Sobukwe's name. They were addressed, at Verster's suggestion, to the Officer Commanding, Robben Island Prison. It seemed that no one would ever contemplate poisoning the Officer Commanding.

It was also Verster who recognised the monotony of Sobukwe's diet, even though he was getting better-quality food. He arranged for greater variety with lunch sometimes served from the warders' mess. A year or so later, I heard that a Cape Town lawyer who had gone to interview prisoners on the island had met a head warder who told him there were two 'great men' in South Africa—Prime Minister Hendrik Verwoerd and Robert Sobukwe. I wondered if the head warder was Verster.

Mentally, I found Sobukwe alert—but not at the same level as before he went to jail. At times he struggled to find words to express himself and laughingly apologised. Our meetings had a dramatic effect: he visibly came more alive as we spent hours talking and sharing thoughts.

On South Africa he believed the Afrikaner Nationalists were then making 'a determined effort to stir up the whites with stories of black hordes so that the unity of the whites will be an anti-black one ... Criticism now of the Nationalist government is equated with criticism of the South African government. I think I have come to appreciate the courage of sections of the English Press and organisations, both political and non-political, which have steadfastly refused to be dragooned. In fact, I think I could even express admiration for *Die Burger* [the Afrikaner Nationalist official newspaper in Cape Town] which is trying at any rate to present an intellectual case.'

In an era when the government was moving remorselessly towards greater authoritarian rule he was surprisingly optimistic about the prospects for change: 'The fact that those who are opposed to apartheid are taking up an uncompromising attitude does mean that the issues will be highlighted,' he said. 'Both the economic development in the country and the intellectual stirrings among the Afrikaner intellectuals in particular will bring about an initial modification of attitudes. Once that is reached, it will be easier to reach a broader agreement. I think the government is quite aware of that, and that is why it is trying to prevent not only contact across the colour line, but also the free circulation of ideas.'

On allegations of his links with Poqo he was sharply dismissive: 'I was behind bars in Pretoria jail when it happened and, when I was allowed contact with the world again, the immediate causes of it were over. So I do not know what gave rise to it. I was not involved in it in any way at all.'

And on his attitude to whites he spoke with passion: 'I know I have been accused of being anti-white, not only by the government but also by others. But there is not one who can quote any statement of mine that bears that out. When I say "Africa for the Africans" I have always made clear that by African I mean those, of any colour, who accept Africa as their home. Colour does not mean anything to me.'

Not only was this a re-statement of his known position but, as we went on talking, what emerged was that he had thought further into some of the practicalities of applying Africanist thinking. By the time my last visit came round in April, I had completed many interviews with political leaders in Cape Town and was especially engrossed in the details I had been given about the role of the Liberal Party in the upheavals of March and April 1960. I told Sobukwe about it. It was a fantastic story, I said, as I referred to the role which the Liberals had played. Yes, he said, he had heard from his men what had happened. In fact, his men were so impressed by what the Liberals had done that they would have been willing to accept the amalgamation of the PAC and the Liberal Party, had the situation arisen.

We talked about the government's current policies. The trouble, he said, was that for all these years the Nationalists had been drumming into their people the idea of keeping down blacks. Now, with the Bantustans—the development, at least in theory, of tribal states in which blacks were to have full but separate freedom—this idea was supposed to be changing. But it was impossible to change the attitudes of people overnight, and this was the problem Verwoerd was facing with his own people.

I was on to him immediately. This was at the core of debates about the future of South Africa. It was the sort of discussion he and I had often had before 1960, I said. We had talked in exactly the same way about African Nationalism with my pointing out that, although I could see the purpose for reasons of expediency in building up black nationalism, this would lead to anti-whiteism; and when blacks eventually won the day it would be impossible to change their attitude to whites overnight. His argument, I reminded him, had always been that it would be possible to accept whites as equals overnight. But, in view of what he was now saying about Verwoerd, had his views changed? Where did he stand on the PAC's exclusion, in 1960, of whites and Asians as members?

Circumstances had changed, said Sobukwe. A number of whites had given clear proof of their willingness to work as equals with blacks in a completely disinterested spirit. One example was that of the Liberals in Cape Town. He agreed with me that they had not attempted to seize control of the PAC campaign, but had merely given full assistance as requested. Another example was Patrick Duncan, the former *Contact* editor who had been banned and then escaped from the country and become the PAC's first white member. By joining the PAC he stood to gain nothing in the foreseeable future, while he had in fact lost a great deal. Thus the actions of these whites made it possible to accept them fully within the PAC.

If the PAC were to be re-formed now, it would in his view be on a wholly non-racial basis.

That was an exciting discussion, and it made saying goodbye at the end of the last visit all the harder. More than ever I was oppressed by the thought of how much he could be contributing to resolving South Africa's problems.

I left him to the daily routine he had developed. In an effort to cut down the length of his day, and the huge loneliness, he was trying to stay in bed an hour longer in the mornings. He was getting up at 7 a.m. or 7.30 a.m. He had coffee for breakfast and studied or read. His university studies were going reasonably well but he was having great difficulty in concentrating. He was getting marks of about 60 per cent for his essays. He felt that when he went through his studies he knew what they meant, but because of his isolation, he was not certain to what extent he was really absorbing the information. At 10 o'clock every morning he listened to the religious broadcast on the radio—always the English, not the Afrikaans transmission, because as he explained with a burst of laughter, 'I suppose I am a spoiled Native.' He spent the rest of the day reading or studying except for listening to a few news broadcasts and to a popular thriller serial—it was called 'No place to hide'—at 7.15 p.m. He went to bed at 10.30 or 11 p.m. He had no difficulty in getting to sleep and slept soundly.

14

The six separate days Sobukwe and I spent together on Robben Island brought us a lot closer. That sharpened my anguish about his detention. It also added to the difficulties of writing to him because I was now more conscious than ever that some or other comments or bits of information could not only cause a letter to be withheld with no notice or explanation, but might actually help to prolong his imprisonment. I spent hours writing and re-writing letters, trying to convey as much as possible but frightened of saying the wrong thing, without a clear idea as to what the wrong thing might be. Blandness and banality was the safe way out, as was discussion about his needs and reports about my young daughter. In addition, it was to be a period of turmoil in my own life—divorce and years-long conflict with the government—and, in retrospect, I wrote some embarrassingly silly things.

During one of my visits I had told him about a smear letter, aimed at me, which had been sent to my wife a few months before. My reporting of the rise of black political power in Swaziland—then still under British rule—was not appreciated by some of the white settlers there and I guessed the poison was from one or more of them. I was touched that Sobukwe devoted one of his rationed letters to write to Astrid, without telling me he was doing so, about the 'disgusting' letter she had received. 'I am sorry you have been caused so much pain and embarrassment,' he said. 'But I do hope that you will regard the letter as the malodorous product of a putrid mind and treat it with the contempt it deserves.'

He told her too about the pleasure his new record player was giving him: '... I had a few turns on my creaky joints in the solitude of my room.' And he wanted her to tell me of his pleasure at my latest choice of clothing for him: 'In future I'll send him my size only and he can experiment to his heart's content with colour-combinations and fashions. Even the shoes which I first viewed with alarm (I am rather conservative, I admit) are extremely comfortable and the pyjamas are a peach.'

After his concern for Astrid, I had to pluck up my courage two months later to break the news to him that we were getting divorced. He delayed replying because, as he explained, the news had stunned him and he had waited for a visit from Veronica—she had again been denied permission to stay with him but had thrice-weekly visits—in case she knew what had happened. She did not. 'I can, therefore, only stupidly but sincerely advise that you do not allow your pride to make a reconciliation impossible. Please remember the long hard road you two have travelled together and then forget and forgive whatever wrongs you think you have suffered.' That was a powerful message, and I wished I could heed it. But things had gone too far for the marriage to be rescuable. He accepted this but later wrote to warn that I would have to answer to him if it turned out that I had been responsible for the break-up.

Repeatedly, his concern was not for himself but for others. He was anxious about my worried feelings about him, especially when newspapers carried reports alleging that he was in bad shape. An echo of the false stories of the previous year appeared in the *Sunday Citizen* in Britain, saying he had to do 'long, exacting manual labour, is given a very poor diet and is not allowed newspapers or a radio'. This time at least, the South African prison authorities could honestly issue a statement describing the report as 'absolute rubbish' and the 'blackest of lies'.

In response to another report, Sobukwe wrote to me: 'I know you are worried about me, particularly in the light of the latest "leakages". But I think you should know me well enough by now to realise that when next you meet me you'll have no difficulty in recognising the Bob you know. That is diplomatic language, isn't it? A lot of words uttered but nothing really concrete said!' Far from reassuring me, however, his letter raised my anxiety level because it ended: 'I'll write more next time. Am not feeling particularly bright today.' An inquiry quickly went off from me and an exceptionally swift passing on of letters meant I had his reply within a few weeks. This time, its evidence of his usual state of mind made cheerful reading: 'I was surprised to learn you found my letter reflecting a mood of depression,' he said. 'I probably wrote it on a day I wasn't feeling too bright. But you can rest assured depression is not my regular mood.'

Evidence of his robust state of mind was in a letter to Veronica: 'I had a quiet Easter but felt strangely elated. Sang some hymns on Good Friday and Easter Sunday, full-blast and was just short of [an] audience (congregation is the word) to preach to. It is all right singing to oneself, but when one preaches to oneself one's sanity is immediately questioned. I am still sane enough to remember that!'

Veronica, after one of her visits, brought back a message for me, later confirmed in a letter: he recommended me to Psalm 91. And reading the Psalm, so much of his beliefs and outlook, then and later, were contained in it: '. . . I will say of the Lord, He is my refuge and my fortress: my God; in him will I trust . . . Because thou hast made the Lord which is my refuge, even the most High, thy habitation; There shall no evil befall thee, neither shall any plague come nigh thy dwelling . . .'

In mid-year, I went to Northern Rhodesia, now Zambia, to cover a church conference and, on my return, wrote to Sobukwe that I had met Professor Z.K. Matthews there. Although I wasn't too sure what Matthews had meant, and whether he was being approving or not, I reported: 'He told me that he had predicted a brilliant future for you, but had warned you to be careful in using the power of your personality.'

During my visits to Sobukwe, we had talked about his needs: he wanted as little as possible from the government—not, in any event, that much was on offer—and I promised that I would ensure that he received whatever he required. Supplies to him were now stepped up. Friends rallied round to provide the money for his formidable list of academic books. Bed sheets, a pillow, pillow slips and clothing were delivered to him. In mid-winter, a telegram request for a heater was swiftly attended to by Peter Hjul.

But the jail authorities did not agree to everything: one of my enthusiastic ideas which got nowhere was for University of Cape Town staff in Sobukwe's study subjects to visit him regularly to give him tutorials for a few hours. On the other hand, no objection was raised to the Defence and Aid Fund sending a monthly parcel of cigarettes, small cigars and pipe tobacco. At that time, unfortunately, the link between smoking and cancer was not known. The fruit deliveries continued and I wrote to thank Colonel Wessels for the official assurance I had been given that the same quality as

Stuttafords would be maintained, and also for the 'courteous cooperation' I had received during my visits.

Even as I wrote that, on 1 May 1964, and although I did not yet know it, the government's wooing of Sobukwe was at an end. Once realisation came that he was not going to change his ways and was not willing to be co-opted, the pleasantness and co-operation were replaced by increasing obstructionism. I was still plugging away trying to bring about his release. At this distance of time I cannot remember exactly what I tried to do. Whatever it was, it was done in consultation with Sobukwe and must have been unorthodox and risky because on 6 June I wrote to him: 'In accordance with our discussion on the last day we spent together, I took up the matter in Pretoria. I did not do it in Cape Town simply because I was too scared! But I was well received and I was promised immediate action.' On 1 September, I reported to him on the results of my 'representations': 'Coming at this stage, it will not surprise you to learn that they were turned down.'

For, by then, he had again been consigned to at least another year of captivity, and with no sign when he might ultimately be freed. The visible turning point in the government's attitude towards him was on 10 June, within only a few days of my writing to confirm that I had made those representations: Justice Minister Vorster announced in Parliament that the Sobukwe Clause was to be re-enacted to keep him in jail until 30 June 1965; more, he would not be allowed to leave the country. Vorster said his department had made a thorough study of what could possibly happen—and 'I decided that in the interests of South Africa I could not permit him to go overseas.'

A week later, the Sobukwe Clause was passed in Parliament for the second time. Even the slight brake on government power in the original formulation of the clause was dropped: from now on, it was no longer necessary for both the lower and upper houses of parliament to go through the formality of extending the clause for another year; instead, the Minister of Justice could simply order the continued detention of anyone jailed for a political offence if he was 'satisfied' that, if released, the person was 'likely to further' any of the objects of communism—as sweepingly defined by the government, that is.

Helen Suzman pleaded for Sobukwe's release. Although, for thirteen years, the sole representative of the Progressive Party in

Parliament, she put up more of a fight against apartheid than the combined dozens in the chief opposition, the United Party. But she was brushed aside. 'I did the best I could about Sobukwe when the General Laws Amendment Bill [the name of the law which contained the Sobukwe Clause] was under discussion,' she wrote to me, 'and the Minister's reply was that he had to be convinced that Sobukwe dissociated himself completely from Poqo and PAC before he would even contemplate releasing him.'

Vorster also said darkly that circumstances which he did not think it wise to disclose made it necessary for him to refuse to release Sobukwe. Earlier in Parliament, Suzman had bluntly asked him: How long are you going to keep Sobukwe locked up? He did not answer. All he said was that a representative of the International Red Cross had visited Sobukwe and reported that his accommodation was equivalent to 'that of a high-ranking officer in time of war'.

That was little solace for him, and even less for Veronica. From the morning of 21 March 1960 when she said goodbye to her husband, she had lived a secluded existence, going to her job each day, keeping up her home and caring for the children. She was not a woman who complained. She showed her feelings in an occasional heavy sigh or a click of the tongue. But she had a hard time of it. For long the relationship between her and me was reserved: we were both shy of the other and in my case it showed itself in formal references to 'your wife' in my letters to Sobukwe. We gradually learnt to unbend with each other and she accepted me as a friend.

Her renewed appeal now to allow the family to leave the country met with no success. Her plea, on Christian grounds, was directed to the 'God-fearing government of South Africa'. It explained that reuniting the family was the main reason for wishing to go. Had Sobukwe been able to emigrate he would have had a support system waiting for him: according to a newspaper report, he had been offered a home and a job in the United States by the National Association for the Advancement of Colored People and a foreign aid fellowship.

No doubt adding to government jitters about the damage which Sobukwe could inflict was the opposition to its rule which it was having to suppress that year. Apartheid was firmly in place and this was a period of consolidation and of making the machine more efficient. Hence a law which provided for stricter influx control by giving more power to government labour bureaux to decide which blacks could work in the cities, and also making it more difficult for wives and children to live with their men working in the cities. Another major legislative effort was the overhauling of the censorship apparatus for prohibiting 'indecent, objectionable or obscene' books, magazines, newspapers, movies and plays, whether domestic or imported. The Population Registration Act was again altered in the constant Nationalist striving for the impossible—a precise definition of a white person. 'Borderline' cases which defied the official classifications for different races kept cropping up, to the despair of orderly-minded bureaucrats. During the Sixties, the law was amended no less than five times.

In the security sphere, imprisonment for refusing to testify in court was increased to twelve months, where previously it had been for up to ten days at a time. The harsher penalty was needed to force people to give evidence in dozens of trials up and down the country as the Security Police smashed the mushrooming underground protest movements. Hundreds of people were detained without trial and many were charged with seeking to overthrow the government. The Defence and Aid Fund reported that lawyers had difficulty in finding out what charges were faced by which people and in communicating with the accused; after months of delay, detainees were suddenly brought to trial.

The most prominent trial concerned Nelson Mandela, already serving the five-year sentence imposed in August 1962. Now, in June 1964, he was given life imprisonment in company with seven co-accused of *Umkhonto weSizwe*. Mandela acknowledged that he had planned sabotage. He had decided it was unrealistic for black leaders to keep up the African National Congress' traditional policy of non-violence when the government frequently used violence to crush opposition, he told the court. 'Africans had either to accept inferiority or fight against it by violence. We chose the latter.' Within a few months, *Umkhonto's* second-level leadership was also given heavy sentences, including life imprisonment, and a major trial was under way of Communist Party leaders.

Hundreds of members of the Pan-Africanist Congress and the African National Congress were jailed for up to three years for underground membership—and at the same time it was estimated that anything from 900 to 5,000 black people had left the country for military training. In Cape Town, members of an odd little revolutionary group called the Yu Chi Chan Club—it was never clear whether it was named after a book by Mao-Tse-tung (Zedong) or a Chinese communist trade union official—were jailed.

The African Resistance Movement (ARM), led mainly by white intellectuals and dedicated to sabotage, was penetrated and destroyed by the police two years after its secret formation. Evidence presented in one trial was that some members had planned to get Sobukwe out of jail. But Baruch Hirson, a former colleague of Sobukwe's at Witwatersrand University who was jailed for his ARM activities, dismisses the plan as a 'dream-fantasy' of Adrian Leftwich, a Cape Town academic who was also in the organisation. Hirson says that when the police raided Leftwich they found his plan to rescue Sobukwe: he had been hoping to use facilities available to ARM for general purposes—a small boat in Britain and a single-engined aeroplane, bought with money provided by Ghana's President Nkrumah.

One episode to do with ARM shocked South Africa because of its uniqueness at that time: a white member, John Harris, set off a bomb in the whites-only concourse of the Johannesburg railway station, killing one person and maiming a young girl. He was tried and executed.

Many friends of mine were caught up in these turbulent events. Some were detained incommunicado, some who had turned to violent protest because of frustration at bringing about peaceful change were put on trial and given years-long prison sentences, and others fled the country and went into exile. Ernie Wentzel was detained for nearly a month; so too was a woman with whom I had become involved in a tempestuous love affair which was to last for several years. There was daily uncertainty about how long they might be detained, about their conditions and interrogation, and who else might be grabbed. Sobukwe knew some of what was happening from newspaper reports.

'It has been a trying time,' I wrote to him in September 1964, in careful terms which did not refer directly to individuals or detentions so as not to upset the censors. 'An atmosphere of crisis, in which one is so deeply involved through close friends, is hardly conducive to sober, academic work . . .' That was as close as I dared get in trying to tell him about the atmosphere of strain in my circles.

What, of course, he did see from inside his sealed enclosure was the growing population on Robben Island. We did not know it then, but the island's prisoners were victims of a brutal regime. The pleasant handling of Sobukwe, while it lasted, and the cordiality shown to me during my visits, were a façade. Monstrous action went on behind the scenes. It took a long time for the stories to start getting around—not until 1965 onwards—and they told of incessant assaults and denial of elementary rights of letters, reading and education. One story published in the London *Observer* I thought was so ridiculous as to be beyond belief: a prisoner was said to have been buried up to his neck in the ground and warders then urinated onto his face. Several years afterwards, however, people released from Robben Island told me it was true: the prisoner was Johnson Mlambo, who more than two decades later was to become Chairman of the Pan-Africanist Congress in exile; the warders were two Kleynhans brothers, notorious for their viciousness.

Even without knowledge of this sort, I became worried about Sobukwe's conditions because the official obstructionism was becoming increasingly evident. In October, I learnt from him that the weekly parcel of fresh fruit, on which I set so much store for ensuring his health, was not getting to him. It took months of letters between him and me and between me and the prison authorities to attend to it. I was also having difficulties in getting a subscription to the London *Observer* delivered to him, and my letters to sundry officials met with varying degrees of truculence. The newspaper was eventually allowed in, and then stopped; we were told he was not allowed to receive newspapers from abroad.

Sobukwe grew thoroughly angry about these and other obstacles, especially as he had come round to accepting in his mind that there was not going to be any swift release from prison so he had to be concerned about conditions which could go on for unknown years into the future. 'You will no doubt recall that I have been complaining ceaselessly about the (to me) inexplicable delay in my mail, almost from the very moment I got here,' he wrote to me on 20 October. 'I thought I would stick it for a while, believing the arrangements to be temporary in any event. But it has proved not to be. And now that letters from, first my children and then my wife, have for a reason unknown to me been apparently held up the possibilities are, to say the least, disturbing.' He argued that neither the Minister of Justice nor the prison authorities had the right 'deliberately so to delay my mail as to render nugatory my right (granted under their own regulations!) to write and receive two letters a week. The reasons for their actions are not my concern. The administrative arrangements they make to achieve their purpose are not my concern either. But I do want to be convinced by a court of law that the right I have referred to can be reconciled with such restriction. And it is not unavoidable, this delay, Benjie. I have been a convict, as you know. And I never had reason to complain about mail delays.'

He wanted a legal opinion from Wentzel about launching a court application to define his rights so as to remove the 'caprice and whim' which appeared to apply to him. 'We have to establish the purpose of censorship and, in the case of so-called subversive material, who is to decide whether words are subversive or not—a court of law or a civil servant? Has that civil servant a right to withhold my letter because he thinks it contains subversive material? These are but some of the questions one would like settled by a court.'

I was surprised that the jail censors let this letter through but decided it was probably because of its references to legal action. It reached me within a fortnight, which was a shorter time than usual. I immediately asked a friend in Cape Town, Barney Zackon, who was a lawyer and Cape Chairman of the Liberal Party, to take instructions from Sobukwe for a court action. But Wentzel told me he believed that 'the law is solid and there is probably little chance of succeeding with an appeal to court', so what I was really doing was attempting to exert quiet pressure on the authorities through the threat of going to court. At the same time I made what I hoped were conciliatory noises to them via my letters to Sobukwe. Hence, on 6 November, my letter said, in the oiliest terms I could muster: 'As we know, the Robben Island authorities have always done their best to ensure your comfort within the limits of your detention. Holding back letters from your wife seems pointless. At the same time, I recall that you have repeatedly told me about the delays in letters reaching you. I assume that you have taken up the matter with the prison authorities, and that you have decided on court action after failing to achieve any satisfactory solution.'

Indeed it was worse than I had realised. For Veronica returned from her January 1965 visits alarmed about his state of health and the extent to which he was being neglected. And I discovered, to my own fury, that the reason for the mysterious problems with fresh fruit deliveries was that the jail authorities had appropriated the money I had sent and used it to pay a dentist. No separate accounts were kept for different purposes, the officer commanding told me coldly in reply to my protest.

A fuller statement came early in February in response to Zackon's approach as a lawyer writing on behalf of Mrs Sobukwe. Letters 'are not delayed unnecessarily', said the prison. Teeth were extracted at the expense of the Prisons Department, but any other dental work had to be paid by the prisoner concerned; Sobukwe wanted to have cavities filled so a dentist was brought out to the island to attend to him—at his (considerable) cost. And, the prison disclosed, a specialist urologist had visited him and examined his prostate gland 'and has prescribed the necessary treatment'; no private specialist would be allowed to examine him unless the District Surgeon—the full-time government doctor who served the island—requested it.

That was as far as we were able to take it. At the end of February the best I could do was to tell Zackon that his approach to the Prisons Department 'has probably served its purpose in showing them that people outside are keeping an eye on what goes on'.

Neither the pressure nor the conciliation seemed to achieve much. We were helpless victims. The prisons and police did what they wanted to do, which meant that Sobukwe's contacts with the outside continued to be as erratic as before.

On the positive side, he was able to send me a telegram asking me to arrange birthday cards for the twins' birthday. I did so and reported back to him, knowing it would please him, that in inscribing the cards from *Tata* (father), 'I tried to make my handwriting as neat and small as possible to make it look at least something like yours'. In December, Fred van Wyk, the Assistant Director of the South African Institute of Race Relations, and I were able to send in a Christmas food hamper: a Christmas pudding, tinned peaches and pineapples, biscuits, dates, nuts, tinned lamb's tongue, salmon, sardines and fruit juices, and even *biltong*, the South African dried meat specialty. I added candles and a few strings of tinsel in the hope of fractionally enlivening his rooms to relieve the sadness he would be feeling at being deprived of family and home.

Towards the end of 1964, the Labour Party victory in Britain drew his applause. He was almost sorry, he wrote, that he had cancelled his subscription to *Time and Tide*, a conservative magazine of the time, because he would have enjoyed reading its 'spluttering fulminations'. In a later letter he said he was 'quite happy' with Harold Wilson as Prime Minister in Britain and L.B. Johnson as President in the United States. 'They'll complement each other with

Wilson providing the ideas, the well-thought-out ideas of a critical, limpid intelligence and Johnson the persuasive skill that is his trademark. Both have been shaped by Kennedy in some way. Wilson hopes to provide the youthful inspiration and vision that Kennedy evoked. And he can: in Britain; where he will not be expected to be a romantic and athletic idol of teenagers. It is the intellectuals of Britain now who will have their chance as the American ones had under Kennedy.

'Johnson, of course,' he went on, 'has inherited Kennedy's mantle and programme. But he wants to be remembered as a great President in his own right. America has the resources to banish poverty completely from the States. And Johnson is going to strain every nerve to do it. He is also going to do everything in his power to implement the Civil Rights Act. In his domestic policy, he is going to be successful, I think. The weak spot in his foreign policy is the hostility towards Communist China which he has inherited. America has no intellectual case against Communist China. She is merely prejudiced. Nobody blames her for being prejudiced against China. She may even hate her if she feels like it. But it is a reflection on UNO if China can be kept out simply because America does not like her policy. It tends to suggest that UNO is America's club to which only those can belong who have America's blessing. And yet she could have China admitted to UNO without in the least compromising her position.'

As events were to prove, Sobukwe was right about Johnson: as President he did try to attack domestic poverty and to uphold civil rights; his vision was the Great Society. But he was mired by the war in Vietnam. As for China, it was to be years before the US came round to accepting the absurdity of its policy of excluding China from the United Nations.

15

One of the first steps in 1965 was to pass on to Sobukwe news which I had only just learnt—that Lincoln University in the United States, which counted Azikiwe and Nkrumah among its alumni, wanted to confer an honorary Doctor of Laws degree on him. 'Has this information reached you?' I asked, and continued tongue in cheek: 'The decision was taken last year and was conveyed to the South African government with a request for information as to when you could attend to receive your degree. Apparently no reply was received.' In due course, his reply came in words in which I could hear the chuckle: 'No, I have had no information about Lincoln University at all. I don't think the government should cause any difficulty over the matter. After all Lincoln is a Negro university: I won't be getting a white degree: I'll be getting a Negro degree.'

But the racial bait wasn't enough and the government never did allow him to travel to the US to receive the degree. Instead, as I wrote in a lengthy report in the *Rand Daily Mail* on 4 May, Sobukwe had, the day before, entered his third year on Robben Island—'and there is no indication when he will be released'. A few days earlier, Justice Minister Vorster had told Parliament that no decision had yet been taken whether to extend the Sobukwe Clause beyond 30 June, when it was due to expire.

The government decided by mid-June. It did not dare free Sobukwe. Newspaper headlines told the story: 'A further year for Sobukwe. Only way I can prevent his escape—Vorster.' In Parliament, even the United Party rejected the law, although its reason for doing so was not entirely clear: a spokesman, T. Gray Hughes —he was well known among blacks as he represented a constituency in the Transkei—said the party strongly opposed the law, especially as it was intended for one man only; the government did not need such a drastic measure for one man. But the arguments counted for naught: the Nationalist majority ensured a comfortable eighty-six to forty-six vote endorsement for reasons explained by Vorster in exchanges which convey some of the flavour of his arbitrary decision-making:

Vorster: 'If I did not have this power, I could not keep him in prison.'

Hughes: 'But you could banish him.' [that is, to a remote rural area].

Vorster: 'I have considered that, but how long do you think . . . he will stay there?'

Sobukwe's attitude was still that, if released, he would continue where he had stopped, said Vorster. He had been organising revolution and bloodshed at the time of his imprisonment. He was a model prisoner but that did not make him potentially less dangerous should he be released.

A Member of Parliament: 'Did you not say you had broken the back of the organisation which Sobukwe led?'

Vorster: 'Yes, but if I let him out he will start again.'

One of the elements affecting the situation, no doubt, was evidence presented in a court in Basutoland, still under British rule. About seventy-five South African refugees, most of them PAC members, were in the country. There was a resurgence of activity among them and six were charged under the Prevention of Violence Abroad Proclamation with conspiring to commit murder and violence in South Africa with the object of securing Sobukwe's release from jail and eventually overthrowing the South African government by guerilla warfare. They were found guilty and sentenced to one to three years' imprisonment, but their appeal was eventually upheld on a technicality.

Even as Sobukwe's future was being decided, he was writing the first examination for his correspondence degree. In view of his existing degrees, the University of London agreed he could aim at two, instead of three, years, and he wrote the first set of examinations inside his enclosure, with a warder acting as invigilator. He was anxious about his chances of passing and the difficulties of writing in those peculiar circumstances were obviously considerable. Despite this, in due course he was able to send me a telegram with the news that he had passed. I telegraphed in reply: 'I will now also call you Prof.' My follow-up letter asked if he was going to treat himself 'to the normal university three-month summer vacation, doing some quiet sunbathing and swimming on the beach near your bungalow, or do you want to start the next year's work immediately?' In more serious terms, another set of fees and books had to be arranged.

Other practicalities of continued imprisonment had to be dealt with. Sobukwe wrote on 17 June, determinedly cheerful: 'I am afraid my needs grow with the years: I certainly will wish to replace the sheets and the shirts and the pyjamas. They're all worn out. The shirts will be size 16½ and please make them striped or checked, but NOT white. No, my friend, it is not a question of colour prejudice otherwise I'd ask for Black shirts, worn, as you will recall, by Mussolini's Fascists, while Hitler's blond Aryans wore Brown shirts ... I should also like trousers I can wear with my black shoes. My grey pair is giving in.' A few days later there was a telegram to say that a heater was needed urgently—and its subsequent arrival, and its quality, were acknowledged by him as putting him 'right in the upper middle-class'.

By this stage I was using the set of measurements which Veronica had brought me, choosing clothing and on occasion receiving a jacket or trousers from the island for alteration by tailors. The measurements were exact—40 inches for the chest of the jacket and 32½ inches for the shoulder to wrist and, for the trousers, a waist of 37 inches and 40½ inches for the outside leg. But other needs also had to be met ... Veronica and the children travelled to Cape Town once a year, and Veronica had a second visit in between; the children were at school in Lesotho and the fees had to be paid, plus the costs of getting them there and ensuring warm clothing for winter.

I did not earn enough to carry the costs so the hunt for donors was ceaseless. As I wrote to Hjul in one of my requests for aid, the number of people in South Africa willing and able to help with financial and other assistance had shrunk because so many people had left the country, while the number of those in need was rising. The first wave of emigration, of white liberals and leftists, had occurred soon after 1948, in response to the Nationalists' election victory. Sharpeville and its aftermath set off what was probably a bigger exodus and, from then on, there was a constant dribble of people, both politically involved and non-involved, who decided they did not want to be part of a Nationalist-run country or feared future chaos for themselves and their children. The numbers leaped with each new major crisis over the years. The loss to South Africa of talented and usually highly educated people has been incalculable. Peter Hjul himself, as well as Barney Zackon, were among those who eventually left, for exile in Britain, after each of them was banned.

Although there was a dwindling number of people I could approach for finance, the South African Council of Churches was regularly available to me. I was also fortunate in having met Dr Robert S. Bilheimer, a Presbyterian Church minister from New York then attached to the World Council of Churches in Geneva. He introduced me to a parishioner, Charlotte Taylor, whose Christian beliefs, and later too her liking for Sobukwe through exchange of letters, made her for some years a pillar of financial support. For a time, money was deposited in a form of trust account at the South African Institute of Race Relations—the Director, Quintin Whyte, was also a friend—and substantial amounts, such as for the children's education, were paid through it. Later, however, I simply opened a No 2 bank account and operated Sobukwe funds through it.

Personal friendship counted, such as with Bennie Rabinowitz, a close friend from schooldays who was becoming a successful businessman in Cape Town. The first time I diffidently asked him for money for Sobukwe he promptly handed me a cheque for a much higher amount than I had requested. From then on, Bennie took the initiative in regularly asking me: 'Do you need money for any of your good causes? You must tell me if you do.'

Sometimes I had feelings of disquiet that Sobukwe was getting relatively so much material support when so many other victims of apartheid and their families were receiving less. That he was the leader of the PAC was important but did not seem to me to be sufficient reason in itself. I met the dilemma in my own mind by trying to give help to others, but ultimately Sobukwe was my friend and I told myself that, whatever I could do for him, and cajole others into doing, I would do.

After my visits to the island in 1964, I was not again given access to him. Early in 1965 an application to visit him was rejected by the Security Police. Nor did I get anywhere by writing to Vorster to appeal against this and to stress that I wanted to see Sobukwe as a friend and not for newspaper purposes. Events now occurred which guaranteed that I would never be allowed to visit him. At the end of June, and in July, I wrote a series of reports in the *Rand Daily Mail* which exposed the cruel and unsavoury conditions in which white political prisoners and black criminal prisoners were kept in jails. The reports detailed everyday assaults on blacks, electric shock torture of prisoners at the Cinderella prison near Johannesburg, appalling food, abysmal medical treatment and the callousness of warders.

The reports created sensation, both in South Africa and internationally, with widespread demands for a judicial inquiry into jail conditions. Vorster's enraged response was to unleash the full resources of the State: the Editor of the *Rand Daily Mail*, Laurence Gandar, and I were vilified and threatened; each of my informants—ex-prisoners and warders—was systematically pursued and prosecuted, and most were jailed, allegedly for not telling the truth about jail conditions. Finally, Gandar and I were prosecuted and found guilty after a prolonged trial. It all took nearly four and a quarter years.

I never doubted the accuracy of my reports. But it was a hard time. It was an awesome and often terrifying experience to be a target for concentrated government attack, which meant the Prisons Department and the organs of state security as well as the Afrikaans Press; in addition, there was a wider hostility among the white public, and that included many colleagues in the English-language Press. Blacks, who had a better idea of jail conditions, saw it differently and were universally supportive.

One early consequence of the government's frantic desire to repair its image where it could was to make Sobukwe available for interview to Aida Parker, a journalist who served as a channel for official propaganda—to put it at its kindest—who was then with the *Sunday Tribune* newspaper in Durban. The Sobukwe interview was at the core of her visit, which was intended to present Robben Island as a home from home. I was never able fully to understand why Sobukwe took part in the interview and posed smiling for photographs: it had to do, perhaps, with his high level of courtesy combined with his isolation from people and a sheer craving to communicate with anyone who was not a warder.

Parker emerged with an interesting view of Sobukwe coming from so crude and antagonistic a source. 'Sobukwe has been described as "The Black Verwoerd". This I can understand,' she wrote. 'As you enter, as you talk to him, you gain much the same impression of power, of leadership, as you do when with South

Africa's Prime Minister. Sobukwe has much the same quiet courtesy, much the same innate charm—and certainly much the same clear, incisive, trained mind. You are left with the overwhelming impression that, if this man is one day released, he will, for good or ill, leave his mark on South African history.'

It was, of course, exactly that assessment by the Security Police which was keeping Sobukwe in jail.

While I was plunged into the wars after publication of my prisons reports, more than a month passed before Sobukwe began to obtain any clear idea of what was happening. The authorities persistently sought to keep the information from him. He was deprived of the *Cape Times*, with which the *Rand Daily Mail* was associated, and which was reporting the saga. But he was allowed to continue getting another Cape Town newspaper, the *Cape Argus*, which was horrified by the *Rand Daily Mail*'s aggression against apartheid and was looking the other way on the prisons story. Radio, serving the government, gave only fragmented and selective news. On 8 August, Sobukwe wrote to me: 'It is only this week that the *Cape Argus* has finally reported on the furore your articles have caused ... The only daily I receive is the *Cape Argus*, which has been trying its damnedest to be "patriotic".' Nor had he received the copies of the *Rand Daily Mail* I had sent him, nor issues of the *Sunday Times* and *Sunday Express*, which carried reports about the furore.

He ended: '... keep your courage high. "You are heir to the promises of God."' A week later, as he began to get a picture of what we were up against, he wrote again: '... I shall feel happier and easier in my mind if you take lessons in karate purely as a precautionary measure. The newspapers are beginning to cause one some concern, particularly as The *Observer* too has failed to arrive for three weeks running. It's my wasted money that grieves me!'

The *Observer* was obviously withheld because it was at this time reporting strongly on the prisons issue. As for his thought about my safety, I was at the receiving end of so many threats that I seldom stayed at my apartment and was often accompanied by a *Rand Daily Mail* man who was both a reporter and a karate expert.

To lighten the atmosphere, I sent a message with two pairs of shoes: 'one pair brown shoes (very good ones to be used when receiving International Red Cross and *Sunday Tribune* representatives), one pair "huskies" for leisurewear (I overcame my religious scruples and bought shoes with pigskin uppers).'

Benjamin Pogrund

Sobukwe was ceaselessly supportive, cheering me on and encouraging me to stand straight. He wrote as much as he could—on 22 September I thanked him for 'a real treat—four letters within a fortnight, three of them arriving on one day'. He was delighted to have seen my photograph in a Sunday newspaper, and noted I was looking 'surprisingly fit and well'. He was contemptuous of a State prosecutor, Dr Percy Yutar, known for fervently carrying out Security Police briefs and who had maligned me in the first of the prisons trials featuring one of my informants, Warder G. Van Schalkwyk, who was railroaded into repudiating his statement to me, only to find that his retraction was then used against him to convict and jail him for lying.

Sobukwe got into the guts of it in writing to me: 'It was you who drew my attention to this dialogue of the deaf: the calcification and ossification of attitudes on either side. In the present case, those who instinctively either disbelieved or resented your articles still do and will continue to do so whatever the verdict of the courts. Similarly, those who instinctively believed or welcomed your articles still do and will continue to do so irrespective of what the courts say or do. The former group sees in Van Schalkwyk's recantation a "rebuttal" of your case—to quote the "zealous" Dr Yutar; the latter, unimpressed, will cynically refer to the 1938 "Confessions" in Stalin's time.

'I am, therefore, not unduly concerned about the court proceedings except only in so far as your integrity, both as a person and as a journalist, is being impugned. That is the object Yutar has in view: and on that score alone I would have him fought every inch of the way, to hell and back. I think I am satisfied now that that will be done.

'There is, of course, the whispering campaign that will be directed against you and for which you must be fully prepared. It is going to be "discovered", Benjie, that you are of Jewish extraction. And racists loathe a fearless Jew. It is going to be "discovered" that you are a very close friend of mine. In a sense I am glad that your divorce is through because Astrid would be getting more of the type of letter you told me about last year. All the advice I could give you on this kind of warfare is contained in *Hornstein's Boy* by Robert Traver, who observes that McCarthy was challenged and routed by a very gentle old Senator, Joe Walsch I think the name is: that, quoting Holmes, "as life is action and passion, it is required of a man that he should share the passion and action of his time, at the peril of being judged not to have lived".'

Later, reading a newspaper report that I was to sue Yutar for defamation, he wrote: 'You know, of course, that if I can be of assistance in any way I shall be happy to oblige. Just you say the word!'

I passed that message to our lawyers, who arranged for Sobukwe to be interviewed in case he could be called as a witness in the then ongoing trial of my original and chief source, Harold Strachan. The government had framed charges against Strachan, a former political prisoner, on narrow grounds, selecting a phrase here and a sentence there from the many thousands of words he had told me, and putting the onus on us to prove the truth. That meant we could only use witnesses able to testify to a specific episode at a specific time in a specific prison. Sobukwe told Tom Walters, a Cape Town solicitor who gained access to him on our behalf, that he could testify about assaults and poor conditions. But as these did not fit into the parameters chosen by the prosecution our lawyers decided against calling him.

Sobukwe was disappointed. He wrote to me on 9 November: 'Your Mr Walters interviewed me some time last week. I commented as fully and objectively as I could on the Strachan article which he read to me. At the end he felt, however, that my evidence would not materially assist the defence and informed me that I would, therefore, not be called as a witness by the defence. I am sorry he thought that way because I was rather persuaded that there was a lot I could substantiate. But then, Mr Walters is an advocate and knows best, presumably, what is relevant and material in a court of law.'

He went on with words which moved me profoundly. Again, as with our discussions on the island eighteen months before, but even more now, he was sealing his fate. He knew as well as I did that what he was now saying would be taken by the government as further proof positive of his intransigence. For a man who was at the mercy of his captors and whose freedom hung on their arbitrary decision, these were astonishingly courageous words . . .

'I want to assure you that I am quite aware of the political implications of this case. And I do not wish history ever to record that for some opportunistic reason or other, I kept mum like Br'er Rabbit, when I should have spoken, at the same time being quite voluble when I should have held my peace.

Benjamin Pogrund

'If then, at any time in the future, at any stage of this case, you should like me to testify please don't fear that your calling me as a witness will jeopardise my position. We have become so anxious to shield and spare our friends that we are virtual "collaborators"!'

We continued efforts to get him full reports of what was happening. I could not send him my original reports on Strachan: the government had blocked all further publication by banning Strachan so that nothing he said could be distributed; it was a criminal offence to give anyone a copy of those issues of the *Rand Daily Mail* in which his story had appeared. But the *Rand Daily Mail* was now publishing copious reports—one to three pages each day—about his trial and Sobukwe asked for these. He had obviously approached the authorities and told me: 'I am certain there'll be no trouble this time. The matter has been resolved even if there still are hedgings and provisos.' Unfortunately, the prison authorities did not keep their word to him. After a lot of effort in putting together the Strachan case reports and sending them in batches, he was never allowed to have them.

Instead, interference with our communication was reaching a peak. Letters he wrote to me on 13 October, 21 October and 29 November never arrived. My letter of 7 December, in which I referred again to sending the Strachan reports, was seized. I sent a copy of the letter but that also did not get through. It took months to work this out. Only in March the next year did I become aware of what had been held. Apart from the disappointment of having letters disappear with no word of explanation, it created havoc in the ongoing, and now extensive, arrangements for Sobukwe and the family.

The meanness applied also to Christmas. I sent a hamper of foods, a bigger one than the previous year, and again included tinsel and candles, plus a modest Christmas stocking. The parcel was returned to the suppliers, a leading food store in Johannesburg, with the note: 'Not allowed to receive any parcels containing eatables.' I wrote to the officer commanding and got a curt note which told me of a new tighter policy: 'Mr Sobukwe may receive parcels from relatives only under very exceptional circumstances.' On checking my files, I realised that my letter of 7 December had said the parcel was on its way, and wondered whether that had been additional reason for it being seized.

The let-down for Sobukwe must have been severe. Two months

later, when he too understood the gaps in our correspondence, he wrote to me that he had been sure in his mind that I would be sending him a parcel for Christmas, and 'when by New Year's Day I had not received it I made inquiries and was informed of the new *ukase*'.

I remember when this letter reached me. I sat for a long time and stared at it, brooding about the desolation he must have endured, shut off from the world, expecting and looking forward to a parcel of special foods to brighten Christmas, and then the gradual realisation that nothing was coming. It would have been so easy for the jail authorities, at the most minimum level of decency, and even if they could not bring themselves to let him have the parcel, simply to have told him of their decision. But their cruelty was too elemental for that.

Our exchanges of views were gathering momentum. Within the confines of our cautious letter-writing I was striving to do what I could to push and prod, to help free his mind from his tiny enclosure. So there was a sense of achievement when he wrote that he felt 'refreshed' after reading my letters and that they were 'constant reminders that I have a self-respect to cherish'. And I felt absolutely triumphant when, in August 1965, he began a letter with a hint of unusual testiness: 'Certain ideas in your letters act as irritants on my mind, compelling me to think them through.'

Midway through the year we became involved in a protracted exchange of views which had as its starting point my gloom about the continuing supremacy of the Afrikaner Nationalist rulers and their racism, and the country's powerlessness at their hands. One of the major political stories of 1965 was a government decision to allow blacks, coloureds and Asians to be served in the transit lounge of the Jan Smuts International Airport near Johannesburg, the country's foremost airport; that was represented as dizzying progress.

More significantly, the law passed in 1963, to allow for detention without trial for up to 90 days, was now extended to 180 days: it was intended to secure potential State witnesses until they testified but was soon used on a wholesale basis for detentions in general. Political trials were running ceaselessly: hundreds of people were jailed, for up to fifteen years, for taking part in banned organisations, or leaving the country to seek sabotage-training abroad, or contravening banning orders. Bannings, further cramping of the right to hold meetings, denial of passports to large numbers of people, and the searching out of nooks and crannies into which to push apartheid were the characteristics of 1965.

'During the year the government has become increasingly intolerant of criticism, and has shown a readiness to flout world opinion, even although international pressure on South Africa has eased,' was how the South African Institute of Race Relations' annual survey later summed up the year. 'New measures have been taken relating to defence and security, and for the control of the activities of individuals. There have been intensified attacks on "liberalists" [the government's term of abuse for liberals], and efforts to bring about conformity of thought in the country.' And underlying it all was the reiterated view of Prime Minister Verwoerd that he believed in separating whites and blacks to the maximum extent. 'I believe in the supremacy of the white man over his people in his own territory,' he told Parliament, 'and I am prepared to maintain it by force.'

My dismal feelings showed themselves in a letter which Sobukwe received when he had just written his exams. He responded with the assurance that there had not been an alarming deterioration in his mental capacities. Again, as before, his concern was not for himself but for my feelings: 'And I know that that is your chief fear,' he said. 'After I had read your letter I felt a heaviness of the soul. This is the first time I have felt sad after reading a letter from you. I detected a wee note of despair and dejection, Benjie, and I was deeply perturbed that my closest friends should feel this way.'

Where I was pessimistic about the future he was optimistic: 'In assessing our position, Benjie, we must not lose sight of the fact that South Africa represents not even a thousand-millionth of the world population. And the ruling caste represents an infinitesimal fraction. In being contemptuous of racial arrogance we represent the distilled product of Western intellectual thought. And the greatest minds of both East and West say it is absolute rubbish to declare: *"Du bist nichts: Dein volk ist alles"* as young Nazis were exhorted to do on waking up every morning. Because if you are nothing, your folk is nothing either.

'And even in this country, the silent courage of thousands of men and women who VOLUNTARILY stand up to be counted is astonishing testimony to the depths of human courage.

> Then it is the brave man chooses,
> While the coward stands aside . . .
> Till the multitude makes virtue
> Of the faith they had denied.'
>
> James Russell Lowell.

He pursued these thoughts in his next letter, arguing that a reappraisal of Western ideas was under way. There was a time, as late as 1913, when the whole world was possessed by European powers and the ideas that prevailed in the world were those of Europe, he said.

'All things were judged by European standards. Even human-beings were divided into those of Europe and those not of Europe. The nomenclature was European. On one side stood the "European" or "white". On the other the "Non-European" or "non-white". And what is significant is that this terminology has been used by the people of Africa, Asia and Latin America without any feeling of annoyance. We have described ourselves as the negative of one-third of the human race!

'The revolution consists in this that two-thirds of the human race are beginning to think of themselves POSITIVELY and MUST SOON describe themselves POSITIVELY!

'China explodes her bomb and to protestations from the West she replies, Why is it "fair" for de Gaulle to qualify as a nuclear man and bad for Chou En-Lai to do so? Why is it good for FOUR European powers to have nuclear arsenals and bad for ONE Asian power to have it? In other words why should two-thirds of the human race be policed by one-third?

'Russia quarrels with China and withdraws all her aid. West Germany quarrels with Tanzania and withdraws her aid. China and Tanzania compare notes and needs must come to the conclusion that the "white imperialists" have behaved like this throughout the centuries.

'But what moves me to the depths of my being, Benjie, is the love that Europe, America and the East bear for Africa, the missionary zeal with which the young people from these lands embrace any opportunity to be of service to the under-developed countries. I feel it, particularly, when India and Pakistan, from their very limited resources, make available technicians for work in Africa and Latin America.

'The youth of these countries have entered into the spirit of the revolution; they understand it; they share it. When they express disappointment or even disgust with certain aspects of African progress, I am grateful—you can only be disappointed by those you love and by those from whom you expect better things.

'From my side, then, I am excising from my dictionary the terms "Non-European", "non-white" and "coloured". I do not know yet how I shall refer to the groups traditionally so described. But the term will emerge.'

He enjoyed a story I told him about a visit I had made to Zululand, to see Chief Gatsha Buthelezi, then hardly known outside the territory but a former university colleague of his at Fort Hare: While talking to Buthelezi about government pressures to get him to accept a tribal authority as part of the 'homelands' policy, a group of elderly tribal leaders came into the room—we were in the sitting-room of his home at Mahlabatini in Zululand—and squatted on the floor listening to us. After a while one of them broke in and, pointing at me, spoke to Buthelezi in Zulu. Buthelezi translated: 'The old man points at your shirt and says you bought it because you saw other people wearing it and you knew it was a good shirt. In the same way we are watching what happens with tribal authorities in other parts of the country: if we like it we will buy it, otherwise we won't.'

Sobukwe said tribesmen were 'extremely shrewd' and the story reminded him of the late S.E.K. Mqhayi, the African 'Poet Laureate' who, during the Second World War, attended in his tribal regalia the opening of the *Bunga* [a form of tribal assembly for blacks] in Ciskei. The Minister of Native Affairs, P. van der Byl, came to press for implementation of the 'rehabilitation scheme' for land, which was strongly opposed by blacks. When van der Byl got out of his car, Mqhayi greeted him with a shouted Xhosa chant: '*Yehla, yehla, yehl'ingwe emthini.*' ('Down comes the leopard from the tree'). Van der Byl and his retinue were flattered, even when the words were correctly interpreted to them. But the tribesmen were warned. When a leopard leaves the tree, while people are around, its purpose is to destroy!

In his next letter Sobukwe returned to the theme of race. America and South Africa represented diametrically opposed, irreconcilable attitudes to the colour problem, he said. If the apologists of apartheid were correct, then wherever black Americans met white Americans on terms of equality there must be friction. The only news that could please them was news of racial clashes in the US as this would prove the correctness of their thesis. 'President Johnson, however, is implementing his policy of complete equality determinedly and successfully: so successfully, in fact, that the African states, despite Afro-Asian solidarity, and despite their conviction that Johnson's Vietnam policy is wrong, will not condemn America because they appreciate Johnson's honesty in his domestic policy.'

That analysis led to an interesting point, he continued. 'The colour or race issue is not, as such, a political issue. It is not confined within the political boundaries of a state. Whether they know it or not, Johnson and Verwoerd now serve as symbols of a divided conscience that spills over their territorial borders. All white supremacists, all over the world, are extremely happy whenever the Verwoerd government takes a step or indicates its determination to "keep the kaffir in his place". When he says he'll have no niggers working side by side with white scientists or flying jets, besides protecting his home crowd from shattering disillusionment regarding the inferiority of "black" men, he also rejoices the heart of klansmen in the USA who are happy to know that the nigger who is beginning to "give himself airs" in the USA has been put in his place by the South African government. Johnson, on the other hand, is the hope of all who stand for non-racialism. His successes are theirs and they endorse his utterances on bigotry.

'Both countries have to maintain a consistent, unbending attitude on matters of colour both for the sake of their domestic supporters and the international attitude they each represent. As a result, at UNO and elsewhere, the USA has had to take an uncompromising stand against apartheid.'

The South African government had of late been turning 'almost gratefully to France as the one country that is sympathetic', he pointed out. At the same time, de Gaulle's France was extremely anti-Anglo-Saxon, touching an historical chord in the Afrikaner's breast.

I sent copies of some of Sobukwe's letters to Bob Bilheimer as a means of keeping him in touch. He was struck by Sobukwe's remarks about President Johnson, racism and Vietnam and sent them to McGeorge Bundy, a Special Assistant in the White House, suggesting that the President might wish to read them; Bundy agreed, but I never had a follow-up.

Liberalism and conservatism were next for discussion in our letters: they were not mutually exclusive but were complementary, he believed. Liberalism was the 'initiating and experimenting force' and without it there could be no progress, in politics and all aspects of life. But, uncontrolled, liberalism led to chaos. On the other hand, conservatism never initiated anything and resisted change— and yet for that reason had a stronger appeal to the ordinary man than liberalism. Conservatism had to be continually prodded by liberalism which in turn had to be continually restrained by conservatism. He went on to express 'severe doubts' about whether it was possible to have states whose economy was 'planned' without ultimately also having their politics 'planned'. 'However, the defreezing in Russia and the countries of Eastern Europe reminds us of the eternal cycle of human development and behaviour. Nature is nicely balanced and the exclusive pursuit of a particular programme or idea leads to an imbalance, the correction of which leads to further imbalance.'

His university studies and the many academic works he was delving into were much in his mind, and as he told me, he was sharing his thinking with me. He was very much the student trying out ideas for size. He was also devouring non-academic books. From soon after his arrival on the island, and apart from what anyone else might be sending, I was shipping cartons of books—ten, twenty, forty or more at a time. They were chosen to be as catholic as possible and to be available, hopefully, for any possible mood in which he might find himself. At times he also asked for a specific author, such as, on one occasion, C.P. Snow, whom he had never read; Goethe, similarly; J.B. Priestley, whose writing he already knew; St Exupery, whose *Flight to Arras* he had read; and Balzac, with the wry comment, 'Suspect his works will be banned, though.' A batch of twenty books by these authors was rapidly posted to him, Balzac among them, and he wrote in due course: 'They are an excellent lot of books, the type I would like my children to know I read in my maturer years.'

The Representative by the German dramatist Hochhuth moved him 'to the depths of my being'. That was understandable because the play deals with the moral issues which men in power must deal with in an age of totalitarianism and war. But *Vicar of Christ* set off a burst of anger. He had been thinking, he said, 'about the total absurdity of a solemn conference of over 2,000 educated and responsible cardinals and bishops discussing whether or not the Jews killed God! How arrogantly stupid can Europe get?'

A while later he wanted plays by Priestley, books by Somerset Maugham, and Leopold Senghor's *On African Socialism*—'if it is not banned, and any other topical books that have escaped the ire of our censors.' He wanted, too, 'literature on Judaism, particularly the Jewish case against the Christian faith'. This last request came after I had been telling him about my own studies of Judaism, and my worries about my daughter, Jenny's, future interest in religion. '. . . I am glad you have on your own found your way back to the Holy One of Israel,' he wrote. 'I am not a racialist, as you know very well. But if I were to be anyone other than who and what I am, I would choose to be a Jew. With all those solemn promises and assurances from God I would walk on air, absolutely certain that "underneath are the everlasting arms".'

I sent him four books about Judaism, all well known and weighty: Baeck's *The Essence of Judaism*, Weiss Rosmarin's *Judaism and Christianity: The Differences*, Epstein's *Judaism*, and Martin Buber's *Two Types of Faith*. Many months later I found they had not been given to him. I never knew why. The Judaism works were among a total of fifty-seven books which I listed in a letter which was not given to him. So he did not know what I had sent. These books ranged far and wide, from Sinclair, Conrad, Pasternak, Tennessee Williams and Joyce Carey to John F. Kennedy and Lyndon B. Johnson. There was equal mystery about these, as I never learnt which were seized.

In this batch, there were also books about communism which, as I explained, for the jail censors as much as for him, 'are all written from the Western side of the fence so I cannot see that there will be any difficulty in their getting through to you. The quality of quite a few of these is rather suspect, I am afraid, so don't hesitate to throw them aside if the opening few pages bore you.' At least some of these did get through. I knew this because, the next year, a group of Members of Parliament visited his quarters while touring Robben Island. One of them, G.F. van L. Froneman, who represented a rural government seat, excitedly told Parliament afterwards that

Sobukwe was a communist. Why? Because he had seen communist books on his bookshelf!

That particular consignment of books had another bizarre consequence. Months later, the Security Police in Johannesburg phoned and invited me to visit their offices. It was the sort of invitation one did not refuse. When I arrived I was confronted by two policemen who produced brown wrapping paper with the address in my handwriting: 'Mr Robert Sobukwe, care of Officer Commanding, Robben Island Prison, Robben Island, via Cape Town.' Then a book was displayed to me: *Africa and World Politics* by Vernon McKay. Published in 1963, it had been banned about six months before I sent it to Sobukwe, they politely told me. I was therefore facing a charge of distributing 'obscene, indecent or objectionable' material. Would I like to make a statement before the papers were handed to the public prosecutor? I asked to phone my lawyer, and had a quick conversation with him to check that I wouldn't be getting myself into deeper trouble by making a statement. Then I went ahead: yes, I had sent the book; Vernon McKay was a professor at Johns Hopkins University, one of America's leading universities, and he enjoyed an international reputation as a scholar; to my knowledge, his book was a serious and academic study; I had not known the book was banned and yes, I was aware that ignorance of the law was not a defence; on the other hand, what sort of a madman would I be if I tried to smuggle an 'indecent etc' book to a prisoner by sending it care of the Officer Commanding the country's maximum security prison?

Even they must have realised how stupid they would look by charging me. My statement was sent to the prosecutor and later I was advised no charges would be brought. But Vernon McKay's book disappeared, no doubt to be destroyed in the same way, by pulping or burning, together with the mountain of other material grabbed by the customs authorities and the police in the course of their daily work. Books, newspapers and magazines covering serious political analysis were treated equally with pornography.

But one book I really did want him to read did get through. That was *Letters and Papers from Prison* by Dietrich Bonhoeffer, which Charlotte Taylor had sent me to pass on. For those who might not know, Bonhoeffer was a Lutheran minister in Germany murdered by the Nazis shortly before the end of the Second World War. While held in prison he wrote these letters to his family and friends.

How Can Man Die Better

He discusses the dilemma of Christians in standing up to tyranny: whether they are justified in turning to violence. I knew the extent to which Bonhoeffer's views were having an impact in South Africa as Christians, inside and outside the country, tried to evolve a strategy against apartheid. I wanted to tell Sobukwe about the agonised debate that was under way, and wrote with what I hoped was enough circumspection to get through the censors: 'In my contacts with churchmen, I have found that Bonhoeffer has become the conscience-prodder of Christians who find themselves in parallel situations. Whether his example should be followed is a problem which many Christians I have encountered torture themselves about.' The book reached him, but not the letter.

Inasmuch as I was later able to discover, four recordings of American folk songs did not get to him either at that time. They were part of a set of records which also included *Porgy and Bess*, opera and, as my personal Christmas gift, the finger-snapping musical soundtrack of *Zorba the Greek*, a movie which was then a hit. 'I had a real hootenanny on New Year's Day,' Sobukwe wrote. 'I played every one of them and enjoyed them immensely. I realise that you young fellows are trying to "modernise" me and I believe you are succeeding ... The opera pieces were marvellous. It was a real musical extravanganza. Yessuh!'

That enthusiasm cheered me enormously. It leavened the sadness of my occasional trips to Cape Town—to carry out investigations for the ongoing Prisons Trials against us—when I was so close to where he was and yet a world away. Once, after I had been in the city for a day, I wrote: 'That was on Tuesday this week. My thoughts were particularly with you on that day; each time I looked across the bay towards the island, I wished we could see each other again. We must wait for happier, freer times ... ' And a few weeks later I wrote that I was planning a holiday in Cape Town with Jenny and would be staying with my parents in Sea Point, 'right across from you'.

One of the roads from the city to the suburb of Sea Point runs across the slopes of Signal Hill, and driving along it, Robben Island can be seen wherever there is a gap in the houses. It is too far for any detail to be visible to the naked eye, but the island is quite close at hand. I always chose to drive on this higher mountain road and it gave me a few minutes of quiet reflection about my friends on the island—Sobukwe, Mandela and others.

There was also the poignancy of his response to my confirmation that Veronica and the children would be visiting him in January: 'Am looking forward to the visit. Around this time of the year I miss the children a lot.'

This was a time, too, for my own personal agonising. An angry government reaction to the prisons exposés had been anticipated. But the actual extent of lying and crookery, the wholesale perjury and attempts to manufacture evidence against us, made me sick to the core of my being. I was already revolted and alienated by the deepening racism in the country; I now felt that continued existence in South Africa was unendurable.

I wrote to Sobukwe: 'In recent months I have become increasingly despondent about the course of affairs in this country. I need not, I know, go into details with you. Let me only say that, as I feel at the moment, I just do not wish to go on living here. I have a growing feeling of sheer physical illness at what I see. It goes without saying that I shall see out the end of the jails issue—whatever happens or is likely to happen to me. But once it is all over, I want to go. When this will be I cannot know for certain, but it should be within the next six to twelve months.'

I was looking for a suitable job abroad, I added, and was putting together testimonials from people I knew well. Would he write one?

I wrote this in my letter of 7 December, which did not reach him. But Veronica carried a verbal message from me. In due course, he wrote: 'I understand your desire to leave this country. But I am afraid I cannot give you a testimonial, Benjie. Such an act would be unethical. I cannot write a testimonial for my brother.' His generosity of outlook made me feel even worse about leaving.

16

Whatever hopes any of us might have had for 1966 were soon ended. The government did not bother to wait for the anniversary of Sobukwe's imprisonment but, as early as 2 February, announced that he would not be released. Parliament duly voted to extend the 'Sobukwe Clause' until 30 June the following year. On this occasion, the explanation given by Justice Minister Vorster was that PAC refugees living abroad still regarded Sobukwe as their leader and efforts were made from time to time to revive the organisation inside the country. There was nothing to indicate that Sobukwe had changed his views or intentions, he said, or that he would not, after his release, start where he had left off before his arrest. It was necessary in the interests of State security that he be detained for at least another year.

The United Party did not object to Sobukwe's imprisonment but opposed the law because it could be used against others too. Typifying the party's role in running in the footsteps of the Nationalists, it again positively egged on the government to act against Sobukwe: a spokesman said it was not beyond the wit of Vorster to find other ways of isolating Sobukwe; he could be dealt with under numerous laws, 'especially as he is a Bantu'.

Suzman again dissented. Sobukwe had now, in effect, served double the sentence of the court, she said. This double sentence had been imposed by the Minister and was a 'travesty of justice' and a 'complete abrogation' of the rule of law. She wondered why the government bothered to put cases through the courts seeing that, regardless of the sentences imposed, the Minister was enabled to keep people in jail. And, referring to Vorster's earlier statement that the International Red Cross had found Sobukwe's living conditions on Robben Island up to the standard enjoyed by a high-ranking officer, she said she did not care whether the accommodation was 'similar to that of a four-star hotel'. The principle was not affected; he had served his sentence and was being kept in jail. Once again, however, her arguments were ignored.

There was by now great anxiety about his health: Veronica had visited him and returned full of alarm. As soon as she contacted me, I wrote to Vorster to convey her concern and to ask for immediate action. She was right to be so worried: unknown to her, in conditions of the utmost secrecy, the authorities had had a prostate gland operation performed on him. The story broke into the open on 9 February with newspaper reports that he had been returned the previous day to Robben Island: a number of Security policemen had removed him unobtrusively from the Karl Bremer Hospital at Bellville, near Cape Town. Newspapers said he had been taken to the hospital about fourteen days before by the Security Police and booked in under a false name. 'His identity was so well guarded that not even the ward sister knew that one of South Africa's best-known political prisoners was being treated there,' said a newspaper. He had been guarded night and day and plainclothes policemen had patrolled the hospital grounds.

The first direct news came to me in a letter from Sobukwe dated 16 February. At the end of it he wrote briefly and matter of factly, no doubt both to allay anxieties and to avoid censor problems: 'Oh, by the way, I was admitted to hospital, Karl Bremer, on 31 January, operated upon on 1 February, discharged on 8 February and have been in my quarters ever since. Am all right.' Later he wrote that he had had the 'delightful company' of a warder and a Security policeman, one on each side of his bed, for twenty-four hours a day while he was in hospital. And on his fourth day there, the 'Medicine for Rhodesia' campaign had been launched—a project for the white rebels in Rhodesia enthusiastically supported by the Afrikaner doctors and nurses at the Karl Bremer Hospital. 'Very congenial surroundings indeed!' he wryly remarked.

He could hardly have understated it more. Karl Bremer, named after a former Afrikaner Nationalist Minister of Health, was an Afrikaner hospital created as the teaching hospital for the University of Stellenbosch, a leading Afrikaner institution. Like other South African hospitals, it was run by whites with rigorous racial segregation of patients. Not surprisingly, the hospital expressed the values of the community which staffed it and which it served. According to a person who worked there (and who wants to remain anonymous), that meant 'a coldness and a neglect and doing the minimum' characterised at least some of the white staff in their treatment of black patients. 'There was no conscious cruelty but there was an expressed belief among some of the hospital staff, though not others, that blacks felt less pain; these staff were therefore reluctant to prescribe painkilling drugs.' He says the attitude was shown, for example, in the remark of a nurse: 'There's no need to give them those drugs. They don't feel pain like we do.'

Unpleasant as Sobukwe's stay there was, he was fortunate. A few years later, after an escape from hospital, it became normal practice to chain prisoners by the leg to hospital beds.

But a lesson was learnt. Nearly a quarter-century after Sobukwe's experience, with the National Party still in power, the Minister of Justice, Kobie Coetsee, revealed that, when Nelson Mandela had first fallen ill in the early 1980s, he was given 'the best possible treatment'. It had had beneficial results for the authorities, Coetsee went on to explain with disarming frankness: 'His exposure to our medical services and nursing staff at the Volks Hospital [a leading, Afrikaans-run hospital in Cape Town] was of such a nature that he became quite appreciative towards, in particular, Afrikaans-speaking people in the medical and nursing professions—to such an extent that he chose local treatment rather than the overseas treatment some tried to force on him.'

And, added Coetsee, 'when it became clear that we were treating him well, there was a change of attitude. When he developed pneumonia and we again provided the best possible treatment ... Mr Mandela's attitude changed.

'I would label it as a more appreciative attitude towards the government, to the Afrikaner and to values like integrity, decency and civility.'

That at least is the way it was seen through government eyes.

In Sobukwe's earlier experience, Veronica was both angry and worried about the secret operation he had undergone. She wanted us to write to Vorster. 'Owing to Bob's health condition which has deteriorated, I think we should be given an exit permit,' she said in a note to me. 'After all, he [Vorster] need not be afraid of him any more, he is finished physically.'

Of course Sobukwe was not finished, and Vorster went on fearing him. But her feelings were understandable. 'I am afraid he is not in safe hands,' she wrote again to me. 'And I want a complete report from the doctors who are attending him. My great fears are complications. What tactful and sympathetic treatment is he receiving? ... We must press that he should be taken to where I must personally supervise his health.'

But I was running into difficulties with Sobukwe. Even before I knew about the operation, I had written to him that Veronica was so upset that she had told me that he was not well, even though he had not wanted me to know about it. I sent him a copy of my letter to Vorster which dealt with his health and raised other complaints too, such as non-delivery of the *Rand Daily Mail*, the Press reports on the Strachan court case, the *Observer* and magazines. I asked Sobukwe not to be angry with me. But he ticked me off for having written that letter; he did not say it but I realised that he felt I had gone too far in bending the knee to the government. The unusual tension between us was a palpable thing. I wrote back, apologising but standing firm in stressing that I had shared Veronica's worries. Finally, with all the delays to our correspondence, the problem was buried in a terse mention by him in a 20 April letter: 'I realise that you wrote out of concern for me, Benjie. No further comment.'

Early in May I had a reply from Vorster to my February letter. To my surprise, he said he had had my complaints investigated, and dealt with them point by point. It did not take matters any further but I wrote to thank him. I sent Vorster's letter to Sobukwe and he was scornfully dismissive: 'It's the typical bureaucratic reply and I am not interested in scoring debating points,' he said. Soon after, Veronica also had a reply: '... your application for the release of your husband received careful consideration,' Vorster's office wrote. 'The Minister regrets that it was not found possible to accede to your request at this stage.'

I was never sure whether to welcome such politeness or whether it added its own layer of horror to these remote administrative decisions which destroyed liberty.

Within a few weeks I tried to trade on the courtesy by writing again to Vorster asking for an interview. I said I wanted to take up 'various matters' which had come to my attention in a letter received from Sobukwe, and to 'submit certain representations which I am certain you will be willing to consider'. At this distance of time I cannot remember what representations I wanted to make; anyway, Vorster refused to see me and said I should put what I wanted to say into writing. I dropped it.

How Can Man Die Better

Despite the lack of success, Veronica was pleased that we had forwarded the complaints and wrote to me: 'At least they know that we are quite aware of them.' Later it turned out that we had actually achieved a small success: the magazine *Economica*, which dealt with economic issues and which had been denied to Sobukwe, was allowed through with as little explanation as its original barring. But the copies of the *Rand Daily Mail*, the Press reports on the Strachan court case, and the *Observer* all disappeared without trace.

What was dawning on me was that a qualitative shift of far-reaching proportions had occurred in the way in which Sobukwe was being handled by the authorities. Two years before, I had been certain that they were leaning over backwards to be nice to him in the hope of being able to bring him across to their side. By late in 1965, I suspected that they had reached the conclusion that he was, in their terms, beyond redemption and that there was not the slightest prospect of him ceasing to be an intransigent enemy of white rule. That was why the difficulties of communication mounted and why the obstructionism became so marked; that was why Vorster was able to announce, as early as February 1966, that he was to be kept imprisoned.

In fact the reality was even worse than I suspected. There were hints from him at the time, as in a letter dated 20 April 1966 in which he said: 'Of course, the last quarter of last year was a very unpleasant and trying period for me.' With fragmentary information available, a full picture was not possible, but the seizing of the three letters from him to me—of 13 October, 21 October and 29 November of the previous year—took on a more sinister meaning. It seemed he was blocked from conveying vital details to me of what he was suffering.

Even our mild letters were too much for his jailers. Veronica returned from her January 1966 visit with a message from Sobukwe that the Security Police had been to see him to warn that we had to stop the 'politics' in our letters. He wrote to me: 'I hope you won't find my letters "dry" as a result.'

Only several years later, after his release, did I learn more of the background to these events. What had happened, it seemed, was that the authorities had walked away from him. He was left to rot. Whatever friendliness had been shown largely disappeared. The authorities were indifferent to him, attending to those essential needs which they believed they had to and no more. That was the official approach. It no doubt opened the door for individual warders to vent their racial and ideological feelings of antagonism and resentment.

Two simple examples to do with his food illustrate a lot of this: his meals were brought to his enclosure, usually by a black criminal prisoner escorted by a white warder. The food was put into his kitchen. For breakfast, it would arrive at any time between about 6 a.m. and 8 a.m. They did not tell him it was there. Often Sobukwe would be asleep in the next room and did not know food had been delivered. The food could start off all right—it might be fried eggs—but by the time he realised it was there it could be unpleasantly cold and congealed.

On other occasions, for supper, he would take the cover off a plate and find steaming-hot, inviting-looking meat; as he cut into it, he would find that the rice underneath was cold, decayed and stinking.

Not everything was negative. One early gain in the year was that Veronica was allowed daily visits during her stay in Cape Town instead of only three days a week. Another was that Eulalie Stott, feeling that the chair she had provided two years before might be wearing out, arranged for delivery of a new one.

Otherwise the year came to be characterised by struggling with delayed letters and parcels and extended lines of communication to keep him supplied. About sixty books had to be obtained for his academic studies: Marvin Wachman, President of Lincoln University in the US, responded to a plea from me by having fifteen shipped to the island, from Adam Smith's *Wealth of Nations*, through the origin and evolution of modern capitalism, to a history of American economic life. Nana Mahomo, one of the members of the PAC national executive sent abroad before the launching of the anti-pass campaign in 1960 and then in London, weighed in with other books after I let him know that someone else had failed to fulfil a promise to send books. But it was all painfully slow and, in April, Sobukwe was anxiously noting that he had already received five lessons in his correspondence course but did not yet have a single textbook. In November that year I was still chasing after missing titles.

But we were still well off because, except for delays and censorship, the books could be sent. For political prisoners in general by this stage, the authorities were restricting access to books. They could not receive books from anyone except libraries. They could buy books only if their relatives sent money to them. No one else, not even their lawyers, was allowed to send money.

The contact with Mahomo did create its own small headache. He was active in exile circles and I worked on the basis that our letters would be monitored by the Security Police. I was uncertain what effect dealing with him—the hated enemy abroad, in official eyes—might have on my own conflicts with the government and whether my contact with Sobukwe might be imperilled. I had a cover name and address for Mahomo in London, but I wrote to him that I preferred to be in touch openly, under his own name. 'In making arrangements for Bob, I prefer to work in the open,' I explained. 'In case your cover address is "blown", I would not like to give the appearance of acting surreptitiously.' It was a safety-first policy I adhered to usually, but not always.

One of the happy events was a face-to-face meeting with Charlotte Taylor and her husband, Thomas, who visited South Africa. They were, as expected, concerned and kind people and in due course another cheque arrived—this time from her mother, who, as Charlotte said, 'spontaneously asked if she could contribute to the account when I told her a little of the story'.

Even with this, cash was in as short supply as ever. Eulalie was always the chief support in Cape Town, arranging hotel accommodation and settling much of the account, while Moira Henderson and Noel Robb were again paying for deliveries of fresh fruit. But, at the end of the year, I had to write a begging letter to Bilheimer to say that 'massive expenses' were looming during the next few months and I hesitated to ask Charlotte again. Could he pass my letter to someone of goodwill? Veronica was to go to Cape Town the next month for a three-week visit and the four children were going with her. I had raised money locally for the train tickets but had to add the cost of meals and bedding for the more than thirty-hour journey. I had the costs of her hotel covered, but not for the children. Then there were the children's school fees—they were at boarding school in Basutoland—and books and clothing for them.

'I feel ashamed at having to write to ask for help because this is something which we should be able to do in this country,' I told him. But repeating the point which was a continual difficulty: 'Unfortunately, there is a limited number of people here to whom one can turn and I have milked them as hard as possible already.' At least I had organised Christmas presents locally, I added. He replied that there was no need to be diffident about approaching Charlotte again.

The occasional small emergency arose, as when Sobukwe sent me a telegram that he needed an electric kettle immediately; Stuttafords posted it to him and I telegraphed him that it was on its way. Stuttafords was so helpful that I finally arranged for him to order whatever he wanted directly from the store and to charge it to me. I never really quite got over being pleasantly surprised at how this select store took these dealings with a Robben Island prisoner in its stride, even to the extent of writing to Sobukwe: 'We shall be pleased if you would advise us about your requirements and shall make sure that these are fulfilled with the least possible delay.' That it could and did happen was one of those crazy South African contradictions.

With all this I still had to press Sobukwe to tell me what he required. I had to behave like a mail order salesman. On 25 April, with the cold weather approaching, I wrote: 'How are you placed for winter clothing? Sheets, blankets, a heater, trousers, jerseys, pyjamas, socks, shoes, shirts, underwear, etc? You notice that I carefully specify each possible item because long experience of you has shown me that you are reluctant to tell me of your needs unless I pinpoint each article. Whatever you need, please let me know so that I can have it sent to you.' In July, I sent a reminder that he had not replied.

Despite being more conscious than ever about the hidden readers of our letters, we were yet able to reach out our hands to each other. It pleased me, and it seemed to me a happy event in South Africa, when friendship meant that the leader of the Africanists, in writing to me, a liberal of another colour, could say: 'Speaking as one African to another ...' It struck a chord in both of us, for I mentioned my reaction to him and, noting it, he described in his turn his reaction to learning of a chance meeting between Miliswa and Mary Moeng, a beautiful and charming young woman who had worked in my home as a domestic servant: 'Imagine my joy then when I received a letter from my daughter informing me that on their way to Jo'burg from Cape Town they met someone she calls "*Ausi* Mary" ("*Ausi*" being the Sotho equivalent of the Afrikaans *ou Sis* = elder Sister), who had for some time been employed by "*Ntate* Pogrund". Now "*Ntate*"—for the benefit of you Zulus—is the Sotho term for "father".

'I have been rather strict, Benjie, in bringing up my children. I have stressed that their responses must always be accompanied by a polite "father" or "mother". In other words I want, "yes, father", "no, mother", "thank you, father" from them and not just "yes", "no" or "thank you", etc.

'I need not tell you, of course, that I have been hard put to it to decide how I can train them to show this politeness to all people irrespective of colour, without making them colour-conscious. And lo and behold, my child, most naturally, without any self-consciousness, writes of "Ntate Pogrund" as she has written of "Ntate Mothopeng" (Zeph) before.

'She reads me like a book, of course, that little girl. And I am afraid she is going to make me dance to her tune!'

These were stressful thoughts for a father. How indeed to bring up children free of racism in South Africa where so many of the ordinary, daily contacts are steeped in racism? To set an example in one's own behaviour is the most obvious way, but even then it must stand up to the powerful countervailing influences of an apartheid society and of school teaching about the superiority of whites over blacks; history has traditionally been taught with that inbuilt bias. I once asked Sobukwe how on earth he had been able to go through his schooling having to study the 'Kaffir Wars', that thoroughly racist phrase for describing the nineteenth-century conflicts between white settlers and indigenous blacks in which blacks are invariably depicted as savage murderers. He said he tried to laugh and then to learn as much as he could by rote so that he could throw it up to pass the examinations.

Sobukwe worried about his children and I worried about my daughter, Jenny, and later, too, about my other children. In Jenny's case, she often asked me if 'Uncle Bob' had ever seen her, to which I would explain that he was living a long way away, but that he had seen her photographs and he was a close friend of her daddy's and therefore a friend of hers. 'This she happily accepts—and sends you her love,' I told him in a letter.

Between ourselves we tried, as much as we could, to climb over the barriers of colour.

In mid-year I went into hospital to be treated for a stomach ulcer and it seemed that I would have major surgery. I telegraphed

Benjamin Pogrund

Sobukwe that I was going into hospital and wrote to him from there that if I had to undergo an operation I would send him a telegram the day before 'and will ask you to bear me in your thoughts and to pray for me. It would mean much to me to know that you were thinking of me then.' The letter, although mawkish, fitted his and my circumstances at the time and I meant every word when, referring to my experiences at the hands of the government since writing the jail exposés, I told him, for his benefit and in the hope and belief of wider distribution among organs of State security: 'I've learned more about evil and corruption than I had dreamed was possible. And I have had to test myself and see how far I was prepared to stand up for what I believe. I would like you to know that in the agony of spirit which I have gone through, the thought of you has been a primary factor. I have looked at your example of courage and integrity and I have drawn strength from it. And underlying it all, I have so often put the question to myself: "If I do this—or don't do that—can I look Bob squarely in the face again?"' (There were indeed two dominating influences: Sobukwe was one, and the other was my daughter, Jenny; I did not want to do anything which might impair her future view of me.)

Back came his response to buoy my courage: 'In my childhood I was a bit of a coward, and my father, who was no mean psychologist, repeatedly advised me: "If you can avoid a fight, then avoid it. Apologise, if that will prevent a fight, even if you are in the right. But if you must fight, then make a complete job of it so that even if you have to be carried unconscious from the field, your adversary should most decidedly not wish for a second encounter." Years later I found Polonius giving the same advice (in *Hamlet*) though not in so many words; proof, if any were needed, that Shakespeare was related to my father. I give you the same advice, Benjie. Choose your ground, carefully; don't dissipate your energies. I have never been worried about you. I've always known you cannot be untrue to yourself. A man must live with himself: and to live with someone you despise is hell.'

I walked a lot taller after getting that letter.

I had told him I was reading Howard Fast's *My Glorious Brothers* and he went on: '... you presumably have by now reached what is to me the whole message of the book: "Tell Rogesh that the Maccabee is in Judaea, the Maccabee and his brother Simon, etc." A similar configuration appears in *Spartacus*: "Tell the Senate . . ." And what a message! And yet I've always felt that the message in *Spartacus* was a political testament. The message to Rogesh was in the genre of the great utterances of the prophets—a timeless message for all oppressed. And when Rogesh, the High Priest, received it, he wept. It reminded him of what he was. I can never forget that passage, Benjie. You owe it to Jenny, on the night of the Passover, to remind her that "once we were slaves in Egypt; and we shall never be slaves again".'

We found that we were both enthusiastic readers of Fast and also of Arthur Koestler. They 'are favourite authors of mine,' Sobukwe told me. 'I still do not believe that *Spartacus* can compare with *My Glorious Brothers*, describing the struggle of the Maccabees. My wife and I read it together, page by page from beginning to end. And we wept as we read.

'I have already read *Darkness at Noon* twice and have read it again. Incidentally it was Koestler who provided me with ammunition to fight the Reds. His *The God that Failed*—he is one of the contributors—*The Yogi and the Commissar* and *Darkness at Noon* as well as *Arrow in the Blue* I got at a time when I was ready for their message! What I enjoy in Fast is just his "unstylish" style. It has a biblical simplicity.'

But James Bond, at another point on the reading spectrum, did not spark any interest. He thanked me for introducing him to 007 but said: 'I fail to see what makes the books bestsellers; but perhaps it is because I haven't seen the pictures. There is a violent revolution taking place in European society, don't you think? With literature coming down from the head and skirts coming up from the knees.'

It turned out that I did not, after all, need an operation so I had a few weeks of rest in a luxury private room in hospital, with excellent meals, kind nurses and many visitors. 'Somehow,' I wrote, 'I feel the food I am getting now is even better than what you eat.' But also: 'Lying here, with friends with me a great deal of the time I have thought back to when you had your operation earlier this year, and how lonely and cut-off you must have felt. Those in whose care you were, were hardly close and dear to you.'

Once out of hospital, I reported to him that I was into a programme of exercises and was again enjoying horse-riding but was finding karate painful and had already suffered a cracked rib. He envied the riding because he had never gone beyond a donkey bareback, he wrote; but my karate experience tallied with his own:

'It got so that I became worried if there were no part of my body aching.'

Quiet encouragement was always forthcoming. I lost the first stage of my action in court for defamation against the government prosecutor Yutar, and Sobukwe sent his regrets: 'I should have enjoyed squandering his millions!' Another time he wrote: 'How's Jenny getting on. You've been rather quiet of late. Don't let *Current Affairs* get you down'—which was to let me know that he was listening to the government's daily propaganda commentary on radio, *Current Affairs*, which repeatedly banged away at the *Rand Daily Mail* and/or Laurence Gandar and/or me.

One of the big personal events of the year was Veronica's fortieth birthday. Nearly two months before the occasion Sobukwe wrote: 'I should like her to know that she is highly appreciated', and asked that I arrange a present from him and the children. We had an exchange of telegrams and he approved my suggestion of a tea service, later commenting in a letter: 'Will use the set when we are entertaining at some future date.' Miliswa, in Lesotho, was also brought into the conspiracy. It all went well and I was able to report to him the day after the birthday that I had delivered colourful sweet pea flowers as a gift from him, an English bone china tea service from the family, a leather handbag from me, and a box of soaps from my girlfriend. But we had overlooked a note so I had done one in my neatest possible handwriting: 'To a wife and mother, for your courage and devotion.'

The words summed it up. With all the strains and the lack of knowledge about the future, Veronica went on doggedly.

She visited the island about five weeks after the birthday celebration and, reported Sobukwe, my message had been 'most appropriate'. She 'was thrilled and arrived here still walking on air. We had a very lovely time together and she laughed just a little more often and more loudly than she usually does.'

In a rare intimate reference to her he said: 'She is very reticent, of course, perhaps typically African. But she is thawing, Benjie, she is thawing. I am, of course, typically non-African (but oh! tell it not in Gath!). I grew up in an environment where African women (my "African" as you know includes so-called "coloureds"), young and old, felt quite at liberty to pick up any child they met in the street, dangle it in the air, plant a resounding kiss on its lips and let it go its way. I have never thought, consequently, that strength of character and dignity cannot be found apart from a grim, unsmiling visage.'

His own emotional tribute, ignoring the eyes that would be reading it, went to Veronica in a letter to her at that time:

> This is the one time that I am indeed grieved that I am not around to express my thanks to and appreciation of you as a wife and mother. I have said it before and I repeat it boldly and gratefully that you are a chosen among the chosen (*mokhethoa hara bakhoelhoa*).
>
> We have come a long way together Little Girl and we have watched each other grow and mature. And we have watched the children God has blessed us with grow. We occupied a building at Mofolo and we turned it into a home. You denied yourself a lot of luxuries and worked uncomplainingly to achieve this. The children and I thank you and bless you.
>
> You've been a widow now for over six years. But you have been father and mother both to our children and they have grown up like other children lacking nothing that you could give them.
>
> You've been regular in your visits to me throughout my years as a convict right up to the present day; ever dignified, calm and cool; ever uncomplaining, never whining. The children and I thank you and bless you.
>
> ... according to the calendar you'll be forty this year. But to me you will always remain the young girl I saw at Victoria hospital and at Fort Hare: the young wife with whom I dug out stones at Mofolo and created a lovely garden.
>
> You have had your share of sorrow. But it has not been in vain. You have discovered new and true friends in quarters that you did not expect. You have come to know yourself: to know what you can bear. And that is a great lesson to learn. Among the Xhosa, as you know, when men doubt each other, they go for a swim in the river so that they may see whether the other fellow has been through the Initiation School. It is a great thing to be able to say, 'I have been through it. I know what it is like.'
>
> I'll say more to you, personally, when we meet. My heart is full because I have come to know what a great woman you are—the true embodiment of African womanhood.

Benjamin Pogrund

Well darling I wish you a very happy birthday and I know that you will be spared to see many many more. I shall get myself a special cake for the occasion and will celebrate. I will do no work that day either physical or mental. I'll just celebrate.

On my side I was usually silent about woman friends—one factor was that I shrank from the exposure to the censors—but a passing reference in one letter led him to write in great glee: 'In your letter you let fall, most casually, the precious news that your girlfriend had given my wife a parcel of toilet soap. And here I had been, deceiving myself that you were living a monastic existence! But my wife whispered the name to me and I was as excited as a schoolboy. I know nothing about the lady in question except that I love her even *in absentia*. Congrats.' And he ended the letter with a flourish: 'Love to the ladies i.e. M. & J.' (M. was Margaret Marshall, president of the National Union of South African Students; through her efforts several cartons of books were shipped to him. She later emigrated to the US and achieved distinction as Chief Justice of Massachusetts.)

In a more serious vein he was excited when the study books began to arrive. The first eight heavyweight titles included *Medieval Thought: St Augustine to Ockham*; *The International Economy since 1850*; and *Capitalism, Socialism and Democracy*. 'You can't imagine how happy I was to receive these books,' he wrote. 'I felt like reading them all at once. I never dreamt I would come to enjoy Economics like this.' Later in the year, when *Economica* magazine was at long, long last allowed to reach him, he said that 'Some articles, while interesting, contain so much maths that they leave huge gaps in my understanding. When I have finished this course I'll have to settle down and learn the ABC of maths, physics and chemistry. Without these one's education is not complete these days.'

He wanted to know whether a book I had sent—*Writing with a Purpose*—was intended as a hint to him. No, I replied, there hadn't been any hidden motive but, now that he mentioned it, I had been wanting for some time to suggest that he have a stab at serious writing. 'I have for long wondered why we have not yet produced any great story about African existence,' I said. 'I am thinking of the African in the city; the amount of material exists on a vast scale, with every conceivable aspect of human suffering and emotion waiting to be set down on paper. There is of course Alan Paton's *Cry the Beloved Country*, which I admire intensely. But without, I hope, being racialistic, I have always been surprised at the lack of penetrative writing by Africans themselves. Zeke Mphahlele, Bloke Modisane and others have written on the subject, but none in my view comes anywhere near the power and insight which Paton displayed. Now how about you dashing off the "great South African novel"?

'I'm not being flippant about this: for a variety of highly complimentary reasons—with which I shall not embarrass you—I have always looked forward to your producing some outstanding fictional writing about people. I remember, when I first met you, that you told me that you wrote poetry. Are you still doing this, and if so, wouldn't you send some of your writing to me?

'There is another point, although I am not too certain whether this is the best time and place to raise the question. What about some autobiographical writing?'

He agreed that no African had produced a great social novel in South Africa. 'But I want to suggest to you, as a verifiable fact of history,' he continued, 'that an oppressed people or class have never produced great literature or art. When we read that such and such an artist was a peasant or worker, what in fact is meant is that he was of peasant or worker origin. He himself was no longer that. It is the middle class that idealises the worker or the peasant or that writes indignantly on his behalf. As Bernard Shaw says, "The worker is concerned with the drudgery of earning a living" and has no time to appreciate the nobility of character assigned to him. Marx spoke of the "stupidity" of the peasant. He, of course, belonged to the middle class.

'Do you know that at Fort Hare we loathed *Cry the Beloved Country*? The Rev Nxumalo typified for us the "Uncle Tom" mentality which we abhorred. In other words no one of us could ever have had such a character as a hero. And yet he is a typical missionary-school product. And Paton took him as he found him. What the oppressed produce is propaganda. If they attempt to be detached, they write superficially . . .

'As for me—well, perhaps I'll take your advice. But I'll never write an autobiography, Benjie. I think this form of writing is being overdone. Yes I wrote some poems and short stories, but they were in Xhosa. Remember I asked you what I could do when the late

Mosaka confiscated my manuscripts from his typist who was typing them during office hours. You wanted me to get Ernie to sue for their return. I recited some of them in jail and the natives were suitably impressed.'

His reply did not satisfy me. 'I don't class you, at the present time, as either a "peasant" or a "worker" (whatever other phrases others might use about you),' I argued. 'This is so whatever your origins in the past.' And, even after allowing for South African restrictions, I noted that there were many thousands of Africans who, despite their peasant or worker origin, had through education and economic advancement become middle class in their mode of living and outlook. This being so, that an oppressed people were too busy merely keeping their bodies together did not explain the lack of good writing.

His answer: 'With regard to my remarks about the social novel, I believe I expressed myself badly. The point is, Benjie, when we talk of European experiences, we talk in terms of class. Except for the great national struggles of the mid-nineteenth century, the dichotomy in Europe has been a class one. But in Africa, particularly, though I believe this goes for Asia too, to a large extent, class interests are either non-existent or irrelevant or muted. The oppression and the struggles are group oppression and group struggles. In Europe, when a member of the middle class wrote about the lower classes he was writing about a different people. In this country the dichotomy is a colour one. Class distinctions within the group are muted and perhaps even discouraged and emphasis is placed on the solidarity and unity of the group.

'Do you think that *Exodus* and *My Glorious Brothers* could have been written by Jews in Hitler's Germany? But your needling is just about getting under my skin and you may irritate me just enough to make me accept your challenge and write this novel if only to see whether and how far I can be truly honest as a writer.'

While this was under discussion he enjoyed the biography of another African leader, Nnamdi 'Zik' Azikiwe. Nell Marquard sent it to him and he wrote to me recalling how much he had admired the Nigerian leader and read his *West African Pilot* newspaper while at Fort Hare University College. 'At that time he could have united Nigeria solidly behind him and his NCNC party. But to do that he had to sever his tribal umbilical cord. He wasn't big enough to do that. George Padmore never forgave him for returning to the tribal fire. "There is a tide . . .".'

And remembering a report the previous year about black riots in the United States caused him to write: 'A number of businessmen in Harlem put up notices to the effect that they were one with the rioters. One notice read "We shall overcome!" I remember thinking, as I read the article, that these businessmen had probably never bothered about anything except making profits. Tomorrow they would be on the side of the police. I don't think climbers on to bandwagons are contemptible: they are pathetic. I have never despised anybody who cringes, Benjie. I have felt sorry for them. I never like to see anyone humiliated—not even by himself.'

A decade later, that attitude was to prove appropriate for South Africa too, as many white businessmen rushed for bandwagons in the aftermath of the mass resistance set off by the 1976 Soweto uprising; and even more so during the 1980s, when violence and threats of sanctions drove businessmen and others at home and abroad, who had cared little before, suddenly to discover a concern for black welfare.

As an admirer of Lyndon B. Johnson, Sobukwe was also unhappy about newspaper reports that Robert Kennedy was squaring up to challenge him for the US presidency in 1968. 'I'll be sorry if he does,' he wrote. 'I like Johnson. I don't think he is devious. I don't think he is very complex either. He isn't an intellectual, but then there are very few in the political field. His touch is very deft in domestic matters and I believe that if, in Vietnam, he had followed his own bent, if he had been true to himself, he would have chosen to negotiate right from the start. He has one outstanding virtue for which I like him. He feels. Some have said he is sentimental. And that is the man for me any day: A man who can be moved; a man who can feel anger; who can feel deep compassion. But above all a man who can weep in the presence of great sorrow and suffering.

'The tragedy of our day is the inability of politicians to read the signs of the times. In the twentieth century we are faced with a situation where "negotiating from strength" is an outmoded maxim—if it were ever valid! It has always been true, I think, and it is more so today, that the person who can afford to lose face is the strong person—provided he does so of his own free will. "Don't crowd me" is a very vivid English expression and it is more apt on the lips of the weak.

'After Nehru's death I wrote to a friend of mine that Shastri could achieve much more than Nehru because the latter's reputed brilliance was a handicap. If he had achieved a settlement of the Kashmir problem the Pakistanis would be looking for a catch all the time. It is a pleasure to submit to persuasion. But somehow it seems to be humiliating to be reduced to silence by Socratic logic.

'Of course, Kennedy stands a better chance to start negotiations with China and North Vietnam. He has not committed himself as Johnson has done. He would be able to withdraw American troops from Vietnam and win American support for the action. But what Americans term the "domino theory" would remain valid. We shouldn't kid ourselves. Cambodia, Thailand and the rest of the Archipelago would face communist bids for power. The most powerful state in Asia is China and she is communist. Co-existence will be on her terms, just as co-existence in Europe will be on Russia's terms and in America on the terms of the USA.

'Oh I could write pages on this, Benjie. But it wouldn't solve a thing. One thing, however, can be said about the USA and it is that she is not in Vietnam for any imperialist purposes. On that both friend and foe are agreed.'

While we meandered around the world in our letters, we avoided the domestic scene. Yet there were weighty events: the Defence and Aid Fund, which provided lawyers to defend the accused in political trials and helped their families, was proscribed. Banishment, house arrest, bannings and detention in solitary confinement went on apace. A new Civil Defence Act gave the government wider powers than the existing Public Safety Act to declare a state of emergency. Prosecutions were made easier of people who returned to the country after undergoing training in sabotage. The law against sabotage was extended to Namibia and it was also made clear that the full range of restrictions of the Suppression of Communism Act applied there—with retrospective effect to 1950.

Then, in September 1966, came the assassination of Prime Minister Verwoerd: he was stabbed to death in Parliament by a messenger, Demetrio Tsafendas. Verwoerd was about to make his first statement after winning a general election with a seventeen per cent swing to his Afrikaner Nationalists. It was the whitest election ever held because all the 1.8 million voters were whites except a bare 351 coloureds, the dwindling leftovers of previously enjoyed voting rights by coloureds in the province of Natal. After Verwoerd, Afrikaners maintained their tradition of choosing a strong, father-type leader and John Vorster became Prime Minister. His toughness and authoritarianism had paid off for him. P.C. Pelser, quiet and colourless in personality, succeeded him as Minister of Justice and Prisons.

Vorster immediately pledged himself to continued racial separate development—apartheid—for different colour groups. And within a few days he proved he meant it with the introduction in Parliament of the Improper Interference Bill, aimed at halting inter-racial co-operation in opposition politics. But protests were so widespread—even among Afrikaners, which was the significant aspect—that the government held back the law until the next year.

None of this was mentioned in letters to Sobukwe. What I did gingerly try to do was to convey a few bits of news. For example, I identified Josias Madzunya—banished to a remote area and apparently destitute—as 'that old friend of yours, the one with the thick beard who always wore a long overcoat'. He was pleased to have news of Madzunya and, reflecting forgiveness of the last-minute betrayal in March 1960, he noted: 'I have great respect for him.'

My last letter of the year to Sobukwe ended: 'I hope your celebration of Christmas will be fortifying your spirit, and I pray for your welfare in the New Year.' I did not know what else I could possibly say.

17

'Greetings', began the letter from a government official to Veronica Sobukwe in January, 1967. It advised her that she and the children could have five visits a week to Robben Island between 9 and 20 January—but that the government would not provide free transport, nor would it refund their rail fares from Johannesburg to Cape Town. At the end of the letter, 'Greetings' again.

This was a period when apartheid went even madder than usual and officials were under orders not to write to blacks as Dr, Mr, Mrs or Miss or to close off letters with 'Yours faithfully'. The instruction came from M.C. Botha, a stony-faced racial ideologue and former schoolteacher, who was the Minister of Bantu Administration and Development and thus applied the myriad laws and rules which controlled the lives of blacks. He was trying to resuscitate black tribalism as a counter to black nationalism: the 'Greetings' thing was claimed to be in line with tribal practice. More revealingly of the underlying racist motivation, officials were told not to shake hands with blacks; touching them was also held to be non-tribal.

But this was also one time that laughter destroyed a government manoeuvre. Botha's order was widely ridiculed and it became a joke for people of all colours to greet each other with hand upraised and the cry of '*Molo*', the Sesotho version of 'greetings'. Eventually, the government restored blacks to Mr and Mrs.

It was an unusual victory against a rampant government. On the apartheid front a major law of 1967 was the Physical Planning Act which gave the government power to freeze the number of black workers who could work in factories in the main urban areas and to decide whether new factories could be opened. This was yet another attempt to hold down the numbers of blacks in the cities. Race classification was once again tightened, especially for whites and coloureds: descent was now made the determining factor with people to be checked for 'appearance' and 'general acceptance'. Somehow, the Afrikaners never woke up to the mockery which their repeated changing of classification rules made of the racial purity they were seeking.

Black deprivation, and white indifference, continued as before. A study showed that 68 per cent of black families in Johannesburg had incomes below estimated minimum living levels. The education of blacks was as starved of money as ever: as the government was simultaneously promoting schoolgoing, at least in the lower standards, less was available for everyone. The South African Institute of Race Relations estimated that, at about this time, the annual expenditure per head of population for education was: whites R74.30; Asians R26.83; coloureds R17.71; blacks R2.39. It could hardly be otherwise with 77.27 per cent of the educational budget devoted to the whites, who made up less than 20 per cent of the population, and 8.9 per cent on blacks, who constituted 75 per cent. Nor did the discrimination end there, for black parents, unlike whites, also had to pay a monthly levy for education, plus pay school fees and buy most of the textbooks. Fewer than 1 per cent of black pupils completed their schooling. Any protests against the system led to swift expulsion.

In Johannesburg, Cape Town and Pietermaritzburg, evening schools for black adults were finally closed down. Government patience at their presence in 'white' areas had run out.

Vestiges of underground black opposition were attacked. Poqo members were brought to trial for offences in 1962 and 1963: fifteen were given the death sentence for killing a white storekeeper and black policemen. Other Poqo members charged with activities in 1963 included John Pokela: he was found guilty of attacking a police station in Kingwilliamstown and planning to kill people, as well as giving training in sabotage. He was jailed for thirteen years. In later years, Pokela would become President of the Pan-Africanist Congress.

African National Congress men, nearing the end of jail sentences, usually of two and a half years, imposed in 1963 and 1964 for belonging to the organisation, were brought to court again to face new charges based on the same period of time as the original offences. In these second trials, charges such as giving money to the

ANC and holding a meeting were deliberately split to ensure heavier jail sentences, of up to five years.

The Nationalists were, however, also facing a new threat—in South West Africa, now Namibia, the neighbouring territory administered by South Africa since 1915 and, after the First World War, under a League of Nations mandate. The government was defying a United Nations order to quit and now faced growing insurgency launched by Swapo, the South West Africa People's Organisation. So the government enacted the Terrorism Act, applying to both Namibia and South Africa. It was made retrospective to June 1962, when, said the government, 'terrorists' first began their training. The government's fears were given further impetus with the news, halfway through the year, that ANC and PAC sabotage teams had been trying to trek through Rhodesia to get to South Africa. They were halted, with many of them dying, by the Rhodesian security forces. One immediate result was that South African policemen were sent to fight in Rhodesia, in support of the Ian Smith government and to gain experience in bush warfare.

The Terrorism Act took South Africa into a new dimension of authoritarian rule. It became the major weapon used by the government against insurgency and to crush internal dissent. A 'terrorist' wasn't only someone who set off bombs and underwent insurgency training, but was defined as anyone who endangered law and order and whose actions resulted in, or could have resulted in, among others, intimidation, promoting 'general dislocation' or disturbances, 'crippling or prejudicing' any factory or industry, obstructing traffic, causing substantial financial loss to any person or the State, encouraging feelings of hostility between whites and others, or embarrassing the administration of the affairs of the State.

The net was cast so wide that no one could be sure of the lines which might be drawn in any prosecution in court. Accused people had the onus of proving that their actions had not infringed the law. So greater caution was vital in political behaviour and particularly for newspaper publication, where lawyers warned that news reports, letters to the editor, interviews, political columns and editorials could be construed as conspiring, procuring, inciting, aiding, or encouraging breaking the law. For anyone found guilty, a minimum five years' jailing was compulsory; the ultimate penalty was death.

How Can Man Die Better

The Terrorism Act allowed for almost untrammelled power: anyone could be detained and held incommunicado, indefinitely. This in turn made torture of suspects even easier than it already was—and was to lead to an increasing number of deaths in detention, the causes of most of which were mysterious only in that they were never officially laid at the door of the police.

In this climate there was no hope of Sobukwe's release. The Sobukwe Clause was re-enacted for another year. Justice Minister Pelser said he was convinced it was not in the public interest to free him. He also said that he had visited Sobukwe.

Years later, Sobukwe told me about that meeting: he said he liked Pelser, and thought him an 'unprejudiced human-being'. I protested: 'How could you have liked him? He is the man who was keeping you locked up on the island. He signed the detention orders.'

Sobukwe, a bit embarrassed but sticking to his guns, replied: 'No, keeping me there was a Cabinet decision. Pelser merely went along with it.'

I argued: 'But he belonged to the Cabinet. He earns his money and his big motor car and all his other perks by taking part in the Cabinet and applying Nationalist laws.'

There was no budging Sobukwe. He had met Pelser, liked him as a person, and would not badmouth him. It was an astonishing tolerance. I often wondered whether this was a strength or a weakness in Sobukwe.

While Sobukwe was on the island my own thoughts about Pelser were anything but charitable. At the end of 1966, deciding to try my luck with the new Minister, I wrote to him asking for a visit to Sobukwe. The reply was that I should apply to the Chief Magistrate in Cape Town. That was a charade. In theory the Chief Magistrate could decide who could visit; in practice it was highly improbable that he would lift a finger without the approval of the Security Police—whose recommendations would also, of course, be followed by the Minister of Justice. So, feeling foolish, I yet wrote a formal application to the Chief Magistrate—and promptly received the expected formal refusal. But I decided not to leave it at that and wrote to Pelser to express my 'very great disappointment and surprise'. Apart from the irritation of being sent round the bureaucratic bush there was again reason for alarm: Veronica's reports of her visits to Sobukwe and her apprehension about his health.

Benjamin Pogrund

After consulting Ernie Wentzel, I wrote a long and diplomatically worded letter in the hope of achieving concrete results. I reminded Pelser that, when Sobukwe was put on the island in 1963, Vorster said he 'will by no means be treated like a prisoner, but receive special treatment in respect of food, movement, using leisure hours, hours of rising and retiring, clothing, etc, and that he would 'be able to receive visitors weekly'. But, I pointed out, he was greatly restricted in the number of visitors. 'Had he been detained in any jail on the mainland it would be a normal occurrence for me, or any other friend, to call during official visiting hours and gain access to him. His detention on Robben Island means that a permit must first be obtained and in this way he is restricted in regard to visitors. As far as I know, the only people who have been permitted to see him during his nearly four years on the island, apart from myself and certain distinguished visitors, are his wife, his brother-in-law and his mother. For financial reasons, they can visit him only seldom.'

Surely Pelser would agree, I said, 'that the imposition of such hardship was not the intention when Mr Sobukwe was first transferred to Robben Island. His situation of virtual solitary confinement is having a serious deleterious effect on him, inevitable perhaps after the passage of so many years, in that he is literally forgetting how to speak properly. He is having, I understand, increasing difficulty in concentrating and in enunciating his thoughts.' Sobukwe was a close friend of many years' standing. I was concerned about him. Why couldn't I visit him?

I ended with a 'special plea' for his release: 'The Republic is secure and at peace ... He cannot, surely, be held responsible for any harmful political developments which may have occurred during the past four years; in this period he has been under close and constant guard, with little contact with the world.'

Seven weeks later, the reply came: no to everything.

At about the same time, several United Party Members of Parliament who visited Robben Island reported that they had seen Sobukwe and he was 'in good health but complaining of limited opportunities to see his family'. And in Britain, thirty-three peers cabled Pelser protesting against Sobukwe's continued detention. It 'cannot be reconciled with justice or humanity', said the cable whose signatories included Baroness Gaitskell, widow of the former leader of the Labour Party, Lord Soper, a leading Methodist, and Lord Brockway, founder of the Movement for Colonial Freedom.

How Can Man Die Better

Nothing helped. On 2 June, Pelser gave notice in Parliament of his intention to extend the Sobukwe Clause. Ten days later, when the clause was up for debate, he said he was convinced that it was not in the public interest to release Sobukwe. However, the complaints about lack of visiting rights had, after all, made an impression because Pelser also announced that Sobukwe's wife and children, in addition to their normal visits, would be able to live with him on the island twice a year for fourteen days at a time. 'I trust he and his family will appreciate this extraordinary concession,' said the Minister. 'We are not insensitive or indifferent to the detention of the man and try, as far as possible, to alleviate the inevitable. Further than I have gone now, I cannot go at this stage.'

Appreciate? Be grateful? It was difficult.

In any event, Veronica made swift use of the new ruling and for a few days became a voluntary prisoner inside the stockade. Sobukwe wrote to let me know that they used the new yellow-flowered sheets.

The information about Sobukwe's condition came from Veronica and was reinforced by Helen Suzman. She was allowed to travel to the island to see the political prisoners and she recalls going to Sobukwe's bungalow, escorted by the Officer Commanding and a few warders: 'It was the first time I had met Sobukwe. We shook hands and I said: "I'm Helen Suzman. How are you, Mr Sobukwe?" He replied: "I am forgetting how to speak." The reply startled me. I just looked at him. "Well, whom do I have to speak to?" he said.'

The meeting set off a thought in Sobukwe, and he wrote to me: 'Helen Suzman visited me here, as you know, and she greeted me with the words "I was with your friend, Benjie, yesterday". I was forcibly struck by the inadequacy if not incongruity of the term. I have friends, of course, of whom I am very fond, and high on the list are Mrs Marquard and Prof. Wellington. But I have long passed the stage of even thinking of you as a friend. I don't want to be sentimental about this. So I suggest that you and I stick to simple Bob and Benjie in our dealings with each other, in the same way as my biological brother, Charles, and I stick to our nicknames.'

I wept over those words. Then I wrote: 'I recall constantly the last times we were able to see each other, of the many hours when we ranged in our chats over every conceivable subject as though we had never not been seeing each other ... so often I berate myself for not doing more for you, and so often too I pray to God that I had the power to act effectively on your behalf. I feel a terrible pain within me about your situation. What more can I say than to agree with you that it should continue to be "Bob" and "Benjie"?'

Our letters were coming through far more rapidly at this stage. Whereas a Sobukwe letter dated 5 February reached me only on 4 March, his letter of 1 March arrived as quickly as 13 March—clearly because Helen Suzman had taken up the matter of the delay in his post. But with my life 'as chopped up as it has been recently', I apologised for not writing immediately; I had in fact written but, as I explained, the letter 'was so dismal in tone that I decided it would be unfair to inflict it on you so I tore it up. So, as you see, you are subjected to a double censorship!'

There were, however, some bright spots: 'You will have seen in the Press that there has been a rush of cases this week. Best of all, from my point of view, is the success I had which has given me new heart. If you lose solidly over a period of nearly two years and then suddenly win, it does something for you! In fact, I have been in a state best described as euphoria.'

I was referring to the Prisons cases which were popping in and out of courts all the time. The success now was against Percy Yutar: after losing the first stage of my defamation action against him the previous year, I went to the Appellate Division, the country's highest court, and won damages. Apart from giving me—and many others—great pleasure, the judgment established the useful legal precedent that a State prosecutor could not gratuitously drag the name of someone into a criminal trial and defame him, as Yutar had done to me.

It was improbable that the jail censors wouldn't understand what I was talking about. But I decided to give the letter a greater chance of getting through by being tactful in not mentioning the words Yutar or prisons.

There were other matters to convey to Sobukwe. My application for the re-issue of my passport had just been turned down again. My hopelessness about South Africa and working as a journalist in South Africa was deepening all the time. My jail informants were being prosecuted one by one but I was left dangling. There was an additional emotional overlay: an earlier relationship had started up again, but at a distance: she had left for Britain the previous year on a one-way exit permit.

She and I decided we wanted to be together and, probably, to marry. She was having a difficult time and urged me to join her as soon as possible. So I decided to give notice of my intention to leave the country—while accepting that my departure could be delayed if, as I wrote to Sobukwe, 'there are still responsibilities which I must face up to'. By that I meant that I would remain if I was to be prosecuted; otherwise I wanted out.

It was a tormented decision, knowing that I would have to leave behind Jenny, my parents, Bob and his family, and walk away from my commitment to helping to seek change in South Africa. 'When I recently conveyed my decision to your wife,' I wrote to him, 'her reaction of dismay pushed into the open all my own concealed fears and guilts. Yet it is a decision which I feel must be taken.'

An emotional exchange followed between us in which he was clearly speaking as much of himself as for me. The references to his own decisions in the past about the course of his life were clear to me: '. . . with regard to your intention to leave the country: I approve wholeheartedly,' he wrote. 'The only stumbling-block I am prepared to consider are personal ties: but true greatness, Benjie, lies in being able to sever those ties in pursuit of the Holy Grail . . .

'The dismay with which my wife received your news is quite understandable. She had come to lean very heavily on you regarding you as a restless younger brother who, unless watched very carefully, could be guilty of extreme extravagance on behalf of Bob and all his . . . My wife is not concerned about material assistance. You know her well enough to know that. She knows and I have told her that I have four brothers: my two biological brothers and you and Dennis Siwisa of Port Elizabeth.

'You have decades of fruitful labour before you, Benjie, and you must make your contribution. The intellect blossoms only in freedom.

'Whether you decide on the UK or the USA, academic life or the typewriter, I should like you to regard that as preparatory work for service to Africa. In fact, once you are settled down I might seriously consider sending the children to you.

'I have no anxieties, whatsoever. We shall meet.'

There was still a great deal of hesitancy within me about going abroad, I replied, but on balance I accepted it must be done. And: 'I most certainly do regard it as "preparatory work for service to Africa", as you put it. My greatest hope is to land up in a US university, where I will have the chance of broadening my knowledge of this continent through study and visits. I am too deeply emotionally involved with South Africa and with Africa as a whole to try to contemplate an existence separated from it. This is my existence ... I am part of this place—the broader Africa of which you are so acutely aware, and it is in the service of that Africa that I would wish to spend my life. Speaking to any other person I would feel that this was a melodramatic statement. I know that I need not have this reservation with you.'

In May, I again applied for a passport, was again refused so applied for an exit permit. I had permission to enter Britain, and booked a flight for late in June. Again I applied to Pelser to visit Sobukwe: 'You will appreciate our mutual desire to see each other, possibly for the last time for some years.' The answer was again no.

Planning to be in Cape Town with Jenny to say goodbye to my parents, I wrote to Sobukwe: 'We shall be thinking of you and will be living in Sea Point right across the bay from you. In fact, at 2 p.m. on 10 June, if you happen to look across at Signal Hill and you see two people standing there—among the houses at the bottom—and waving to you, you will know that it is us.' Jenny and I did exactly that at the appointed hour—even though it was only a game for her to wave to Uncle Bob, and symbolic for him. I had the idea from a newspaper report that Signal Hill was in direct line of sight of his quarters, even though at a distance; but he later explained that I had been misled by 'imaginative reporters'.

In June, Sobukwe and I were finally pinning down the fate of books I had sent eighteen months earlier. It was now certain that the authorities had not allowed him to receive Weiss Rosmarin's *Judaism and Christianity—The Difference*; Epstein's *Judaism* (although he had received an earlier copy from me); and, even more incredibly, Lewisohn's *Selection of Jewish Short Stories*. It was impossible to work out how the official mind had decided that these were dangerous books. It was more laughable to find that at least six books—all militantly anti-communist—had also been seized. They included Carew's *Moscow is not my Mecca*—which was the story of an African student's experiences of racism in Moscow; Honey's *The Road to Vietnam*, and Appleton's *The Student Trap*.

He ended that letter with words which, all these years later, have been a prime motivation in writing this book: '... you are undoubtedly going to be quizzed about me. You knew me when I was a timid lecturer at the Wits in my early years. You know the pressures to which I was subjected and you saw me react to them. You were, yourself, a struggling, frequently frustrated beginner on the *Rand Daily Mail*. I saw you react to the pressures to which you were subjected. In other words, I am not a superman and it will be your task, more than anybody else's, to keep my proportions true. On my side, too, I'll keep yours true.

'A safe and pleasant journey, old man, and success attend your work.'

In giving him my address in London, I had added a nervous note: 'It is, of course, my hope that nothing untoward will occur to delay my departure. I imagine you will know of it should it occur.' It was justified. Some four days before I was booked to leave, two policemen came to my apartment late at night and served charges under the Prisons Act on me, thus pre-empting the exit permit application.

That also made history of a sort: it was the first time, as far as I knew, that an exit permit was not given as a matter of course (Sobukwe's earlier application had been turned down because he was a prisoner on Robben Island). Until this time, the government had been only too glad to give exit permits to any people denied a passport who could not stand being cooped up inside South Africa. It made no secret of its view that this was a convenient means of ridding itself of dissidents—so much so that, built into the law controlling passports, was a clause giving passportless people the positive right to an exit permit if they applied for one. So, after all, I had no choice but to remain in South Africa.

The first of what were to be many appearances in court followed, with a letter from Sobukwe several weeks later—delaying his post was back to what it had been: 'It appears that you will be around for quite a while, after all, as I assume that whatever the outcome the case will be taken on appeal. You know my feelings on the matter.'

I had given up my apartment and sold most of my furniture in expectation of leaving the country. My books and papers had been shipped abroad. Trying to get back to any normality was difficult and, in regard to Sobukwe, I was without the extensive files which I had established to keep track of his affairs and letters.

But no filing system was needed to attend to his request about his three sons. He was a strict traditionalist. 'At a later stage they will have to undergo, like me, the *rite de passage* of circumcision,' he told me, referring to the Xhosa tribal ceremony whereby manhood is attained, with young men undergoing a ceremonial period in the bush including circumcision. The idea struck a natural chord in my Jewish breast, although I felt sorry for the boys having to endure circumcision in their teen years rather than Judaism's ten days or so after birth. Sobukwe was alive to the trauma and went on: 'But I shall feel happier if the surgical operation is done now while they are young, under hygienic conditions—unlike with me! You will have to overcome Veronica's objections. I am going to tell her I have given you those instructions.'

And so the male plot was carried out. I arranged for a surgeon, and the jobs were swiftly done.

Despite having to attend to this instruction, my relationship with Veronica grew closer. It began with the fact of my profound admiration for her. She was inflexibly dedicated to her husband's interests. She wrote again to Vorster as Prime Minister but he referred her to Pelser. He gave her an interview but her request for her husband's release was once more rejected. I wrote to Sobukwe: 'I need not again tell you, because you well know it, what a magnificent wife you have. Her quiet courage and strength is awe-inspiring.'

Occasionally there was a sudden glimpse into some of what she was suffering, as in Sobukwe's response to my suggestion of a set of tape recorders to extend communication between them: '... I would encourage the idea if it were somebody else,' he said. 'But she, who takes months to answer a letter, knowing that it would be weeks reaching me, would not be improved by a change in the medium of communication. The honest truth about Veronica is that she is undemonstrative by nature and upbringing. It must be hell for her to tell me that she loves me in letters she knows will be read by eyes other than mine. It is that knowledge that tempers my impatience and annoyance at her casual attitude to letters.'

He wanted me to meet his mother, who had a visit scheduled. But it proved impossible for me to be in Cape Town at the same time. Regretfully, we never did meet. I do not know whether, even if we had, we would have become friends. Perhaps the generation gap and the cultural divide would have been too great. Sobukwe, on his side, never met my parents—essentially because of geographical reasons for they lived in Cape Town. But had they met, there would have been a considerable divide between them too.

One bit of fun, at least for me and the children, was derived from the official prohibition on taking photographs of prisons. It was, and is, a serious offence under the Prisons Act. While on holiday in Cape Town, and with the children also there, I took them on an outing to the top of Table Mountain. A cable-car climbs steeply to the summit and, from that height of a few thousand feet, there is a glorious panoramic view around the mountain and the sea. On that summer's day, Robben Island was clearly visible in the shimmering ocean below. I carefully positioned the children for photographs so that the island was in the background, and sent the colour prints to Sobukwe. In such small ways was there very occasional satisfaction in beating the system.

He was excited about a set of records of music by Beethoven, Bach, Mozart and Haydn which the Wentzels and I sent. 'I never tire of the music of these fellows,' he wrote. 'Have you experienced this acute pain, a straining of the nerves of the heart, as Mozart piles music upon music? "Why is all lovely thought a pain?" asks Walter de la Mare.'

But he was not allowed to have a record of work by the American poet Carl Sandburg. As usual, no reason was given and the record simply disappeared.

At the purely practical level I noted my 'sense of triumph' in finally wheedling his clothing needs out of him. This was the shopping list he sent: 3 pairs of pyjamas, size 42, dark preferably; 3 shirts, 16½; 2 pairs coloured or striped sheets; 1 pair Huskie shoes, 9½; 1 khaki shirt and trousers 5½; 1 slop pail; 1 balaclava cap, black or grey, 7¼. And I gravely acknowledged the list: 'I shall try not to go too mad in the choice of colours and materials.' The sheets, we later agreed, should be winter-weight, for as he explained: 'The previous winter sheets most certainly were a boon. Winter can be quite nasty out here.'

By this stage my judgement about his clothing was fully accepted. He sent trousers to be altered—he had lost weight—and left it to me to get others for him too: 'I have confidence in your taste,' he said. And on another occasion: 'It amuses me the regularity with which you disregard my instructions completely and buy clothes of your own choice which, invariably, appeal more to me than my own choice had done. I say it amuses me because if you were that type of person, you could claim, as many do, that you know better than I what is good for me.'

A new overcoat was welcomed because he said that, when his sister-in-law had visited, she 'had very uncomplimentary things to say about my overcoat. It was unfashionably long she thought.' The sister-in-law was Veronica's sister, Florence, who was married to Dr Fabian Ribeiro and lived in the Mamelodi ghetto near Pretoria. Many years later, on 1 December 1986, husband and wife were shot to death at their home. Suspicions were openly expressed that it was the work of official assassins. As always in such killings, no one was prosecuted.

Emboldened by Sobukwe actually expressing his wants, I enthusiastically suggested a few ideas for his 'greater comfort' ... what about occupational-type activities such as a painting kit, or carpentry or tapestry work? what about sounding out the authorities to see if they would allow a 16 mm film projector so that two films a weekend could be sent in? what about brightening his quarters with a few paintings, a bedspread or a small carpet?

He gently brought me down to earth. He hadn't ever had time to develop hobbies, but he was a card fan whose 'plebeian' tastes ran to the game of patience. The 'occupational therapy' items, he felt, should be left until the next year when he had completed his examinations: 'It requires a great effort, as it is, to concentrate on the lectures and I am afraid that if I had something more interesting to do I might neglect my work.' The film projector was out—even if the authorities approved the principle, which he doubted, there would be constant censorship of the films—'And, I am afraid, some humiliating experiences would be unavoidable.'

He said he needed replacements, not additions, for his quarters. The radio was giving trouble, and the plastic chair was uncomfortable on the neck. He would like to have his own bedspread but a small carpet was not necessary as he had a felt mat for his feet. Nor did he want pictures: 'You see, all these, after a time, become part of the environment. And it is a jail environment. And there is something in me which does not wish to forget that either.'

Eulalie Stott again provided a new chair—which proved to be so good that Sobukwe said he wouldn't take it to sit under the tree outside: 'It belongs in a polished lounge.' A new radio was sent in with the agreement of the prison authorities and after yet another exchange of telegrams. It was FM and medium-wave only so that he would not be able to listen to foreign broadcasts.

As always, books were going to him in large batches of up to several dozen at a time, from a history of Germany and another of Russia, both of which he found 'delightful reading', to *Sophocles the*

How Can Man Die Better

Dramatist, Letters from Jack London, and Mayakovsky. As a Christmas gift from the Wentzels, there was Koestler's then newly published *The Act of Creation*—which for the usual unknown reasons was handed to him only several months later. Books were also coming from friends abroad and from Nell Marquard. He was now on first-name terms with her: 'I am very happy about that because though we have never met I've grown very fond of her.'

By mid-year it had got too much and there was an urgent plea from him: 'My shelves are bursting at the seams—so don't send any more at this stage.' As if to relieve him, the prison authorities failed to give him about three dozen books I sent from my own library: a series of letters to them over many months failed to draw any explanation.

He also warned me against sending the literary supplements from the London *Sunday Times*, with their mixture of serialisation of major new books, such as Manchester's study of John F. Kennedy, new book reviews and reports on the arts: 'It is a "foreign" newspaper and foreign newspapers are forbidden, irrespective, I believe, of their contents.'

Sobukwe dropped a religious bombshell during the course of a renewed discussion about the German theologian Dietrich Bonhoeffer. He had read all Bonhoeffer's published works, he wrote. Bonhoeffer's writing had influenced Britain's Bishop of Woolwich, whose book, *Honest to God*, had rocked the Christian church.

'You'll be shocked to learn and so will many of my friends that these authorities and others of their school have forced me to face the fact that I am not a Christian and do not desire to be one.'

It was a shock. I knew that he was intensely hurt by the failure of the churches, his own and others, to minister to him, but I thought that he was still drawing spiritual sustenance from his religious beliefs. He had told me about his disillusionment with clergymen when I saw him on the island during 1964 when he spoke so warmly about his friendship in Pretoria prison with Father Webber of the Roman Catholic Church. Sobukwe's status as the country's leading political prisoner apparently frightened off the local clergy, who dealt with the island's prisoners. They were part-time chaplains, with the exception of the Dutch Reformed Church minister, who attended chiefly to the white warders. The chaplains, apart from an occasional contact, stayed away from him. I was disgusted and took up the matter with Eulalie Stott: breathing fire and brimstone, she went to see the Anglican minister of a city church, and asked him to visit Sobukwe. But it was to no avail: he said it would be a burden because he suffered from seasickness.

Late in 1965, the position changed after the Methodist Church appointed the Rev Theo Kotze, its minister in Sea Point, as part-time chaplain for Robben Island. Kotze, a white, was an exceptional minister, well known for his public speaking out against government policies, and a man of warmth and compassion. It was surprising that the Department of Prisons accepted him as a chaplain; it must have been a mistake.

But having the job, Kotze set about doing his best to 'minister spiritually' to Methodist prisoners as his official letter of appointment required him to do. He was also—it was a specified 'duty'—determined to find out from the jail register the names of prisoners of his denomination. 'I had great difficulty in discovering this information,' he recalls. 'On my first visit, without any opportunity of access to registers, I was marched under escort through the main building into a large barrack square with its typical barbed wire fence and watchtowers with armed guards keeping constant vigilance. In the middle of the square was a hall where about a hundred prisoners, of course under armed guard, were gathered. After the service, I was not given the opportunity of greeting anyone. I was taken to lunch in the officers' mess, and seated at a solitary table. After that I was escorted back to the ferry. On subsequent visits I simply went ahead and did my own thing.'

On each of his monthly visits Kotze pushed for access to the register. Knowing that Sobukwe—and also Nelson Mandela, who was by then with the political prisoners on the island—were Methodists, he specifically asked to see them. In about January 1966 he finally succeeded in getting to Sobukwe—but was accompanied by a senior prisons officer during the visit of twenty to thirty minutes.

'As this was the first time we had met, Robert obviously greeted me with some reservation, but on the other hand he did know about me and obviously knew where I stood,' says Kotze.

He saw Sobukwe about three times after that, until August, when the Prisons Department cancelled his appointment as a chaplain. The Methodist Church demanded an explanation and had a rambling reply which said 'techniques and methods of treatment that are often crowned with success in free life often fail in prisons' and that 'religious workers, as human beings, may also sometimes fail to conform with the Department's views on the correct approach to prisoners . . .' Kotze suspected that the objections to him included his habit of shaking hands with prisoners and inquiring after their health; from his standpoint he was not meeting prisoners but human-beings, and behaved accordingly.

During the short time he spent with Sobukwe, 'we established a bond of friendship which in later years developed into a very deep relationship, certainly one of the most precious of my life,' he says. He remembers one incident in particular, on what proved to be his last visit: 'In all the time Robert had been on the island, no one had given him Holy Communion. I discussed this with him and he requested that, on my next visit, I should share this Sacrament with him. Every visit or interview with any person was always in the presence of an officer with at least the rank of captain, so picture a scene in Robert's tiny cottage with him, the captain and me:

'It is the custom in the Methodist Church to invite all those "who sincerely love our Lord" of whatever denomination to partake of Holy Communion. I asked the captain if he was a Christian, to which he made an emphatic affirmative reply and I therefore invited him to join us in the Communion. He refused to do so, but when Robert and I knelt at a little wooden stool to share the elements of bread and wine, the captain came and stood over us. Obviously he was suspicious that I might pass a surreptitious message or something. It was an extraordinary feeling, I should think not unlike the early Christian experiences in the catacombs of Rome.'

But, with Kotze denied access, his successor—the Rev Francis MacCreath—wreaked great harm to Sobukwe's beliefs. For Mac-Creath had a rigid fundamentalist attitude which would cause him to view Sobukwe as a 'sinner'. On his first visit he lectured Sobukwe, saying he deserved to be where he was. Sobukwe refused to see MacCreath again.

Nor in fact did he wish to see any Christian ministers at all. He wrote a formal letter to the commanding officer that he did not wish to have any 'priests or padres' visit him, at least in their official capacities. But there was some embarrassment in this because in the afternoon of that same day, only a few hours after writing the letter, his eldest brother, Ernest—then an Anglican priest—unexpectedly came on a visit. In the circumstances, it must have been a rather strained meeting for Sobukwe wrote to me afterwards: 'He is a very good man, but has always had certain prejudices and biases that I do not share. He thinks I am annoyingly stubborn.'

Veronica, too, was not pleased about his change in outlook. Not long after, she stayed in Cape Town with an Anglican priest, Father Clive McBride, who said Mass for her before she went off for an interview with Pelser. 'As usual she is being rather perverse,' Sobukwe wrote. 'All these years she's been a rather indifferent Anglican and a more indifferent Christian. But now, because I abjure this faith, she's beginning to swear by it.'

It was against this background and the reading he was doing that, not much more than six months after taking Holy Communion, Sobukwe severed his emotional and physical links with the Church. He wrote that his break with Christianity was 'fundamentally doctrinal'—'Even if everybody around me were to live a truly Christian life, I still would reject Christianity. And after sober reflection, Benjie, I don't think you should be bewildered. After all, we are Christians because we were subjugated by Europeans, whose cultural religion Christianity is. If we had been subjugated by Turks we would be fanatical Mohammedans as are eighty million Africans on the continent. Similarly, if Indians had subjugated us we would be fanatical Hindus. There is nothing inevitable, therefore, in our being Christians.

'In South Africa, hardly a quarter of our people are Christians, in spite of the fact that, as in Nigeria, it is those who professed Christianity who got the most lucrative jobs. They were the "good boys"—trustworthy, obedient and loyal.'

He said he agreed with what I had written to him about Bonhoeffer: that, after initially placing Bonhoeffer on a pedestal high above other mortals I had come to see him as a very simple, ordinary man who stood up for basic beliefs, and who lived, and died, for them simply and sincerely. It was a disappointing thing to have to accept, I thought, because one liked to see one's heroes cast in a giant mould. I also realised that his writings presented a challenge to faith: to have believed so implicitly and yet to what end? Nor was I certain that his opposition to Nazism was all that clear or effective: I rather suspected that this aspect of him had become inflated; the opposition to Hitler which developed in the 1940s was motivated by feelings and drives which, in a way, had been responsible for bringing the evil originally to power.

Yes, said Sobukwe, in the early years of Hitler, Bonhoeffer like many others was impressed by the dramatic change that came over Germany. Many church leaders admired the appeal of Nazism 'to the best in German youth'. They applauded a movement that made so much of purity.

'Two days after Hitler's assumption of power Bonhoeffer spoke against the "leadership principle". But his sermon was academic. He did not seek a clash with Hitler. He was pushed into it . . . It is not at the beginning, then, that his greatness lies but at the end, as with Churchill.'

Bonhoeffer, he went on, said Christians had made of God a *deus ex machina*, a God of the gaps, to explain whatever men's reason and experiment could not. With the increase in scientific knowledge, God's sphere had decreased. Bonhoeffer did not define God nor did he question the Christ doctrine. It was the legalistic, tradition-encrusted Christianity that he rebelled against. Bishop John Robinson in *Honest to God* went further: he said there was no God 'up there', but that God was the 'depth of our Being'. He too did not question the Christ doctrine; he questioned traditional interpretations of Christianity.

'Now I've been brought up in a home where to even think of questioning anything in the Bible is scored up as a success for Satan. I've suppressed all questioning. "Believe!" I've told myself. And when I found these theological minds asking the questions I've always wanted to ask, I applied my intelligence and found that they, too, were skirting the problem. They feared their own conclusions.

'Central to the Christian doctrine is acceptance of Jesus Christ alone as saviour of the world. No one who rejects Christ as his personal saviour can be saved. Now, whatever its origins, Christianity today is the religion of Europe. So to me, an African, this statement means that only Europeans, whose religion Christianity is, and those of other nations who are the "spiritual assimilados" of the Europeans qualify for salvation. I reject that.

'In the light of present-day knowledge I cannot accept the story of the ascension.'

All that the critics of Robinson had said was that he caricatured Christianity, said Sobukwe. Not one critic had refuted any point he made. Christianity still had to say, unequivocally, in public: Is God a being? When we say Jesus Christ is the son of God, what do we mean? Do Christians believe in a geographical heaven from which Christ came and to which he returned? Do they believe he physically ascended through the atmosphere and stratosphere against the pull of gravity?

He ended: 'Do I believe in God? I don't know. Robinson quotes Tillich with approval as saying: "The name of this infinite and inexhaustible ground of history is God" and that belief in God is a matter of "what you take seriously without any reservation, of what for you is ultimate reality". How many Gods does such a definition not permit? So much for that.'

Our discussion died out, but not before a mention from him that he was 'reading Stephen Neill's history of the Christian church—"red in tooth and claw", bearing out Epstein's contention that Christianity, unlike Judaism, has been spread by the sword and not by the pure strength of its message.' And towards the end of the year there was a terse reminder of his outlook when he wrote: 'Please don't send me any Christmas card.'

On the world scene, he believed, after the end of the Middle East war of 1967, that 'vicarious Israeli heroes are individually and severally telling us what lessons are to be drawn from the conflict. Unfortunately, the lessons are merely a rationalisation of prejudices. I would have felt happier if Levi Eshkol [Israel's Prime Minister] didn't have a Dayan [Moshe Dayan] to put up with. As one correspondent has said, Dayan is no Churchill. I am afraid he is allowing the ululations of the vicarious heroes to go to his head. And yet the touch that is needed is the toning down of the humiliation under which the Arabs smart. Somebody has said a man will forgive you, after some time, for defrauding him or even taking his wife away from him but no man will forget or forgive a humiliation. Eshkol has the personality and the ability, I think, to wash his enemies' wounds.'

Israel's stunning victory and its capture of vast amounts of tanks and other war material led me to send him some of the jokes doing the rounds—such as Egypt's Nasser phoning the Soviet Union's Kosygin, asking for 200 tanks and being told: 'Look, if Eshkol wants tanks, let him phone me direct.' At the political level, I reflected the intense Jewish pride of the time when I wrote about the profound effects which events were having on Jewish behaviour; writing long before reading books by Primo Levi and benefiting from his insights into why people in ghettos and concentration camps behaved as they did, I said: 'The 2,000 years of being quietly led to extermination are past. Today, among Jewish youth, there is almost anger—in fact, it is anger—at the six million who went without a fight to their deaths. The real original turning point, I suppose, came with the uprising in the Warsaw Ghetto and it has reached its climax in modern Israel and more particularly in the recent war.'

My chauvinism drew reproof. 'You are an intellectual,' he replied. 'And that imposes upon you the obligation not only to think but also to carry about with you an awareness of history ... What you young fellows must remember is that the Jews that Hitler murdered were citizens of Nationalist Socialist Germany. A new Hitler with an equivalent military power could do the same thing today AND GET AWAY WITH IT! Israel couldn't save them: nor could UNO. Why didn't they resist? Hardly a tenth of the population and facing the most efficient and scientific tyranny the world had ever produced!

'And was the Warsaw Ghetto's resistance so unusual? It was remarkable, yes; but unusual? Jewish military strategy has always been suicidal in its recklessness, from the time of David to the Maccabees. As for resistance to the last man, woman and child you have the recent excavations at Herod's temple ...

'Now for the point I made about peace. In the American Civil War it is recorded that Grant treated Lee when he came to surrender, as though he were his superior officer. When he left the hall, Grant and his men saluted. Quite recently, in a boxing championship in Britain, the Scottish champion McGowan was forced to retire because of a badly cut eye. The defending champion, an Asian, who was defeating McGowan for the second time, went to McGowan's corner—and they say McGowan was in tears—and knelt before him. The grand gesture, Benjie.

'A further illustration. Moshoeshoe 1 (nineteenth-century King of the Basuto), when attacked by the Zulus, inflicted a crushing defeat on them at Thaba Bosiu and, as they retreated, sent a large herd of cattle to "his brothers". The Zulus never again attacked him. He cut the English forces to ribbons in 1859 and while Warden, the British Commander [in fact, Cathcart in 1852], was in a state of bewilderment and humiliation, sued for peace! I am not saying Israel should be "magnanimous". If I were Nasser I would want no magnanimity from the Jews. All I am saying is that it is Eshkol and not Nasser who can afford a diplomatic rebuff, it is "adulations" that might go to Dayan's head, not "ululations". I love the sound of the latter though!'

Then Sobukwe set out an unusual pan-Africanist line of thought: 'It had been my intention in 1959 to have Egypt and the "Arab north" taxed with the direction of their loyalty,' he wrote. 'Are they African or Arab? If they are Africans then the Middle East problem is not theirs except in so far as Egyptian territory is concerned. Algeria, Morocco and Tunis have no reason whatever to be involved. I have asked myself whether that would be my attitude regarding the Afro-Americans and the West Indians and I can honestly say "yes". As soon as Hitler saw himself as the guardian of Germans anywhere and everywhere he chose the path of war for he was bound to find it irksome that Germans anywhere should be under non-German rule.'

While making these comments he was pushing himself to study for his examinations. The required fees for the University of London were paid to the British Embassy in Pretoria and arrangements were again made for him to write the examinations on Robben Island. Was he managing to study? I wanted to know. To which he replied: 'Yes I am still finding it difficult to concentrate; and I expect the trouble to get worse, not better. It is unavoidable in the circumstances, I think.'

I was struck, as I so often was, by the absence of self-pity.

He was saddened by the death of Patrick Duncan. After Duncan's role as a Liberal in the Pan-Africanist Congress' positive action in Cape Town in 1960, his newspaper, *Contact*, was banned for a time and later he was himself banned and restricted. He escaped to Basutoland, and from there travelled north. He made history by being the first white to apply for membership of the PAC. He was accepted and was sent to the organisation's office in Algeria.

'It was very painful for me to read about Pat's death,' Sobukwe told me. 'I hadn't known, you see, that he was ill.' A few months later he wrote again about Duncan, expressing what I thought was an eloquent epitaph: 'Strange as it may sound, Pat was the first man, after PAC was founded, to accuse me of racialism! Came up to the Wits to tell me I was a racialist and he would fight me. I spent a whole afternoon trying to persuade him I was not a racist. He was very honest. I liked him.'

A year after I had first challenged Sobukwe to get into serious writing, he suddenly revealed that he had been working, on and off, on Xhosa short stories and poems and on an 'unambitious' English novelette. He thought the novelette 'has beautiful descriptive passages and I think its chief characteristic is the conveyance of smell. Its defect is that the story does not hang together. I shall have to work longer and harder on that aspect. I am quite certain you would love it.'

However, he found he could not translate the Xhosa stories, and suggested that he should send them to me to be translated by Mrs Bernard Friedman, wife of a noted former liberal Member of Parliament, who could render it into 'the most delightful English'. She and he had done a few Xhosa and Zulu poems together.

Unfortunately, he did not send any of this to me; or if he did, none of it got through. When he eventually left Robben Island, the authorities would not allow him to take any of his writings with him.

But one poem came through in a letter. He said he had read it to Veronica during a visit, 'but dammit, she's puritan! . . . She thought it was not "nice". I ask you!'

Truth to tell, I also found it rather odd. This is the poem:

They all say so

I'm not going to keep quiet
I'm going to tell you what you are:
Oh you can beat me, to your heart's content.
You're very brave when it is women you face.

I've been holding my peace too long
I must speak or I'll burst.
The water in which
The midwife washed you at your birth,
Was a whore's water.

Don't promise me; hit me;
Your scowl doesn't scare me this bit.
What's that? That's your mother!
Yes I say so; I say that's your mother.
I was a virgin, me, boy,

Benjamin Pogrund

When I met you
'They all say so?'
I am not concerned
With what others say.
I . . . What's that?
'My breasts had already fallen?'
I have a high bust, that's what I have.
But as for carnal knowledge of a man
That I acquired when I met you.
What is it you say? You're insulting me!
You are going to produce the woman
Who helped me to procure abortions.
'It's my mother?' You say it's my mother
Who has removed my stomachs? (procured abortions)
Oh no you've gone too far today.
My father's house is intact, you know;
The roof does not leak.
What's that? 'I shouldn't come back
I shouldn't come back
Until my manners have improved?'
Sis! Look who's talking!
I beg your pardon? I don't hear:
Bah! That doesn't disturb me
You can collect all your whores
And accommodate them here:
But all this is mine
I am taking away with me.
You will lie on the bare ground
For you do not have a mat even;
O! Is that what you say!
'You're going to change us,
Trade us in like motor cars?'
I'm going to stay; just for that reason;
This gall that you have
I'm going to empty you of it!

18

As 1967 drew to a close, Sobukwe was looking forward to Veronica and the children spending fourteen days with him. It led to a crazy episode. He wrote to me to say he had asked Veronica to bring him hard cheese and honey—'And I wonder what typical Jewish dish you could prepare for me. It will form part of their provisions.'

I chose a *kitke*, also known as *challah*—a plaited bread associated with the Sabbath—plus a kosher polony, chicken fat (to be spread on the bread in eating the polony), pickled cucumbers, a jar of rollmop herrings and a cheesecake. In other words, Jewish soul food. I was on holiday in Cape Town and was to meet Veronica when she arrived by train from Johannesburg and to give her the parcel. But the arrangement went awry so, in late-afternoon, I rushed to the ferryboat quay in the docks and persuaded the bemused warders on duty to accept most of these Jewish foods on behalf of their prize prisoner. It was too late to send the parcel over to the island that day but they promised they would put the polony in a refrigerator overnight.

Sadly, the polony never reached him. Whether the half-metre-long dark-red sausage raised official suspicions and it was cut to pieces, or whether it was devoured by hungry warders, I never discovered. But in due course Sobukwe reported to me: '... as I had had no instructions I ate the bread first and found it absolutely delicious. But the fish! I finished it out of loyalty to you.' I replied to express my disappointment: 'Imagine a nice Jewish boy not liking rollmops ... One day you will have to try the non-bottled variety and see if it is more to your taste.'

He was happy and relaxed after having the family with him. I liked the twinkle in his letter when he said: 'I've looked all over for your last letter but can't find it. I remember that Veronica read it as she read all your other letters to me. It's just possible that she put it in some other place. That's the price one has to pay for company.'

The children took toys with them, given for Christmas by wellwishers, and Sobukwe played badminton with them, and also introduced them to tennis, inasmuch as he could do so inside the stockade. He put aside a car rally game because of the lack of glue and said he would assemble it when his examinations were over later in the year.

But one result of his close contact with the children was increased anxiety about their education. Months before, I had written to him that I was worried they were not learning enough English and I was trying to arrange special tuition for them. 'Whatever steps you take to improve their command of the language will meet with my approval,' he replied. In the circumstances, I believe, all one can hope for, in the immediate future that is, is greater fluency even if the accent remains a "separate development" accent.'

He was delighted with Miliswa's willowy gracefulness, saying she 'is growing into a glorious Watusi woman.' When she wrote to him in English and asked him to let her continue to write in English, he remembered his own background: 'Times have changed, of course, and I do not offer it as an excuse, but believe me, she writes much better English than I did when I was in Standard 4. Admittedly I was much younger. I was eleven then.'

But now, after a fortnight with the children, he felt frustrated at his inability to help: 'It was the first time I could talk to the children without feeling rushed and I found myself sharing your concern: they are almost completely inarticulate in English ... I tried to drill them in a few of the vowel sounds but I soon realised the hopelessness of the task. For a whole year they pronounce "bird" as "bed" and what possible hope can I have to correct that in a fortnight?

'It appears also that their teachers complain that they are weak in Arithmetic. I made a few tentative moves but as I do not know what methods are being pursued by their teachers, here, too, I retreated. We played plenty of scrabble, though, and at least here I had the pleasure of seeing them use their heads.'

This letter was held by the authorities for several weeks and reached me on 4 March—and its references to newspaper subscriptions and a heater brought realisation that his letters were again being seized. His letters written on 23 November and 14 December had not got through. Veronica and I were able to reconstruct some of his urgent needs—the heater, repairs to the record player and two pairs of trousers, to be suitably altered to meet a loss in weight and his 'paunchless state'. Telegrams went back and forth as to whether bar heaters, which were cheaper, provided enough warmth, or whether he needed fan heaters. We settled on one of each, and Eulalie Stott rushed through buying and delivering. Thoroughly irritated, I once more wrote to the Officer Commanding to ask that letters not be withheld and delayed—and asking, again, what had happened to the carton of books I had sent to Sobukwe ten months before. 'I wish to inform you that the matter will receive the necessary attention,' was all the reply that came. Nor was there improvement.

Only in mid-May, when it was too late to do anything about it, did I discover that Sobukwe had wanted copies of previous examination papers, and for his studies, a pamphlet about Britain's Department of Economic Affairs and an article by Douglas Jay on the European Common Market.

As May came and with it the approach of a sixth year on Robben Island, it was clear to me that he had no illusions and no hopes: he accepted that he was to be in jail indefinitely. Mentioning his need for heaters he was speaking about having 'to space my "requisitions" over the year in future'; he also suggested sending me his toiletry and washing needs so that I could supply enough for a year in advance. Instead of using his slender funds kept in the prisons account for these items, as he was doing, he wanted the money 'for luxuries like cheese, peanuts, sweets, etc.' A year's supply went to him, from washing powders, steel wool and scouring powders to blades, toothpaste, deodorant, toothbrushes and shoe polish. In April, he was writing to me that, as soon as his university examinations were over the next month, he intended to resume work on Xhosa poems and to start studying Dutch and Swahili.

On my side I was anguished about the absence of hope. Early in April I wrote: 'Bob, May is nearly upon us. Throughout the year you are in my prayers, but never more so than at this time. I pray for your speedy release, for you, Veronica and the children to continue to have strength, to have the courage you have shown for all these long years.'

On 12 June, Justice Minister Pelser confirmed in Parliament what we were already certain was going to happen. 'The man on the island', as he put it, was to remain there. In the ensuing debate on the law to extend the imprisonment, Pelser and other government spokesmen offered the by now familiar Nationalist litany: how much they hated keeping people in jail without trial, but that they would steel their hearts to do it for the sake of the nation's security. What they were getting at was that they knew Sobukwe had not changed in his thinking, or his commitment, and that they feared him.

It was within this context that Pelser's specific words were that Sobukwe's fate was 'not a matter to be decided by capricious decision one way or the other. I weighed the pros and cons very carefully before deciding what I should do. In the final result it was a matter of choosing between the interests of the country and those of an individual.' With the information at his disposal, he continued, he would have failed in his duty if he were to let the interests of the country give way to the strong humanitarian impulse to bring about a change in Sobukwe's fate. His conscience was at rest, he assured Parliament—'because I know that the powers that are seeking our downfall are gathering their forces to destroy us and are at this very moment assiduously looking for a star to give lustre to their nefarious schemes. The man concerned would, if he were given the opportunity, not hesitate to do everything in his power to make up and regain what he has lost during his time of detention because in his life and aspirations, he has in no way changed his attitude or his aims.'

Continually stressing that he was acting on information at his disposal—but without disclosing what it was—Pelser said he could not be expected to play into the hands of the enemies and to give them the opportunity to rally round the man whom they thought could unify them to bring about the downfall of South Africa.

In a re-run of previous years, total rejection came only from Helen Suzman. Sobukwe had not originally been sentenced for terrorism, treason or crimes against the State, she said. He had been sentenced to three years' imprisonment for incitement against the pass laws at a stage when the Pan-Africanist Congress was a lawful organisation and before it became violent. He was still suffering from the 'tragedy of Sharpeville', where it had not been his followers who opened fire, but the authorities.

On the Afrikaner Nationalists' major bogey about communism, Pelser had this to say: he had visited Sobukwe on the island and 'I shall not say he is a communist [but] he will incite people to commit the deeds of communism.' In another breath, he said it was well known that the PAC were the lackeys of communism.

A fellow-Nationalist, G.F. van L. Froneman, was more extravagant in his claims. He too had visited Sobukwe the previous year with other MPs, he said. In Sobukwe's quarters, he had seen books on communism and Marxism; he had asked Sobukwe about this and Sobukwe said that he liked reading Marxist literature—it was his ideology. Having expressed that improbability, Froneman reported a further slice of conversation which might perhaps actually have happened: 'Will you ever change your views?' he said he had asked, to which Sobukwe allegedly replied: 'Not until the day of resurrection.'

The mishmash of ignorance and smear shocked even the United Party. Mike Mitchell, who had been with Froneman on the island visit, said he had asked Sobukwe about the books of Marx and Engels on his bookcase: Sobukwe said he was studying economics.

Parliament duly rubber-stamped the enactment of the Sobukwe Clause for another year.

A few days later *The Star* newspaper in Johannesburg published a reader's letter. 'Puzzled' asked: How did the books on communism described by Froneman come into Sobukwe's possession 'when such literature is totally banned by the Nationalist government in South Africa?'

Sobukwe made the same scathing point with greater force in a letter to me. Whatever Froneman said had to be taken 'with a ladle of salt', he said. At no time had he been alone with Froneman during the visit. Whatever was said was said in the presence of five other MPs and the Commissioner of Prisons and there was no 'confession of Faith'. In any case, books on Marxism and Leninism were banned—'and if they can't get into the country, how, except in a James Bond film, can they get into Robben Island. It is you who sent me the books that examine communism and you know that they are all, WITHOUT EXCEPTION, anti-communist books on communism. Sorry to waste your time: but I resent the implied slur on the efficiency of the Security Branch!'

In speaking as they did in Parliament, both Pelser and Froneman showed how uninformed they were about Sobukwe. They didn't have the slightest insight into, for example, his view of communism. Yet this wasn't surprising: as whites and Afrikaners they had no understanding of the depth of black resentment, let alone the aspirations of African Nationalism; in their everyday lives they never dealt with blacks except as servants or, if they owned farms, as near-serfs. Mitchell and his United Party colleagues had the same emotional blinkers and lack of experience of personal contact with people who were black. The scene on Robben Island when that group of white Members of Parliament clustered around to gawk at Sobukwe and awkwardly to question him must have been rich in unconscious humour. He would have been only too aware of the nuances in the encounter and, in his nature, he would have played along with his visitors in the gentlest and kindest way.

Now, in mid-1968, the Afrikaner Nationalists had just marked twenty uninterrupted years in government. Led by Prime Minister John Vorster, they were more securely in office than ever, and were constantly enacting measures to ensure that they remained so. It was difficult to think of a time in the future when the Nationalists might not be in control. They were overbearing and menacing towards anyone who stood in their way.

But a number of strands were in place and were slowly unravelling, to have significant consequences in the years to come. Vorster was as dedicated as his immediate predecessor, Verwoerd, to the fundamentals of apartheid and in particular the concept of racial separate development; but even while holding to this he was beginning to move away from what was called 'petty apartheid'. Over the next decade he would do so at an accelerating pace because he believed that was the best way to protect the core of Afrikaner interests.

A major aim at this stage was what became known as the 'outward policy'—an attempt to make friends and establish diplomatic links with black-ruled states in Africa; another was the effort to gain the support of the country's English-speaking whites. These and other departures from Afrikaner orthodoxy created internal stresses which led to whites smearing and attacking each other with a bitterness usually reserved for dealing with their anti-apartheid opponents. The fashionable Afrikaans terms were *verligte*—the 'enlightened' ones who backed Vorster—and the *verkramptes*—the opposing 'conservatives'. A year later the divisions precipitated a split in the Nationalist Party and a breaking away of verkramptes led by a former Cabinet Minister, Dr Albert Hertzog.

How Can Man Die Better

But none of this diverted the Afrikaner Nationalist effort to ensure the purity of whites. The Mixed Marriages Act of 1949, one of the earliest racial laws and which prohibited inter-racial marriage, was extended: from now on, if a South African man married, outside the country, a woman who was not white, the marriage would be void inside South Africa. Husband and wife could face prosecution under the Immorality Act, which barred inter-racial sex, if they returned to South Africa and lived together. At the same time, however, the Immorality Act was not succeeding in entirely stopping people of different colours from doing what came naturally: during this year alone, 671 white men were charged and 349 convicted for inter-racial sex; 18 white women were charged and 11 convicted.

In race classification, most people had by this stage been assigned to their colour category. But hundreds of objections were still being considered by the special race classification appeal board. During the year, 69 coloureds were reclassified as whites, three whites became coloureds, and 41 blacks were transformed into coloureds by the stroke of an official pen.

In the political sphere, the chief apartheid law of the year was the Prohibition of Political Interference Act: this barred racially mixed political parties and made it a crime for people of one colour to help the political parties of people of another colour. With this, the remnants of representation of coloureds in Parliament—a few whites elected by them—was also ended. The Liberal Party, about half of whose 2,500 members were not whites, voted to go out of existence.

The Afrikaner Nationalists, however, were slowly being pushed into accepting the unreality of their ideological dream of total segregation to be achieved by reversing the numbers of blacks in cities and towns. Instead, the policy then evolving, and which was to run through the 1970s and beyond, was to strip every single black person of his or her South African citizenship and replace it with citizenship of 'homelands' which were to be given their 'independence'. The creation of 'tribal authorities' was being speeded up, and blacks in the Transkei 'homeland' were running fast to be the first to gain 'independence', partly out of belief in a restored tribalism and partly for the spoils of office.

At this early stage in 1968 the full implications of the policy were understood by only a few. But everything that was done was geared to it. And that included trying to limit black numbers in the cities. Thus pressure was put on blacks by zealous enforcement of the pass laws: a study of the Bantu Commissioners' courts in Johannesburg found 123 cases were heard in 225 minutes. *The Star* estimated that about 600 blacks a day were arrested in the city for pass offences.

New regulations bore down hardest on women and the aged. A study of 70,000 people in 'resettlement' villages—the places in far-flung rural areas which became compulsory homes of those blacks ordered out of cities because they were not 'active labour units'—showed that about 50,000 were women and children, and the rest mainly boys and elderly or disabled men. With hardly any work, living conditions were primitive and water was delivered by a tractor once a week. A doctor described one of the camps, Sada, as 'rotten with tuberculosis'.

There was smugness among Afrikaner Nationalists and it was understandable. Blacks had no say in their own lives, and resistance barely existed. More than 1,000 people of all colours were locked up in jail under 'security' laws. Hundreds of others were politically emasculated through banning orders, and the occasional prosecution of transgressors helped to keep everyone in line.

19

Sobukwe wrote the final university examinations—eight papers in a tough timetable from 20 to 28 May—and reported with relief: 'The exams are over, thank God.' He wrote under the shadow of knowing that the government was once more deciding his future. But he never referred to the strains. Instead there was a cheerful message that the papers were fair and he had scrupulously obeyed instructions and had no ink splashes or scratchings-out. The most he would admit was: 'I wasn't at my best so instead of a First Class Honours I shall be satisfied with a plebeian pass.' He was, however, confident enough to add: 'I think I have passed. If I fail I authorise you to arrange for a re-examination of the scripts!'

In the same positive vein he said: 'I don't want to waste time and so I want to start on the next course immediately.' He was choosing between a Master's degree in English or a basic course in Mathematics, Physics and Chemistry. He was also thinking of a Master's in Economics, for which he would need Mathematics. He preferred doing English 'for the next two years or so', provided he wasn't first required to do French.

A batch of thirty-two books I had sent arrived shortly after the examinations and he wrote delightedly: 'I lost my head, I am afraid, and approached them greedily. I was reading a stolid volume—*Reichswehr and Politics*—when they arrived and it has demanded tremendous self-discipline to continue with it in the face of the blatant coquetry of Shaw, Somerset Maugham, Oscar Wilde, George Orwell and other luscious characters.' Others he received in this batch included Evelyn Waugh, John le Carré, John Steinbeck, Edgar Allan Poe, Aristophanes, Ovid, James Michener, Sinclair Lewis, Dylan Thomas, Jean Cocteau and Scott Fitzgerald.

A few days later he wrote that he was reading the Russian poet,

Mayakovsky, and that these 'stupendous lines' appeared in *A Cloud in Trousers*:

> Wherever pain is—there am I;
> On every single tear that's shed
> I myself have crucified.

The examination results reached him early in September and he sent me a telegram: 'Just made respectable ranks. Third class honours.' To confirm that, the pass list of the University of London for Bachelor of Science, Economics, for 1968 included the entry: 'South Africa (Robben Island)/Sobukwe, Robert Mangaliso.' It was a thrilling achievement. He now had three degrees—Bachelor of Arts from Fort Hare, Bachelor of Arts Honours from the University of the Witwatersrand, and B.Sc.(Econ.) from London.

The presumption that he would be on Robben Island into the future was evident in his decision to write immediately to the University of London for a syllabus for a Master of Arts degree in English. It was equally clear that his strength of purpose was undiminished. 'Mind you I wanted to study Netherlands and brush up my Linguistics,' he said. 'But these are for pleasure and will not provide sufficient incentive to keep me wholly and completely occupied. I feel the same about my novel and short stories. I don't want my mind to get accustomed to prolonged relaxation lest it becomes slothful.'

But some academic disappointment followed because it turned out that, unlike South African practice, the University of London would not accept his Honours from the University of the Witwatersrand as the first stage of a Master's degree. As he did not have a University of London Honours he could not be admitted to their Master's degree, they wrote. They were sorry but 'there can be no exceptions made'. I thought that, in the circumstances, it was a narrow and bureaucratic response. But there was nothing else Sobukwe could do but apply to register for London's Honours degree.

On my side, I was in a state of limbo while waiting for the State to start its prosecution of Gandar and me. Several years' jail seemed certain: that was the way a judge would be expected to fulfil the government's expectations. I was on bail, with occasional brief appearances in court for remand. I was without a passport and was probably under Security Police surveillance. With one of the remands imminent, I wrote to Sobukwe: 'By the time you are reading this, I shall have made another of my public appearances. It isn't quite an applauding public, but then the appearances are against my own desires.'

The tension was probably reflected in my rather volatile relations with women. Sobukwe got to know some of this and, very much the elder brother, made his displeasure known through a sentence tucked inside a paragraph dealing with other matters: 'The reports I received concerning your skirt-world aren't particularly sublime, you know.' I felt bad that he was upset.

At that time I was concerned about making arrangements for his future care, especially in light of the belief which I shared with him that no end to his detention was in sight. After checking with Veronica, I wrote to Eulalie in April: 'As you know, my time here is limited: either we shall soon be going on trial with a jail sentence likely to follow, or else I shall be leaving the country. In either event, I am most anxious to have secure arrangements for looking after Bob's interests—and I wonder whether you would be willing to take over the supervisory work? . . . To be frank, I just cannot say if there are any risks involved in it. I have been doing this for quite a few years now, and certainly have not experienced any difficulties that I am aware of as a result of it. But then I have been having so many other difficulties that perhaps any arising out of this have simply been obscured.'

Eulalie was bothered about fund raising: if I went abroad or to jail, she would wish to know the sources of money. Her suggestion that whatever money was collected be administered by Social Services, the prisoners' welfare organisation, was totally rejected by me. Institutional care for Sobukwe was out of the question, I told her: 'I believe very strongly that Bob's affairs should be attended to by friends.'

I drew up a rough budget of the money involved: school and hostel fees for the children and their train fares, Sobukwe's clothing, train fares for the family to Cape Town, Veronica's salary for a month so that she could have an extra visit to the island, and treats at Christmas. It came to quite a sizeable amount. Where possible, I explained, I raised money locally by going to people I knew and asking for a specific amount, say for a pair of shoes. Money for rail fares and suchlike came 'from Christians who give it as a Christian duty', and from Charlotte Taylor in the US. And: 'I avoid like the plague any approach to political or similar-type organisations.'

The 'Christians' were the mainstays of the financial support: they were in the new national council of churches being formed then, and in the person of the Anglican Dean of Johannesburg, the Very Rev G.A. ffrench-Beytagh. Thereby a tale was to hang, because some three years later his help for apartheid victims in general was to make him a target for government attack, and I was dragged in too.

Sobukwe was also concerned about my leaving the country and he suggested that an account he had had at a leading men's outfitters, Markhams in Johannesburg, be moved to their Cape Town store. And, in what he termed 'Stock exchange' matters, he proposed regular payments into his savings account at Barclays bank near the University of the Witwatersrand which he said he had never closed. With a healthy sense of business he noted that the money could earn interest and he could operate a cheque book for payments. But, even as his letter arrived, there was a swift telegram from him saying not to go ahead. It turned out that the jail authorities would not allow him to have a bank account; perhaps the thought of cheques being signed from a jail cell proved too much for them. Instead, they said he could have a post office savings account.

Meanwhile, I was still buying his clothing and he found my choice of trousers, vests and shirts 'faultless'. I was taking him into brighter colours than his usual dark ones and he joked: 'It really appears as though you are determined to make it quite clear that you are no admirer of the "Black Power" cult ... you went as far from charcoal as you could! We'll accuse you of racism, if you don't look out.' A mustard-coloured turtle-necked shirt drew the protest—'a bit mod, don't you think? You can't modernise me forcibly, you know!' But within two months he had decided that it was 'not at all as loud as I thought at first it was', and he was also reassured because he saw in newspapers that the style was worn by Britain's Lord Snowdon, husband of Princess Margaret, and Robert Kennedy in the US—who 'could not be described as a mod ... So, I apologise.'

It was my turn to apologise a while later because by mistake I sent him all-white underwear instead of the colours he had requested. 'Anyway, I console myself with the thought that the white ones will at least look colourful on you,' I wrote.

Through Eulalie, everyday needs were attended to: his record player repaired, the heaters delivered, plus a new folding chair so that he could sit outside, a hot plate and pots for his kitchen, an iron, slop pail and bath. He was receiving the two local English-language newspapers, the *Cape Times* and the *Cape Argus*, and the *Sunday Times*, and was still enjoying the *Reader's Digest*.

For a change, the jail authorities actually returned a book to me which they said he could not have. It was *Allied Intervention in Russia*. I was as puzzled about it being prohibited as I was about the courtesy of returning it.

Early in the year I sent him prints by Michelangelo, Lautrec and Cézanne. Later I sent photographs of my recent purchases of a painting by Bill Ainslie and a sculpture by Dumile, both South Africans. He praised the works but confessed that he fitted Sir Malcolm Sargent's description of the English: they loved music; they didn't understand it but they found the noise pleasant. 'Same with me. I am moved by music and pictures without being able to analyse them—more so with pictures.'

In checking through our letters I noticed that he had not replied to my questioning many months before about religion. So I put a set of questions to him: What about the many Africans—and other non-Europeans, in the non-South African use of the term—who had a profound and sincere acceptance of Christianity? What of the Roman Catholic Archbishop of Maseru who was an African, the Sinhalese who was an Anglican bishop, etc? Where did they fit into the view of Christianity as a religion of Europe only? They could not simply be dismissed as 'stooges'. These were intelligent, believing and devout men. And did he reject Christianity as such or the entire concept of God? And why should he show a preference for Judaism, as he said he did?

His responses, I thought, revealed a less emphatic attitude than before towards God and Judaism:

> My faith in God remains unshaken, Benjie. At the moment I don't care to know what He is like and where He resides. It is enough to know that He is and that His will will triumph.
>
> It is not Judaism that I show a preference for, Benjie. It is the uncluttered God of the Old Testament—of Moses and Joshua and Isaiah and all the prophets—that appeals so strongly to me. It is Moses I think who says: "Blessed are you, O Israel. What people are like you whom God has chosen for His own?" With

such a faith, Benjie, one could go through Dachau and Belsen with a song on one's lips. The chief contribution of Christianity has been to assure the whole world that the promises made to Israel apply to all who confess Christ as their Lord.

Intelligence has nothing to do with faith, Benjie. Just the other day I was reading how Fortescue, a fifteenth-century Chief Justice, boasted that there were more men hanged in England in a year for robbery and manslaughter "than there be hanged in France for such manner of crime in seven years. There is no man hanged in Scotland in seven years together for robbery. But the Englishman is of another courage." Men accept the norms of their time, by and large. You just read what the nineteenth-century British industrialists said of their men! And how many professors of religion supported Hitler.

Finally, what is it, Benjie, that people believe in? To most people God is a talisman; an additional spirit. In Ghana, for instance, many Christians worship their own fetishes as well. I have read the Koran through and through; and I can't see what it is that Muslims find in it to give comfort or spiritual enlightenment. And yet they worship their Allah fanatically. In the Christian religion I think that my difficulty is that Christ is hidden behind the pretensions, superstitions and arrogance of Western Europe. By himself, alone, he is as lovable as Isaiah. But the claims made on his behalf by Western theology are unscientific. I don't even mean the mystical claims. I mean the purely historical. To say he was the one and only perfect man is unhistorical.

'Full many a flower is born to blush unseen
And waste its sweetness on the desert air.'

He is the only one about whom the West has a record. That's the most that can be said.

The Christians of Africa and Asia are not stooges, Benjie. I agree. But usually we speak of them as Westernised, to indicate that we associate Christianity with the West. But these are matters best discussed in a person-to-person situation, not by post over vast distances.

The issue of religion arose again briefly late in the year: I started a fortnightly feature in the *Rand Daily Mail*, called Talking it Over—a discussion with two or three ministers of religion at a time.

How Can Man Die Better

The ministers were drawn from different denominations and I would get them debating topics such as immortality, Christmas, or the moment of death. Was there anything Sobukwe would like to have debated, I asked him; I would do it and send him the published report.

He liked the idea and asked for the reports already published, adding: 'I should like you to pin these fellows down on their conception of heaven. Is it a geographical locality? If not what is it? If not, where was Christ from then? Where did he return to? Pin them down to concrete, unambiguous categorical statements! I'll look forward to that. Let them reconcile the historical Jewish Jesus with the eternal Christ in unmythical language. It's time they did!'

By this stage his family were aware of his altered views. His mother told Ernest of the change: she noted that he had not called her to prayer while she was visiting him.

There was a burst of enthusiasm from him after having one of his rare visitors: it was Lord Walston, Chairman of the British Institute of Race Relations, who had given a lecture at the University of the Witwatersrand and was, unusually, invited by Prime Minister Vorster to visit Robben Island. This came about, says Walston, because during a meeting with Vorster he chided him for his inhumanity towards Sobukwe and Mandela; Vorster replied that 'they were in fact kept in admirable conditions and told me that if I doubted this, I should go and see for myself'.

That's what Walston did and he found that Sobukwe had 'decent and fairly spacious living quarters, with a desk and plenty of books. He also had a yard which gave him ample room for exercise, and a glorious view across the water, to Table Mountain. I am afraid that this occasioned a tactless remark on my part. As we were strolling up and down the yard I remarked on the beauty of the view and said that at least he should draw some comfort from that. He replied, "I suppose you are right: but you may not realise how much I long to see what the view looks like from beyond the wire enclosure. Yet I know I shall never be able to see it."'

Sobukwe 'appeared devoid of hope, and resigned to staying on Robben Island indefinitely,' Walston concluded after his hour to an hour and a half meeting.

But that did not come through when Sobukwe wrote to me about the meeting. 'I enjoyed the few minutes we had together,' he said. I wasn't sure why, but the visit triggered the thought in him:

Benjamin Pogrund

'The essential thing in life is to be committed, Benjie: success or failure are mere by-products. Of course, you will always find that the other man is committed to evil and you to the good. I suppose intolerance, if not the essence, is a major ingredient of commitment.'

Current events in the world drew comment from time to time. Fresh tension in the Middle East caused him to say: '... if you have any influence, you'd better warn Dayan. He'll be seeking to talk genuine peace when Arab humiliation has rendered such a prospect impossible.' On the other hand he thought a newspaper article by Dayan's daughter, Yael, 'very well balanced ... with none of the arrogance that characterises her father's references to Arabs. I say it once more, Benjie: Nobody is going to be "taught a lesson" by anybody. The days for that type of mentality are over: between nations and between individuals. Our own children demand that we justify our "right" to teach them a lesson.'

I sent him an interview, one of my few writing efforts of the time, which I had done with Shimon Peres, then in a faction opposing the Israeli government and much later to be Prime Minister. I was impressed by Peres, I said, although 'I was unhappy about the extent to which his cold logic took him in regard to the terrible problem of the Arab refugees. I felt at times that I was talking to an alien being, that this was not the sort of Jew to whom I was accustomed and in whom I believe. Perhaps this is the metamorphosis in the modern Jew to which I referred in previous letters. Perhaps it is due to the fact that Peres and his countrymen must be like this simply to survive. But I cannot ever accept that, even in the fight for survival, there can be no room for compassion. And even apart from this aspect, I agree with you fully that Israel must show compassion, if only for reasons of expediency, if it is ever to live in peace with the Arabs.'

Because of Sobukwe, I said, I had blundered: I was vague about Peres' background when I first met him and mentioned what Sobukwe had said in his last letter to me—about influencing Dayan to be compassionate towards the Arabs. 'I was a bit surprised at the coolness with which Peres responded. Only later, during the interview, did I understand why—when I learnt he was Secretary-General of the party to which Dayan belongs and they are close friends!'

My letter and interview got through and Sobukwe replied by referring me to the works of C.P. Snow: 'They are brilliant. And yet I always read them reluctantly. He is pitiless. His characters stand before you naked and vulnerable. And my chief weakness—and strength—is that I never enjoy looking on the nakedness of another. I am tempted to cover them ' Secondly, he continued, in Sheridan's play *The Rivals*, when Sir Anthony gives his son a tongue-lashing, the son goes on to lambast his page who complains to himself that it is unfair for superiors to work off their frustrations on their subordinates—and then, when the 'boy' comes in and is cheeky, the page kicks him down the stairs and tells him to remember his place. 'That was in the eighteenth century I think. But you can see how well the dramatist knew human nature

'C.P. Snow and Peres have this in common that they claim to be realists. But such a creature does not exist. Life would be impossible for the realist. We all of us live because we hope for better things to come. When, under the reign of Nicholas I, Vissanon Belinsky said: "Our lot puts the cowl on us. We must suffer, that life may be easier for our grandchildren. We must renounce all happiness, because destiny is cruel to its instruments"; and when Robespierre, on the occasion of the Austrian invasion, addressed himself to posterity, they were being extremely optimistic: "tomorrow will be better". The only "realists" I have known are victors who are preening themselves and those who climb on the bandwagon.

'Throughout his speech [interview] Peres says: "We told them ...". Just imagine Hussein in Peres' place, with the roles reversed, saying "We told the Jews" and taste it in your mouth.'

His disapproval of Dayan was later repeated in a reference to *The Last of the Just* by André Schwarz-Bart—a novel about the persecution of Jews which made a deep impression on me and which was one of the first books I had sent to him on the island. I did not understand the connection which Sobukwe now made but, apart from anything else, his reaction was a powerful testimony to his belief in a Supreme Being. It also reflected his own modesty and his rejection of the arrogance of leadership:

'If you've read it (*The Last of the Just*) you will understand why Dayan antagonises me,' he wrote. 'One has to be careful, at all times, not to allow the Press and other publicity media to create an image of one to which one finds oneself compelled to conform. It happens so often and so easily. Herod addresses a public meeting and the people shout: It is a God that speaks. He doesn't correct them. And God strikes him down. As soon as you appropriate to yourself the glory that belongs to God, he strikes you down. Once you say my arm, my wealth, my wisdom have brought me this, you already belong to the scrapheap of history . . .'

He remained sympathetic towards Lyndon B. Johnson and, on his withdrawal during the year as a candidate for re-election as President, wrote: 'I'm sorry about that: particularly as it is only now that he thinks of playing the role which the whole world thought he was singularly cut out for, at the time of his election. I have always had the feeling that he was acting out of character on that Vietnam issue.'

But he was 'rather disgusted' with Robert F. Kennedy, who was running for President: 'His behaviour smacks too much of opportunism, calculating, ruthless opportunism. I am always ready to forgive a mistake, however serious, if the intention was good. Johnson's blunders I can, therefore, understand and forgive. But I hate the statistics-watching "hero". I really wish McCarthy beats him. McCarthy had the guts at least to challenge Johnson when nobody thought it could be done.'

Two months later, in mid-year, Kennedy was assassinated. Sobukwe said he was sorry about it: 'I did not want him dead. I wanted him to be beaten by McCarthy. Failure would have done him a lot of good.'

During the second half of the year, Veronica spent a few weeks with him inside his stockade, and she and the children went there again early in 1969. As with him, their meals were provided from the warders' kitchen; before each visit the prison advised Sobukwe of the total cost, he let me know and I sent the money to the Officer Commanding. I was annoyed about it: I thought it was miserly for the government to demand payment, apart from adding that much more to our financial needs. So I wrote to the Officer Commanding to ask if it was 'necessary to send money like this for meals'.

I told Sobukwe what I had done and he shot back at me: 'Do you mean is it necessary for Veronica and the kids to pay for their meals or do you mean the account could be sent to you after the visit? If it is the necessity for paying that you are questioning then you must direct your question to the Minister of Justice. That is one of the stipulations he made. And I am glad he did, Benjie. I feel happier knowing that Veronica and the children pay for their meals. And so does she: ask her.'

I liked his fierceness and I liked his insistence on as much independence as he could possibly maintain even though a prisoner of the State.

After all the delays, and the prosecution of my informants—.with jailing for most of them—the Prisons Act trial, with Laurence Gandar and me as the accused, finally began in November. Speaking for both of us, Gandar made an opening statement in which he repudiated utterly the charge that he and I had knowingly published false information about jails. It was an essential part of the tradition and philosophy of the *Rand Daily Mail*, he said, to safeguard the interests of the less privileged and more vulnerable elements of society, and to stand ready to expose injustices and malpractices where these were found to exist. Not to have published the information which I had found, and which we were satisfied was true, would have been a dereliction of duty, 'a suppression of matters of vital public concern'.

By 11 December, when the case was adjourned for the Christmas recess, the State had already called ninety-seven witnesses. Truth was largely absent. It was an eerie experience to sit in a courtroom day after day and to realise that we were the centrepiece of a public show trial. Assisting our lawyers in preparations for the case and attending at court each day proved a considerable ordeal, emotionally and physically. I was still the South African correspondent of *The Sunday Times* of London and was also writing the Talking it Over series. Filled with contrition at having neglected Sobukwe's interests for nearly two months, I wrote two letters in quick succession to him while rushing around to attend to what needed to be done, such as getting another copy of Irving Wallace's book, *The Man*. 'Stupendous! I should please like you to get Veronica a copy: I'd like her to read it,' he had written to me.

In fact we were not as totally doomed in the trial as we had anticipated. Our redoubtable lawyers, led by Sydney Kentridge—later to act in the Steve Biko inquest—and John Coaker and Kelsey Stuart, did more damage to the State's procession of schooled witnesses than we had thought would be possible. At the same time, we had the judge—Cillie, rewarded with the job of head of the Transvaal provincial bench just before our trial opened—to contend with, so prison at the end of it still appeared certain, whatever we did to the State's case.

But I was able to write to Sobukwe: 'It has all gone far, far better than expected and we are very cheerful. Winning is another matter, but that is not the important thing. But it has left me feeling terribly tired and drained.' I resisted the temptation to add: 'Copies to Security Police/Prisons Department Security/State Prosecutor/Attorney-General/Bureau for State Security/Minister of Justice', believing it was unnecessary as my letter would be circulated anyway.

'It relieved me,' he replied, 'to note that your attitude to your case was quite relaxed. I had written to assure Nell Marquard that the Jew boy who's been through his *bris milo* [circumcision] and bar-mitzvah shouldn't mind a year at Pretoria Central [prison]—at least not now!'

I also conveyed the news that Charlotte Taylor had come through a bad time because her marriage had broken up after twenty-five years. 'She is as generous as ever,' I said. 'She sent me a note for you and I am glad to be able to enclose it with this letter. Its warmth and concern reflects her spirit.'

He replied to that: 'Is it good to attempt to bandage every wound? Aren't some wounds a private concern: what they term *umvandedwa* in Xhosa (That which I feel alone); the type which we nurse like some secret disease?'

For Christmas, the Wentzels and I jointly sent him a huge dictionary. It was superbly printed and we were excited about it, and wished him 'much happy delving'. Inevitably, though, it was not handed to him until a few days after Christmas. I also sent the *American Judaism Reader* and he said: 'Without sounding like Oliver Twist, may I ask you for more books by Jewish authors—particularly Malamud, Golden and others. Only don't send anything by Leon Uris. I have become allergic to him.'

He was cheerful about his plans for studying. He thought he might have to do a foreign language and intended writing to the University of London to find out whether he could do it at the same time as a post-graduate degree or whether he first had to have the language. And, he said: 'After much thought I have decided to attempt Arabic, in spite of the emotions such a choice might arouse! The reason is, really, that it is an African language in which a great deal of early African history has been written.'

I was trying to get the government to contribute towards the costs of the family travelling to and from the island, and was in touch with a United Party Member of Parliament, Japie Basson. He approached Pelser but reported back that he was not hopeful of success.

Early in January, Veronica and the children stayed with Sobukwe on the island for several weeks and he wrote to say how happy they were to be together. Later, when Veronica was home again, she too wrote about their 'lovely holiday', adding: 'He looks fine although he has lost weight as far as I am concerned.'

On 5 February, Sobukwe wrote: 'As you know I have no urgent studies this year and I have learnt to appreciate Lord Walston's references to a "purposeless" freedom. I am, however, studying Netherlands—a year's course—with the Maxwell Instituut of Utrecht. Theo Kloppenberg [a Durban man who had been banned and then returned to his native Holland] arranged for me to take the course.'

He said also that his mother and sister-in-law were due to visit him: 'It's something to look forward to.'

It took four weeks for that letter to reach me. I replied the same day and there followed, until well into April, as brisk a turnaround of letters as the prison authorities allowed. The letters dealt largely with practical matters. The usual arrangements were in hand for the children's schooling, for pen pals abroad, and for their other needs—Dini had asked for quality books and a selection including *Oliver Twist* and *Julius Caesar* was on its way to him. Sobukwe told me that, instead of merely sending them money to spend, they should be encouraged to start saving, through piggy-banks or savings accounts, and should be told it was for their university education.

My days in court were 'tedious and dreary except for the occasional high spot', I wrote. But, 'I suddenly got the idea of not allowing this to be a wasted year. And I thought to myself: if that brother of mine on the island can do it, so can I.' So that morning, I told him, I had registered for an Honours degree in African Studies at Witwatersrand University.

Behind this decision was the fact that most of my research papers had been shipped to London, in anticipation of my being there, so I could not continue with a Ph.D. But I could at least improve my knowledge of Africa. The lecturers and my fellow-students were helpful and classes were arranged to fit in with my court schedule—which meant rushing to the university late in the afternoons, and spending the whole of Wednesday afternoons there when the court did not sit. For the next few months I crouched behind heaps of law books in the courtroom and worked away at university essays. It helped to keep me sane.

There was an exchange of information about trousers he had sent for alteration. In letting him know two pairs had been returned to him, I asked whether a white shirt had been included—if so, would he please send it to me as it was mine. We were also dealing with the delays in getting him started on the next round of university studies. There were details to be sorted out about our new system of sending monthly cheques to him. I told him about my pleasure at Jennifer's glowing school reports and how much she had enjoyed seeing a movie version of the opera *La Traviata*.

In a letter written on 27 March, Sobukwe noted that his mother and sister-in-law were having their last visit to him that day. He said he had sent his sister-in-law to make use of the new arrangement for clothes to be bought at Stuttafords in Cape Town on my account. 'Her tastes are expensive—as are mine,' he recorded, 'and she has run up a formidable debt.' But he liked what she bought and thought he would not need any other clothing that year. In the same letter he said he wanted me to give Veronica advice about land she was planning to buy.

And there was one of those sentences which was so revealing of him: 'I shall write again later. But so far, this has been really a blessed year for me, with unexpected pleasures following closely on one another.'

I thought this was probably mainly a response to the family visits he had had. I had come to accept it as typical of him that, amidst the lack of hope, he could yet speak about a 'blessed year'.

This letter reached me on 18 April. Everything seemed normal—as far, of course, as the word could be used in Sobukwe's abnormal circumstances.

But less than a week later, on 24 April, suddenly and unexpectedly, with not a hint in advance, Justice Minister Pelser issued a statement for publication at midnight announcing that Sobukwe was to be released. A letter, said Pelser, had been sent 'advising him it is not intended to detain him beyond 30 June, but to release him at the earliest possible date subject to such restrictions as are deemed necessary for the safety of the State'. Certain administrative arrangements still had to be made, but 'as soon as these have been completed the necessary steps for his release will be taken'.

How Can Man Die Better

I wrote, sending the letter to Robben Island: 'There is little I can say, or need to say, at this stage. Just that I share your happiness, and the happiness of Veronica and the children. And that in saying a prayer of thanks, I have prayed also for your future. There is a life stretching ahead of you: may it be as useful and purposeful as so much of your life has been up to now . . .'

Even amid the eruption of relief and joy among family and friends, there was apprehension. Even as I sent what I hoped was the last telegram to him—'Please telegraph Eulalie regarding requirements suitcases and boxes for packing'—it remained to be seen how onerous the promised restrictions were going to be. In addition, there was clearly something odd going on: the government had made public its decision to release Sobukwe, but had not decided what to do with him. It did not add up.

We did not have long to wait. On 2 May, Veronica phoned me in a state of fear: she had received a registered letter from Sobukwe that day. It was dated 16 April but the authorities had not posted it until 29 April.

Halfway through what was otherwise a straightforward letter dealing with mundane issues, Sobukwe said: 'Yesterday I wrote to Ernie Wentzel on a rather serious matter, affecting my health. I have also written to the Minister of Justice on the same. I may require you to come down some time soon, for a week or so. If it becomes necessary I shall send you a telegram, but I should like you, meanwhile, to find out whether you can get a week's leave at short notice. Better still, discuss this matter with Benjie.'

I shared Veronica's panic and acted immediately: I phoned General van den Bergh and demanded information about what was going on: what had they done to Sobukwe?

Although van den Bergh wasn't easy to read, it seemed to me that my call took him by surprise and that he did not know anything about the matter. He promised to investigate. I sent a telegram to the Officer Commanding Robben Island seeking immediate access by a doctor of our choice; there was no reply. I alerted Helen that something was very wrong and she contacted Pelser—who gave her his personal assurance that Sobukwe was fine.

Pelser was hiding the truth. For what later emerged was that the effects of six years of solitary confinement were showing themselves. Sobukwe had developed the idea that the authorities were using a machine which was influencing the functioning of his body.

The details were in the letter to Wentzel. But that letter was also held back, for even longer, by the authorities and arrived only in mid-May, a day or so before Sobukwe was let off the island. Wentzel immediately sent a telegram to the Officer Commanding demanding access; again there was no reply.

What had happened? An understanding of events comes from John Schlapobersky, a psychotherapist who has specialised in studying and treating victims of repression. Since 1985 he has been with the London-based Medical Foundation for the Care and Treatment of Victims of Torture. He brings his own personal experience to bear on this work for he is a South African exile living in Britain; in June 1969, while a 21-year-old student at the University of the Witwatersrand, Schlapobersky was arrested by the Security Police, tortured and held in solitary confinement for two months.

He notes that South Africa first began to use solitary confinement during the 1960s as a containment process—as a way of stopping trouble, and/or as an intermediate form of punishment. As the anti-apartheid organisations went deeper underground, the Security Police increasingly studied and exploited solitary confinement as a weapon against the government's opponents. They developed techniques which start with what Schlapobersky describes as the 'worldwide bread and butter of torture'—beating a victim on the head and face with a mix of hands, fists, feet, wooden batons or iron bars—and going on to the extensive use of electricity for inflicting pain, plus intensive interrogation techniques.

In Schlapobersky's own detention, after initial violent abuse and beating, he was made to stand on a brick while teams of interrogators questioned him. That began on a Friday afternoon and went on non-stop, except for breaks for meals and occasional short sleep periods, until Wednesday afternoon. Then followed nearly two months of solitary confinement.

'From the people we see at the Medical Foundation,' he says, 'the South Africans are much more sophisticated than just about all the other torture agencies with which we are familiar, such as those in the Argentine, Chile, Iran, Iraq, El Salvador, Ethiopia or Somalia. The level of physical violence used by the South Africans is less than in these countries but the capacity for controlled terror and manipulation of minds is much greater.'

Considerable information is available, he points out, about the effects of solitary confinement. The first major research emerged from the debriefing of United States soldiers who were prisoners during the Korean War at the start of the 1950s. Since then, the experiences of many other victims have been studied and there have also been extensive laboratory experiments. It is now well known —and no more so than to torturers who use solitary confinement— that, as a person's contact with others is reduced, so psychological functions become distorted. In Sobukwe, the first effects were apparent when he said that he was forgetting how to speak, and in the difficulties he had in concentrating on his studies. All this was predictable, says Schlapobersky.

Still more effects were inevitable when Sobukwe's confinement went on day after day, month after month, year after year, and with no end in sight. He was in a hostile environment, surrounded by warders who viewed him either with malevolence or indifference—and who on occasion gave him decayed food. He was an alien being who was guarded round the clock. He and his organisation were being persecuted. He was not only singled out for punishment but had the extra punishment of being kept in a stockade where he could see and hear other prisoners but was separated from them.

'He knew that the authorities were destroying him and his mind developed the metaphor of a machine,' says Schlapobersky. 'The machine was Robben Island. It was the apartheid system. The thought was an accurate description of what was happening to him. It was an apposite image which captured the ubiquitous, pernicious quality of the system which was bearing down on him.'

There was a further confusion of reality because during this era the Security Police were modernising and were bringing into play the latest available surveillance technology, from simple bugging of conversations in rooms and cells and miniature tape recorders and cameras, to ultra-sensitive directional microphones which could pick up conversations at a considerable distance or through windows. So there was less and less absolute certainty about what the police could or couldn't find out and do.

This is a view in retrospect. Harking back to 1969 it took a while to understand what had probably brought about the decision to release Sobukwe. Reconstructing events, it seems that his mid-April letter to the Minister of Justice set off alarm bells and that psychiatrists were rushed in. Some of what they reported is known: that his personality was intact, his volition was intact, his emotional responses were appropriate, and his behaviour did not reflect a break with reality. This was confirmed by examinations after his release. Thus the damage he sustained was not as serious as it might and could have been and, once he was released, everyday living took over.

But, equally, there was a distortion in his thinking process and it was clear to me at the time that, the moment the government came to realise this, they moved swiftly to get him out of jail. Hence their announcement that he was to be released even before they had decided what to do with him. Hence the delay in letting Sobukwe's letters through to Veronica and to Ernie Wentzel. The government did not want to be blamed for what they had done so they hurriedly set about dumping him.

On our side we kept silent and let them get away with it because of concern for him: at that stage we did not know how extensive or permanent the damage to Sobukwe might be.

20

Sobukwe was taken on the prison ferry boat to the Cape Town docks on the mainland. From there, two Security policemen drove him nearly 1,000 kilometres to his new home outside the city of Kimberley. He had no choice. That is where the government decided he had to be. On 14 May, he sent me a telegram: 'Address is 6 Naledi Street, Galeshewe, Kimberley. Would like meeting soon.'

In the dry west of the country, blazingly hot in summer, Kimberley was no doubt chosen because, although a small city, it was away from the major urban areas: Johannesburg is 470 kilometres to the north. It was large enough to offer reasonable living amenities; it was also small enough so that Sobukwe could be closely watched. He would not be in jail but there was clear intention to maintain invisible barriers for his isolation: the city's black community was not only conservative and out of the mainstream, but the dominant language among them—Tswana—was largely unknown to Sobukwe. He had only once before been to Kimberley, as a prisoner in chains while serving his jail sentence, to give evidence for the defence in a trial involving Poqo members.

The city is on one of the two highways which run from Johannesburg and the Witwatersrand, the commercial and industrial heart of South Africa, to Cape Town in the south. Traffic on the Kimberley route is usually sparse, except during the summer holiday season. For most travellers, the city is then a place to rest for a night or to stop for a meal. Some take time to visit the Big Hole—which is literally what its name says it is. It also represents the history of the city, and much of South Africa's too.

In 1866, children on a farm in the district—then in the Cape Colony ruled by Britain—were playing with stones which they had picked up; a neighbour thought one of the stones was interesting and offered to buy it but the children gave it to him as a gift; it turned out to be a mammoth 21¼-carat diamond, later called Eureka. The discovery drew diggers and adventurers from throughout the world. In 1869, diamonds were found on an even more dazzling scale forty kilometres to the south. This site, at first known as New Rush, was named in 1873 after Lord Kimberley, Britain's Secretary of State for the Colonies. The digging into the earth went deeper and deeper and the walls—used as roads—between the 1,600 staked-out claims, some as small as 7 square metres, grew narrower and finally collapsed. The eventual oval-shaped hole measured 305 metres by 183 metres. Out of this came 22.5 million tonnes of soil which yielded 14.5 million carats—2,722 kilograms—of diamonds, before the treasure chest was exhausted in 1914.

By the mid–1880s the hundreds of small claims had been consolidated under the single ownership of De Beers Consolidated Mines, headed by Cecil John Rhodes. The discovery and mining of diamonds transformed the Cape Colony's agricultural base. This brought greater controls over blacks: a form of 'pass' law had begun in the Cape nearly one hundred years before, and was now extended to control the black men who went to the diggings to work as labourers. They were forced to leave their rural homes in search of work through the imposition of poll taxes which required them to make cash payments. The pattern for modern South Africa was set in place, with skilled white workers contrasted with blacks doing menial work, and blacks as cheap, exploited labour.

The diamonds established Rhodes' fortune, enabling him to extend British rule into Africa, although he never did succeed in his dream of a Cape to Cairo rail link, to run entirely through British territory. The discovery of gold in 1886 in the Johannesburg area, in the Boers' Transvaal Republic, confirmed minerals as the economic mainstay of the region and set events in train which not only entrenched the economic dominance of whites over blacks but led to the war between Britain and the Boers in 1899. During that war, Kimberley was besieged by Boer forces for 124 days before it was relieved.

Although the Big Hole has long been played out, underground pipes of diamonds are still mined nearby. Kimberley remains the richest concentration of diamonds the world has known. It has enabled De Beers to grow into an international cartel, making a glittering addition to the coffers of the owners, the Anglo American

How Can Man Die Better

Corporation of South Africa and the controlling Oppenheimer family. There is little obvious evidence of the wealth in the appearance of the city's modest business centre; the outstanding building is a modern glass-faced structure put up by De Beers as a diamond-sorting centre. But life is comfortable in the leading whites-only suburbs: the streets are wide, the houses are large and the gardens bloom with flowers under the high blue sky. As usual, residential apartheid applies: the 36,000 whites live in their designated suburbs and the 1,000 Asians and 36,000 coloureds have their areas, and so do the 66,000 blacks.

A few minutes' drive from the business centre, off the main tarred road, is Galeshewe, the ghetto for blacks. Streets are untarred and rutted; the poverty of the people is evident. The house in Naledi Street to which Sobukwe was brought stands out among what are mostly typical tiny ghetto houses: it is large, with white-painted walls. The roof is corrugated iron, a hard material which fits in with the hardness of the land; it can withstand the battering of summer hailstorms but provides poor insulation against the local extremes of temperature. A verandah of light-brown faced-brick fronts on the street, looking out on a small lawn and a wire fence. The size of the house makes it likely that it was originally built by a white person and was taken over by the Kimberley city council as Galeshewe spread out.

There was little in the house when Sobukwe was dumped there: a narrow iron bed and prison-issue blankets, a locker and a small wardrobe, a small pot, a kettle and a spoon. He was alone for several days before Veronica was able to get away from work to travel to see him. She cannot remember his first words to her: they were both simply 'happy and excited'.

His existence was severely shut in by the multi-bannings served on him before he was removed from Robben Island. The six-page administrative decree signed by the Minister of Justice was issued under the Suppression of Communism Act—a point of irony in light of Sobukwe's hostility towards communist influence.

It ordered him, for the next five years, to remain within the boundaries of the Kimberley municipality. Even more specifically, between 6 p.m. and 6 a.m. every day he had to remain inside the Naledi Street house. No one was allowed to visit him there, except a doctor and a small number of family members whose names were set out. This was known as 'house arrest'.

He was also prohibited from entering any hostel or compound for black workers, any factory premises, any newspaper premises, any university or school premises, or any courts of law unless he was a party to proceedings. He was ordered not to give any educational instruction to anyone except his children. He was prohibited from communicating 'in any manner whatsoever' with other banned people or anyone listed as having been a member of a proscribed organisation—which, of course, would mean being cut off from those listed as having been members of his own Pan-Africanist Congress.

He was ordered not to write anything for publication, or prepare any publication, or help in any way in the 'preparation, compilation or transmission of any matter for publication in any publication . . .' He was barred from preparing or publishing any document—defined in the decree as including any book, pamphlet, record, list, placard, poster, drawing, photograph or picture—in which 'any principle or policy of the government of a state is propagated, defended, attacked, criticised, discussed or referred to'. In other words, he was excluded from the slightest involvement in political activities.

The penalties for non-compliance were up to five years' imprisonment.

His release came as the Prisons Trial was drawing to a close, nearly eight months after its start. The evidence was ended, Laurence Gandar and I had each gone into the witness-box and been traduced and browbeaten by the prosecution, and we had put in a few witnesses. Legal argument was under way and, as I wrote to Helen Suzman on 28 May, the prosecutor had flung 'garbage' at us the previous week but 'we are now enjoying ourselves immensely: Sydney [Kentridge] is thundering away, and is quite magnificent'. Indeed, the defence led by Kentridge had been so brilliantly handled that, by this stage, although there was as little chance as ever of an acquittal, it seemed unlikely that even Judge Cillie would be able to jail us.

It was strange to write to Sobukwe without having to worry about upsetting the jail censors. But I remained mindful that there was no doubt that the Security Police would continue to be interested readers of his correspondence. My first letter to him began: 'Welcome, welcome. It's not quite home, but it's a big step anyway . . . Do I welcome you back to freedom? That would be silly. But what I can do is to wish you well out of what you were in.' And within what was for us the astonishing time of four days he was replying: 'Your welcome and welcoming letter arrived this morning and Veronica and I read [it] with joy.' He did not have a telephone, he said, and hadn't yet found his way around. 'But as soon as I find my land–1egs I shall phone you. In the meantime I shall write often, if only to convince myself that my letters can reach you before fourteen days!'

That letter, written within only a few days of his arrival in Kimberley, conveyed his familiar sunniness of outlook: 'Quite a few people have already tried to make me feel welcome, and I am grateful. I am quite certain things will work out well. God has been too good to me, Benjie, to leave his promises unfulfilled. I have no anxiety on that score.' Not long after, in the same happy vein he was also to tell me that Veronica 'smiles more often now and to me has never looked lovelier'. It was a busy time, with the children coming from school—they were now in Lesotho and Swaziland—and his mother and brother and other family planning visits.

After a few days he noted that he was still sending letters to me by registered post: for, as he explained, 'habits die long. It'll take me some time I think to believe that a letter of mine will travel "incognito" to wheresoever and to whomsoever I send it.' He was also uncertain about phoning me: 'I've been out of circulation a long time and I am not familiar with the operation of your telephone service. Wouldn't it be a TRUNK call to Jo'burg? As soon as I am able I'll phone you, be sure.'

Settling into everyday life after nine years in jail also meant becoming reacquainted with a simple tool of everyday existence: a watch. I chose one and it went to Kimberley together with my personal gift of a homely dressing-gown to welcome him.

Problems abounded. The immediate ones concerned employment and furnishing the house. After Veronica's initial quick visits to Kimberley, she was to move there as soon as she could obtain release from the Johannesburg municipality—she was still employed as a midwife in Soweto. She would buy curtains in Johannesburg for the house, but what to do about all the furniture needed? They still had their dining-room furniture and some other items from their Soweto house, but a lot else would have to be bought.

What work would he do? He said that a local lawyer, H.Z.M. Nzimande, who was a friend of long standing, had sounded him out about serving articles to qualify as a solicitor: 'We'll discuss this when you come. I am not sure that law appeals to me. I am a teacher, Benjie. I love the classroom and to see the look of comprehension on the faces of children.'

We had to delay our first meeting. I could only get away from Johannesburg and the trial over weekends, and he was available for only part of the time because of his house arrest restriction. It was a tough period in the trial, I told him, as the prosecution was summing up its case 'with a flood of abuse flung at Gandar and me and our attorney [Kelsey Stuart, who had, four years earlier, cleared my reports on jails for publication in the *Mail*]. Had it been justified and related to facts one could not and would not mind. But it has all been entirely unrelated either to actual events or to our evidence, so I have found it sick-making ... and at an extraordinarily low intellectual level.'

Sobukwe was now following the trial day by day as the *Rand Daily Mail* reached Kimberley by lunchtime on the day of publication. Once more he stepped in to give comfort, at the same time reflecting his own ability to retain tranquillity in the face of the poisonous attacks on him over the years: 'Yes,' he said, 'the prosecution had a field day: a real *stryddag* [an Afrikaner party political rally]. But what my attitude has always been, Benjie, that what matters is what my friends think of me. It bothers me not a damn what my enemies think of me or say of me. They would not be normal if they showered me with compliments.'

Early in June, the moment the trial adjourned for the judge to prepare his case, I flew to Cape Town to see my parents and then went on to Kimberley. The happiness of our reunion was in no way dimmed by the circumstances: I was not allowed to visit him at home because my application to do so had been rejected; nor was I even allowed to enter Galeshewe, for this too had been refused. As it was a black ghetto, whites needed a permit to go in.

I did not trust the police. I had had more than enough experience of official deceit and frame-ups to be wary of landing in any situation which could be twisted to harm either Sobukwe or me. For myself, I suspected the authorities could be itching to seek to compromise me during the five weeks that the trial was adjourned for judgment. Trapping me into an illegal meeting with the country's foremost ex-prisoner seemed within the bounds of possibility. Kelsey Stuart warned me to be careful not to give the authorities any excuse to arrest me. So in discussing seeking permission to enter Galeshewe, I told Sobukwe: 'I think it is essential, for both your protection and for me, that any such permission be given in writing.' But, of course, my worry about a possible trap proved groundless as I was not even allowed to set foot inside the ghetto.

We had three days of incessant talking and sharing emotions and thoughts. My dominant sense about him was his optimism about himself and South Africa. It helped him to endure the experience of being plunged back into the reality of everyday apartheid living. We also went through the details of a brotherly pact. I would continue to do whatever my means allowed to help him and the family, whether financially or otherwise; there would be a minimum of thank yous. In due course, if our roles were ever reversed and I landed up in need of help, he would help me to the best of his ability—and again, with a minimum of thank yous. Both of us would be frank in stating our needs and what each of us could do for the other. As Sobukwe was to say in a later letter, 'the truth between us; that is our bargain'.

The pattern for visits which developed was that I flew to Kimberley and hired a car at the airport, or drove in my own car from Johannesburg. The five-hour drive became more difficult in the aftermath of the oil crisis of the early 1970s: feeling the simultaneous effect of anti-apartheid oil sanctions, South Africa had an 80 km/hour speed limit, which made it an ordeal to travel the long country stretches. But, whichever way I got to Kimberley, I would collect Sobukwe at an agreed time at an agreed spot near Galeshewe and, at the end of each day, drop him off again so that he could walk home in time for the start of his 6 p.m. house arrest.

Those end-of-the-day goodbyes, as the sun was setting and as I watched the tall figure of my friend set off on the sand road to be home on time, were poignant moments, leaving me to spend evenings alone in the hotel, feeling drained and depressed about his closed-in life.

Early on, his state of health was a priority issue. It wasn't only his saying that he did not feel his legs were strong enough to cover the distances he wanted to walk, but we did not trust the government's doctors in whose care he had been. We agreed that I should arrange for him to be thoroughly checked over by doctors of our choice. A leading local physician carried out a full examination and pronounced Sobukwe in good physical shape. The physician's ethics, incidentally, proved to be wanting: word got back to me that he was gossiping about Sobukwe's psychological state.

The next step, we again agreed, was to check his psychological condition. The police confirmed that the banning orders allowed doctors to go to the house; the Galeshewe officials in turn said they would issue permits to doctors to enter the ghetto to get to the house. So Dr David Wynberg, a Johannesburg psychiatrist who was a friend of mine, flew to Kimberley and, after a day with Sobukwe, said that he believed one of three things could follow: the belief in a machine would either grow so that it dominated his existence, or it would recede into the general pattern of emotions and thinking, or it would disappear completely. The chances were greatest for the second or third alternatives, he thought, now that Sobukwe was living in a more normal situation. And, in due course, that is what did happen: he essentially recovered from what he had endured on the island.

Some small twinge of conscience must have flickered among the few inside government who knew what the solitary confinement had done to Sobukwe and that he was now being abandoned in a friendless place. Or perhaps it was only a rare instance of the government trying some public relations to soften its harsh image. Whatever the reason, there was an offer to find him employment and to subsidise him until then. The employment offer came through the Kimberley city council: a job was to be made available as a clerk in its Department of Bantu Administration—that is, the council's section which controlled the lives of the local black people. The salary of R720 a year, rising to a maximum of R900 a year, was at the very low level considered suitable for blacks.

To Afrikaners, this was all extraordinarily generous behaviour. So much so that there was anxiety in Nationalist circles that some whites might be offended that a black man, and a political enemy at that, was being afforded such treatment. Thus a government newspaper took care to explain that Sobukwe's salary would not actually be drawn from money paid by white taxpayers, but, as with other officials in the Department of Bantu Administration, would be paid from the income received from the sale of 'Bantu beer'—the maize-beer for blacks profitably brewed and sold by white-run municipalities.

It was demeaning, and he could never have accepted such a job. It was also personally and politically unthinkable for him to become a cog inside the apartheid machine. Seeking another way, at Sobukwe's request, I wrote to Suzman to ask whether Harry Oppenheimer—whom she knew well—might be able to offer him a job with De Beers. She replied that she was writing to Oppenheimer. But nothing came of this.

Nearly a year later, Pelser was still having to soothe his National Party supporters. At a meeting in a rural town he was asked why Sobukwe received R100 a month and a free house while some (white) railway workers, so the questioner said, were getting salaries of less than R100 a month.

Pelser offered a medley of justifications: it had cost the government R12,500 a year to guard Sobukwe on Robben Island, he said—five warders and two warders with dogs, twenty-four hours a day. When Sobukwe was released, the government 'could not just put him anywhere as he was an educated person who had earned a good salary before his arrest'. And the government had to safeguard itself 'against criticisms from abroad and that was why we gave him a house and R100 a month for three months'.

On my visits to Kimberley, the police were almost always with us. It was no surprise because we made most of our arrangements over the phone, and it was more than likely that our phones were tapped. At the airport, as I drove out in my hired car, another car would usually follow—and keep following all the time. If I arrived in my own car, a Security Police shadow was soon with me. Nor did the end of the day, when I checked into an hotel, bring relief. One time, while having dinner in the hotel, a waiter—an Asian—whispered as he was serving me: 'The *Boere* are watching you. They are at the front and the back of the hotel.' He went on dishing out the vegetables and I whispered back: 'Why are you telling me?' He hissed: 'They locked up my son for IDB.'

That was enough explanation why he was tipping me off about the *Boere*—he meant the police—because what he was conveying was that his son had been jailed for Illicit Diamond Buying, a serious offence in a city and country where a special police unit is constantly trying to halt the profitable trafficking in stolen diamonds. The trade is dangerous for not only do the police set traps for the greedy, but so do criminals: con men are on the lookout for the unwary who can be made to believe that a chunk of smooth glass from the thick bottom of a Coca-Cola bottle is an uncut diamond of huge value.

When I finished dinner and walked into the lobby, there was a Security policeman, whom I recognised, talking to the desk clerk. To judge from his startled reaction when, standing behind him, I asked for my room key, he had been talking about me.

But police efficiency was thankfully not always what it was supposed to be, as another episode revealed. I was going to be visiting Sobukwe and phoned him to arrange for him to meet a visitor from abroad—whom I did not name—while I was there. We fixed the day and the time. At the last moment, the visitor's plans changed and he arrived in Kimberley a day earlier. The three of us met in a museum, using the interleading rooms to make sure we were not being followed. He and Sobukwe talked, and the visitor departed. Exactly twenty-four hours later, at the originally scheduled time, there was a flurry of Security Police activity around Sobukwe and me. They seemed to be expecting him to meet someone, and were eager to know the stranger's identity!

I was mentally a captive of South African laws and mores, so did not dare take Sobukwe to my hotel. Strict apartheid still applied and we simply accepted that, if we walked in together, he would be ordered out. Neither of us wanted that sort of unpleasantness. Apartheid also applied to tea-rooms and restaurants. So we spent the days together driving around, always taking great care to remain inside the city boundaries. That meant we could drive for a few minutes from the city centre into the countryside, and especially in the broiling summer days, try to find a patch of shade under a scraggly thorn tree. The city's art gallery, small but with an impressive range of work, also gave us many hours of shared pleasure.

The Security Police, usually two men in a car, drove a short distance behind. When we went off the road and parked in the thin bush, they followed and sat in their car twenty or fifty metres away, a silent and baleful presence, their faces hard to see with the sun shining off the windscreen. We did not know if they were using directional microphones to listen to our conversations, or if my car—especially if I had hired it—was bugged. But we had to assume that they might be able to listen to us and so had to be careful when we spoke about politics, and especially about underground politics.

Only twice did I risk taking brief notes of our discussions: it was an offence for Sobukwe to prepare anything for publication. We could never know whether the silent watchers might suddenly descend on us and search us. I was also too scared to make notes in my hotel room at the end of the day in case there was a knock on the door and the police were there; or perhaps they might stop me as I was leaving Kimberley.

It was an existence on the edge of uncertainty. It also contributed towards maintaining the notion of the police using a 'machine' on Sobukwe: directional microphones, telephones tapped, a listening bug in a car... what else was possible?

Having police escorts could make others nervous. One time, I met local coloured people whom I knew and arranged to meet them later at a hotel for coloureds. When Sobukwe and I arrived there, we had our usual police car behind us—and the people waiting took one look and hurriedly went off.

He was under constant surveillance. The Security Police often drove past his home and office, just keeping an eye on him. And he was in no doubt that, where they left off, informers were busy. He accepted that a number of people in Galeshewe had been suborned into spying on him. This has been a normal part of ghetto existence: whether through the use of pressure, such as the threat of 'endorsement'—eviction—out of the city area into rural poverty, and/or payment of money, the police have been able to rely on networks of informers. The system has broken down at times because of community retaliation, such as after the 1976 uprising, only to be re-created.

Now and again we speculated about the possible informers around him. Some he was sure were informers; others had question marks over them. But he was always relaxed about it. Let them do their worst, was his attitude. He expressed more sorrow than anger for those who had landed up working for the Security Police, and saw them as victims of pressure and human weakness. He delighted in reminding me of a joke illustrating a difference between Western and African attitudes towards entrapment...

In Moscow, the KGB used a beautiful woman to seduce a Ghanaian diplomat, and photographs were secretly taken of him in a compromising situation. For Western diplomats, the threat of making such photographs public was usually enough to open the victim to blackmail. But it didn't work in the same way for the

Ghanaian. For, shown the photographs, he said excitedly: 'Those are great. Can I have six copies of each?'

At the same time, Sobukwe's personal relations with the local Security Police were cordial. It seemed to me that they had the same deep respect for him which had been shown by the warders on Robben Island. The men in charge were even willing to bend his restrictions a bit: he loved boxing so he was allowed, from time to time, to attend fights staged in the city on Saturday nights; he was also allowed to go to the local drive-in movie-house.

During one of my visits, the unceasing sight in my rearview mirror of a large green car irritated me more than usual. It seemed more than coincidence that, on a Saturday morning in Kimberley, there were two white men driving around in the same aimless way as we were, always a block behind us. With a swift bit of acceleration and rapid turning of corners I lost the green car. That was no mean feat given the smallness of the city centre, and I was pleased with myself. We drove to the outskirts and parked in the shade of a tree, for once without anyone in sight. Later, returning to the city centre, there was the green car again. Now there was no attempt at pretence, and they stayed right behind us: when we parked, they parked, bumpers almost touching, and two faces glaring at us.

But once more, with nifty driving, I went one way through traffic lights and got them to go another way. A few minutes later, like a scene from an early comedy movie, the green car roared past—but going in the opposite direction, with two astonished and unhappy faces staring at us. My self-congratulation did not last long, however, because I soon discovered a grey car was behind us; later I found there was a third car also. Three cars and six men followed us for the rest of the day. That evening, my wife and I strolled from our hotel to the local cinema: there was one of the cars again, wheeling around the streets, seeing us safely to the movie.

Sobukwe was most disapproving of me that day; he did not think I should be playing these games. Apart from anything else, he was probably right because he had to go on living there and would have to put up with the enraged policemen when I went away.

In fact it had different consequences. The next morning, coming out of the hotel, I saw a car parked down the street with two men sitting in it. I behaved totally irrationally and walked up to them, bent down to the window, and demanded aggressively: 'Who are you? Why are you following me?' The only answer was a dismissive wave of the hand and a muttered *'Ag man'*, which can be loosely translated from Afrikaans as a derisive 'Oh man'. But they must have radioed in a report because a few minutes later the town's security chiefs, whom I knew as a major and a captain, arrived and expressed their own aggression in wanting to know what my complaint was.

Anger from Security policemen is not to be treated lightly, and I was frightened. I was dressed in shorts and sandals and was embarrassed that my trembling knees would betray my inner feelings. So during the discussion—or argument, because there was soon a shouting match on the pavement—I continuously hopped from one foot to another to disguise the signs of my fear. It must have been a strange sight.

As the argument grew more heated the captain used a four-letter word to tell me what he thought of me. 'How dare you talk to me like that,' I yelled, 'I shall report you to your superiors for using foul language to me.' Incredibly, the captain blushed and fell silent. The major became placatory: 'Please Mr Pogrund, you must understand that we are doing our duty. When you come here, Pretoria wants to know what you are doing and we must tell them.' That led me to more yelling: 'What do you think I am doing? You know why I come here.'

The set-to actually led to an easing in the surveillance, at least in its visible form, with far less Security Police intrusion from then on. There is no rational explanation for this. It is the sort of wacky thing which happens in South Africa.

There was another sequel. The captain—T.G. du Plessis—in due course was promoted to major and was put in charge in Kimberley. Later on, when Sobukwe was preparing for his final law examinations, I arranged for a friend, Raymond Tucker, a Johannesburg attorney with a fine record in acting for the defence in political trials, to spend a weekend in Kimberley as a tutor. The major gave Tucker permission to spend an entire Saturday at Sobukwe's home. I was barred, however, so remained in my hotel room. Du Plessis called in at Sobukwe's house during the day to check that there were no problems, and was given a message from me thanking him for his help.

He responded by coming to see me. He seemed surprised that I was willing to thank him for anything. We sat in my hotel room—I think neither of us particularly cared to be seen with the other in the open—and chatted over tea. He told me how much he tried, without referring back to his headquarters in Pretoria, to make life for Sobukwe as tolerable as possible. I was able to express appreciation of a particular incident of which Sobukwe had told me: Veronica and the children had been on a train arriving in Kimberley at 2 o'clock in the morning and Sobukwe had applied for exemption from his banning so that he could fetch them; not only had du Plessis arranged the exemption but had himself fetched Sobukwe and driven him to the station and collected the family.

This conversation, a mixture of warmth and some strain, culminated as he was leaving by my asking about the personal tragedy which Sobukwe had told me of: he did not have a wife and had a son who was a cripple. Yes, said du Plessis, he hoped he would not be posted away from Kimberley because he had bought a house there and had had a great deal of expensive work done to adjust the bathroom and so on to cater for his son's needs; he wanted to spend the rest of his police career in Kimberley and to retire there.

Standing in the doorway, we had this friendly, very personal, conversation for about ten minutes. Suddenly, du Plessis appeared to realise that he was speaking to someone who was the enemy. He broke off, almost in mid-sentence, and hurriedly walked away.

It wasn't often that one encountered a human face in a Security policeman.

Major du Plessis did not live to retirement. He died a few years after our meeting. I never found out what happened to his son.

In spite of the friendliness, or whatever else it was, the real nature of the relationship—the watcher and the watched—was always there. If any reminder was needed, it came as a result of Sobukwe's return to formal religion. On Robben Island, it will be remembered, he had broken with Christianity although his faith in God remained unimpaired. In Galeshewe, he began to attend a Methodist church on Sundays. And because he was a gifted linguist, he was used as an interpreter—standing in front of the pulpit to translate the minister's sermon into one or other language.

Word of this got back to the Security Police. They told Sobukwe they were considering bringing a criminal charge against him for transgressing his banning because he was addressing the congregation. In fact they never did prosecute him, probably realising how ridiculous they would look for doing so. But they also went to the church's minister and warned him that he could be prosecuted as an accomplice. The minister took fright and stopped using Sobukwe as an interpreter.

There was another incident which was a reminder of the need for caution. Patrick Laurence, a reporter on *The Star* newspaper in Johannesburg, wrote an article in which he quoted Sobukwe. He mailed it in a normal street letter box to a colleague in London, with a covering letter explaining it was intended for possible publication in *The Observer*. The letter never reached the colleague. Instead, according to the official version, it was opened by an unknown person in Britain and posted back to South Africa—to the Commissioner of Police. In fact, it was more than likely that Laurence's letter had simply been intercepted in the extensive system of checking letters in force in South Africa for many years. Either way, the police had the evidence to prosecute Laurence: he was charged with attempting to publish the statements of a banned person, and was sentenced to eighteen months' imprisonment, suspended for three years. After this, people remembered to be more careful what they wrote in letters.

When Sobukwe moved into the Galeshewe house, he had to buy his own furniture. It was a large house and furnishing it was costly. The South African Council of Churches stepped in with a substantial grant of R2,000. The council, through its General Secretary, Bishop B.B. Burnett, also relieved the pressure on Sobukwe by saying that it would make money available for a year to supplement his earnings, and that it would be willing to consider any further request for funds after that.

Veronica looked at furniture in Johannesburg; in Kimberley, Sobukwe and I toured the local shops looking for what was needed—principally a lounge suite, bedroom suite, refrigerator, stove, linen and carpets. The lounge suite created the biggest problem: while on Robben Island, he said, he had set his heart on one day having a black, leather-type suite. It epitomised what he described as a 'posh lounge'.

We did find such a black lounge suite in a furniture shop—and it was expensive. Veronica was using her pension money but I was also conscious that I could be called to account to the Council of Churches for how the donated money was spent. I went with Sobukwe to a whole series of furniture shops—just about every one we could find in Kimberley—trying to steer him towards other, less expensive lounge suites. But, despite my coaxing, his emotions were fixed on that black one. Finally, after two days of shopping, I decided that anyone who had spent six years' solitary imprisonment on the island was entitled to a lounge suite of his dreams and we went ahead with the purchase.

The house was simply too big to furnish entirely. It was also unpleasantly cold on winter nights, and heating was always difficult and inadequate.

The Prisons Trial finally ended in July 1969: as expected, Judge Cillie found us guilty. In sentencing, he took care to separate us to avoid a joint reaction from us: Gandar was given a fine, alternatively imprisonment, while I was sentenced to six months' jail, suspended for three years. If we had both been sentenced to a fine, alternatively imprisonment, we would have elected to demonstrate our views about the trial and the judge by refusing to pay the fines and instead to go to jail.

In any event, the mere fact that the judge had not been able to give us outright jail sentences was hailed as a great victory in non-government circles. One small example was the crowd which cheered us when we came out of the court. Later, when Gandar and I decided after long discussion that we should take the sentences, even though they were mild, to the Appeal Court, our friends and supporters talked us out of it: 'Why bother?' they asked, 'You've won.'

Free for the first time in four years from the threat of going to prison and back at full-time work on the newspaper, as night editor, I resolved my 'skirt world': Anne Sassoon and I decided to marry. She was an artist and we had met the year before, shortly before the trial began. She had two small children, Amanda and Daniel, from a previous marriage and this led to a certain amount of embarrassment with Sobukwe. For, in February that year, while he was still on the island, I had let him know that a previous relationship—with a woman who also had two young children—had ended and he had written in rollicking style to say how relieved he felt: 'In a way I prayed for it. I don't see why you should get yourself a house-broken mare. You're young enough to house-break and tame your own wild mare. No hand-me-downs, Benjie!' Now here I was, having to confess that I was marrying 'a house-broken mare'. He took it well.

Anne and I were married in October. Sobukwe applied to travel to Johannesburg for the wedding. A few days before, he sent a telegram: 'Permission refused. Welcome to Anne. Joining glorious brothers. Shalom. Bob.' He was also denied permission to visit Johannesburg for the consecration in the following month of his brother, Ernest, as Bishop Suffragan of the Anglican Diocese of St John's, Umtata, in Transkei—only the third black bishop in the church of that time.

I drove with Anne to Kimberley for the meeting that meant so much to me. She was apprehensive. 'Many South Africans,' she remembers, 'if they had been me, speeding along the road to Kimberley, would have felt excited at the prospect of meeting the famous Robert Sobukwe. But I had never especially wanted to meet famous people as such, least of all politicians. I had certainly been moved by his solitary state on Robben Island, so much so that it had given me the idea for a painting. But I wasn't at all sure we would have anything to say to each other. Benjie loved him so much, but I was secretly scared that I might not warm to him at all. We might find each other completely boring.

'To make our meeting even more nerve-wracking, Benjie couldn't be part of it. Because of the banning orders it was just going to be me and Bob. First Benjie collected him and left him sitting on a bench outside the municipal art gallery, and then fetched me from the hotel, so that Bob was never with both of us at once.

'He stood up as I approached, a tall elegant man with such life and kindness shining in his face that my shyness immediately vanished and so did my misgivings. I liked him enormously, straightaway.

'We found ourselves walking through the gallery and conversation was no problem. Politics didn't come into it. We spoke about art, the paintings in the gallery, what I was trying to do with my paintings, and about books.'

Her feelings were matched by Sobukwe. For, as he was later to write to Anne: 'When I heard Benjie was coming with you, I had coached myself to smile appropriately and show the required amount of enthusiasm when I met you, in order not to disappoint Benjie who was obviously and helplessly head over heels in love with you.

'It was a relief and a pleasure to find that I did not need to dissimulate. I was happy to meet you and look forward to seeing you as mistress of your own house "in freedom".'

We always did ensure that the three of us were not together at the same time in public. Had we been found together it would have opened him, and us, to prosecution. On one occasion, Anne and I and our collection of children were returning to Johannesburg by train from Cape Town: Sobukwe was given permission to go to the Kimberley railway station at dawn and we had a brief reunion on the platform while the train engine was changed. I decided, whether correctly I have never been sure, that our young children did not count for purposes of defining a 'gathering' in terms of the banning so we stood in a small crowd on the station with Sobukwe.

Once more or less settled into the house he turned to gardening again. 'So far it is more of an archaeological excavation that we are engaged in, unearthing layers of rock,' he wrote. 'Now and again we come across an interesting formation and our hearts beat fast—Diamonds! we think. But we have unearthed no hidden treasures, so far.'

From Cape Town, Moira Henderson and Eulalie Stott went to Kimberley at the start of 1970. After having done so much for him over the years, they now met him for the first time. 'I thought he was the most super person I'd ever come across,' remembered Moira, who died in May 1989. 'He had the gift that top Englishmen have got, such as Robert Birley [the late former headmaster of Eton who, in his retirement, went to South Africa to work in education], and John Maud [a former British ambassador to South Africa]. When you are with them they make you feel you are the only person they are interested in, and that what you say is terribly important, whereas it is probably something mundane that they have heard a hundred times before.'

Although both women were publicly and actively anti-apartheid —Moira played a leading role in helping the families of detained and jailed people, and Eulalie was a city councillor—they were also part of Cape Town's white English-speaking social establishment. Moira knew Julian Ogilvie Thomson, the head of De Beers, and he had offered her the use of a company apartment in Kimberley if she went there.

Now, planning to visit Sobukwe, she contacted Ogilvie

Thomson about the apartment. But he backed off and instead offered to have a caravan hired which would be sited at the municipality's caravan park. Moira rejected this, if only because of the summer heat. She was then offered—and accepted—a shed, apparently usually used to garage a car, on the edge of the De Beers museum at the Big Hole. It had an earthen floor; two tables and chairs were provided for the lunch which the museum restaurant was to send in. But the restaurant manager was embarrassed about the heaping on of indignities, and burst out, 'To hell with the lot of them, you'll have your lunch in the restaurant.' They had their lunch on the 'white' side: the two women, Sobukwe and a friend at two adjoining tables placed a foot apart so that his banning orders would not be infringed.

It says much about De Beers and South Africa that this giant corporation behaved like this. There is hardly a more powerful organisation in the country than De Beers, or at least its parent, the Anglo American Corporation. It was inconceivable that the government, even if it wished to, could do the slightest thing to 'punish' De Beers if company officials had behaved with a modicum of respect towards Sobukwe. But Sobukwe was black and radical and that was enough to frighten the men at the head of the corporation. Even the social connections of Moira and Eulalie could not overcome this.

Nor was this the only time that De Beers was craven in regard to Sobukwe. Two years later, Robert I. Rotberg, then Professor of Political Science at the Massachusetts Institute of Technology in Boston, went to Kimberley to study the De Beers mine and archives. He was a privileged guest because the doors had been opened for him by Harry Oppenheimer. Rotberg and I met while he was in Johannesburg and I arranged an introduction for him to Sobukwe. In Kimberley, Rotberg had lunch at the home of the De Beers manager and asked whether he could be given a lift afterwards as he was meeting Sobukwe. But he was told that De Deers wanted no connection with Sobukwe. At the end of the lunch he was escorted to the front gate and left to make his own way to Sobukwe.

They had tea together in Rotberg's room at the Savoy, then the best hotel in town. It was the first time Sobukwe had been in it. Rotberg thought he was 'alert, sensitive, open, amazingly un-bitter, determined but not overtly militant, and absolutely charming'.

Even stronger impressions were left with two other American

visitors, Jim and Diana Thomson. Jim was Curator of the Nieman Fellowship for Journalism at Harvard University, and went to South Africa in July 1975 because he was worried about the presence of South Africans in the fellowship programme, and wanted changes in the selection process if they were to continue. Diana taught writing at Harvard. At my urging, they went to Kimberley to meet Sobukwe, had five hours with him, and then Diana spent more hours with him a few days later at my home in Johannesburg.

'He was tall and soft-spoken. His English was surprisingly unaccented. There was a largeness and a gentleness that I remember being struck by,' says Jim Thomson. 'He sat back and talked quietly. He was relaxed. The central fact that emerged to me was his defence of non-violence.'

To which Diana adds: 'What he talked about almost nonstop was the beauty of democracy and the beauty of America because we represented democracy, and how much it meant to talk to us because we were Americans and we understood democracy. I imagine that no one had ever defended democracy like that since Thomas Jefferson.

'There was a strong religious component: he was deeply religious and deeply spiritual. He was a profound Christian. But he was not the kind of religious person who hits you over the head with God all the time. It was so deep in him that it pervaded everything he said without being blatant.'

Jim: 'And there was an unshakeable faith that God's good purposes would ultimately prevail in South Africa.'

Diana: 'I felt his own personal trust in God made him trust in what his own life had been, and to me it seemed he accepted it.'

They had both been struck by what they say was the 'religious-spiritual' quality they found in many black and white anti-apartheid leaders they met during their visit to South Africa. But, says Jim, 'in this man there was the serene confidence one associated with Martin Luther King in the US'.

Diana: 'I felt that the two most saintly people I met in South Africa were Bob Sobukwe and [the Rev] Beyers Naude. But I picked up that Bob, perhaps because of his suffering, came across as the joyous type of saint, whereas Beyers was also a saint but absolutely ridden with guilt and suffering.'

The Thomsons were already well on the way to achieving notoriety—among whites, that is—for not bothering to conceal their disgust about apartheid. Meeting Sobukwe added to their feelings and reputation. On the night of the second meeting with Sobukwe they went to dinner at the home of an Afrikaner Nationalist editor: 'We were incensed on behalf of Bob when we got to that dinner party because that beautiful man had been treated like that,' says Diana. 'When all those white ladies there asked me how I liked South Africa, I told them. That created tensions.'

A year later, in the US, a white exile came to Diana, took her hand and said: 'I hear you behaved abominably in South Africa, and I'm proud to shake your hand.'

A visit to Kimberley in 1974 by two other Americans had far-reaching consequences for the Sobukwe family. They were Andrew Young, a black Congressman noted for leadership in the US civil rights movement, and Arthur Ashe, a tennis star who was to go on to become the first black winner of the Wimbledon singles championship. 'There are people who shape history. I put Robert Sobukwe in that class,' Young said in a Press interview. Ashe said: 'He is a real leader of the African people. It is so evident, so obvious, after spending two hours with him . . .'

What particularly struck both of them was what others saw too: Sobukwe's lack of bitterness and the complete absence of hostility. 'There are people with limited or no physical resources who fight injustice through the sheer force of their personalities,' said Young. 'Like Martin Luther King, Robert Sobukwe is one. I was even thinking during my talk with him that one of these days the South African government may have to go to Sobukwe like the British went to Kenyatta. There is a need for strong men to pull the people together around common goals.'

Young offered to take the two oldest children, Miliswa and Dini, to his home in Atlanta, Georgia, and ensure they were given the schooling they deserved. By coincidence, a few months later, I made my first trip to the United States and contacted Young at Sobukwe's request. Sobukwe wanted the children to have the chance of going to the US. I told Young that he had unusual power to get the children out of South Africa. The government was against young blacks going abroad to study; it was bothered about the ideas and modes of behaviour they would pick up and bring back home; in white parlance, they would become 'cheeky'.

But Young had made a great impact: he was a black leader—one of the few to have been admitted to South Africa—and while he had been highly critical of apartheid he had not supported a violent response but had instead spoken in Christian terms about the need for racial reconciliation and a non-violent resolution. The government would have difficulty in refusing anything he asked, I thought. If he supported applications for passports for Miliswa and Dini, I was sure the government would not dare to turn them down.

Others must have made the same point to Young and he went ahead. In June 1975, Miliswa, then nearly 21, and Dini, who was 19, did get out. Young ensured VIP treatment for them: the United States Consul-General in Johannesburg went to the airport to make sure their visas were in order. They lived in Young's home for a long time. It was generous behaviour. I was even more impressed when, at the end of 1976, while working for six months at the *Boston Globe*, I visited him at his home and also asked whether I could interview Dini. 'That's entirely up to Dini,' said Young. I liked him for that: his appointment as US Ambassador to the United Nations was to be announced by President-elect Carter the next day. It would have done Young's political career no harm, and perhaps even some good, to have had media publicity about his guardianship of these children of a South African black leader.

Regretfully, neither Ashe nor Young entirely stayed the course. A year or so later Ashe was on another visit to South Africa and told me he was going to Kimberley to visit Sobukwe. But he did not go, and nor did he send an explanation. And Young, too, returned, this time in a blaze of publicity and with a sizeable entourage of officials and friends: he was no longer only a Congressman, but a high-profile Ambassador visiting the country at the invitation of Harry Oppenheimer and having talks with leading businessmen.

He did not contact Sobukwe. He had Sobukwe's two children staying with him in the US, he knew that Sobukwe was not allowed to leave Kimberley, but he failed even to put through a phone call to Sobukwe. Nor did any member of his large entourage do the job for him. On the Sunday that Young flew out of the country, I was in constant touch with Sobukwe on the phone: I felt desperately sorry for him as shocked realisation grew in him that Andrew Young was not bothering about him. The hurt over the phone line was a palpable thing.

How Can Man Die Better

It drove me that night to get hold of Steve McDonald, the member of the US Embassy in Pretoria whom I knew had been the official assigned to the Young trip. McDonald was an exceptional diplomat who had many friends across the colour line. He had told me that he had personally given Sobukwe's telephone number to Young. But, although he had no part in Young's omission, poor Steve had to endure my angry tongue that night: I asked him to convey to Young, with all the expletives I was using, exactly what I thought of him as a human-being. Young was at that point in mid-air, in an official US plane. I never discovered what followed upon my call. It is possible that McDonald got a message through to Young; later that evening, Sobukwe's phone rang twice but there was only garbled sound on the line. Possibly Young, made aware of what he had done, tried to put through a call.

Over several years, the Anglican Dean of Johannesburg, the Very Rev G.A. ffrench-Beytagh, was a consistent helper of the Sobukwe family. When Sobukwe was still on the island, I turned to the Dean for winter clothing for the children, and whenever else there was need. His help was always given openly, with a cheque handed to me—together with a card of Christian greetings which I would pass on to Veronica Sobukwe.

The Dean was helping many people and in February 1971 the government went after him, detaining him and then charging him—under the Terrorism Act no less—with taking part in the activities of illegal organisations. Another charge related to underground leaflets which the police claimed to have found in his home. Those who knew the Dean said the leaflets had been planted there. Then, in trying to make the charges stick, the police went in search of more information by raiding many people and organisations. I was among these: we had a raid which began at around 6.30 a.m. and went on for the next nine hours, with eight Security policemen crowding into our apartment, searching even the children's toy box.

They were quite excited because they found a huge amount of documentary material to do with black politics: it stood from floor to ceiling in a wall cupboard. During the Prisons Trial, I had completed the Honours degree in African Studies at the University of the Witwatersrand and was now working on these papers for an application to register for a doctorate. Among the papers were three copies of the (South African) *Guardian* newspaper which had been a communist paper before it was banned. My copies were of issues of twenty-five years before.

Apart from removing the *Guardian*, the police took books and many research and personal papers—my Sobukwe files among them. Many, many months later I applied for the material and most was returned to me: but each document had on it—and still does—the scrawled initials of a Security policeman. I had a sense of violation. I put the papers away. It was a long time before I felt able to bring myself to handle those papers and file covers again.

During the hours of the raid, a number of bits of paper found their way out of the apartment. A few sheets of paper—my notes of an interview with a banned person—were among them. Robert Botha, a newspaper photographer who was among the journalists standing in the street to cover the raid, took these sheets of paper to his office. Unfortunately, a police spy in the office, or it might have been in the local pub used by journalists, told the Security Police about the documents; the police rushed in and seized them.

In due course, I was joined to the Dean's trial: the charge sheet listed me as a 'co-conspirator'. It didn't seem to mean much and was probably intended, in official eyes, as some kind of smear. I saw it differently: I was proud to be linked with ffrench-Beytagh. Cillie, the same judge who had presided in the Prisons Trial, was in charge. The main State witness was a Security Police agent who had insinuated himself into the Dean's circles by posing as a man seeking religious guidance. Cillie found ffrench-Beytagh guilty and sentenced him to five years' imprisonment. On this occasion justice did triumph: on appeal the next year, the Dean was acquitted. He left the country.

But I had my own troubles, because the police charged me with possessing 'indecent, objectionable, etc' material—the banned newspapers. For good measure, in a real attempt at a smear, I was also charged with theft: of having stolen my own documents—the sheets of paper which the police had grabbed from Robert Botha. Of course, those documents had never been in the possession of the police: they knew that as well as I did; the documents had gone out of the apartment before the police could lay hands on them. But that meant nothing: a police signature was simply put on the documents, and a Security policeman gave perjured evidence that he had actually seized the documents during the raid. I was found guilty on both charges, and given suspended sentences.

This was serious because the prosecutor was speaking of 'deliberate defiance of the State', and I now had two sets of suspended sentences in a row. Imprisonment would be likely if I was ever charged with anything else. So I went to appeal and succeeded in having the theft charge thrown out at the next level of the courts—not because the judge found that the police had lied, but simply because the warrant to raid me was held not to have covered the documents concerned. The conviction for possession remained, even after an appeal to the highest court.

During the first court hearing, I was incensed at listening to the Security Police lie under oath. During a tea interval I went up to a group of them outside the court and upbraided them for doing so. It drew a swift and unanswerable response. One of them looked me straight in the face and said coldly: 'We'll stop at nothing to get you.'

At first, Sobukwe wrote worriedly that he did not want to see me in the dock again. 'These boys are after your blood,' he said. But once the trial went ahead and I was found guilty, he poked fun at me—and at the absurdity of the theft charge. 'There's an excuse for a Bantu to indulge in theft because he can at least argue that he acted under the pressure of necessity,' he wrote. 'But for a white man, and a white man of your standing at that, there is just no excuse. "Disgraceful" is the word that came to mind immediately I read the report in the paper. Honestly you are building up a reputation for yourself that is becoming extremely embarrassing to us of the family in defying the law (as the prosecutor correctly observed) and stealing your own property . . .

On my trips to Kimberley, as I was not allowed to go to Sobukwe's home, there was nowhere we could have a meal or even a cup of tea together. The best we could do was to buy a pie or sandwiches and a carton of milk from a corner shop and drive to one of our spots outside the town. Later, De Beers happened to open a modest café at the Big Hole, as part of a village which imaginatively re-created the early days of diamond mining. The café was split into two equal sections, with the kitchen in between; one part was for use by whites, the other for those who were not white. The staff would not allow us into the white section, but said we could go into the 'non-white' section. That was the sort of oddity one had to expect in the nature of racial discrimination: Sobukwe could not be accepted as white, but I could be accepted as not being white.

But it was exciting for us. For the first time in more than twelve years, since we had first met, we were able to sit at a table in a public place and share a pot of tea. We also ate sausage rolls as we marvelled at the progress being made in South Africa! The Big Hole's café became a regular haunt for us, until overtaken when Sobukwe became friends with a local family, Fatima and Achmat Laher, who made their home available to us. This too became something for astonishment: 'Look at us,' we would say to each other. 'Isn't it amazing actually being able to sit in comfortable armchairs in a pleasant lounge and have tea brought to us!'

Eventually I was put to shame by an American visitor who told me he had simply invited Sobukwe to his hotel room and had sat and talked to him there; no one had bothered them. This coincided with the slow process of opening quality hotels to black visitors. So I also used my hotel room—but, still inhibited by my South Africanness, always first told the hotel manager what I was going to do. He would politely tell me that it was all right as long as none of the other white guests objected.

Now and again we strolled through the city centre, and I was struck by the friendly way in which local coloureds and blacks always greeted him—and his gravely courteous hello to them. Whites largely ignored him. He told me that that was the pattern of his everyday contacts. But he never encountered rudeness. What did irritate him was the treatment he suffered from a white teller in the local bank he used who persistently addressed him as 'Robert'. Sobukwe finally said to him: 'We haven't even been introduced so why do you call me by my first name?' The teller blushed and apologised. It was a polite 'Mr Sobukwe' from then on.

21

The major disagreement between Sobukwe and me was over the Bantustans. Starting early in the Sixties, I had become friendly with the Zulu chief Gatsha Buthelezi, and both liked him as a person and thought him a significant force in fighting against apartheid. Sobukwe had known him for even longer as they had, for a time, been students together in the 1940s at the Fort Hare University College. I believed that Buthelezi was playing to a clever stratagem, gaining stature and visibility through taking part in the government's separate development apparatus, while using the platform to fight against apartheid.

Sobukwe totally disagreed. He argued that non-collaboration was the only weapon which blacks should use and that it was the only way to block what the government was trying to do. Blacks should simply refuse to be involved. Whatever Buthelezi's intentions might be, he was playing into the government's hands by giving credibility and a form of respectability to separate development. Sobukwe was anxious, too, about Buthelezi's role among blacks: he feared that Buthelezi's claims to be a black national leader ran second to his Zulu nationalist outlook and this had dangerous implications for unity.

I maintained my view over several years and many discussions. Gradually, however, Buthelezi's behaviour confirmed Sobukwe's anxieties. Buthelezi was co-opted into the Afrikaner Nationalist system; he failed to make any real headway against apartheid; and he did become more Zulu than nationalist, with what were finally to prove murderously divisive results, with many deaths in clashes between his followers and anti-government groups.

After a lot of thought I finally told Sobukwe I agreed with him, and that I had been wrong in my assessment. I had reached the conclusion that Buthelezi was doing more harm than any good in collaborating with the government. I felt humble about making such a major retraction; he was kind about it.

Another equally key issue was that of violence. It grew more important all the time, as blacks sought ways of opposing a government so determined to hold onto office. Because of uneasiness about what the Security Police might be able to listen to, violence did not feature as a regular topic of discussion. But it arose often enough for me to have the impression that, in essence, Sobukwe's view had not changed since 1960: he did not like violence; he was disturbed about it not only on grounds of principle but because of his consciousness of the lives it would end. In 1976, during the 'children's revolt' which flared in much of South Africa, his attitude was a mixture of admiration and pride in the children, and acute worry about just how many protesters the government would be prepared to kill.

Years later, while visiting Zeph Mothopeng in Johannesburg Prison, where he was serving his current fifteen-year sentence, I questioned him about Sobukwe's views. With a jail warder listening, I spoke in roundabout terms: Had Sobukwe believed in 'non-Gandhian methods'? I asked. 'No,' said Mothopeng with a smile, 'he was too much of a Christian.'

Mothopeng, ill with cancer, was released from jail late in 1988. He travelled to Britain for treatment the following April and we were able to continue our conversation there in more direct language. 'Sobukwe believed in the concept of non-violence,' said Mothopeng, 'although he was forced over the years, by what happened, to accept that the ruled could not avoid turning to violence. When you talk of non-violence, you presume that the other side has a conscience and understands the nature of non-violent protest. But the rulers in South Africa have not had a conscience. The ruled, of course, will ask what's the point of facing people who are armed to the teeth and ready to use their arms, if we don't also have arms.

'Sobukwe did not like it and I don't think that he would ever have been commander of the army.'

How indeed to resist the government? As Sobukwe came off Robben Island, the Nationalists still gave every impression of being more invulnerable than ever. The decade of the Sixties had begun with John Vorster the Minister of Justice strengthening security laws and the Security Police; it closed with John Vorster the Prime Minister bringing a new security apparatus into being. The Bureau for State Security was created by Parliament in 1969 and was immediately dubbed BOSS by the opposition Press; or, as my friend Ernie Wentzel quipped, the real meaning was in the initials, BO and SS. Headed by the Security Police chief, General Hendrik van den Bergh, BOSS was intended as a super-duper umbrella intelligence agency, something akin to the CIA, MI5 and KGB rolled into one, and responsible only to the Prime Minister.

Its creation marked the high point of police power. But, although BOSS had pervasive influence, it did not have quite as much as Vorster and van den Bergh had planned. One of their major goals was to place military intelligence within BOSS' orbit so as to bring the army's growing and unchallenged demands for money and arms under scrutiny. Behind the scenes, however, the military leaders warned Vorster not to interfere in their affairs and he backed away from this provision. There was still enough left in BOSS to make it powerful and feared.

In the same year, the grip on information was tightened yet again by changing the Official Secrets Act to include the phrase, 'security matter'—which, as usual, was so widely defined that it could mean almost anything the government wanted it to mean. Another law gave the government the power to prevent evidence being given in court for reasons of the interests of the State or public security. And censorship of newspapers and magazines outside the mainstream was made easier by stipulating that not only could a current issue be banned, but all future issues too. There was even the Prohibition of Disguises Act, making it an offence for anyone to be found disguised in circumstances in which it could be deemed that he or she intended committing an offence.

On the racial front, the scheming for 'grand apartheid' went on apace, but the wording changed. Government leaders spoke of racial 'differentiation'; it sounded better than 'discrimination'. Instead of apartheid, there was 'separate development' or 'multi-nationalism' to stress the latest official notion of South Africans as a series of different nations of different colours. The word 'homelands', denoting the rural tribal areas, was assiduously promoted for the Bantustans until it entered everyday language. It conveyed the political concept fundamental to the government's racial ideology although, in reality, countless numbers of black people in the cities had little or no connection with their supposed homelands.

Step by step, through the early 1970s, laws were enacted to provide 'homeland' blacks with their own citizenship as the prelude to stripping them of their South African citizenship. Adding to dispossession through the clearing of 'black spots', another estimated 400,000 were uprooted because of the phasing out of the labour tenant system on white-owned farms; they were sent packing, taking their few goods and their cattle with them, but with nowhere to go. Buthelezi described it in hauntingly mournful terms: 'There is unfolding one of those great human tragedies for which South Africa is becoming well known ... Thousands of evicted Zulus are wandering homeless through Northern Natal and Zululand—a great black trek—preferring to keep on the move rather than lose their cattle.'

These were inconsequential details to the government. It was intent on its strategy to safeguard white interests.

Yet, with all this confidence and ruthlessness, the signs were there that Afrikaner Nationalists were beginning to bend under the weight of events. The process had begun tentatively as Vorster settled in as Prime Minister and it then speeded up considerably during the 1970s. A new chapter was beginning, it seemed at the time, when President Hastings Banda of Malawi came on a state visit in 1972. There was high drama in a photograph on the front page of the *Rand Daily Mail*—I placed it there—showing Vorster flanked by two Malawian women at a banquet hosted by Banda. White extreme right-wingers bought 5,000 copies of that issue of the newspaper for what they saw as its propaganda value for their cause.

The reforms carried out by President P.W. Botha during the 1980s, and which drew so much international attention, obscured the fact that Vorster was responsible for the first Afrikaner Nationalist break from the past. As early as mid-1975, I tried to project the mood of the time in an article in *Africa Special Report* magazine: 'Change is the word of the moment in South Africa. Seldom in the country's history has there been such insistent widespread demand for change. Never before has a South African government shown itself so willing to effect change.' The country, I noted, no longer presented the monolithic, granite-like structure of the Sixties. Since Banda's visit there had been 'a steady, if irregularly spaced, train of events'. Among the changes I listed: most leading hotels now accepted black guests; in Johannesburg, municipal libraries and park benches had been desegregated; dining and lounge cars on luxury trains had dropped apartheid; whites and blacks were competing in sport on a widening scale; there were more than 1,000 works committees, to give black workers a voice, and the training of blacks for industry had begun.

But, the article went on, South Africa remained a racist society. What was happening could be described as 'significant insignificant change'. The Bantustan policy was being pushed forward as fast as possible; in the social sphere there was as much rigidity as ever in blocking private contacts across the colour line; and government control remained absolute at all levels of society: 'this is still a government determined to control change—where it happens, when it happens and how it happens'.

It was at this time too that the sub-continent was creeping up on South Africa. With unexpected speed, Portugal lost its hold on Mozambique and Angola. By 1975, its rule was ended, creating hopes of new pressures on the South African government. The changing scenario, at home and on the borders, refreshed Sobukwe's optimism.

His thinking appeared in the pages of *The Times* of London. Nicholas Ashford, the newspaper's correspondent in South Africa, went to Kimberley and his insightful report—carefully and cleverly written to avoid actually quoting Sobukwe, even while going beyond what any local journalist would have considered safe for publication—appeared on 27 October 1975 under the headline: The Silent Triumph of a Black South African:

> A new sign has just been painted on the window of a small shop just inside the boundary line of Galeshewe African township on the outskirts of Kimberley. It says quite simply, 'Robert Sobukwe, Attorney'. The sign represents a personal triumph for one black South African over myriad restrictions on his freedom that would have cowed a lesser man long ago . . .
>
> Mr Sobukwe is a man of great intellectual vigour who possesses three degrees . . . A conversation with him covers not only the political situation in southern Africa but also Mr Harold Wilson's brand of socialism and the historical background to the Northern Ireland problem, with quotations

Benjamin Pogrund

from Dr Kwame Nkrumah and the [BBC's] Reith Lectures.

He talks about the early days of African Nationalism, when there seemed a real chance that the winds of change would blow as far as Pretoria. He coolly analyses the differences that developed between the all-African PAC and the ANC which, he felt, was too dependent on its white left-wing supporters. He still sees a need for an all-black nationalist movement but is worried that black racialism—a charge of which he used to be, incorrectly, accused—could develop if Africans continue to be denied political rights.

He speaks with sadness of the homeland leaders, many of whom he admires but who, he feels, have made unacceptable compromises. Chief Gatsha Buthelezi is an old friend, a man of intelligence and ability. But he no longer speaks on behalf of Africans as a whole, only one tribe—the Zulus. Inadvertently Chief Buthelezi has become identified with the government's policy of separate development rather than the African unity he once stood for.

Mr Sobukwe is not impressed by the changes said to be taking place within South Africa. The whole apparatus of apartheid not only remains intact but has been strengthened. But he does detect a modification in white attitudes and this, he believes, could be of great significance. The 'monolithic arrogance' of the ruling Nationalist Party seems to be starting to crumble.

Small changes have struck him. Whites are now more respectful towards Africans. He has received dinner invitations from white lawyers who had never previously communicated with him. White South African journalists have suddenly 'rediscovered' him and ask for audiences. He invariably refuses because he thinks the change in attitude has been dictated by the government rather than coming from the people themselves.

He also notices a shift in emphasis from politics to economics in discussion about South Africa, inspired no doubt by the government, which constantly stresses the need to develop a middle class among the blacks. People now appear to be more concerned with economic development rather than political freedom. For instance, critics of the government's homeland policy tend to attack it because the homelands are seen to be not economically viable, rather than because the whole policy is politically and morally abhorrent.

He accepts that it is important for people to have full stomachs, but would personally prefer to have fewer meals and more freedom.

Mr Sobukwe talks about freedom with an idealism that has not been dulled by years of repression. He wants people, both black and white, to be consulted, not just told what to do. He describes himself as a socialist but believes in consensus politics; he does not want to see one form of totalitarianism replaced by another.

His critics believe that it is already too late for his type of idealism: that the days when blacks and whites would have engaged in constructive dialogue have long since passed. But Mr Sobukwe is more optimistic. He senses that the youth of all races wants to see change. He considers that the collapse of the Portuguese regime, which most Africans thought was indestructible, has raised hopes that the Nationalist government is itself not totally impregnable. He remains confident that the inexorable advance of African Nationalism will manage to reach its goal in South Africa within his lifetime.

While men like Mr Sobukwe are around there is still hope that real change may take place in South Africa without recourse to violence and bloodshed. The tragedy is that so long as he remains a 'banned person' he is inaudible to the people who ought to be heeding his words.

Ashford wrote during a period when South Africa was generally not a major story in the world's media; but there was still a fair amount of interest and foreign correspondents were always coming through. Those who went to see Sobukwe have provided a form of running commentary on his thinking.

Thus Anthony Lewis of the *New York Times* was some years later to recall meeting Sobukwe: 'A few times in his life a newspaper reporter meets a political figure and senses authentic greatness: a magnetic external presence combined with a sense of inner serenity. That happened to me on 9 June 1975, in the South African mining town of Kimberley. I met Robert Sobukwe.

'He was despised and rejected by those who hold power in his country. He lived in enforced obscurity, unable to travel, his countrymen forbidden to read his words. But there was a power in him that shone through all the petty cruelties of official suppression. It was the power of belief in humanity, in non-violent change toward justice...'

Robert Sobukwe 'suffered indignities that would destroy most of us,' said Lewis, but none of it showed in him.

'Meeting him, one saw a man utterly at peace with himself—and with his tormentors. He laughed a lot. And when he spoke of some ingenious twist of racial discrimination in South Africa, he shook his head as if in amazement at human foolishness and said: "Honestly..."

'I said I thought the Afrikaners who rule South Africa still had a strong sense of having been treated unfairly by the English-speaking whites. "I agree with them," Mr Sobukwe said. "I think there's a lot in that. But then why don't they understand how we feel when we suffer discrimination? Honestly..."'

Lewis went on to note Sobukwe's view that whites and blacks had to live together in South Africa: '"A non-racial society. 'That remains my goal. I would make racism a crime, no matter from which side it came—like an American civil rights law."'

But Sobukwe saw 'that time was running out for his ideas, that anti-white feeling was growing among blacks. He noted with quiet irony that whites were shocked at expressions of black antagonism: "Until now it has been the white prerogative to hate." He predicted, correctly [what was to burst out in Soweto almost exactly a year later], that students would lead the way in expressing black feelings, and that they would be suppressed. The government would discount the students' protests, he said, "but they are in fact the barometer of black opinion".

'He had no illusion of quick change in South Africa. No easy revolutionary slogans came to his lips. He thought it would be a long, hard struggle to persuade the white minority that its own true interest lay in treating non-whites as fellow human-beings. In the end, he said, as whites felt the pressures of the world, they would find themselves needing "the loyalty of the blacks. That will be the crucial dilemma".'

Jan Tystad of Norway's *Dagbladet* newspaper also went to Kimberley and in February 1976 reported Sobukwe's optimistic belief that there would be black majority rule in Rhodesia within a year and in South Africa within five years. 'Sobukwe is convinced that a guerilla war will break out in southern Africa; it has started in Rhodesia and it will start in Namibia and spread to South Africa. African rule in Angola and Mozambique has started a movement which will spread across the whole of southern Africa.' On South Africa, Tystad recorded Sobukwe's view that blacks were becoming more politically aware and that this would result in more strikes and demonstrations—and that 'The young are getting increasingly impatient and demand changes. They want part of the wealth and political influence.'

Sobukwe sounded the same themes in an interview with Bernard D. Nossiter of the *Washington Post* who wrote of him, also in February 1976: 'For a man starved of intellectual companionship in this sleepy backwater, Sobukwe bears his existence with great cheerfulness and an unlooked-for sense of humour. Trim at 51, he has a remarkable physical resemblance to the late Martin Luther King and an almost religious certainty in the rightness of his case and its eventual triumph.' Sobukwe troubled the government like an 'aching tooth', said Nossiter: 'Just the other day, [Prime Minister] Vorster felt compelled to explain to Parliament that he had not let Sobukwe accept an invitation to the presidential inauguration in Liberia because no one had "elected" Sobukwe a leader.'

It was clearly necessary for Sobukwe to accept that there was to be no early remission from Kimberley. Soon after arriving in Kimberley and being approached by H.Z.M. Nzimande, he decided on a change of career: he would undergo articles for three years to qualify as a solicitor. Sobukwe checked with the local Security Police, who indicated that they would agree to his studying law: their approval was necessary because his banning orders had to be altered to allow him to enter the courts.

Nzimande profited through having Sobukwe working for him: the clients rolled in. That might have been why he dragged his feet about having Sobukwe's articles of clerkship registered with the Cape Law Society. The period of service could not begin until the articles were registered, so the longer the delay the longer Sobukwe would be tied to Nzimande's office. Nzimande kept promising to prepare and sign the articles, but always had excuses for not having done so. At the beginning of 1970, Sobukwe enrolled as a correspondence student with the University of South Africa for his law studies. The National Union of South African Students met the cost of the courses. Its General Secretary, Sheila Lapinsky, was always helpful and perhaps this played a part in the banning which the government later imposed on her.

Still Nzimande stalled. He was quite shameless. I resorted to repeated phone calls: 'Mr Nzimande, when are you going to register Bob's articles?' It took months of this sort of harassment before he finally signed the papers—at the end of March 1971.

Although the police had indicated they did not oppose Sobukwe doing his articles, there was some worry that he might run into difficulties from white lawyers and in the courts, with objections that his political challenge to the structure of the State made him unfit to be an 'officer of the court', in the phrase used for lawyers whether in government employ or in private practice.

But there were friends behind the scenes: during a visit to Cape Town I bumped into Philip Herbstein, who was a highly respected solicitor there and a leader in the Cape Law Society. I knew him because, years before, while still a student, I had served two years of legal articles with him. He promised that he would support Sobukwe's application for registration and help to get it through as rapidly as possible.

There were no problems once Nzimande signed and forwarded the necessary papers. While serving the articles, Sobukwe completed the law examinations—and, equally necessary, had to study enough Afrikaans for a school-leaving certificate. Raymond Tucker, during his weekend coaching visit, found that Sobukwe was well up with all the study material, except for a blind spot in company law. He had no experience of handling a company, either in concept or practice. 'His greatest difficulty was in comprehending company law—how you created a company out of nothing, gave it life and then wound it up,' Tucker recalls. 'Liquidating a company, for him, meant simply tearing up the company documents.'

It was a long day's work in going over the practicalities which an aspiring attorney had to know. 'He had had to learn in isolation, without the benefit of studying in a classroom or doing articles with a solicitor who had trained him properly,' says Tucker.

Writing the examinations, Sobukwe passed all the subjects—except company law. He succeeded at the second try a few months later, in January 1975. Then preparations began for what was normally a formal application to the Supreme Court for his admission as a solicitor.

Nearly six years had gone by since Sobukwe's release from Robben Island, but he remained under the same strangling restrictions. The banning orders imposed on him had expired in May 1974, but were immediately re-issued for another five years. Even though he did not attempt to play an open political role, the government clearly viewed him as a hovering threat. A report in the *Rand Daily Mail* on 27 January 1975 conveyed the sense of his place in the political firmament: 'Even while under banning, Mr Sobukwe has been a dominant figure looming over the political scene.' Although the government had not blocked him from studying law, would his jail sentence and his bannings under the Suppression of Communism Act now be raised in court to debar him from practising law?

Jack Unterhalter, the senior barrister in Johannesburg who had seen Sobukwe in leg-irons as a witness for PAC colleagues and who had since dealt with him when briefed by Nzimande in various cases, was chosen to draw up the application papers for court. He worked with care, even having available, should the judge wish to see it, a copy of the record of Sobukwe's trial for incitement in 1960.

But there were no difficulties and, on 13 June 1975, Sobukwe was admitted as a solicitor.

For some months before, Nzimande had been suggesting to Sobukwe that, once he qualified, they go into partnership together. But Sobukwe was sickened by the high fees he saw Nzimande levy on clients—black people, and often extremely poor. Sobukwe writhed at the prices they were paying, especially knowing that many of the people had been drawn to Nzimande's office because of him. He was himself also a victim because he was paid a paltry salary. Indeed the only way he was able to survive through his articles was because Randolph Vigne, as always a supporter, made discreet arrangements in London for a regular flow of financial help. It was provided by a church-based charitable fund controlled by Canon L. John Collins of St Paul's Cathedral. The late Canon Collins took a leading part in ensuring that fighters against apartheid, and their dependants, were cared for.

Offered a partnership, Sobukwe told me that he was tempted to accept it and to remain for six months—for the specific purpose of inflicting what he thought would be the greatest hurt possible on

Nzimande, and that was to charge reasonable fees. It was the one and only time that I ever heard Sobukwe give vent to vindictiveness. But he finally decided he couldn't bear it and, as soon as possible after qualifying, he went off and started his own practice.

He ran a one-man practice, operating from a small office in a single-storeyed building in Galeshewe. It had an equally small waiting-room, usually crowded with clients. It was a typical small-town practice, handling at a direct personal level the problems and conflicts of the local people—petty criminal cases, divorce and work and accident cases. But there was also a much wider dimension because of who he was and where he was. He drew cases from long distances, from a football club in a town several hundred kilometres away and from Graaff-Reinet. Unterhalter, whom he briefed a number of times, remembers getting 'very competent, very clear instructions ... You wouldn't have thought this was a man who had so recently come out of articles.'

The cases tell some of the story: fighting the forced removal of a tribe from its traditional living grounds in the district; opposing rent rises in Galeshewe; the inquest into the death of a detainee who was said to have fallen from a window on the seventh floor of Security Police headquarters in Kimberley—this at a time when there was a run of strangely sinister deaths in incommunicado custody in the country.

In this particular episode, the window was the only one on the entire floor said to be open at the time: the police offered the explanation that it was open because there was an unpleasant smell from the air-conditioning. This sort of limp explanation which explained nothing was standard practice in detainee deaths; and, as equally standard practice, the magistrate in the inquest hearing found that no one was to blame for the death.

By August 1977, there had been forty-four deaths. The explanations included claims that a detainee slipped on a piece of soap while showering and smashed his head on the wall.

After his release from the island, Sobukwe remained interested in leaving South Africa. He felt a heavy sense of responsibility to the family; he felt he owed them the chance of living a normal life. He thought they could all flourish in the United States and he asked me to find out what might be possible. So, within a month of his release, I wrote to Marvin Wachman, the President of Lincoln University, Pennsylvania, which had once conferred an honorary doctorate on Sobukwe, about an appointment at Lincoln or other US universities. Letters went back and forth and, in March 1970, Sobukwe accepted the University of Wisconsin's offer of a research and teaching fellowship; he would be able to work for a Ph.D. in African linguistics while having an income from teaching. This was to combine with part-time teaching at Roosevelt University and the Adlai Stevenson Institute in Chicago.

But the South African government refused to release him: his application for a passport was turned down. So he again applied, as he had done while on Robben Island, for an exit permit to leave the country.

Once again there was obvious fear on the part of the government that, if he went out of the country, he would be the focus of resistance; a free Sobukwe in exile could be more dangerous to white rule than a captive Sobukwe at home. The previous time, it had been possible for the government to refuse an exit permit simply because he was in jail. But now a new legal reason for rejection had to be found. So the Secretary of the Interior wrote to Sobukwe to say that, of course, he was entitled in law to an exit permit and could have it—but he first had to produce proof that, in terms of his banning orders, he was able to leave Kimberley to go to the international airport at Johannesburg. And in due course, when Sobukwe applied to the Minister of Justice, P.C. Pelser, for relaxation of the banning orders to enable him to go to the airport so that he could obtain an exit permit, he was turned down.

Would Sobukwe be allowed at some stage to leave the country and lead a normal life, Suzman asked in Parliament. 'You can't surely punish him in perpetuity,' she said. 'That was not the sentence imposed on him by the courts.' Pelser gave the same sort of unyielding explanation as before: 'I cannot give the honourable member a reply to that,' he said, 'except that I can tell her that we cannot release him or lift the restriction on him as long as there is no change of heart on his part. That is certain ... As long as Sobukwe persists in holding the convictions he does, we simply cannot allow him to be set free altogether.'

The cat and mouse game was dragged out for a full year after Sobukwe put in his application for a passport. During that time, another banned person, Shantavothie ('Shantie') Naidoo, also applied for an exit permit and was made to suffer the same bureaucratic evasions. She had been jailed the year before after refusing to testify against twenty-two people charged with terrorism and now wanted to leave Johannesburg to start a new life in Britain.

Raymond Tucker acted for both of them and asked the Supreme Court to order the Minister of Justice to release them from their bannings so that they could get to the airport. The Minister was frustrating the common law right of South African citizens to leave the country, their lawyer argued: 'The Minister is using his powers to restrict Sobukwe to Kimberley for another purpose. He is guilty of an abuse of his powers because he has misconceived them.' Not so, countered the government's lawyer: the common law right was subject to qualification and was not absolute; the common law rights of Sobukwe and Naidoo had been 'swept away' by their banning orders.

The court agreed with the government's submissions. The case went to the Appeal Court in December 1971—only again to be turned down.

Sobukwe reacted with total calm. The decision was to be expected. 'I know these people,' he said to a friend, speaking of the judges. It seemed to come as a relief to him. He had felt it necessary to seek to leave South Africa, but had been prevented from doing so. He accepted it as his fate.

Earlier, well before this, he had believed that whatever befell him, Veronica and the children should go to the US. 'If they can't return to South Africa,' he wrote, 'they can settle anywhere in Africa should they later desire to leave the States. And, of course, they'll return to South Africa one day when the Nats are dead and forgotten.' In the event, once he was kept penned inside South Africa, Veronica stayed too.

Nearly four years after losing the appeal, out of the blue the government sent him a letter demanding payment of R1,102.91 within fourteen days. It was a large amount of money and was the State's costs awarded against Sobukwe in bringing the application to leave the country. Sobukwe's own considerable legal costs had been met at the time through contributions from sympathisers in Britain and from the Lawyers Committee for Civil Rights in Washington DC. Why the government decided to dun him later was a mystery; the Security Police must have known that he possessed little and was in no position to pay. They must also have been aware, if only because he expressed it to me with some heat in phone calls and a letter, that he was defiant and would refuse to pay anything. No action followed; but the demand was left to hang over his head.

Later, he was very occasionally given permission to visit Johannesburg. The first time was in July 1973, when Dalindyebo was in a Johannesburg hospital. In June 1974 he was again allowed a one-day visit because Veronica was having a major operation, and later that month he was given approval for a three-day visit to be with her. Apart from this latter visit, the conditions allowing him to travel were stiff: he could be away from Kimberley for twenty-four hours, from midnight on Friday to midnight on Saturday. He had to report to the police on leaving and returning. Each time, Achmat Laher drove him through the night, on occasion coming straight to our home so that Sobukwe could wash and have breakfast. The family business done, they had to leave in the afternoon for Sobukwe's Cinderella deadline in Kimberley.

He usually wanted to do some shopping, and Anne would take him to the shops in Rosebank, the well-off suburb nearby. Our son, Gideon, had been born in January 1973 and Sobukwe would put him on his shoulders and stroll with Anne among the white shoppers. No one gave them a second glance, she told me. It was one of the puzzling oddities of South Africa that it was so.

I have a memory of Sobukwe in our sitting-room, playing with Gideon and bouncing him on his knee. 'You'll spoil him,' I said. To which there was a fierce look in response and Sobukwe said: 'And why shouldn't I spoil him? I wish I had had the chance to spoil *my* boys.'

One Saturday—it was 14 July 1973—he wanted to go to the city centre, to John Orr's, a large department store which was the epitome of middle-class English shopping. We drove in and I dropped him at the store while I went in search of parking in the morning traffic. That done, I was walking through the store in search of Sobukwe when I met Buthelezi, also shopping, in company with a group of guards and assistants. 'Bob's here,' I told him. 'Here, in the store.' Buthelezi wanted to see him—but made clear that he would not go in search of Sobukwe, but Sobukwe should come to him. I went off and found Sobukwe—who made clear that Buthelezi should come to him. Having got the ball rolling, I landed up as a go-between, muttering curses under my breath as I shuttled between the two of them in different parts of the store. Along the way I was able to dash to my car and fetch the camera which I happened to have brought.

It was in fact a fraught situation, and I quickly regretted my involvement. Not only was it obvious that Sobukwe was anything but eager to be seen in public with Buthelezi, but my friendship with Buthelezi was by now much cooler. A major reason for this, on my side, was not only political but my disillusionment with him as a person because of the way he had behaved since Sobukwe came off Robben Island. Whenever I saw him he asked about Sobukwe—and always said how much he would like to see him again. And I would always say, 'Why don't you phone him?', and give him the number. But he never phoned and never contacted Sobukwe. It became a bit of a game for Sobukwe and me: 'Heard from Gatsha lately?' I would ask him, and he would reply with a grin, 'No, I'm still waiting.' I felt sad about this failure by Buthelezi: it revealed an unpleasant side of him.

But there was one communication, when Buthelezi posted to Sobukwe a copy of his letter to a writer, John St Jorre. What had happened was that St Jorre wrote an article about South Africa in the American journal *Foreign Affairs*. He wrote rather disparagingly of Buthelezi, comparing him unfavourably with Sobukwe and Biko. Buthelezi, who was then (and even more now) hyper-sensitive to any criticism, fired off a lengthy and furious letter to St Jorre. It was a copy of this letter which Buthelezi sent. It amused Sobukwe, who wrote to an American Mennonite, Jack Purves, with whom he was in touch: 'He sent me a copy of a blistering letter to a journalist . . . who had dared to suggest that the late Steve Biko and I were not overly impressed by Gatsha. He said, among other things, that there was nothing in our background which he could envy—we are Xhosa Commoners.'

The momentum of the reunion begun, it finally took place on the pavement outside John Orr's, with a curious crowd gathered to watch the two men embrace each other and stand chatting for a short time. I took a picture and it appeared in Monday's *Rand Daily Mail*. It was a happy portrait of smiling faces. Buthelezi phoned me a few days later to say how glad he was to have met Sobukwe. He begged for a copy of the photograph. I sent it to him, my doubts overcome in the pleasure of having been able to record the historic encounter.

There was a sequel: a few months later, Sobukwe, in a rare state of anger, told me that word had reached him that Buthelezi had visited Tanzania. He had not been well received because his role in the 'homelands' was under severe attack. In addressing a meeting of students at the university there, Buthelezi had held up the John Orr's photograph and spoken about 'me and my friend, Robert Sobukwe'. He used it to gain political respectability.

Even as I had taken the pictures, I was saying to myself that the Security Police would never believe that the meeting had been as fortuitous as it was. The Pan-Africanist Congress certainly did not believe it: the version given in an official publication—a collection of Sobukwe's speeches, issued in 1989—is that 'some white liberals contrived an "accidental" meeting along the street with Chief Gatsha Buthelezi of KwaZulu. The latter subsequently spread rumours that Sobukwe approved of his collaborative activities.'

My work at the *Rand Daily Mail* included handling books for review and, in 1975, I was sent *South Africa: A skunk among nations*, published by International Books in London. The author was Les de Villiers, who had been in charge of the South African government's Information Office in the United States for five years. De Villiers, it later turned out, was among the officials caught up in South Africa's Information Department scandal of the late 1970s, in which huge amounts of money were secretly used to try to buy a favourable image abroad. The skunk book aggressively proclaimed itself as devoted to exposing what it termed 'the hypocrisy and double-standards' of the world and 'unscrupulous journalistic and political behaviour' in dealing with apartheid. This 'scrupulously researched book', it said, told the real truth.

I leafed through it and found it anything but scrupulous or accurate. Then I found a couple of distorted references to myself, went on and came across a far grosser statement about Sobukwe: a claim that he had once said that 'Other races should be exterminated or sent packing . . .' It was too outrageously libellous to be ignored. Sobukwe and I agreed we should act against it. Randolph Vigne in London took legal advice and wrote to us: 'I am told Bob simply can't lose if he sues the publishers here.' It cheered us up: 'For once we seem to be on the side of the angels,' I wrote to Sobukwe. He went ahead, and the publishers immediately withdrew the book, issued an apology and paid him R1,500.

In South Africa, the local distributors, Purnell, dropped the book—so hastily that it never got into the bookshops and Sobukwe was therefore deprived of the chance to sue again. To make sure that this was the end of the story, I wrote to friends in the United States, Canada and Australia, asking them to watch for the book. But it disappeared from sight, which is what it and de Villiers deserved.

Sobukwe was envious about the efficiency with which the Post Office installed a telephone in my succession of apartments, and then in my house. Each time, it was done on the day that we moved in. 'What an advantage to be a big shot!' he wrote. 'Here we are, with no hope of having a telephone installed for at least three years and yours is installed in a matter of days. Behold the power of Jewish capitalism!' In fact, it was a private joke among my friends—whether true or not I never did discover—that I was among those who enjoyed an unusually efficient telephone service, including swift repairs, because the Security Police wanted to know what we were saying. If true, the same principle was eventually applied to Sobukwe and he was given a phone at home. With improvement in South Africa's telephone services, it meant that we spoke more and more on the phone, and letters became infrequent.

For Sobukwe, Kimberley was a time of waiting. His analysis convinced him that Afrikaner Nationalism, under the dual pressure of forces building up internally and externally, was running its course. He remained thoroughly committed to every one of his Africanist ideals. He believed as deeply as ever in his own relevance and that circumstances would inevitably draw him into the politics of power. This was a theme he constantly voiced to me, always in the most matter of fact way, as something which was so obvious that it did not bear elaboration or discussion.

His followers, who had waited so long for him, went on waiting. They put aside their disappointment that, once again, he could not lead them. They accepted that he was in a state of enforced suspension; the general view seemed to be that he had endured so much that he deserved protection and should not be involved in anything which could jeopardise his safety. Some went to visit him. Among them was Lennox Mlonzi, who had walked with Sobukwe into imprisonment on 21 March 1960. But he was so anxious not to cause him any difficulties that he first went to the local Security Police to check on Sobukwe's banning details. Many, however, deliberately stayed away. Hamilton Keke, an unswerving adherent after serving his Robben Island sentence for Poqo activities, decided against visiting him 'with a view to protecting him from the viciousness of the Security Police'. His reasoning was simple: 'If the police were so vigilant about watching someone like me, who was a small-fry, what would they be doing with our National President?' He was disapproving about those who did go to Kimberley as he thought they were 'careless' in exposing Sobukwe to unnecessary risks. Mothopeng had the same sense of diffidence and made only one visit.

The caution was maintained even though Sobukwe's followers were in acute need of his leadership. The PAC had never recovered from the wholesale jailing of its leaders in 1960, and the decimation of its ranks following the formation and crushing of Poqo. Leballo operated from the exile movement's headquarters in Dar es Salaam, and was acting President. The PAC was cleaved by feuding, power struggles, expulsions, walk-outs, corruption and murder.

Although the PAC was in disarray, the African Nationalist lineage it represented was once more gaining acceptance within South Africa. The government's post-Sharpeville repression had been successful, but fresh resistance gradually built up. It came from students, especially those at the new apartheid universities for blacks. The same colour dilemmas existed for them as for the African Nationalists of the 1940s and the Africanists of the 1950s: how to express black self-respect and organise black struggle while retaining non-racial aspirations? By 1969, the South African Students' Association, SASO, was in existence and it rapidly developed a coherent set of views known as Black Consciousness, or BC. If anything, it was even more critical than what had gone before in regard to white participation in the struggle. As Sobukwe had done thirteen years earlier, Steve Biko, the father of BC and the first Chairman of SASO, used a liberal publication to challenge white liberals about their role. Even those whites 'who see a lot wrong with the system make it their business to control the response of blacks to the provocation', he said in the 26 March 1972 issue of *Reality*, the magazine which kept alive liberal thinking after the demise of the Liberal Party. Many white liberals did not understand the thrust of his argument and took it as an affront.

A BC leader, Saths Cooper, says that Sobukwe was viewed 'as a very significant national leader who had a symbolic role as well as an immediate practical role in leadership and in creating a very necessary national unity'. Through the whole decade of the 1960s and into the early 1970s, when new political activity began, Sobukwe 'was one of the most popular leaders and was looked up to by people, whether or not they were supporters of the PAC. They looked up to him because of his charisma, his commitment and his integrity, and his ability to rise above a partisan polemical position.'

BC leaders regularly visited him, in defiance of his bans, slipping in and out of Kimberley under the noses of the Security Police as part of their consultations with leaders of different organisations. The contacts increased as plans developed for founding a new political organisation. 'Quite a few people went to see him,' says Cooper, who was elected Publicity Officer of the Black People's Convention when it was created in 1972, and was President of a late BC movement, Azapo (Azanian People's Organisation). 'He was consulted. His opinions were solicited and in effect his encouragement and blessings were received ... He was seen as one of the progenitors, one of the key thinkers, in the run-up to the development of Black Consciousness.'

It did not take the government long to recognise the BC movement for the threat that it was, and to act against it. SASO leaders, including Biko, were banned. In 1975, Cooper was among a dozen SASO leaders charged with trying to overthrow the government, and jailed on Robben Island the next year.

But 1976 was also the year when, despite repression, widespread resistance again broke into the open. Dr Andries Treurnicht—who later led a breakaway from the Nationalists to form the Conservative Party—was the Deputy Minister in charge of black education; he was blind and deaf to black opposition and plunged ahead with enforced extension of Afrikaans as a language in which other subjects had to be studied. On 16 June, school pupils in Soweto went into the streets to protest against this. The issue reflected their wider rejection of their inferior schooling, and their still wider rejection of white rule and apartheid. The police opened fire and that was the

How Can Man Die Better

start of the 'children's revolt'—as with Sharpeville, a fundamental turning-point for South Africa.

In May 1975, Sobukwe's mother died, at the age of 90. He was given permission to drive to the east of the country, to Umtata, 800 kilometres away, where his mother had died; then 500 kilometres to his birthplace, Graaff-Reinet, for the burial; and then 400 kilometres on a direct run back to Kimberley. He had to report to the police when he reached and left Umtata, the same in Graaff-Reinet, and when he returned to Kimberley. He had to be back the day after the funeral.

The Umtata to Graaff-Reinet route took him through Kingwilliamstown, which was the home of Steve Biko. At that time, Biko was also banned so a meeting between them was illegal. They could both have been jailed for it. But they met, without the police knowing about it.

I knew of their meeting because when I next saw Sobukwe he said to me with a smile: 'Steve sends regards.' It was one of those situations where it was best not to ask questions or to seek to know too much.

They kept in touch. The 1,500-kilometre round trip which separated them was a barrier to personal contact. But at least half a dozen times, messages were exchanged between them.

Biko took appalling risks. On 18 August 1977, he was stopped at a police roadblock outside Grahamstown while on his way back home from an underground visit to Cape Town. He was killed in Security Police detention on 12 September. The government revealed his death the next day.

The news appeared in newspapers while Sobukwe was in hospital, about to undergo surgery.

22

In June 1977, during our frequent phone calls, Sobukwe repeatedly said he was not feeling well. He was feverish and had a bad cough which went on and on. He thought he had flu, but was unable to shake it off. He was seeing doctors at the local Kimberley hospital—the 'non-white section' of course, for public hospitals were as segregated as jails. Veronica was worried and as my concern grew I urged him to apply for permission to come to Johannesburg for a full medical examination by a competent doctor. I said he should fly up. He was reluctant to ask for such a favour but finally gave way. Such applications were made to the local magistrate, who was supposed to have the power to decide on it; in practice he was merely a functionary and the real decision was taken by the Security Police. Sobukwe applied, and was refused.

I went to Kimberley as soon as I could. It took a few days to arrange. I found Sobukwe coughing a lot, but he looked well. The photographs of us taken that weekend show him smiling and seemingly all right. As soon as I returned to Johannesburg I spoke to Dr Bodo Koch, a specialist physician. He knew more than most about totalitarianism: half-Jewish, he was born in Germany and qualified as a doctor; one of his professors saved his life by helping him to get out in 1939, very soon before the start of war; later, his mother was murdered. He was married now to Ellen Hellman, a social anthropologist who was a noted liberal and former President of the South African Institute of Race Relations. I had been a frequent dinner guest at their home during the darker times of the Prisons Trial, when many other people thought it best not to have me around.

So I was assured of Bodo's support when I contacted him. He agreed that he should give Sobukwe a thorough examination. He was willing to go into his consulting rooms on a Saturday morning so that Sobukwe would not have to miss a weekday in his one-man legal practice. He asked me to tell Sobukwe to bring with him the X-rays which had been taken at the Kimberley hospital.

Now, with Sobukwe's approval, I took a deep breath and phoned Jimmy Kruger, who was the Minister of three formidable portfolios—Justice, Police and Prisons. He was both in charge of the police and decided on banning orders.

I knew Kruger through my work on the *Rand Daily Mail*. I had been appointed an Assistant Editor in 1972 and became Deputy Editor early in 1977. The joke among my friends was that I needed one more conviction to become Editor, although I doubt that the directors of South African Associated Newspapers, the company owning the *Rand Daily Mail*, would have shared in the laughter (and as time went by, it was obvious that they were as astonished as I was that I was occupying such senior executive positions). For some years I had made an annual visit to Cape Town to spend a week at Parliament, having background discussions with government and opposition members. The doors of most members of the Cabinet were open to me; I had lengthy discussions, and some tough arguments. That they were willing to see me and for some to spend many hours having me disagree with them was again one of the oddities of South Africa. They loathed the *Rand Daily Mail* for its flailing of Afrikaner Nationalist dogma and its exposure of apartheid uglinesses; but they also recognised the newspaper's weight and, if not its influence, then what they believed was its potential for influence, especially among the black people who by now made up 60 per cent of the nearly one million daily readers.

Laurence Gandar had left the editorship, and South Africa, when the Prisons Trial ended. He went to Britain and, carrying forward the humanitarianism with which he had inspired the *Rand Daily Mail*, he became the founding Director of the Minority Rights Group, set up to research and publicise the plight of oppressed minorities throughout the world. It still exists, but Gandar left after a few years, to retire to South Africa. He was replaced on the *Mail* by Raymond Louw, who took the newspaper to a new height of professional journalism.

As I became more senior on the paper and played a larger role in shaping policy and helping to run it from day to day, so my personal conflict increased as to whether I was a friend or a journalist in regard to Sobukwe. Over the years, as our relationship deepened,

I was more uncertain in writing about him for publication. I didn't feel I should be using my special access to the newspaper's columns; it would have been an abuse of my responsibility towards the *Mail*. It could also have given the newspaper's many enemies—ranging from the government to its own management—that much more ammunition to use in the near-unceasing attacks, criticisms and pressures to which we were subject. We lived with the consciousness that the paper was on borrowed time, and many staff members had an attitude of protectiveness towards it. On the other hand, I had a privileged position in regard to Sobukwe, knowing so much about his circumstances, and was therefore better able than anyone else to write authoritatively about him. In my uneasiness it is very likely that I landed up writing less about him than I could have and should have.

The dilemma of my dual relationship was illustrated in another way when Sobukwe was awaiting the Supreme Court's decision on his application to leave the country to go to the US. Had the court ruled in his favour there was just the remotest chance that there might be a gap of an hour or so between the judgment being made public and the police re-formulating and tightening his restriction to Kimberley. That might just make it possible for Sobukwe to leave Kimberley legally and, if I was on the spot, for me to drive him at speed to the west, across the border into Botswana. Had I done it, and succeeded in getting Sobukwe out of the country, the effect on the government would have been akin to putting a dart into a mad bull. The scheme was entirely unrealistic as it was improbable that the police would let him get away, but I did think about it seriously enough to mention to Raymond Louw, who was not only editor but a friend, what I was cooking up. His response was simple: what I did in my private life was up to me, he said, but he had every belief that I would always be mindful of the effects of whatever I did on the *Mail*. I abandoned the idea.

That there was a difference between private and public life was in fact acknowledged by the government. Over the years I was also in touch with Nelson Mandela and regularly applied to visit him, always to be turned down. My latest request for a visit was still pending when I had one of my annual round of meetings at Parliament. While with the Minister of Justice, Kobie Coetsee, I asked about my application. No journalists were being allowed to visit Mandela, he said. I don't want to see him as a journalist but as a friend, I replied. Even more, if the government were to invite me to visit him as a journalist I would decline unless I knew that it was with Mandela's consent. Coetsee seemed surprised, but still would not agree to a visit. Later that day I was asked to see the Commissioner of Prisons, and we had exactly the same conversation. Then, suddenly, several months later, I was allowed a visit—on condition that I promised not to write about it.

So it was on the basis of a private approach that I phoned Kruger. He was a man self-confident in the untrammelled power he had over people's lives. He would always tell me how much thought he gave to examining the files the Security Police put before him, and how he acted with the greatest reluctance to curb a person's liberty. In my eyes, however, he was like Vorster and their other colleagues in crude abuse of the administrative powers which they rammed into law to safeguard their hold on the country.

It took several days to get hold of Kruger at his office in Pretoria. When I did, he was friendly and helpful and said he would go into the matter immediately. He phoned back less than an hour later to say that Sobukwe could travel to Johannesburg to see a doctor. But not that weekend; it was 'too soon'. It would have to be the weekend after. I was worried about the further delay; but I did not question it because I was too happy at having got permission.

There were conditions: there was to be no publicity; Sobukwe could arrive on the Saturday and had to stay overnight at my home; he was not to go anywhere except to see Bodo Koch; the only people I was to allow at my home while Sobukwe was there were members of my immediate family. I agreed to it all.

The restriction to my home had its funny side: blacks were not allowed to stay as guests in 'white' suburbs; but the authorities were so keen not to have Sobukwe overnight in Soweto that they were breaking their own apartheid law so that he could stay in my home in the white middle-class suburb of Parktown North.

A few days later, a formal letter was served on Sobukwe setting out the conditions, even specifying which flights he had to take—and adding that Koch had to examine him at my home. I chased after Kruger again, to explain to him that Koch wanted the examination in his consulting rooms because he needed to use the equipment he had there. There was a flurry of phone calls. On the Friday afternoon before Sobukwe was due to fly, the Security Police phoned me: all right, Sobukwe could go to Dr Koch's rooms but once finished there we had to drive straight to my home.

I knew Sobukwe was having difficulty in prising his X-rays from the Kimberley hospital and it was uncertain whether he would be able to bring any with him. But I did not ask the Security Police to let us have new X-rays taken in Johannesburg. It wouldn't have meant much effort because Koch's rooms were in the city centre's Jeppe Street, where many scores of specialist doctors, including radiologists, had their rooms. To have X-rays taken, however, would have meant asking to see another doctor across the street. Unfortunately, I was intimidated. I was scared that, if we asked for anything more, for another concession, the permission for him to come to Johannesburg might be withdrawn. This might sound ridiculous. But it was the atmosphere in which I was operating. I was begging for favours, always aware that anywhere in the apparatus of power someone could peremptorily say no.

The extent of the danger was shown by a small request which I did put in: that Sobukwe be allowed to fly back to Kimberley on the 3.30 p.m. flight on Sunday instead of the 9.30 a.m. flight stipulated by the Security Police. I explained that, as he was ill, it would be helpful if he did not have to get up first thing in the morning. I put the request to Kruger. The reply came a short time later in a phone call from an anonymous Security policeman: abrasively and curtly, a voice told me that if I didn't like the 9.30 a.m. flight, Sobukwe would have to fly back early on the Saturday afternoon. There was no room for argument or pleading. I swallowed my pride and shut up.

So I did not dare ask for permission to have X-rays taken. It was to prove a fateful omission.

I met Sobukwe at Johannesburg's Jan Smuts Airport and drove him into the city. A car with two men followed us all the way. I drove carefully, watching them in my rearview mirror, making sure they had no difficulty in keeping behind us. I didn't want them to have the slightest reason to believe that I might be trying to get rid of them. This was no time to play any games.

Sobukwe had not been able to bring his X-rays with him. Bodo Koch, warm and concerned, did a lengthy examination and then sat the two of us down to give his diagnosis. He started by emphasising that the lack of X-rays meant there were limits to his knowledge; he had had to rely on the lighted screen in his rooms. But from what he had seen he believed that Sobukwe was suffering from a weakening of the heart muscles caused by a bacterial infection. It was serious, but it could be treated medically. Had it been left to continue unchecked, it would have had grave consequences. Bodo said he would write a letter to a Kimberley doctor to keep up the treatment he prescribed; he also wanted Sobukwe to return for regular check-ups.

It was a happy outcome, at the time. We were relieved that it was something tangible which could be treated. We smiled and joked that now Sobukwe had a valid reason for applying to spend weekends at my home. We drove home. I did not spot any car following us and wondered whether they were being discreet or whether they were working on the thesis that I was so intimidated that I would follow orders strictly. We spent the rest of the day at home. I had passed the word round to friends to stay away so there were no visitors except my mother-in-law, Hazel Sassoon, who wanted to meet Sobukwe. It was a sunny day and we ate lunch in the garden, in the shade. Sobukwe drank a glass of wine—for the first time in his life. It was by way of celebrating the medical diagnosis. I served him one of my favourite South African red wines, *Oude Libertas Pinotage*. He said he enjoyed it. But he thought it safest to remain a teetotaller.

During the day I went to Bodo's house and collected the report which he had typed out himself so that Sobukwe could return to Kimberley with it. By 8 a.m. next morning, despite his illness and tiredness, we were on the road to the airport.

His visit went unpublicised. I told my colleagues at the *Rand Daily Mail* about it and explained the promise of silence which Kruger had forced on me. The difficulty of my situation was accepted. It was by no means unusual to suppress information. The purity of journalism, with its impelling force to strive for maximum publication, could not always be maintained in an authoritarian state. It had to yield to the principle of protecting people. Examples which I often came across had to do with blacks who fell foul of the pass laws or the allocation of houses in the ghettos, both integral elements of the official system of control. There was ample evidence of vast corruption within the system. But to expose it would have meant reporting the details of individuals who had used short-cuts to get a pass or a house. That would certainly lead to them losing their pass and/or house. So I would look the other way about corruption, as we all did. Similarly with information, say, that a well-known banned person had been a guest at a Saturday night party.

The problem, from day to day, was to decide when a Nelson's eye should be applied, and to keep suppression of news to the absolute minimum.

I sent a copy of Koch's report to Kruger. I wanted to ensure that there would be no difficulties in Sobukwe coming to Johannesburg. I marked my letter 'confidential' and wrote: 'Although I am sending the report to you on a confidential basis I believe that it will be helpful for you to see it so that you have full understanding of Mr Sobukwe's condition.' Dr Koch wished to see Sobukwe regularly, I added, and I asked for permission for another visit to Johannesburg, and a stay at my home, in September. And 'it would be much appreciated' if he could return to Kimberley on the Sunday's 3.30 p.m. flight.

Everything seemed under control. A few days later, I went off on a trip to the United States. But on Tuesday, 6 September, Anne tracked me down there. She was anguished. Bodo Koch had phoned her. The X-rays had finally arrived from Kimberley, he had examined them and seen cancer in a lung. He recommended urgent surgery. I told her to phone Kruger immediately, to give him the information and to say, from me, that Sobukwe had to have the right of access to any doctors or hospitals that he wanted or needed.

The official response was to offer him surgery in hospital in Bloemfontein. This city, a couple of hours' drive to the east of Kimberley, is the country's judicial capital in that it is the seat of the highest Appeal Court. It is a featureless, unattractive place, devoid of any discernible creativity. It is also thoroughly Afrikaans and to Sobukwe it was a wholly hostile environment inhabited by people who wished him only harm. In no way would he agree to put himself under someone's knife in the hospital; he thought he would not come out alive. There was probably little substance to this, but he believed it. Faced by his rejection, the government backed off and agreed to his wish to go to Cape Town, to the Groote Schuur Hospital made famous by the world's first heart transplant operation performed by Dr Chris Barnard a decade earlier. Contradicting any stereotype image of Afrikaners, Barnard—himself an Afrikaner—was later to give invaluable support when Sobukwe needed it.

On 9 September, Kruger issued a statement to the Press to say that Sobukwe could have medical treatment by any doctor in any hospital in the country. He gave no details of the illness but said he had been approached by Sobukwe's medical adviser.

That statement appeared in morning newspapers the day I returned from the US. I was immediately in contact with Bodo Koch. He confirmed the gravity of Sobukwe's condition. The cancer had had time to grow. More than three vital months had been lost. He was not hopeful about recovery but believed surgery had to be undertaken. My shock was mixed with a huge rage that Kruger was now seeking to polish his public image, by presenting himself as a caring, co-operative minister, and was trying to escape responsibility for his behaviour and that of the police.

I spoke to Sobukwe that day: he was calm and accepting of the ordeal that lay ahead. He was, however, upset about Kruger's statement, if only because of the effect on Miliswa and Dini in the US.

I wrote to Kruger:

> On returning from overseas on Saturday I was shocked to find that you had issued a statement the day before in which you made public the fact of Mr Robert Sobukwe's ill health.
>
> I cannot understand why such a statement was necessary. My letter to you of 12 August, in which I gave you the then known details, was confidential and indeed (as it made abundantly clear) was sent to you entirely on that basis. When my wife, acting on my instructions, telephoned your office last Tuesday to convey the new information about Mr Sobukwe's condition, she repeatedly stressed that this too was being imparted confidentially.
>
> Mr Sobukwe's illness should surely have been his own private concern until such time as he (or his family or close friends acting on his authority) chose to disclose it.
>
> Throughout my recent dealings with you in this matter I believe I have acted in the best of faith, observing the restraints on lack of publicity and access by people to him as set out in our telephone discussions. The issuing of your statement is therefore all the more surprising and distressing.
>
> I feel that I must also take this opportunity to point out to you that, looking back from this stage in time, the delay during July/August in obtaining permission for Mr Sobukwe to come

to Johannesburg for a medical consultation could prove to have been tragically decisive.

As you will know, his first application to come here was refused. Only when I approached you directly was permission granted and even then a further week's delay was imposed.

You will recall the additional difficulties when your Department sought to limit the nature of Mr Sobukwe's access to a doctor when he came to Johannesburg.

And underlying all this is the terrible thought that, had he not been confined to Kimberley, but had been free at any time to obtain the best possible medical advice, the exact nature of his condition could have been detected far earlier, with immeasurably better prospects for treatment than now exist.

It is against this background that I wish to express the hope that he will now be allowed normal freedom to obtain medical assistance. But the medical view is that the harm has already been done.'

For what it was worth, that letter did penetrate Kruger's skin, as his reply revealed: 'I think you should have realised that I would not have issued a statement on Mr Sobukwe unless background circumstances warranted it. In any case I never disclosed the nature of his illness.

'The whole trend of your letter is such that in future you will have to make any representations you wish to, through the normal channels of my Department and not to me directly.'

He signed the letter himself, instead of the usual form whereby his Private Secretary wrote on his behalf. I took that to be an indication of how personally he had taken my letter, which was what I had wanted to achieve. It was our last contact.

Meanwhile, faced by the crisis, the old network of support came into action again. Moira Henderson, who had kept up visits to Kimberley, was at the airport in Cape Town when Sobukwe and Veronica flew there. It was late afternoon and *en route* to the hospital she asked whether he wanted to see Robben Island again, nearly eight years and six months since he had been there. He said yes so she detoured along De Waal Drive, which runs along the mountain above the city; he sat for a few minutes, staring at the island in the middle of Table Bay, his first view of it from the mainland.

On Wednesday, 14 September, less than two days after he was

admitted to hospital, a lung was removed. Rodney Hewitson, rated as probably the best thoracic surgeon in the country, did the operation. Sobukwe was put into Ward C10, on the second floor, used for lung and heart surgery patients. It was a segregated ward for blacks, coloureds and Asians; a separate ward for whites was on the same floor. The leading doctors were whites. Despite the apartheid, the operating theatre was non-racial and served both wards.

One of the doctors was Joe Nobrega. He had many fans among the hospital's workers because he had once been the star goalkeeper in the Cape Town City soccer team. Now he was a surgeon in the heart unit headed by Chris Barnard. His wife, Nita, was also a doctor, working in community medicine.

Joe returned from holiday a couple of days after Sobukwe had had the operation. Dedicated to the long hours of his work, Joe had little interest in politics. He knew the name Sobukwe and was aware, rather vaguely, that he was a political leader who had been on Robben Island. He says he heard on the grapevine that he was a patient in C10. During his daily ward rounds he would pass Sobukwe's bed and greet him: 'He was not well and that was one of the reasons I got involved with him. He was on a painkiller, codeine, and I told Nita about it. She gave me dried prunes to take to him for the constipation he was suffering. I introduced myself and said if he needed anything, he shouldn't hesitate to ask me. He thanked me, but said there was nothing.'

By this stage, says Nobrega, Chris Barnard had cleared the Security Police out of the ward. At the beginning, Sobukwe had been under twenty-four-hour guard, with two Security policemen always at his bed. They ordered the doctors not to allow Sobukwe any visitors except his immediate family. The doctors were incensed at the police intrusion: 'Barnard told them: "This is my ward, I take responsibility for my patients." And he chased them out. For a while they sat outside, in the passage opposite the lifts, and then they disappeared.'

There was a constant flow of visitors. Some were old friends; many were people from Cape Town's black ghettos who came to pay their respects, often standing quietly at the door to look at him. Moira kept him stocked with flowers: 'He adored roses and I would take a couple of dozen of them, heavy-scented. It was a year of roses in Cape Town.'

Whatever the segregation in the wards, Sobukwe 'got the best treatment that Groote Schuur had to offer,' says Nobrega. The facilities for blacks and whites were identical.

As he began to recover he walked around the ward, talking to the other patients, or sat on the side of his bed, reading. Barnard, who was a considerable television personality, wanted to interview Sobukwe for a foreign station. Barnard's media role was erratic. He sought publicity but, at the political level, he veered between criticisms of apartheid and attacks on the country's critics. Sobukwe would have none of Barnard's attempt to charm him into being interviewed and he simply laughed when Barnard finally burst out at him: 'It's obvious you're not prepared to listen to reason.'

A month after the operation, Sobukwe was still in pain. But it was time to leave the hospital temporarily, to recuperate for a fortnight until his wound had healed sufficiently for the start of radiotherapy treatment.

As early as 3 October, Veronica—who was staying with Moira Henderson—had delivered a letter to the Chief Magistrate in Cape Town applying for Sobukwe to stay at the home of Bishop Patrick Matolengwe, a Suffragan Bishop in the Anglican Church. He was black and was contradicting apartheid laws by living in an official church house in the well-off 'white' suburb of Newlands. Veronica twice asked the authorities about the application but without result. On 12 October, Alex Boraine took up the matter for her. Boraine, a former Methodist Church minister and Chairman of the church's Conference, was now a Member of Parliament for the Progressive Federal Party. He spoke to Kruger's secretary and was told the application had been referred to Kimberley, from where it had been referred to Pretoria. No decision was yet available. Veronica phoned the Security Police in Kimberley, but got no further.

On 14 October, Matolengwe fetched Sobukwe and took him and Veronica to his home. Everyone believed they had done everything possible to seek permission for this. Sobukwe intended staying until 28 October, when he was due to return to Groote Schuur. He immediately went into the garden to savour the sun.

The nightmare began twenty minutes later. Two Security policemen arrived and demanded Sobukwe. Veronica told them he was in the toilet and asked them to sit down and wait for him. But they would not—they tried to push past her to get to him. There was a scuffle as she blocked them. It ended when Sobukwe himself appeared. 'My husband was a man of peace,' explains Veronica.

How Can Man Die Better

The police presented an order from Kruger in the form of a letter signed by the Chief Magistrate: Sobukwe had either to return to Kimberley or to the hospital. Immediately.

He was weak and barely able to walk properly. It was his first day fully on his feet since the operation. Veronica begged that he be allowed to rest. He also had a dread of returning to hospital. Despite the care he had had there, Ward C10 was dreary and confined and the windows faced onto an inner courtyard. He yearned for the sun.

The police insisted. They told the Bishop's secretary to phone the airport to book seats on the first available flight to Kimberley. She refused. Sobukwe was not fit to travel, she told them. The policemen themselves phoned. The only flight that day was full, they found.

The police left, but before going they gave Sobukwe two hours to decide what he intended doing. Late in the afternoon they phoned to demand his decision. Sobukwe decided to return to Groote Schuur.

The next morning, the police sent a message forbidding him from leaving the hospital grounds. Then permission was given for Joe Nobrega to take him for a drive; but he was too exhausted to want it. Veronica succumbed to the strain and in a rare display of her inner feelings, wept and cried out, 'Please, somebody help us.'

She appealed to Chris Barnard. He was in an operating theatre, watching an emergency heart operation. As the afternoon wore on, he was in and out of the theatre as he put phone calls through to Prime Minister Vorster and to Kruger from the adjoining doctors' room, striving to persuade them to be flexible. 'Look man, why can't you guys do something to make this man comfortable,' he was overheard saying. Joe Nobrega, aroused by the official handling of Sobukwe and encouraged by Nita, had offered the Sobukwes hospitality in their home in the suburb of Oranjezicht, on the slopes of Table Mountain. Barnard conveyed this to Kruger and said he would accept responsibility for the arrangement.

Finally, at about 5 p.m., Kruger agreed—no doubt after the Security Police had checked out the Nobregas' lack of political involvement and overcome suspicious incredulity that two ordinary white South Africans could actually be willing to have a black couple live in their home.

Nobrega conveyed the plan to Sobukwe: 'Professor Barnard has spoken to Mr Kruger and Mr Kruger says it's OK for you to stay at my house,' he told him. 'It's OK with Kruger but it has to be OK with you. If it suits you, it's an option open to you. If you accept, it will be a pleasure to have you at our home.'

The next morning, the Sobukwes moved in, meeting Nita for the first time. It was a perfect setting with the front of the house facing the glorious view of the city and the bay; from his bedroom, Sobukwe could look straight up at the looming mountain with its light grey rocks and the dark green trees on the lower slopes. The police made one formal visit—and, as Joe explains, 'the gist of their message was that they were very apologetic that we had to have a black man in our house'. How little the police understood the sort of people the Nobregas were, their instant liking for the Sobukwes and the friendship which had rapidly developed.

Again there were many visitors. But even though there was no visible police presence outside the house, everyone carefully observed Sobukwe's banning orders: one person at a time could be with him.

One of the visitors was Alex Boraine, who had first gone to see Sobukwe in hospital. He found him now dressed and propped up in a chair. 'I knew he was dying,' says Boraine. 'I thought I would just ask him how he saw the future and what he thought about the past. I expected a sort of outpouring of bitterness about the way he had been treated: the Sobukwe Clause, his banishment, and so on. But he was remarkably gentle. Not that he was weak. He was gentle with a strength that was very humbling.

'He said that he felt desperately sorry for the government because they were "blind to the realities". And then he also used this phrase: "We must forgive them because they really don't know what they are doing. We must pray for them that their eyes will be opened."

'He then asked me: "Will you pray for them now?"

'So I knelt next to him and said a prayer. I prayed for him, although he hadn't asked me to. I also prayed for the government. Then he prayed and said again, "Father, forgive them." He also said: "Take away all bitterness from us and help us to work for a country where we will all love each other, and not hate each other because hate will destroy us all." '

On a Sunday night, Nita took him to a Methodist church service in the suburb of Sea Point. In the manner of South Africa it was a service for blacks—probably mainly people who worked as domestic servants for white households. At the end, the minister announced a collection: a hatful of money—the total of the small amounts given by the poorly paid workers—was handed to Sobukwe.

To Nita, he was 'so real and so human that you could only respond totally to him; you couldn't have a wishy-washy relationship with him. There was no false pride in him and no false gratitude; he accepted everything with grace and dignity.' Joe remembers Veronica's total devotion to Sobukwe: 'She obviously felt she had been cheated of him for years.'

The Nobregas had sold their house and were going on a visit abroad; Sobukwe would be without accommodation for two days before re-entering Groote Schuur for radiotherapy. So new applications were submitted, for him to stay either with Bishop Matolengwe or Moira Henderson, who also lived in Newlands. 'I've given them the choice of a white or a black home,' Sobukwe told Moira with a smile. The government rejected both, but agreed he could stay at a Holiday Inn on the outskirts of the city.

It was anything but a congenial environment for a convalescent. He wanted to get into the open so Moira looked around for a suitable house where he could at least spend a day in the early summer weather. It could not be her house because Sobukwe was not allowed to leave the magisterial district of Cape Town and her home fell in the adjoining Wynberg district. She approached a white journalist, well known for his anti-apartheid writings, who had been telling her he wanted to meet Sobukwe because people were always asking him about him. He had a beautiful home overlooking the sea. She phoned him and the calls went back and forth. He finally rang her to agree to the arrangement: to Moira's astonishment, he said he had taken the precaution of checking with the Security Police who had told him it was all right. Moira, exercising self-control, drily told him she would not tell Sobukwe about his contact with the police. She later learnt that the journalist had also sought the approval of the Chairman of the board of his newspaper.

She took Sobukwe to the house, and he spent a restful day on the verandah. The journalist wasn't there: he had left before Sobukwe arrived, and he hadn't returned by the time that Sobukwe left.

That's how the souls of people were corroded by the apartheid society. It reveals much about how the Nationalists have been able to keep their grip on power for so long: certainly they aggressively coerce people; but the overwhelming number of whites connive and collaborate out of fear of losing their status and privilege.

The course of radiotherapy over, Sobukwe returned to Kimberley. His illness did not save him from an unpleasant and quite incredible experience at the hands of a foreign diplomat. It came about in this way: Gerald Reilly, head of the *Rand Daily Mail*'s bureau in Pretoria, phoned me to say that a member of the Australian Embassy based in that city was driving to Cape Town and wanted to stop in Kimberley to meet Sobukwe. Would it be all right? No, I said, I had spoken to Sobukwe only a few minutes earlier and he was in great pain and had specifically told me he did not want visitors.

I gave no further thought to the matter—until a few days later a distraught, near-hysterical Veronica phoned to say that a man who said he was an Australian diplomat had knocked on the front door and asked for Sobukwe; she had told him her husband was very ill and did not want to see anyone; but the man had brushed past her and got into Sobukwe's bedroom before she could get him to leave. It had happened only a minute before she phoned me.

I fired off an angry letter to the diplomat asking how he dared behave so callously. He replied—basically telling me to go to hell as it was none of my business. I wrote another letter, this time a complaint to the Australian Ambassador. Later, I heard on the grapevine that the diplomat was known for his rudeness and insensitivity and that my complaint was the last straw; he was moved out of South Africa shortly afterwards.

After two months in Kimberley, Sobukwe went back to Cape Town for more treatment. By an astonishing coincidence, his elder brother, Ernest, was in an adjoining ward for a leg operation.

Once more, what should have been the simple issue of accommodation was a source of aggravation. The government again rejected the Matolengwe and Henderson homes, and instead insisted—it was part of the written order issued by Kruger—that he stay at the Holiday Inn. But it was holiday-time and the hotel was full. Fortunately, the Nobregas were back and Sobukwe was allowed to stay with them in their new home—which happened to be in the same Newlands suburb as the vetoed Matolengwe and Henderson houses.

The government did not only determine where he could stay, but also hemmed in his travel movements. Kruger's original announcement, that Sobukwe could go anywhere for treatment by anyone, was not as generous in practice as the fine words had promised. Each time Sobukwe left Kimberley, he was required, by written orders, to report to the police—which meant going to the local police station and signing a special register. On arrival in Cape Town, he had to go straight to the central Caledon Square police station and sign in. Leaving Cape Town he had to report to the police, and also when he reached Kimberley.

Moira, who always fetched and delivered the Sobukwes at the Cape Town airport, remembered the scene outside Caledon Square: 'He looked old and ill, and had quite a lot of trouble getting there. He shuffled across the pavement with Veronica, an arm around him, supporting him. It was terrible that he had to be subjected to that. There was never a word of complaint from him.'

And in Veronica's words: 'He struggled to move slowly to the charge office to report that he was around. It was painful.'

Despite the surgery and the follow-up treatment, there was no stopping the cancer. In December, he wrote to Jack Purves, the American Mennonite working in Botswana who had been to visit him, that he was 'making good progress though I have an excruciating backache that has recently made itself felt. The doctors diagnose arthritis but that does not help—the pain remains excruciating!'

By January, the 'arthritis' was clearly the cancer. He was extremely sick during his January return to Groote Schuur, and back in Kimberley his days were filled with pain. As his body began to go into crisis, he was admitted to the Kimberley hospital. On Friday, 10 February, Veronica phoned me to come to Kimberley immediately.

He was so terribly ill when we got there the next morning. We spent a day in his darkened room, talking quietly; when he slept, which was often, Anne and I sat still and watched him.

At one point, a local priest and his wife came in, and we stood around the bed. The priest—I did not know his denomination—prayed aloud, asking for life. I held Sobukwe's hand and marvelled at the small smile on his face as he lay with eyes closed, murmuring 'Amen'. Amid my own prayers, I reflected on the scene: a black man, a priest and his wife who were coloureds, Anne and I who were whites, and the cluster of blacks, coloureds and Asians in the corridor outside. This was the South Africa that should be, I thought, and the South Africa that could be once apartheid was ended. When the priest left, Sobukwe said to me: 'I know I am going to live. God put me in this world for a purpose and that purpose is not yet ended.'

By the end of the day he was vastly better. The next day the improvement was maintained and we left Kimberley feeling heartened. But he sank again, and as Veronica phoned me with daily reports I frantically tried to organise an air ambulance to get him back to Groote Schuur. It was an act of desperation, and the doctors there, as well as Bodo Koch, brought me to the reality of it. They said he was unlikely to survive an air trip and that, even if he did, there was nothing more that medical science could do for him. I turned to prayer and had a sympathetic response from Desmond Tutu, who was then general secretary of the South African Council of Churches, when I suggested the council call a national day of prayer.

Anne and I planned another trip to Kimberley. But early in the morning of Monday, 27 February, the phone rang at our bedside in Johannesburg. It was Veronica. 'Your friend has died,' she said through her crying.

Medical opinion was divided. Bodo Koch said that, from the moment the cancer was found, there was no hope for Sobukwe. Marius Barnard—younger brother of Chris and also a surgeon in the Groote Schuur heart team—made the point to me that the earlier a cancer was caught the greater the possibility of halting it.

It is evident that the delays in diagnosis which had resulted from Sobukwe's confinement to Kimberley, and the obstacles put in his way by the authorities, had fatal consequences.

But was it more sinister even than that? The Pan-Africanist Congress believes so. Within days of Sobukwe's death, Peter 'Molotsi, the former PAC executive member, told a tribute meeting held at the United Nations building in New York: 'The death certificate indicated he had died of cancer. We, however, have reason to believe that the cancer was induced ...' In 1982, John Pokela, then PAC Chairman in exile, said in Tanzania that Sobukwe was 'maliciously eliminated by the Boers in a bid to weaken the movement'; he promised an investigation into the 'real causes' of the death.

It seems that the origins of the PAC's claim, apart from natural suspicion about the perfidy of the South African authorities, could derive from Zeph Mothopeng's visit to Kimberley: Sobukwe told him the government had 'poisoned' him. That would seem to be a reference to the 'machine' which Sobukwe believed had been used on him on Robben Island. When he was afflicted by cancer, this was taken by PAC members to be a result of his having been 'poisoned'.

The suggestion is not entirely in the realm of science fiction. On 26 September 1989, *The Independent* newspaper in London reported that Dr Michael Lewis, a researcher at University College Hospital, who injected a cancer-inducing compound into rats for twelve years, had died from a type of disease similar to that developed by the animals. An inquest was told of his lengthy exposure to a low dosage of fumes from the compound coupled with an unusual sensitivity to the effect.

But there is no evidence at all that Sobukwe was the victim of any deliberate exposure to cancer-inducing elements, and to suggest that it actually did happen is far-fetched.

From birth to death: the funeral was to be held in the town of Graaff-Reinet. Veronica phoned about the arrangements: 'Will you please arrange for the cattle for the funeral,' she said. That is an African custom, to slaughter cattle for a feast for the mourners. But I had never before been actively involved in the custom and, sitting in my study in my Johannesburg home, wild thoughts raced through my head as I wondered how to go about finding and buying six live cows and shipping them to the other end of the country.

Veronica reassured me that the minister in Graaff-Reinet who was arranging the funeral would attend to the technicalities. I checked with him and he said he would buy six head of cattle locally, at a cost of R750. It was a sizeable sum and I did not have it. I put through a call to London, to Randolph Vigne. 'You are the only person in the world I can phone and say that I urgently need R750 for cattle for Bob Sobukwe's funeral without asking me questions,' I said. Randolph, as always, took it well. 'Let me see what I can do,' he replied. He cabled R1,000 the next day.

Benjamin Pogrund

Among the many public tributes to Sobukwe was one from an unexpected source—his jailer. In an enterprising feat of journalism, Patrick Laurence, who had a few years before been convicted of writing a report presenting Sobukwe's views, succeeded in getting in to see Colonel T.G. du Plessis, the Kimberley Security Police chief, at his office. 'I did visit him at his home on occasion,' du Plessis told him. 'I was received like a gentleman and treated like a gentleman. His wife can confirm that.'

Du Plessis likened his role in supervising the twenty-four-hour surveillance of Sobukwe to a 'business transaction': it was a duty to be fulfilled without allowing personal feelings to intrude, he said.

Kruger, however, declined comment when approached by the Press. That was probably just as well, for the best that could have been expected from him would have been something unctuous and mealy-mouthed.

An editorial was required for the *Rand Daily Mail*, and I said I would write it. I did so on the basis that I was sufficiently in control of myself and that in any event the then Editor, Allister Sparks, and other colleagues would check it so that it would not be my personal statement but the newspaper's point of view. Published on 28 February, it picked up the theme of the phrase 'Father of the nation', which had been used in a statement by Mrs Sally Motlana, a leader in Soweto and wife of Dr Nthato Motlana.

The editorial went on to say that, coming after the recent deaths of Albert Luthuli and Steve Biko, his passing 'could prove to have been the last chance for white South Africans to deal directly, peacefully and constructively with a black leader straddling the national scene and enjoying wide populist respect and support. This will inevitably reduce the chances of South Africa ever being able to reach towards a non-racial, democratic society. Which would be the ultimate tragedy—for the country and for the memory of Robert Sobukwe.'

Miliswa and Dini were studying in the US, and now so too was one of the twins, Dalindyebo. All three had been home for Christmas. Raising money for their air fares to get to the funeral would have been a giant problem—except that it never even arose. The day that

How Can Man Die Better

Sobukwe died, Chris Barnard offered Veronica the R4,000 needed for their fares. She and I talked it over. Was anything behind it? we wondered. Should she accept? Would she be compromising herself in any way? I recommended acceptance, and she agreed. The children flew out; Anne and I met them at Johannesburg's airport and put them on the next flight to Kimberley.

It remains a puzzling episode: Marius Barnard told me several years later that Chris could not have afforded so much money at the time. His wife was wealthy but his own financial resources were limited. Marius said he was convinced that the money had been put up by the government.

But why should the government do any such thing—and especially anonymously, using Chris Barnard as an intermediary, so that it could not reap kudos for its generosity? In retrospect, it might be that there was a connection with what later burst into the open as the 'Info Scandal'—revelations about the wholesale misuse of public funds by the minister and high officials in the Department of Information who were seeking to buy and to manipulate a better image for the government at home and abroad. Their crookedness ranged from setting up *The Citizen* newspaper in Johannesburg and hiring prominent blacks to put a gloss on apartheid sport, to putting up funds to try—unsuccessfully—to buy a newspaper in the United States.

An Information Department connection with the air fares is pure speculation. In an effort to get to the truth I wrote to Chris Barnard and asked him about it. He replied, politely and pleasantly, that it was true he had been responsible for bringing the children to the funeral. But he went on to say: 'Unfortunately I am not at liberty to give you any information as to who provided the funds for the air-ticket. What I can tell you is that I phoned Mr Andrew Young who was then United States Ambassador of [sic] United Nations and was looking after the Sobukwe children, but he was not prepared to provide the airfare.'

Saturday, 11 March was dry and baking hot in Graaff-Reinet. Anne and I had driven there the day before—which wasn't as easy as it seems because South Africa was under the twin pressures of international oil sanctions and soaring prices, and petrol sales were restricted. Long-distance trips over weekends and at night could be made only by obtaining a government permit for buying petrol; that meant an application to the magistrate's offices in Johannesburg. Despite my anxiety about being turned down, to officialdom's credit a permit was issued authorising me to buy petrol for *'Begrafnis van Sobukwe'* (Funeral of Sobukwe).

As soon as we reached Graaff-Reinet we went up the hill to the black ghetto to call on Veronica who was staying there.

She had at an early stage asked me to be one of the speakers at the funeral. I accepted and thanked her for the honour. At Veronica's request I phoned several other people to invite them. She also asked Bishop Matolengwe to invite Helen Suzman. He did so through Moira who phoned a surprised Helen, who twice phoned her back to ask: 'Are you absolutely certain they want me?'

But forces beyond Veronica's control were gathering force and were to disrupt the planned programme. They were to project the country's racial and political entangled divisions, and were in turn to have disruptive effects for years into the future.

Going into the Graaff-Reinet ghetto in the evening I had a sense of tension in the air. It was formless but I knew it was there in the way people responded to Anne and me. But the first firm indication of what was afoot was next morning, shortly before setting off for the funeral ceremony. Moira returned from visiting Veronica and brought me a message from Matolengwe. He had taken her aside and told her: 'The children have taken over and they won't have Mr Pogrund and Mrs Suzman speaking.' He asked her to find us and tell us.

The mere mention of 'the children' was a signal in itself. After the 'children's revolt', which had begun in Soweto in June 1976, anything which they did, or threatened, had to be treated with deadly seriousness. 'Children' was a broad concept covering those of school-going age, whether or not they were in classes or had dropped out for whatever reason. It could take in youngsters of eight or nine to people in their early twenties.

Later I learnt from Matolengwe that the youngsters in this case came mainly from Soweto and Port Elizabeth. They insisted that neither Helen Suzman nor I was allowed to speak. Whether the issue was precipitated by her role in the Progressive Federal Party—an all-white political party in an all-white parliament—or whether our shared offence was simply that we both had white skins was never entirely clear. The basic complaint of the youngsters was: 'We are tired of liberals.'

There were some heavy scenes during the night: the Sobukwe family and members of the organising committee tried to stand up to the militant youngsters—who were backed by some former Pan-Africanist Congress members—but were forced to give way under threat of disruption. The youths removed the prepared programmes for the ceremony, and cyclostyled their own sanitised version.

In a newspaper interview, Desmond Tutu was later to throw more light on what had occurred. Tutu was then the general secretary of the South African Council of Churches, based in Johannesburg. Until two years before he had been the Anglican Bishop of Maseru, in Lesotho. He was, of course, to achieve world-wide fame as he successively became Nobel Peace Prize Laureate, Bishop of Johannesburg, and Archbishop of Cape Town. He was already a highly influential figure. Tutu had first met Sobukwe when he was teaching at Standerton in the early 1950s and says he was impressed at how 'he remained behind at school to give the students extra tuition—so utterly selfless and dedicated to people'. Later, at Witwatersrand University, Sobukwe gave the same sort of help to Tutu who was preparing for a Zulu examination at another university. Tutu also saw him in Kimberley and was again impressed—'with his lack of bitterness and prodigal gift of himself to serve others'. He visited Sobukwe at Groote Schuur Hospital 'and my admiration for him just grew'.

In the interview, Tutu said that former PAC members had thought that speeches by Helen Suzman and me were 'inappropriate', for as he explained: 'They believed—quite rightly—that the funeral was not a private affair; that their leader had been a public figure who belonged to the people; and that they had a say in the drawing up of the programme. They were deeply incensed that Mrs Suzman and Mr Pogrund were scheduled to speak when so many of those who had worked with Sobukwe had to be left out.'

He went on to say that he had great regard for Helen 'who has earned respect as virtually the only opposition politician for . . . such a long time'; but he believed that, as a politician, she would be sensitive to the feelings of the mourners. 'However, I advised those re-organising the programme to let Mr Pogrund speak. He was a personal friend of Mr Sobukwe and a representative of a newspaper that had always presented him in a positive light.' His views were not heeded.

I was disappointed. But the shock of Sobukwe's death was deep inside me: I was feeling numb and detached, so the hurt was not as great as it might otherwise have been. I accepted it as part of what was happening in South Africa (except, a few days later, when I read what Tutu revealed, I could not help wondering about those who had spoken so loudly but who had done little to help Sobukwe when he was in need). In any event, on the day itself, there was really nothing to be done except to feel apprehensive about what the rest of the day might bring. Anne and I, together with Jennifer, who had come from Cape Town where she was studying, drove to the venue—a large arena with rudimentary stands along the sides, and usually used for agricultural shows. A covered platform, for special guests, stood in the middle.

As we walked into the arena, I met Gatsha Buthelezi. We exchanged civilities. He seemed uncertain of himself and I wondered why he had come: not only was I only too aware of how little of a friend he had been to Sobukwe, but his role in the government's separate development apparatus was increasingly controversial and overshadowed his articulation of black rights. I thought he was out of place as a leader of the Bantustans in attending this funeral, even though he had been quick to issue a statement lauding Sobukwe as a 'political giant whose leadership and sacrifice will stand out in the history of the liberation struggle in South Africa'.

In fact, Buthelezi was there because he had phoned Matolengwe to say he wanted to attend as he had been with Sobukwe at Fort Hare. Ernest Sobukwe, told this, said Buthelezi was welcome—and told Matolengwe that if Buthelezi was at the funeral he should be given the opportunity to speak. Adding to this, Buthelezi was telephoned from London by A.B. Ngcobo, the former PAC national executive member, who told him he should go to the funeral. It does not seem that Buthelezi knew he was supposed to speak. But his name was on the first programme, and when the militants saw it they would have none of it. 'To hell and gone with him,' they shouted.

In the arena, Ernest arrived—stretched out at the back of a station wagon as he was still recovering from his leg operation, and this indeed had been a reason for delaying the funeral by a week. I went to greet him and while he was being lifted out he told me how upset he was about my exclusion: Would I agree to speak after all? He and others wanted me to speak and he intended making sure that I did. I was in his hands, I told him, and would do whatever was thought best.

We were asked to take our seats on the platform, together with the Sobukwe family, the ministers in charge, and Bishop Matolengwe, the scheduled speakers, and Moira, Eulalie and Helen, and Buthelezi, and William Bowdler, the United States Ambassador. No one seemed to object to the presence of whites.

It was already a noteworthy day for the sleepy town. As Zwelakhe Sisulu—who was, in the late 1980s, to spend several years incommunicado in jail to prevent him editing a black newspaper, *The Nation*—reported in Monday's *Rand Daily Mail*: 'The little town of Graaff-Reinet woke up with a shock at the weekend to black power salutes and endless doses of freedom songs from a highly politicised black youth.' For two weeks, students had kept a vigil in the location, and on a hill nearby police set up camp to keep watch on them, he wrote.

'At the crack of dawn on Saturday, cars and buses began a steady stream. Within an hour the township on the outskirts of the town was a hubbub of activity which soon developed into freedom songs ... Thousands of people milled in front of the Sobukwe homestead, singing and chanting slogans. The older people gave the open palm salute of the Pan-Africanist Congress, the young gave vigorous clenched fist salutes.

'The crowd stirred as the coffin was brought out of the house—the open palm salute of the PAC carved on it. Then the march to the oval showground in town began. The solid phalanx moved down the winding dusty street—spearheaded by students. A group in front started a song which was immediately taken up by the winding body. The crowd surged forward and there were intermittent shouts of "One Azania, one nation". A lanky man, sweating heavily, shouted: "Freedom", and the crowd roared back: "Now".'

Sisulu wrote that the march moved into town where it 'was business as usual, but as soon as the crowd was spotted, the street cleared and shops shut down. White traffic officers and police were the only ones who remained to direct traffic, but their services soon became useless as the crowd submerged them. They stood still. The crowd broke into song, "We shall kill the dogs", but still the traffic officers did not move.

'White families in tidy white houses kept indoors, peering through the curtains or sitting on their verandas. Abuse was hurled at them, some were even spat upon . . .'

As the spearhead of the procession entered the arena, Buthelezi was spotted by the youths: 'They broke into a song, "When I see Matanzima [head of the Transkei Bantustan], I see a stooge, when I see Mangope [head of BophuthaTswana] I see a puppet, when I see Gatsha I see. . . ." (a derogatory word was used).'

A young barefoot boy approached Buthelezi 'and extended his hand: "Here, take this," he said as he handed over a two-cent piece, which was flung away.'

The tone was set. The proceedings—an opening hymn and prayers—had barely begun before there was a rush—more a stampede—of people towards the platform. And it was only too clear that they were angry and that the chief target of their anger was Buthelezi. There were upwards of 200 screaming and shouting people from the crowd of 5,000 who made it impossible for anything to be heard. Appeals by religious ministers for calm were ignored. Even the time-honoured method of restoring order by starting the singing of the African national anthem did not work.

The situation looked uglier by the minute. Violence was imminent. Jennifer was holding tightly onto me. I thought that if an outright attack was launched I might, with luck, be able to run fast enough to get away, but what of Anne and Jennifer? I turned round and saw Ambassador Bowdler's two bodyguards leading him off the back of the platform. That really worried me. Someone passed me a hurried message from Ernest: there was no possibility of my speaking.

Finally, after a long half-hour of pandemonium, Buthelezi gave way to the pressure and the urging of Tutu that the funeral could only proceed if he left. Tears streaming down his face, he walked off the back of the platform. As he went past, a metre from us, I turned to Anne and said shakily: 'That man with his enormous pride has been totally humiliated. God knows what price South Africa will be made to pay for it.'

As Buthelezi crossed the uneven ground, hordes of people rushed at him. He ran a gauntlet of scuffles and kicks. Some spat in his face. The jeers and screams cursed him as a 'stooge' and a 'sell-out'. At least one stone was thrown: it hit a journalist on the head. Watching from the platform, I grew more frightened, knowing that one blow bringing him down could set off a mass murderous attack on him. I rushed to Dini, who was standing on a chair looking out over the confusion. 'Dini,' I told him urgently, 'you must get out there and save Gatsha before he is killed.' But Dini was as stunned as all of us at the torrent of hatred. Just then, several shots were fired—possibly by a Buthelezi bodyguard. As the mob hesitated, Buthelezi was hustled away to his car and safety. He escaped with a leg injury.

Others were also ordered to go or were advised to leave because more trouble was feared. They all went quietly. Each was associated with separate development and was labelled a 'black collaborator': Sonny Leon, from Kimberley, of the coloured Labour Party who had recently formed an alliance with Buthelezi's movement; Professor M. Njisane, Transkei's Ambassador in South Africa; the wife of Tsepo Letlaka—the former PAC leader who had deserted and become a Transkei Cabinet Minister. Even black Lennox Mlonzi, who had been jailed with Sobukwe in March 1960 but had later taken part in a government body in Soweto before moving to the Transkei, had to leave.

The uproar ended, the ceremony wended its way through seven speeches—some, such as by Godfrey Pitje, in fiery language both in praise of Sobukwe and in condemnation of white liberals. Feelings were still touchy: I was using a tape-recorder for the speeches but was aggressively challenged by some young men about it. I switched it off.

By mid-afternoon it was over. The crowd marched to the graveyard—the one reserved for those who were not whites. But we did not go. By then I did not feel that this was Bob Sobukwe's funeral: the remains of his body were there but it was not a tribute to the man I knew; it had been hijacked by people intent on sharpening their political axe and I had no particular wish to be associated with it.

What would I have said had I been allowed to? The text of the speech was published in *Reality* later that year:

Robert Sobukwe. My brother and my friend.
It did not matter that our skins were of different colours; that we came from such different backgrounds—he from a woodcutter's home in this village, the descendant of people who have spent centuries in the African continent; me a first generation African, from a middle class home in Cape Town. It

did not matter that we did not have the same father and mother. We grew to be brothers. Over a period of twenty years our relationship of love and caring developed and deepened.

That Bob Sobukwe saw me as his brother and that I saw him as my brother already tells a great deal about him and about the South Africa he believed in and wanted. A country without blacks or whites, but of human beings. A country where racism will be outlawed.

Many words about the greatness of Bob Sobukwe are being spoken today. They are true words. Many wonderful words have been spoken about him since he passed away two weeks ago. They are true words.

It is tragic that, in his lifetime, so many in South Africa spurned him; that so much of what he had to offer us was suppressed and locked away—in Pretoria prison, on Robben Island prison, in confinement and banning in Kimberley.

But the test of a man can be seen in what he leaves behind him, in what he has left for us who remain in this world.

And we have from Bob Sobukwe that belief in South Africa of which I spoke earlier. One united South Africa, free of colour or tribal divisions. A South Africa devoted to justice and democracy for all its peoples, without totalitarianism, communism or any other crushing of the human spirit. It was a dream in his lifetime; yet it is more than a dream for in it lies the future and the salvation of all of us.

In all the years of his life, Bob Sobukwe did not deviate a fraction from his belief and always he wanted it to come about in peace.

Going closely with this, what we have from him is a love of people.

He practised this in his life to an extent that was incredible to behold. Even for his oppressors, for those who held him captive, there was no bitterness or hatred. Only a sympathy for them, a pity for them because of the way they behaved.

When we were together, it was I who would express the resentment, the anger, at the way he was treated. He would simply be amused, tolerant about those who had done humiliating things to him.

I would feel ashamed and embarrassed, as a person and as a

South African, about the things that were inflicted on him—whether the cruelty of forcibly keeping him year after year on Robben Island in isolation, or the ugliness of the apartheid system in forcing us, when I visited him in Kimberley, to go and drive out among the thorn bushes to seek shelter from the sun, drinking our cool drinks and eating our pies. It was one of our moments of joy when, after several years of doing this, we discovered a café that actually did not mind if we sat down together to share a pot of tea. Provided that we sat in the black section of the café.

For Bob Sobukwe these were things to be taken in his stride. To him, they were examples of the weakness of his oppressors, of the desperate and ugly things that they had to do to maintain themselves.

He rose above it all; he was the giant; those who tried to debase him were themselves debased.

Whenever, during the dark times of his life, I went to give him comfort, I came away amazed. Because it was not I that gave him comfort, but it was he who gave me comfort.

And even in the last few months of his life: he could not but know then that it was the bannings enforced on him, confining him to Kimberley, which had prevented him from travelling freely to obtain the specialised medical attention which could perhaps have prolonged his life. Even then he did not lash out, as a lesser person would so naturally have done.

Yet none of this, as we well know, meant that there was any trace of weakness in Bob Sobukwe. For what he has also given us is the example of his strength and courage in sticking to what he believed. He applied this to a super-human extent. He asked people to do only what he himself was prepared to do. He was the first to lead the way—and to accept the consequences of what he did.

Many years ago I shared in his dilemma when Rhodes University offered him a full-time job as lecturer. At that stage, Bob was called a 'language assistant' at Witwatersrand University. Now he had the chance of a well-paid, status position to do the teaching and the writing that he loved. But he turned it down. He decided that his task was to give himself to his people. And he stuck to that unwaveringly to the end of his life, never regretting, never complaining, never losing his faith in his mission and in God's purpose.

Bob Sobukwe has also given us his thinking. Under the laws at present inflicted on us, I cannot quote his words. Even in his death the Nationalists are so frightened of the power of his thinking that they cannot be directly referred to. But we all know that it was he who took the ideas of black consciousness—so vital towards the gaining of freedom for all our peoples—and developed and refined them.

He applied his intelligence and his perceptions to our problems. The philosophies he presented are still with us; they have been carried along by another generation.

It is because of his thinking and the way that he lived it out that he has been rightly described as the 'Father of our nation'. That is a nation which will come in South Africa. When it does, it will be, more than to anyone else, a memorial to Bob Sobukwe.

As we mourn him today, we need also to think of his wife, Veronica. In the years of fighting and struggle, Veronica stood like a rock, always there, bringing up the children and giving support to her husband. She fought with him and for him.

As we share in her grief, we give her honour and admiration. She is the mother of the nation.

And Bob's children. What does one say to children—young adults—whose father has been such a mighty figure?

Their grief is our grief. We give them comfort as we seek comfort from who Sobukwe was.

I grieve for my brother. South Africa grieves for its father, for this son of Africa.

Bob Sobukwe has passed away. But he lives. He is belief, love, hope—and a great gift to all who knew him or of him.

We returned to the hotel—the Drostdy, a gracious and luxurious place, with the main section restored to its original 1806 design when it was built as the *drostdy*, the seat of local government, and the rooms created out of a row of cottages which were once the homes of coloured labourers, and possibly of freed slaves. The cool and comfort of the hotel came as a bizarre contrast with the dust and heat of the ceremony—and even more so because all the guests at the hotel were whites, as required by the law. Among them was the small group of whites in the town for the funeral, including Nita and Joe, whom I met for the first time (and since then, friendship with them has been one of Sobukwe's legacies to me); Alan Paton, the author, and Peter Brown, who had led the former Liberal Party with him and had endured years-long banning for it. (Peter was Editor of *Reality*, a small magazine which provided a forum for liberal thinking after the demise of the Liberal Party, often publishing articles which could find no other home in South Africa.

On that day, the Drostdy wasn't a totally colour-fast world so close and yet so far away from what we had experienced in the preceding hours: Neville Alexander, who was coloured and who had been a political prisoner on Robben Island while Sobukwe was there, could not attend the funeral because he was banned and restricted to his Cape Town home; but his mother came on his behalf. Moira, who was looking after her, went into the bar to get her a drink and found a black woman there. Moira discovered the hotel had been declared 'international' for that day: in terms of the current laws, that meant it was open to people of all races. To press home the point, Moira took Mrs Alexander to have her drink inside the otherwise usually whites-only bar.

Suzman had her say about her exclusion. She told the *Rand Daily Mail* that it was obviously regretful because Veronica herself had extended the invitation—'But I respected their decision that it should be a black people's occasion.' She added: 'One had no means of knowing how representative the militants were. It would have been interesting to hear the crowd's reaction had they heard what I had to say.'

My published comment went to the heart of my outlook: 'I feel sad about it, of course. It was a negation of the non-racialism for which Robert Sobukwe stood. It reflects how far down the road we have gone in South Africa. White racism has inevitably spawned black racism. Both are equally abhorrent.'

I carried that theme forward when it was again thought appropriate for me to write the *Rand Daily Mail*'s view of the weekend's turbulent event. It was also a helpful cathartic process for me—as writing for the *Mail* so often was—enabling me to get my thoughts together and to work through my emotions. 'Glimpse of an Ugly Development' was the editorial's headline in Tuesday's issue:

Benjamin Pogrund

Those who precipitated the violent and disturbing events at Graaff-Reinet on Saturday did no service to the memory of Mr Robert Sobukwe, whose death they had supposedly come to mourn.

In confronting Chief Gatsha Buthelezi and chasing him away from the funeral service they behaved contrary to the gentleness and the peaceful outlook which were such outstanding ingredients of Mr Sobukwe's character. In imposing their will on the funeral and refusing to allow two invited whites to speak ... they were both discourteous to Mr Sobukwe's family and they betrayed the nonracialism which was the basis of his political beliefs.

But was it merely a case of 'political thuggery', as Chief Buthelezi says it was? And can those responsible be dismissed as a 'few delinquents' from the townships who were used on the spur of the moment, as he also says?

We fear that this is only partly correct; that in fact the youths who turned to these distasteful actions reflect the wider and growing attitude of intolerance and anti-whiteism among blacks.

Can this really be cause for surprise? White racism has inevitably spawned black racism. White rejection of blacks is leading to black rejection of whites. Even such a courageous fighter for black rights as Chief Buthelezi is despised by some because of his role in the white man's separate development apparatus.

It is the Nationalist creed that white and black must be separated. That is what Nationalist rule is all about. Apartheid has deliberately fostered racial exclusivism—with rank discrimination to sharpen the black sense of grievance—and now we are having to cope with the monster.

How to do so? Certainly the government's answer in locking up and banning and resorting to ever-tougher restrictive laws is not the way. As pointed out by Mr Sonny Leon, who was also ordered away from the funeral: 'Once you remove the recognised leaders then the mob becomes a leaderless rabble and anybody can influence them.'

Indeed the stern repression so favoured by the Nationalists inevitably becomes counter-productive, setting off greater anger, passion and activity which are then met by even harsher official retribution.

The spiral of hatred and violence, frightening in what it portends, must be halted. That can only be done by the Nationalists seeking a new path of racial reconciliation: not in the debased politics of separate development but through true racial consultation and sharing.

In life, Robert Sobukwe was shunned by most of his white countrymen. There can be hope for all of us if the events surrounding his burial alert whites to the need to act swiftly and positively.

Epilogue

South Africans won freedom sixteen years and two months after Robert Mangaliso Sobukwe's death. After the turning point of 21 March 1960 came the next major outburst of resistance to apartheid, the schoolchildren's revolt of 16 June 1976. Then the mass protests which erupted in September 1984. Each time government suppression grew fiercer; each time protest rose again, wider and more determined, until the country was eventually engulfed by mass action. The black townships became ungovernable, and the police were able to enter only in groups and heavily armed. The United Democratic Front was created and quickly became a popular movement linked to the African National Congress in exile whose Umkhonto weSizwe (Spear of the Nation) movement waged guerrilla war. International boycotts and disinvestment took their toll, weakening the economic ability of whites to maintain their rule and undermining their morale. During the 1980s the name of Nelson Mandela began to emerge from the confines of his prison cell. From early in 1985 the government of President P.W. Botha was in secret contact with him; when Botha was deposed and replaced by F.W. de Klerk, the pace speeded up as Afrikaner Nationalist leaders came to recognise that they could no longer hold on to power, at least not without plunging the country into catastrophe. In February 1990, amid tumultuous scenes, Mandela was released from prison, and the bans were ended on the African National Congress and the Pan-Africanist Congress, both illegal since 1960, and the Communist Party, illegal since 1950.

The collapse of the Soviet Union in 1991 was the final tipping of the scales: the ANC lost its patron and whites were dropped by the West. The two sides had no choice but to deal with each other.

The ANC was the dominant body in the struggle. It also commanded the moral high ground: when, in 1961, it had switched to armed resistance, it decided that white civilians were not to be targets for killings. That stemmed from adherence to the Mahatma Gandhi principle of non-violence in which the ANC was steeped, and also for strategic reasons on the basis that whites would be more likely to yield power if they did not fear being swept into the sea. The policy was maintained, with only a few exceptions, for the next thirty years, and events proved its worth. Only during the last three years of apartheid did violence occur on a massive scale with some 12,000 deaths, nearly all of them black people.

The Pan-Africanist Congress never recovered from its post-Sharpeville disarray. It never succeeded in developing leaders of Sobukwe's quality. Through the 1960s, 1970s and 1980s the PAC in exile repeatedly tore itself apart through savage internal feuding, murder, thuggery and theft. A book, *Struggles Within the Struggle*, which was said to spell out the lurid details and written by Henry Isaacs, the PAC's former director for foreign affairs, was printed in Britain in 1985 but was withdrawn from publication under threat of defamation action.

In 1986 the PAC elected Zeph Mothopeng as president: it was a token move because he was in prison in South Africa. 'Uncle Zeph', as he was known, had worked closely with Sobukwe and was a man of exceptional commitment and courage: once a high school teacher, he had devoted himself to destroying apartheid; almost the day he came out of prison after serving one sentence he began anew until he was again jailed. That was the pattern of his life. It was said that he joked that he first went to jail with his contemporaries, went back with his children, and went back once again in 1979 with his grandchildren when he was 74 years old.

He rejected a government offer of amnesty on condition that he renounced armed struggle. But he was released two years later, suffering from cancer. He visited London and was given the best possible hospital treatment—it seemed the British government picked up the tab. I saw a lot of him and it was sad. He was old and spent. At a public meeting, Mothopeng was swept along emotionally by radical American blacks on the platform and ended up repeatedly yelling out an invitation for all black people everywhere to 'return to Africa'. He clearly did not know what he was saying. When the PAC became legal in 1990 it confirmed him as president, but he died later that year.

Like the ANC, the PAC turned to armed resistance. But the

violence of its military wing, the Azanian People's Liberation Army (Apla), which had emerged out of Poqo of the 1960s, was specifically directed against white civilians. Its slogan was 'One settler, one bullet'. Settler meant whites. In the closing years of apartheid, while most white and black leaders met and argued and negotiated to end white rule, Apla played an ugly, spoiling role with massacres of whites, notably inside a church and a tavern in Cape Town.

Representatives of black organisations and of the government and other white parties finally reached agreement and set 26 to 29 April 1994 for the historic first one-person, one-vote elections. The Pan-Africanist Congress dithered about what to do. Arguments raged internally as to whether to boycott the elections and continue the armed struggle. There was also division about the leadership of the PAC president Clarence Makwetu.

'When the PAC finally decided to be part of the elections, it was too late,' Nomavenda Mathiane later commented in *Business Day* newspaper on 27 May 1999. 'It had sent conflicting messages to its supporters and sympathisers and there was not enough time to campaign. Neither was there time to produce a sound election manifesto. They ended up campaigning around the slogan: "The land first and everything will follow." This led to people ridiculing the PAC, saying they were archaic and were stuck in the past like a scratched long-playing record which kept on repeating the same old tune. A joke doing the rounds in the Eastern Cape, where Raymond Mhlaba was the premier-elect for the ANC, cost the PAC dearly. The ANC took advantage of the PAC slogan to vote for the land—or "mhlaba", which means land in Xhosa. By telling rural peasants to vote for "mhlaba", the ANC's Raymond Mhlaba was the one to benefit.'

Some commentators thought there was a strong undercurrent of Africanist belief waiting to be tapped in many parts of the country. If there was then the PAC did not get to it and instead suffered a humiliating defeat: it polled 1.28 per cent of the votes, winning five seats in the Parliament of 400 members. The ANC won 62.6 per cent.

The next PAC president, elected in 1996, had credentials that were impeccable, astonishing really: Mmutlanyane Stanley Mogoba had just been re-elected as Presiding Bishop of the Methodist Church when he agreed to lead the PAC. Mogoba, once a high school teacher, served three years on Robben Island in the mid-1960s for underground PAC activities. He went on to be ordained as a minister and in 1988 was elected the Methodists' leader. He was also at various times President of the South African Institute of Race Relations—his theme was 'Harmony: Key to National Reconstruction'—Chancellor of the Medical University of South Africa and President of the Boy Scouts of South Africa.

This gentle cleric was now leading what was supposed to be the radical PAC, with policies that focused on the main grievances among people at the time (and now too): economic justice for all, fighting crime, housing and land distribution for agriculture. I was at the conference that elected him and noted the enthusiasm among delegates about the PAC's new future. Many young men were there: one of them was wearing a black T-shirt with the slogan, 'One settler, one bullet'. I was surprised and asked him: 'Isn't that message out of date?' He was embarrassed and said it was the only shirt that he owned. I was also amused by the young black militants who, when they learned my name as Prof's friend, were plainly astonished to see that I was white and were uncertain what to do about it. They would probably have been even more astonished to know that the lapel badge that many delegates wore with Sobukwe's face on it was from a photograph I took at my home in Johannesburg in August 1977.

Confidence within the PAC was bolstered by the return to South Africa and appointment now as national organiser of Philip Kgosana, the legendary hero who in March 1960 had been the young Pied Piper in frayed shorts and a jacket who led a crowd of thousands in a march on Cape Town. Kgosana had escaped from the country, studied economics and public administration at universities in Ethiopia and Uganda, undergone military training in Ethiopia, and spent twenty years working for the United Nations Development Fund and Unicef (UN Children's Emergency Fund) in Sri Lanka, Tanzania and Botswana.

Now he told me in an interview for the *Mail & Guardian* newspaper: 'In 1960 I was a young rebel fighting against apartheid; my feelings almost bordered on hate. Over the years I spent with the UN I came to appreciate human beings for what they are and what they can contribute. I have come to understand what Robert Mangaliso Sobukwe called the human race. This outlook is what I would like to see myself bringing into our country ... Sobukwe is a kind of messiah to some of us.'

Inside the PAC some expressed their worries to me as to whether Kgosana still had the personal power and magnetism that he had demonstrated in 1960. I asked him bluntly whether he could do for the PAC now what he had done 37 years before. 'During the Cape Town days I was a crusader,' he said. 'I think I have matured.' He did not speak in terms of street politics but of 'hard work' and 'restructuring the party so that it is a machine that can win elections'.

Kgosana did not succeed in giving new life to the PAC. He was probably too nice a man for the brawling and backstabbing inside the leadership. Mogoba, too, after starting well and seeming to draw wider support—he even held parlour meetings for whites—was tormented by internal strife. He also changed: in February 1999, with the country's horrifying level of crime high on the political agenda, he issued a press statement endorsing amputating the limbs of criminals as a means of deterring crime. It was strange talk for a Christian leader. The Methodist Church distanced itself from him. Peter Storey, also a former Methodist bishop, described his statement as 'bizarre'. Four months later, on 2 June, voters gave their views: the PAC won only 0.78 per cent of the vote, with three seats in Parliament. The ANC won 66.4 per cent.

The PAC continued to be its own worst enemy. Its December 2002 congress was suspended because of allegations that the deputy president, Motsoko Pheko, had brought in under-aged voters. Pheko went on to be elected president the next July. Schisms continued. Patricia de Lille, a Cape Town trade unionist, a member of the PAC national executive since 1990 and a vigorous critic of the government, broke away in 2003 to form her own party, the Independent Democrats.

In the next general election, on 14 April 2004, the PAC placed Mogoba at number 83 on its list. Whether this open insult to a leader affected voters cannot be said. In any event, the PAC drew 0.73 per cent of the votes with three seats in Parliament. The ANC drew 69.7 per cent.

In the general election of 2009, the PAC sank to 0.27 per cent of the votes. Infighting went on unabated. In May 2013, the president, Letlapa Mphahlele, was expelled amid accusations of trying to cause divisions inside the party, financial impropriety and poor leadership. With Alton Mpethi as president, a mere 37,784 South

Africans—0.21 per cent—voted for the party in the 2014 general election. It had no members of Parliament.

The Pan-Africanist Congress has doomed itself to having little meaning in the South Africa of today. There is little trace of Sobukwe's vision.

In the closing years of apartheid, government policy changed and blacks were allowed to buy the houses they could previously only rent. Veronica Sobukwe tried to buy her house at 6 Naledi Street in Galeshewe township, Kimberley. First a high price was set; then months passed and her attempts to get an appointment to finalise the issue were repeatedly sidestepped with officials telling her it had been referred to Pretoria. Meanwhile, the rent was raised by nearly 40 per cent. 'This dilly-dallying is intended to make us throw up our hands in despair ...' she wrote in a letter. Then a final cruel blow: when Sobukwe's estate was wound up, she says that the authorities told her she did not qualify under the pass laws to live in Kimberley and had to get out.

She decided to move to Swaziland. But the Swazis, with as little compassion as the South Africans, invoked their law dealing with the transfer of property to foreigners and denied her permission to buy land. She tried Edendale, near Pietermaritzburg, then Sobukwe Street in Graaff-Reinet, but could not settle in. She moved into an unfinished house in the town of Alice, where Fort Hare University is situated. Finally, in 1998, she returned to Graaff-Reinet and bought a house in Stockenstroom Street, in what had previously been a neighbourhood for whites only and now has residents of all colours. She says that she wants to live there and be buried there because that is where her husband was born and is buried. Her home is in walking distance of the site where Sobukwe was born, but illness prevents her from walking there and she is largely housebound. Once a month a Methodist minister comes to give her Communion. The black leather lounge suite which fulfilled Sobukwe's dream in Kimberley way back in 1969 after his release from Robben Island still graces her living room. In her eighties, Veronica Sobukwe is the same quiet, indomitable woman as always. Laughter comes easily, even after the adversities she has endured in her life.

For the children, being deprived of their father, and not knowing for so long when he might be home again, left its marks.

Miliswa completed her psychology studies in the US, married and lived in Africa before returning to South Africa. Dini married in the US, worked for a legal firm in Washington, DC, and then returned to South Africa; he has established the Robert Mangaliso Sobukwe Trust. Dalindyebo obtained a diploma in business studies in the US and returned home, finally enlisting in the post-apartheid South African National Defence Force. He held the rank of captain. He died in 1999. Dedani has for many years had a troubled existence; it was already in evidence when his father was released from Robben Island, and it has continued.

I decided to donate all my papers dealing with Sobukwe—the letters that had passed between us and the files which had been built up in dealing with his affairs—to the Africana Library at the University of the Witwatersrand (Wits) in Johannesburg. This was the university where Sobukwe had taught and was the place where we had first met. I was a graduate of the university and from experience over the years in dealing with documentary material of anti-apartheid groups I knew that the Library stood out in South Africa for its courage in ensuring that the material would be available for future scholars. The university gladly accepted the papers and a date was set in September 1997 for the formal handing over. It was combined with a reissue of this biography of Sobukwe.

Nelson Mandela, who was then president, was invited. But he did not respond—until the night before, when the university was urgently phoned by one of his staff who said that the president had only just learnt of the invitation and insisted on attending. A flurry of activity followed. The Wits principal said he was coming. Security men descended on the Library and the grounds. Guests streamed in.

Mandela came. He clearly meant it as a gesture of reconciliation to reach across political divisions.

As usual, his sense of humour bubbled up. As he walked into the Library he saw Stanley Mogoba, then PAC president and in opposition to the ruling African National Congress. Mandela raised his arms in greeting and called out, 'My leader!' As Mandela came through the crowd in the lobby, people—both black and white—pressed to get close to him and to touch his hands. I watched their faces, the glint in their eyes and the looks of respect and admiration.

How Can Man Die Better

Jules Browde, who chaired the event, was an old friend with a distinguished record as a lawyer for the defence in apartheid trials and as Chairman of Lawyers for Human Rights in South Africa. He became a Senior Counsel and a judge on the Appeal Courts of Swaziland and Lesotho. He never met Sobukwe but in 1960 was approached by Joe Slovo who asked him to lead the appeal to the Supreme Court against Sobukwe's sentence of three years' imprisonment for the 21 March anti-pass demonstrations, as well as for his fellow PAC leaders.

'In preparing for court,' says Browde, 'I was given a great deal of information by the instructing attorney, Godfrey Pitje, about Sobukwe's past and his philosophy. This enabled me to approach the court with passion because I believed in the character of Sobukwe and was sympathetic to his motives. I could not challenge the merits of the case because they had been convicted of doing what they had set out to do, to offer themselves for arrest. But the point was to highlight the degradation imposed by the pass laws and to argue against the severity of the sentences.

'Judge Lammie Snyman was one of the two judges who heard the appeal and from the moment I stood up to argue he was extremely hostile and began throwing questions at me and making statements about the need for blacks to have passes. "This man disrupted the whole social fabric of this country," he said. "If Natives could walk around freely it would lead to great hostility between the races of this country. Therefore it is essential that the Natives have passes."'

Browde replied, in the archaic language of South Africa's courts, then and now: 'Perhaps Your Lordship is under a misapprehension. I am here to attempt to persuade Your Lordship that the sentence is disproportionately harsh. Your Lordship does not have to persuade me about anything.' That angered Snyman, says Browde: 'He did not like me after that. I had several brushes with him in different forums. He was nasty to me in later, other cases.'

The appeal was dismissed and Sobukwe and his comrades remained in prison. As is known, the fact that he broke his 'no bail, no defence, no fine' pledge was overtaken by recognition that the PAC had rendered itself leaderless and did not seem to damage his public image.

In the very different atmosphere of the ceremony at Wits, after Browde spoke in praise of Sobukwe, recalling his sincerity and his fight against the humiliation of blacks under apartheid, Mandela shook his hand and told him: 'I am very pleased that you paid that tribute to Robert Sobukwe because, although I did not agree politically with him, I thought he was an outstanding man and deserved what you said about him.'

Yet the event still carried bitter echoes for some. Nhlanhla Maake, Professor of African Languages at Wits, referred to it a few weeks later in a newspaper review of the biography, describing it as the 'final posthumous irony' of Sobukwe's life: 'This is the same institution that had failed to accord him and other African academics who worked in the African languages department a fitting status, following apartheid to the letter. The launch was attended by President Nelson Mandela, but other Africans of Sobukwe's hue were merely observers. Staff members of the department were conspicuous by their absence.'

Whatever the validity of the criticism, Wits laid the past to rest twenty-five years after Sobukwe's death: in May 2003 the university broke with tradition and, for the first time, conferred its highest honour, Doctor of Laws *honoris causa*, posthumously in 'recognition of his singular and significant contribution to South Africa'. The citation said that Sobukwe's 'call for a Pan-African identity has been resurrected in this new century in the concept of an African renaissance. Through processes such as the African Union (AU) and the New Partnership for Africa's Development (NEPAD), African leaders are attempting to give practical substance to his vision.

'We live in an Africa that faces huge challenges—xenophobia, racism, ethnicity and tribalism, dictatorship, corruption, poverty, disease, war, famine and a paralysing timidity and resistance to the general processes of transformation. In meeting these challenges African leaders in every field in every country would do well to remember Robert Mangaliso Sobukwe's call to his fellow Africans: "We must be the embodiment of our people's aspirations." What better embodiment could there be of the best of Africa's aspirations than Robert Mangaliso Sobukwe?'

In mid-1982, a letter reached me from Dennis Siwisa. 'We are unveiling Robert's memorial tombstone on 15 August', it said. 'The ceremony will be at Graaff-Reinet, starting at 10 a.m. I'm in the Committee that is handling the arrangements ... We in the

Committee have unanimously agreed that we should request you to be one of the speakers on the occasion ...'

This time, unlike the funeral, it went off as planned. The tombstone, a map of Africa etched into black marble, was unveiled. Graaff-Reinet's tranquillity was again shaken by a crowd of more than 2,000 black and coloured people who marched through the town from the Methodist Church in the ghetto—the same building where Sobukwe as a boy had begun his school studies—to the cemetery.

I spoke about Sobukwe's legacy and so did representatives of Black Consciousness organisations. They spent a lot of time criticising white liberals. But no one seemed to object to me personally. I thought Bob Sobukwe would have smiled at the wryness of it.

There were other public occasions on which to speak about Sobukwe: in February 1988, the Pan-Africanist Congress asked me to go to New York to a meeting of the United Nations Special Committee on Apartheid, an arch-foe of the South African government. The meeting, with its tributes to Sobukwe, was addressed by representatives of member states of the Special Committee, by the PAC and an assortment of others from US radical black groups to the PLO.

It was an unusual grouping for me and no doubt my attendance found its place in my Security Police dossier. But I thought that a point was being made about a future non-racial South Africa by a white person speaking in praise of a black friend and leader at the invitation of the Pan-Africanist Congress with its image of being anti-white. Johnson Mlambo, the PAC's then chairman, later told me that, in inviting me, he had had the same view.

Another act of reconciliation took place on 28 February 1998: Veronica invited Chief Mangosuthu Gatsha Buthelezi to speak at the commemoration of Sobukwe's death. As Sobukwe had feared, Buthelezi and his Zulu Inkatha Freedom Party had become a highly disruptive force. The struggle for power between him and the ANC during the waning years of apartheid brought the country close to explosion. A last-minute peace was effected just before the 1994 election, and Buthelezi became Minister of Home Affairs in the new South Africa.

At the commemoration he began by recalling how what he termed 'some misguided youth' had forced him to leave the funeral twenty years earlier: 'On that day, their blindly fervent and violent attacks threatened my life, forcing me to leave our brother Mangaliso's funeral. I have always regretted that and have carried a very heavy burden in my heart. By being made to leave, I never had the opportunity to deliver my condolences and offer my tribute to a man whose life rang true to the meaning of his name: "man of wonders".' He hailed Sobukwe as 'one of Africa's greatest sons'.

It was only after the end of apartheid rule that I was able to go into Galeshewe and visit Sobukwe's house; previously, I had been refused the permission which whites needed to enter black townships. The house, I was told when I went there in 1997, was five years old when Sobukwe was dumped there. It had been built by a local man who sold it to the municipality. On either side of No. 6 I saw other substantial-looking houses; across the street were small semi-detached houses for workers.

The street was known as the 'Rich Block' because it housed the small number of professionals in the black community such as doctors and school principals plus shop owners. But contradicting its nickname, the street was still unpaved and rocky even twenty years after Sobukwe had lived there. Cocks crowed in the middle of the day as they had done years before. Giant overhead electricity masts lit up the area at night. Because of increases in robbery, murder and rape—problems besetting South Africa's cities—residents said that it was no longer as safe to walk the streets at night as it had been when he was there. Sobukwe's house always had piped water but in his time most houses in the township had shared communal taps; later, each house had its own cold-water tap in the yard.

The memory of him remained strong and warm among the people of the township although admiration sometimes enlarged their recollections—such as those, for example, who said that they had often visited him at his home at night in defiance of his house arrest and banning orders. However, Veronica Sobukwe says that did not happen. She and Sobukwe spent evenings and weekends alone: he studied and they tended their chickens and the garden in which he planted flowers and fruit trees, including peach.

Alice Makaud says that Sobukwe rented his office from her husband. It was a small building that included a trading store and had a receptionist in the front section and an office for Sobukwe at the back. He stepped from the building into a street that was paved at the time. A short distance away was the municipal building where residents—mainly blacks but also coloureds—paid their rents. Years later, there was still a trading store, as well as the giant bluegum tree across the road, the same small, run-down township houses, and lots of sandy open spaces.

Joyce Makhele recalls that she owned a small café when Sobukwe began to work for attorney H.Z.M. Nzimande. Sobukwe came in each weekday to buy newspapers—the *Rand Daily Mail* and the local *Diamond Fields Advertiser*. Then he stopped doing so and she asked one of the secretaries about it: 'She said, "You won't believe it but we are getting a better salary than Prof." So I decided I may just as well supply newspapers to Prof because he is used to them. He came one day and asked why I was doing it and I told him I suppose I am continuing the goodness that you did for our people. He said, "I won't call you Joyce anymore, but Mtshana (Xhosa for Niece)." I called him Malume (Uncle).'

Makhele says that she cooked for Sobukwe when he arrived in Kimberley and before Veronica came: 'I gave him samp, with dumplings and tripe alternately with it.'

Sobukwe attended local funerals but, she says, he never sat with the VIPs. And when food was dished up outside in big bowls he ate with the ordinary people. He arrived early for the Sunday services at the Methodist Church in the township. He gave up his seat if an elderly person or a woman came in and instead went to sit with the children in a small space in the front.

In the same strain, his eldest son, Dini, remembers going to town by bus with his father: 'He was seated at the back and I was in the middle. I was absent-mindedly looking outside as the bus moved along when I was aroused from this daydream by his angry booming voice calling my name. He never talked this way … I turned around to look at him and immediately saw a lady standing next to me. I jumped up to let her sit. He never would abide disrespect.'

As I had always seen him do, he had a friendly greeting with hand upraised for everyone he met, irrespective of who they were. A memory for one man is that Sobukwe always greeted the workers on the night-soil trucks and they called out, 'Hello, Prof.'

Gabriel Manong, who took over 6 Naledi Street from Mrs Sobukwe, was a prosecutor in the Bantu Commissioner's Court, which dealt only with blacks. Sobukwe acted as a lawyer in divorce and civil cases, and defended people who fell foul of apartheid's influx control, the same laws that had caused him to call the anti-pass protests in 1960. He was also a defence lawyer in criminal trials in the magistrates' courts. He was a good attorney, says Manong, meticulous in his preparation of cases and he knew the law.

Sobukwe got to his office by 8 a.m. each day, say local residents, and usually found people waiting for him outside. They came because they knew he would be leaving for court and arranged to see him in the afternoon or the next day. He was given a lift by car by friends to the courts, a few minutes' drive away in the town. He had to leave for home before 6 p.m., when his weekday house arrest started.

Yvonne Mokgoro, born in Kimberley, was a university student and Black Consciousness activist when Sobukwe was banished there. 'Prof was our father-figure,' she says. 'We were like students. We called him the Prof, as did everybody, even women and children. He gave us a first-class political education. When we emerged and started with matured political activities, many of us were ANC; others were PAC. My husband and I were ANC. I can't remember Prof ever trying to recruit any of us. He would conscientise us and talk about history and people and world events. Prof would give us the facts. He spoke well about everybody, he would never speak badly about anybody.'

She says Sobukwe acted for her when she was held by the police for protesting against the arbitrary arrest of a young man who had been standing in the street. When she was freed she said to Sobukwe: 'I spent the whole weekend in the cells and I am standing here with you because you got me off the hook. I am trying to imagine, where is the young man? Where are all the people who were beaten up? Who is standing up for them? Who is representing them?' Sobukwe told her: 'Law is a male-dominated profession but you don't have to be a man to study law. Why don't you study law?' At that time, there was probably one black woman lawyer in the country, in Durban. 'You question why more men don't study law,' he said. 'Why don't you become the first black woman lawyer in Kimberley? You can do it.'

Mokgoro duly switched to law studies. 'Prof sowed the seed of feminism in me, he sowed the seed of legal activism in me,' she says. 'And he did more than inspire—it was also the way he operated: he would represent people, and money never came into the equation. I do not know if people went to him because they knew that he would not charge them. It was because of the heart. Prof never mentioned money. We used to scold him: he was this wise Prof and we used to say to him, "How do you think you will live? You have to take money; you can't do work for nothing. You are spoiling these people." We used to call him the "social worker lawyer".

'We saw Kimberley as a blessed place because Prof was banished to it. We saw ourselves as lucky because he was banned to our place.'

Mokgoro climbed the legal ladder. In 1994, in the new South Africa, she was appointed a judge in the country's highest court, the Constitutional Court.

With the end of apartheid it became safe to reveal details of underground contacts between Sobukwe and Steve Biko. A couple of times Sobukwe had said to me with a smile, "Steve sends regards." In those days one knew when not to ask questions so I merely said thanks. Sobukwe was in fact saying that he had had an illegal meeting; if it had become known, both of them could have landed in prison. Biko was banned and confined to King William's Town in the east of the country while Sobukwe was banned and confined to Kimberley, nearly 700 km (435 miles) away on the direct route.

One time that they met was when Sobukwe returned from his mother's funeral in Graaff-Reinet. He drove through King William's Town and secretly met Biko. On another occasion—I do not know if it happened more than once—Biko took the immense risk of driving to Kimberley. He did so by reporting to the police in King William's Town—he was required to do so every weekday—then driving across the country, meeting Sobukwe at night in Kimberley and driving back home in time to report again to the police.

Biko, in fact, regularly defied his banning orders to carry out political work. It ended tragically: on 18 August 1977 the police detained him at a roadblock; three and a half weeks later this gifted leader died as a result of massive head injuries inflicted by the Security Police.

Biko's travels were funded by John Rees, then General Secretary of the South African Council of Churches in Johannesburg. Rees and I were close friends and he told me about Biko's work. He twice provided funds for Biko to visit Sobukwe but did not know if the visits had actually taken place. He said that he had funded other political activities too but would never reveal the details so as not to compromise the Council of Churches and the people he was helping. He said he realised that he might, one day, have to face the consequences of his actions but had made up his mind to remain silent.

He was indeed called to account: the government was implacably hostile towards the Council of Churches because of its moral opposition to apartheid and the financial aid (using millions of rands Rees raised abroad) it gave to the large numbers of people and families who were repressed after the 1976 schoolchildren's rebellion; the government seized the chance of financial disputes inside the Council of Churches to investigate the organisation. Rees, who by then had given way to Desmond Tutu as general secretary, was charged with fraud and theft. He denied the charges but did not disclose his secret activities. I knew Rees as a devout Methodist, a man who lived his Christian beliefs in every moment of each day, and I did not believe the charges. I was certain he had been set up. His attorney, Raymond Tucker, told me that he had not the slightest doubt that Rees was innocent. However, Rees was found guilty. He was not jailed, but was heavily fined.

John Rees died young. In what was effectively a deathbed statement he wrote letters to the judge who tried him, the prosecutor and others, to say that he had not stolen a single penny of the money and would carry to the grave the names of those whom he had helped. Shortly before his death Rees told me that he had a tape recording with information that exposed the case against him. Someone whom he would not identify had contacted him and confessed. His family later told me that they did not want this pursued. Nineteen years down the line, I received a letter – from the son of whom I assume was the someone – giving details of how Rees had been the victim of a Security Police agent inside the Council of Churches.

Sobukwe's belief in leadership by example, which had terminated his freedom in March 1960, extended also to personal behaviour, at least in public. Father Aelred Stubbs, the white Anglican priest who was close to Steve Biko and other South African Students' Organisation (SASO) leaders, reports a long talk with Sobukwe during a visit to Kimberley in 1972. Stubbs was concerned about 'heavy drinking and excessive womanising' by the students. Sobukwe told him that he too 'did not like the stories he was hearing about the social habits of the SASO leaders. He said it would lead to a loss of respect from the rank and file for the leadership ... African men might have different standards to Christian norms as far as drinking and women were concerned ... but they expected the leadership to be beyond reproach in these areas.'

Criticism from Sobukwe carried weight because, as Stubbs notes, he was 'a hero and an elder' to the new generation of political activists in SASO; they 'admired his unflinching integrity as they did his intellectual pre-eminence, his perception of the need in the South African situation to keep leadership in black hands without in any way being anti-white, and his legendary eloquence'.

So Stubbs conveyed his views to SASO leaders, first to Barney Pityana, 'and found support'; and then to Steve Biko, who 'reacted vigorously', saying that theirs was a student movement, that student mores had changed over the past twenty years, and that in this respect Prof was out of date. Whether Sobukwe pressed his views on anyone is unknown; knowing him, it seems unlikely. It was probably left to Stubbs to argue out the issue with Biko.

Sobukwe's alma mater, Fort Hare, which is now a fully fledged university, has honoured him several times with a memorial lecture. In 2003, the Vice Chancellor, Derrick Swartz, spoke of Sobukwe as 'one of the most outstanding political and intellectual figures of 20th century South Africa', as 'a giant among his peers' whose vision and foresight remained relevant to the debates about transformation twenty-five years after his death.

The Steve Biko Foundation, co-host of the lectures, noted in the memorial brochure that Biko had been 'greatly inspired' by Sobukwe: 'There's a wonderful story that Steve once walked into a room where Sobukwe was holding forth. Surprised and overwhelmed by the sight of this great leader he simply exclaimed: "*Tyhini no Thixo Ulapha*" (Xhosa for "What! Even God is here!"). Steve was using this figurative expression to show the kind of awe and respect in which he held the Prof ...'

Steve Biko's elder brother, Khaya, was secretary of the underground Pan-Africanist Congress cell in Ginsberg township, outside King William's Town, and was jailed for his activities. 'The PAC presence in Ginsberg, and especially in his own home through his brother, made an impact on Steve,' said the brochure. 'When he founded the Black Consciousness Movement he was simply building and expanding on some of the tenets of pride in identity that Sobukwe had articulated. Like Sobukwe, Biko believed that the raising of consciousness was the most vital step in the journey towards individual and collective self-realisation.'

The Anglican Archbishop of Cape Town, Njongonkulu Ndungane, spoke about Sobukwe's legacy in the struggle for liberation in the memorial lecture in 2004: by focusing on the pass laws he had 'addressed what was at the very heart and core of the oppression of black people in South Africa'. Sobukwe's 'eloquence, charisma, decisiveness and clear objectives caught the imagination of many'. And, going on to a personal note, said Ndungane, his encounter with Sobukwe had changed the course of his life: 'It marked the beginning of a journey which saw me involved in political activism and landed me on Robben Island for three years. A journey which began in chains and has now ended in freedom; a journey which saw a prisoner from Robben Island becoming an archbishop.'

Ndungane, renowned for his liberal views on homosexuality and his urging of action to tackle South Africa's HIV/AIDS scourge, had been a student at the University of Cape Town in 1960 and took part in the PAC's anti-pass demonstrations. He continued working underground after the PAC was banned and in 1963 was jailed for three years. He was on Robben Island while Sobukwe was there.

Ndungane assessed Sobukwe in the context of the grave problems in the liberated South Africa: 'I wonder what he would have made of the continued economic conditions in which most black people still live, and of the fact that the rich in South Africa are getting even richer? Over half the African population is living in poverty—even in destitution. Would he have applauded the fact that the rich—even the mega-rich—in our country now include black people? I am sure that he would have been glad to see that black people have the opportunity to develop their capacities to the full—including their entrepreneurial capacities.

'But my own feeling is that he would have been shocked by the continued lack of freedom in South Africa today. I think he would have been shocked that so many human beings live without freedom. A person is not free if they do not have enough to eat, if they have to hear their children cry in vain for food. A person is not free if they have to sell their bodies in one way or another for a very tiny mess of potage. A person is not free if they cannot read and write in a society that rewards only the literate. A person is not free if they must beg on the streets, or go irredeemably into debt, or steal from others—in other words, beg, borrow or steal. That is the condition of the majority of our black population— and some from other population groups as well. The astonishing thing is how many do NOT resort to crime, considering the alternatives.

'In other words, I think that Robert Sobukwe would have mourned the continued economic injustice in South Africa today. Black Consciousness was not only about dignity and self-respect— though that was the personal, individual core of it. It was also about justice. I don't think he would have thought it is enough to have a vote—though that is a basic human right and essential for our dignity. I think he would have thought a vote, to be useful, should be able to carry in its wake justice for those who were marginalised.

'I believe Sobukwe would have moved on from the emphasis upon equality and reconciliation between the races to an emphasis on economic justice. That indeed IS the struggle that lies ahead of us.'

Graaff-Reinet remembers him. The old library has been turned into a museum and includes the Robert Sobukwe Wing which was opened by Veronica Sobukwe in 2000. She donated Sobukwe's desk from their home in Kimberley. His pipes lie on it. Framed photographs of Sobukwe are on the walls and there are copies of his letters. There is also a replica of the bronze bust of his head by a local artist which was commissioned by the town council. The original stands in the Mangaliso Robert Sobukwe building, built in apartheid times for the local commando, the militia for whites. It was originally named after President P.W. Botha and was opened by his wife, Elize.

The year after Robben Island ceased to be a prison in 1996 it was declared a national heritage site and was transformed into a popular tourist attraction. At one stage, overnight stays were offered in rooms which had once housed warders. In 1999, Unesco named the island a World Heritage Site. The boats ferrying tourists from Cape Town harbour have included the *Susan Kruger*, formerly used to transport prisoners and now, these many post-apartheid years later, still carrying the name of the wife of Jimmy Kruger, the notorious Minister of Justice, Police and Prisons, whom I had held responsible in 1977 for the fatal delay in getting medical treatment for Sobukwe and who is remembered for his 'It leaves me cold' public comment about the killing of Steve Biko.

Visitors tour the island by bus and are shown through the prison buildings. Their guides are former prisoners and warders. Nelson Mandela's cell is a prime attraction and a photograph of it also features on keyrings sold at the shop on the jetty. The Robben Island Museum spent years researching and restoring the small bungalow, known as T159, and compound in which Sobukwe was detained. The restoration was completed in 2009. The house has shiny cement floors; in one room there is a simple metal bed and coir mattress and grey blankets and a small table and chair; in the other room, a table with a kettle and an iron. The nearby T158 was his ablution block, and T160 was where the four Sobukwe children slept when they were allowed to stay on the island.

It seems that the T buildings were constructed by the Department of Defence during the Second World War as barracks for non-commissioned officers; T159 was the hygiene office and store. For a short time after Robben Island became a prison, T159 was the classroom for the children of coloured warders. But in 1962 the first political prisoners were moved to the island and a few months later an official report worried that the Prisons Department 'could not rely on the coloureds in time of need'. It said that they could be open to bribery; they might also link up with coloured fishermen from Cape Town to help prisoners escape; and the white warders on the island were concerned about the safety of their families. A policy of white-only warders was swiftly decreed and the coloured warders were removed a few weeks before Sobukwe arrived.

Later, eight years after his release, the compound was devoted to housing the prison's guard-dog unit: T159 was the office complex, twenty-five dog-handlers lived in other buildings, and kennels were built for the dogs. With change coming to South Africa, plus the growing problem of ensuring a supply of fresh water, the last of the political prisoners were released in 1991, and only criminals were held there for the next five years. During the restoration the kennels were an issue of much debate – whether or not to keep them. Rightly or wrongly, they have been retained so the compound is not exactly as it was during Sobukwe's imprisonment.

The restoration was marked by a public ceremony in March 2009. The museum flew me from Israel to speak. It was not a happy event. The leadership of the Pan-Africanist Congress attended in strength and they should have been sensitive to the emotions of the moment, the opening to the public gaze forty years later of the place in which Sobukwe was subject to his lonely ordeal. Instead, they linked the event with the PAC's 50th anniversary and used it for PAC propaganda aimed at the general elections being held the next month. They emotionally denounced the ANC and criticised the lauding of Nelson Mandela as the only liberator. They used Sobukwe for their narrow purposes, forgetting that his achievements went beyond political parties and that he belonged to all South Africans. I felt embarrassed and depressed. However, as much as the PAC was to blame, fault also lay with others: the Robben Island Museum said it sent invitations to the ceremony to every Member of Parliament and to the Mayor of Cape Town and other dignitaries; as far as I know, not a single ANC MP came, nor the Mayor, nor a single leader of government.

These days, buses stop for a few minutes outside the fenced-in compound and the guides speak about Sobukwe. But visitors remain in the buses and do not see the interior of the Robert Sobukwe House. It cannot be said whether this is for political reasons in downplaying Sobukwe's historical role or if it is because of the rushed nature of the tours.

Unfortunately, Robben Island is the victim of serious administrative failures. The continued use of the *Susan Kruger* ferry, despite its age and name, is one result. In January 2015 the ship's radar malfunctioned and with its load of tourists it sailed past the island in thick fog and had to be rescued. That led Marianne Thamm to write, on the Daily Maverick website later that month, that Robben Island had been beset 'by problems too numerous and too depressing to list entirely. These include gross mismanagement, the theft of fuel intended for the ferries, staff defrauding the souvenir shop and exorbitant salary increases for executive management.

'The continual breakdown of ferries in particular has had an enormous impact on the island's tourist potential and its ability to generate an income over the years. It is quite extraordinary that in 2015 those who wish to make the pilgrimage to the University of Robben Island have to do so in boats procured and built during the Apartheid era.

'In 2007, the modern *Sikhululekile* ferry was acquired for R26 million as a flagship in what was later found to be an irregular tender award. It took a year before the boat transported its first load of tourists to the island but only a few weeks later it was in the dry dock undergoing repairs.

'The ferry was then attached by its manufacturer Farocean because of non-payment and then suffered seven major breakdowns between 2008 and 2010. The repairs totaled around R10 million and at some point these were attributed to "sabotage". The ferry was eventually taken out of service last year. In 2013 the then Minister of Arts and Culture, Paul Mashatile, informed Parliament that the museum had spent R2.6 million on hiring private boats.

'However, the truth of why the *Sikhululekile* was unsuitable finally emerged last year when a Council of Geosciences underwater study of Robben Island's Murray Bay Harbour showed that a rocky outcrop was causing the damage and that the boat's hull was too heavy, particularly at low tide. Previous museum management had failed to conduct a proper study before commissioning the boat.'

Referring to 'The metaphors lurking in the lost ferry', Thamm said that 'the hidden rocky outcrop symbolises all the currents that lurk below the contemporary political surface and which have emerged and continue to emerge and bubble forth ... the devastating legacy of Apartheid and how much this has scuppered and continues to scupper current progress ... But part of the challenge in making redress is also how to prevent the disturbing haemorrhaging of public money due to corruption, incompetence and mismanagement by the current government over the past 20 years.'

Research has yielded glimpses into Sobukwe's life on the island, his loneliness, his strength and his courtesy towards those who held him there. Jan Moolman was one of the warders who shared the perpetual twenty-four-hour guard duties outside Sobukwe's compound. 'We were not allowed to talk to him,' he says. 'If they found you talking to him then you were in big trouble. But there were a lot of trees so they could not see me from either side ... at 10 o'clock or 10.30 in the morning, I would be sitting there, then he whistled and shoved a plate towards me with either an apple, or a pear or an orange or something sweet ... cookies. He knew that a warder was always hungry ... He knew that I was not allowed to take something, that's why he put it on that side ... He never ever tried to get me into trouble.'

Moolman says that when he did speak to Sobukwe, 'he never led me into political talk. Only how are your father and mother? How are your family?'

The shelters for the guards, at the front and back of the compound, were simple structures of four poles with a corrugated-iron flat roof and open in the front. The first guard shift began at 7 a.m. and ended at 5 p.m. The next shift ended at midnight, and then went through the night to 7 a.m. Dogs were at that time housed elsewhere but the compound was the starting point for the night-long patrols which went north and south. T159 was not locked so with each change of guards at night they checked that Sobukwe hadn't escaped. At first the guards went inside and spoke to him but this stopped after he complained that they were waking him up and he could not get to sleep again.

Moolman says that there was a large spidergum tree next to T159 in whose shade Sobukwe sat on hot summer days, studying and reading, and protected from the strong south-easterly wind. Each morning, in shorts and a vest, and whatever the weather, summer and winter, he went to the ablution block for a cold shower. He could at least boil water in a kettle for shaving. He slept on a plain iron bed, with an old mattress with blue-and-white stripes and grey blankets.

Dini, Sobukwe's eldest son, remembers his visits when the family was allowed to spend two weeks with him, locked into the compound. With his mother and three siblings they were driven from the jetty in a van with bars on the darkened windows. They were escorted by two to three warders.

When their father met them and took them into T159, 'the first thing he'd do is pray for us'. Prayer was part of every day: 'In the evenings after supper, we'd finish the dishes, talk for a while and then around his bed we'd pray. And even later, after prison, it was basically the same prayer. He'd pray for the prisoners here and he'd mention them by name. Of course, Mandela, Sisulu and all of those and also his colleagues and those who were out fighting for the liberation of this country. He would mention them by name and hope that God was with them.'

Dini says that his father warned them that the rooms might have bugging devices. 'But then he'd say, "Of course, I'm not afraid of saying what I want to say. It's ideas I have and have had and I can always say them again, whenever I must."'

Dini says his father was 'very funny' and told a lot of stories. He put music on the record player and the children danced for him. The family reunions occurred once a year in the last two years of his imprisonment, for two weeks around Christmas time. 'It was very good to be with my father and all of us together but every moment you realised that this was a very harsh place. You never escaped that. It was a very, very harsh place.'

It was barren and stark. The ground was sand and crushed shells. Nothing much could be seen except the surrounding trees and the sea. 'It was a very sad place. It was fun to be here but ... you'd think the very first day you were here, this is all going to end very soon.'

After meals, the family washed the dishes in the ablution block and put them inside the box in which the food had been delivered, for a warder and prisoner to collect.

Sobukwe had the prison habit of continually polishing the cement floor: inside the door of T159 there were two pieces of cloth and whenever he came in from outside he stepped on them and shuffled around on them to keep the floor shiny. 'One of the children came in and did the same thing,' says Dini, 'and he said, "No, no, no, don't worry about that. Just walk in."' He also polished the tiles in the kitchen area; he said he did it for exercise.

The compound was brightly lit up through the night, say Dini and his sister Miliswa. T160, where the four children slept, did not have any curtains so it was like daylight all the time. A lot of rabbits were running and hopping in the light and the children stood at the window and watched them.

Dini recalls his father telling them that 'we should always be proud, even though it may not seem a very good thing that we are without a father, but we should be proud of his presence here. He was going to come home some day. That he was doing it for a reason. It was not just abandonment. There was a reason he was here and it was something to be proud of.'

Dini notes that, even on the island, his father was a disciplined person. 'He wasn't always well when we came here but he was strong. And above all he was a very loving person. It was always good to be around him. We, of course, did understand why he was here. It did make sense.'

Both Dini and Miliswa remember that their father 'used to tell us all the time how he loved us … he said a lot of things through prayer … he prayed for all his friends and for his enemies too.'

South Africa is radically and wonderfully different from what it was. The pass laws have long gone and only memories remain of the state's racism which used skin colour to condemn people to inferiority in every detail of their lives from birth until death. Bob Sobukwe made his contribution. If he was alive today he could revel in the freedom and non-racism which he did so much to secure.

But he would not be able to rest easy. There has certainly been colossal progress. Many black people are wealthy. The extent of economic transformation is reflected in a Johannesburg Stock Exchange statement that by the end of 2013 blacks owned at least 23 per cent of the Top 100 listed companies, up from 21 per cent two years earlier; whites owned about 22 per cent and foreign investors about 39 per cent. (Strangely, President Jacob Zuma puts black ownership at only three per cent.) However, in the country as a whole the gap between haves and have-nots is distressing and alarming. It is made worse because many of the haves have turned their backs on the recent past and don't care about the plight of the have-nots. They flaunt their wealth through super-luxury cars and ostentatiously extravagant living. Black empowerment, needed to overcome the past, has been an easy cover for massive moral and material corruption and cronyism. Sobukwe, sternly believing in leadership by example, would not have approved.

Archbishop Ndungane's damning comments in his Fort Hare lecture in 2004 are as valid, if not more so in some respects, in 2015. As he said, Sobukwe would have mourned the continuing social injustice. Crime remains at terrifying levels. Much of the problem is inherited from the past, from the dislocation of families under apartheid and the continuing lack of job opportunities. Yet, as time goes by, more blame attaches to the leaders of the present because they give every sign of living expensively in safety and comfort which cocoons them from reality. The government rightly points to giant steps in ensuring housing, clean water and electricity, but those without these basic amenities live in their millions in deprived shanty towns, known euphemistically as informal settlements, around the cities and in the rural areas. The country's electricity supply is in crisis, with major shutdowns affecting everyone's daily lives, damaging industry and mining, imperilling water supplies and frightening off foreign investment. Shorn of all the excuses, government incompetence is to blame.

In education, money and effort have been poured in and progress is evident in the numbers who complete their schooling. But poor standards have consequent effects in jobs and universities; a report in 2012 said 80 per cent of schools were dysfunctional with inferior teaching, lack of buildings, books, toilets, water and electricity. The AIDS denial of the presidency of Thabo Mbeki has ended; his Minister of Health, who rejected anti-retroviral drugs and propounded beetroot juice and olive oil as a cure, is a bad memory. But their legacy is shown in statistics such as 270,000 AIDS deaths in 2011 and more than 2 million orphaned children.

Poverty and despotism elsewhere in Africa have driven millions to South Africa. Porous borders and corruption allow them in: a taxi ride from the Zimbabwean border to Johannesburg costs R750 (about $65) for those with valid passports; without a passport the cost is R1,500. Domestic poverty has spawned envy and hatred of foreigners who own small shops in black townships. 'Xenophobic demons linger in South Africa', said the *Mail & Guardian* newspaper in 2012, reporting that during that year at least 140 foreign nationals were killed, many of them grotesquely and intimately, and 250 seriously injured. In 2013, at least three major xenophobic incidents were reported each week, most rooted in business competition; killing and looting of shops continued in 2014 and 2015. There is little counter-action by the country's leaders. It's a long way from Sobukwe's vision of pan-Africanist brotherhood and a United States of Africa.

While visiting South Africa in 2010, I felt impelled to write a report about the deeply troubling state of the country. It appeared in the *Sunday Independent* in Johannesburg: 'During more than 50 years as a journalist, I have reported or heard about every possible human vileness in dealing with other humans. Now, in Johannesburg, in the actions of striking workers, I have found a new low in human behaviour.

'The details have been revealed by Gauteng's Premier Nomvula Mokonyane: she is reported to have told the provincial legislature that some 53 premature babies were left unattended in Gauteng hospitals during the strike. She said she had been told "shocking stories" that the babies were left unattended "when striking workers forced nursing staff to leave their posts".

'She noted: "Some of the babies were literally locked in the wards with no one bothering to make alternative arrangements for their care."

'Not just babies, note, but premature babies who cling to life and need constant care and attention. Denying them nursing care was like sentencing them to death.

'How can strikers explain this?

'Other reported incidents are also depressing and worrying: such as the nurses who have violently prevented colleagues from going to work to look after patients; or the woman who begged to be allowed through a hospital picket line to visit her dying father in intensive care but who was turned back, with strikers cheering.

'Something has gone badly wrong in South Africa. A moral rottenness is evident.'

Relations between people form the bedrock of the new South Africa. Nelson Mandela's five years as president put that foundation in place. It remains strong but needs more than lip service to counter growing intolerant talk and behaviour which can slip into violence. A particular aspect is abuse levelled at the Jewish community because of its support for Israel; the anti-Semitism is plain. There is also clear danger in failure to meet the needs and dreams of the have-nots. They express their despair in more than two hundred violent outbursts a year, blocking roads with burning tyres and attacking municipal buildings. The door is open to wild populism, such as that of Julius Malema's Economic Freedom Fighters. If the have-nots grow too restless and angry it will also be tempting for a future government to try to divert them by turning to racial scapegoating; that would be calamitous.

Meanwhile, South Africa has not been kind to Robert Sobukwe. The magnitude of his deeds and beliefs is largely ignored. The

African National Congress in government has done much to airbrush him out of the freedom struggle. He is seldom referred to. A rare exception was a television series by the state's South African Broadcasting Corporation about five struggle icons, Sobukwe among them as 'A great soul'. The anniversary of Sharpeville, on 21 March, is officially Human Rights Day, but to watch and read references to it is to believe that it was really an ANC effort. Sobukwe has not been honoured with any major naming of public institutions. His post-island home and office in Kimberley are unmarked.

'Consider that the only person who was so greatly feared by the apartheid regime that they had to craft a law especially to chain him, appears to continue to suffer the ignominy of non-recognition by the new mandarins,' wrote Dr Themba Sono, a one-time Black Consciousness leader and now a well-known liberal commentator, in a letter to *The Star* in January 2015. 'There is virtually nothing of national significance or prominence named after Robert Mangaliso Sobukwe. No university, municipality, dam, highway or monument is named after him.'

Nor is it only the ANC. Patricia de Lille was once so much an admirer of Sobukwe that I asked her to speak at the initial launch of this book, in 1990; many years later, she led the Independent Democrats into an alliance with the opposition Democratic Alliance (DA), and in 2011 became Mayor of Cape Town. I wrote to her, twice, to suggest that an important road be named after Sobukwe, but she did not reply; a third e-mail to her private address drew the response that the city's street-naming committee would look into it. A couple of years later, in 2013, Modderdam Road (Muddy Dam Road) became Robert Sobukwe Road. It was not a great honour, although the naming is appropriate because the busy road leads to the University of the Western Cape, with its sterling history of resistance to apartheid. In contrast, in 2015, the DA-controlled city named a major highway, Table Bay Boulevard, after the last apartheid-era president, F.W. De Klerk. The decision was controversial, but his courage and vision in ushering out apartheid certainly made him worthy of recognition. However, heaping such praise on De Klerk underlined the DA's tepid attitude towards Sobukwe.

Significantly, a resurgence of interest in Sobukwe was developing in 2015. It is described by Dr Derek Hook, a South African-born social psychologist at Duquesne University, in Pittsburgh, who is writing a biography of Sobukwe. Hook notes that another major study is being written in South Africa, with other asssessments under way in universities and political circles. He offers this thoughtful analysis of the resurgence of interest in Sobukwe: 'Many of the reasons undoubtedly concern the politicaltimes South Africa is living through. J. Brooks Spector, on the DailyMaverick website, provided a neat précis of the sense of politicalunease and social dysfunctionality pervading the country in 2012,including: the Marikana massacre [the deaths of 44 people, mainlystriking platinum mineworkers, by police shooting, in August2012], rampant service delivery protests, obvious systematic corruption,glaring inefficiencies of government, and the growing disengagementwith the contemporary political landscape by disaffectedcitizens. Heroic appeals to Sobukwe's memory are oftengrounded precisely in the analysis of such political failures.

'Take these words by Malaika wa Azania, an activist devoted to pursuing the African Renaissance agenda: "[T]here is a rapture happening in our country. There is an awakening of black people. There is a sense of consciousness that is slowly but surely creeping into our communities ... [T]he increasing number of service delivery protests ... are a result of disenfranchised masses fighting for the right to humanness. These are people who are refusing to continue living in squalor, to being accessories to corruption, maladministration and mediocre leadership, obese with immorality and a lack of integrity ... These are Sobukwe's disciples, blacks who refuse systematic dehumanisation."

'We might frame these issues in a broader historical context by noting that the honeymoon of the Nelson Mandela era, with its hopefulness, its aspirations to racial reconciliation, and the hopes for building a new "rainbow" nation is well and truly over. This reflects a prevailing mood in the country. For many, the celebrations in 2014 of 20 years of democracy resulted in a period of reflection.

'A new political direction is being sought. The advent of the Economic Freedom Fighters and its early electoral successes seems to make this abundantly clear. One way of understanding the protracted mourning of Mandela and the desperate clinging to his memory concerns precisely this dilemma of direction: what is the new political dream? what co-ordinating principle will prove the compass in the unsure times ahead?

Benjamin Pogrund

'Social discontent at the pace of transformation has sullied the ANC's image somewhat, as has the perception that the organization has turned its back on the poor, for whom the promises of a better life have not yet materialised in as substantive a manner as might have been hoped. To this consideration we must add that of the problematic character of the ANC's leader, President Jacob Zuma, who can by no stretch of the imagination be considered a leader of the same moral integrity as Sobukwe. One of the reasons that Sobukwe is revered today concerns his unbending integrity as an ethical leader, a man of principles, who increasingly, in today's South Africa, strikes us as an image of an altogether different world, where political leaders could still be "uncorruptible". That is to say, the return to Sobukwe today should not be understood simply according to the moral attributes of Sobukwe himself—outstanding as they were—but in terms of a contemporary crisis of political leadership, and in view of the perceived decline in the moral authority of the ANC.

'Two related problems come to the fore here concerning the possible misuse of Sobukwe's memory. There is, on the one hand, the prospect of an excessive idealization—a type of over-the-top aggrandisement—in how we retrieve the historical image of Sobukwe. By treating Sobukwe as somehow more than a man we, ironically enough, do a disservice to a heroic yet humble man who had little time for the histrionics of political showmanship, and who ultimately put more trust in the people themselves than in leaders presenting themselves as saviours.

'There is too what I term the "consensus of forgetting" affecting Sobukwe's memory. The dual political hegemonies of the African National Congress and the Democratic Alliance voting-publics appear to agree on this point: Sobukwe's political legacy is best consigned to the dustbin of history. The reason for such an unlikely alliance of forgetting is not difficult to surmise. Sobukwe's vision of African Nationalism offers biting critiques of key ideological commitments underpinning both such Congress and Democratic Alliance constituencies. Sobukwe attacked not only the self-serving interests of paternalistic white liberalism. He was strongly critical also of the ANC's turn—via the activities of the Freedom Charter—to a politics of multi-racialism that turned its back on the priorities of African Nationalism and the 1949 Programme of Action. The sad result of this consensus of forgetting is that Sobukwe, a man known for his utopian vision of a Pan-Africanist future, was for many years, seemingly better known during rather than after apartheid.

'There are of course a varied range of references to Sobukwe's name in the (left-leaning) South African public sphere. These scattered references are anchored to a variety of injunctions: to celebrate the language and culture of the African continent; to heed issues of gender violence and equality; to prioritize learning and the ideal of truly African educational institutions; to herald the coming revolution of the dispossessed. Rather than taking issue at the diversity of such appeals—which at times seem to diverge somewhat from Sobukwe's own political aspirations, to claim something different to what Sobukwe himself proclaimed—we might take this as a positive sign that "Sobukwe" now stands not simply for the memory of a single man, but as the embodiment of a wide array of political aspirations.

'It is in this sense that Sobukwe as an idea provides a form of radical social critique, increasingly prominent in South Africa, which is both new, and yet not, representing as it does a historical continuity of sorts with many of Sobukwe's most profound commitments.'

More than three decades of freedom have failed to fulfill the dreams and hopes of millions of South Africans for a better life that is their right. The African National Congress has betrayed the people. It has inflicted disaster through arrogance, greed, incompetence and corruption, made worse by its Stalinist policy of cadre deployment – giving jobs to party members without regard to their ability and suitability. The presidency of Jacob Zuma was the era of state capture, of unbridled looting of government resources. Disappointingly, President Cyril Ramaphosa, has failed to meet expectations for repair and redemption. Much has even grown worse: crime is at truly frightening levels; municipal government, health, education, transport and the military, to mention only some key spheres, are often abysmally and dangerously defective. A crisis in water supply looms. One bright spot is that electricity availability is being restored. The *Susan Kruger* ferry boat, referred to on pages 403 and 404, still exists but has been retired from service and is to be put to quayside use for the 1 600 visitors who make the journey to Robben Island each day.

South Africans expressed themselves in the May 2024 elections: the ANC's share of the vote dropped to 40.1 per cent from the previous 57.5 per cent. It was surprising that it got so much, reflecting the strength of traditional allegiance to 'Congress'. The ANC promises to reform itself. Whether it is capable of doing so is an open question.

It is hard to be optimistic. Hope was embedded during the long years of white domination and apartheid: as South Africans suffered and struggled, they believed they could and would overcome. They did. Now, somehow, hope and optimism still exist. But how much more will the have-nots endure, and for how long?

The 100th anniversary of the birth of Robert Mangaliso Sobukwe was observed on 5 December 2024. His words and deeds remain the exemplar for South Africa.

For the original documentary material about Robert Mangaliso Sobukwe in the University of the Witwatersrand Library, see: www.historicalpapers.wits.ac.za/?inventory/U/collections&c=A2618/R/6325.

Sources

Interviews Conducted With:

Barnard, Chris*
Berman, Monty
Boraine, Alex
Browde, Jules
Caley, George
Caley, Helen
Cheminais. Gaby
Cole, D.D.T.*
Cooper, Saths
Dagutt, Merton
Fort Hare, University of (Registrar Academic)
Henderson, Moira
Hirson, Baruch
Hjul, Peter
Huston, Perdita
Keke, Zolile Hamilton
Kotze, Theo
Madzunya, Josias
Maimane, Mike
Makaud, Alice
Makhele, Joyce
Manong, Gabriel
Matolengwe, Patrick
M'Cwabeni, W.S.M.*
Mda, A.P.
Mgxashe, Mxolishi 'Ace'
Mlonzi, Lennox
Mngqono, Sephai 'Bushie'
Moabi, Joe
Mokgoro, Yvonne
Mokoape, Aubrey
Molete, Z.B.
'Molotsi, Peter*
Mothopeng, Zephaniah
Motlana, Nthato

Nobrega, Joe
Nobrega, Nita
Ngcobo, A.B.
Ngendane, Selby*
Nkoana, Matthew
Nkomo, W.F.
Nodada, Butana Eleazor
Ntloedibe, Elias
Ntloko, Cecil
Nyaose, Jacob Dumdum*
Pitje, Godfrey
Pitts, Stanley
Pogrund, Anne Caroline
Pokela, John*
Rees, John
Rotberg, Robert I.
Schlapobersky, John
Sekgoro, Daniel 'Schoolboy'
Siwisa, Dennis
Sobukwe, Ernest
Sobukwe, Veronica
Stott, Eulalie
Suzman, Helen
Thomson, Diana
Thomson, James C.
Tobias, P.V.*
Tucker, Raymond
Tutu, Desmond*
Unterhalter, Jack
Vigne, Randolph
Vilakazi Martin
Walston, The Lord*
Witwatersrand, University of the (Mrs D.M. Anderson, Deputy Registrar, Academic)*

*By correspondence

Benjamin Pogrund

Newspapers and Magazines

Africa Report, New York
Azania Combat, Dar es Salaam
Azania News, Dar es Salaam
Bantu World, Johannesburg
Beeld, Johannesburg
Die Burger, Cape Town
Cape Argus, Cape Town
Cape Times, Cape Town
Contact, Cape Town
Dagbladet, Oslo
Dagbreek, Johannesburg
Daily Dispatch, East London
Daily News, Dar es Salaam
Drum, Johannesburg
Evening Post, Port Elizabeth
Golden City Post, Johannesburg
The Independent, London
Inkundla ya Bantu, Verulam
Liberation, Johannesburg

The New African, Cape Town/London
New Age, Cape Town
The New York Times, New York
Observer, London
Pace, Johannesburg
Rand Daily Mail, Johannesburg
Reality, Pietermaritzburg
The Scotsman, Edinburgh
The Spectator, London
The Star/Sunday Star, Johannesburg
Sunday Express, Johannesburg
Sunday Times, Johannesburg
Sunday Tribune, Durban
The Times, London
Tribune, London
Die Vaderland, Johannesburg
Die Volksblad, Bloemfontein
Washington Post, Washington D.C.
The World, Johannesburg

Books and Reports

African Claims (African National Congress, n.d.)
An African Explains Apartheid by Jordan K. Ngubane (Frederick A. Praeger, New York, 1963)
Black Politics in South Africa since 1945 by Tom Lodge (Ravan Press, Johannesburg, 1983)
Black Power in South Africa by Gail M. Gerhart (University of California Press, 1978)
Days of Crisis in South Africa compiled by Muriel Horrell (South African Institute of Race Relations, Johannesburg, 1960)
Each Man Must Play a Part by Isadore Frack (Purnell, Cape Town, 1970)
Encyclopaedia of Southern Africa, 7th edition by Eric Rosenthal (Juta, Cape Town, 1978)
Freedom for My People by Z.K. Matthews, Memoir by Monica Wilson (Africa South Paperbacks, 1983)
From Protest to Challenge: Documents of African Politics in South Africa edited by Thomas Karis and Gwendolen M. Carter (Hoover Institution Press, Stanford, 1973/1977)
Handbook on Race Relations in South Africa edited by Ellen Hellman (Oxford University Press, Cape Town, 1949)
Hansard of the South African Parliament
Healdtown 1855-1955: Centenary Brochure (Healdtown Missionary Institution, 1955)
Inside BOSS by Gordon Winter (Penguin, London, 1981)
Kimberley: Origin and Growth (Kimberley Municipality, n.d.)

How Can Man Die Better

Law, Order and Liberty in South Africa: by A.S. Mathews (Juta, Cape Town, 1971)
Laws affecting race relations in Africa: 1948-1976 compiled by Muriel Horrell (South African Institute of Race Relations, Johannesburg, 1978)
Let My People Go by Albert Luthuli (Fontana, 1982)
Letters and Papers from Prison by Dietrich Bonhoeffer (Macmillan paperbacks, 1962)
The Newspaperman's Guide to the Law 3rd edition by Kelsey Stuart (Butterworth, Durban, 1982)
The Oxford History of South Africa edited by Monica Wilson and Leonard Thompson (Oxford University Press, London, 1969)
Paarl Riots Commission Report, R.P. 51/1963
Patrick Duncan: South African and Pan-African by C.J. Driver (Heinemann, 1980)
The Plays of John Galsworthy (Duckworth, 1929)
The Politics of Inequality by Gwendolen M. Carter (Thames and Hudson, London, 1958)
Regina vs Robert Sobukwe and Others, L173/60
The Rise of African Nationalism in South Africa by Peter Walshe (C. Hurst, London, 1970)
The Rise of Azania, The Fall of South Africa by David Dube (Daystar Publications, Lusaka, 1983)
The Rise of the South African Reich by Brian Bunting (Penguin African Library, 1964)
Robert Sobukwe: A Tribute to Integrity directed by Kevin Harris (Produced for SABC TV by Kevin Harris Productions, Johannesburg, 1997)
Shooting at Sharpeville by Ambrose Reeves (Victor Golancz, London, 1960)
Sobukwe Complex: Primary Research (Robben Island Museum Heritage Department, 26 August 2003)
South Africa: A Skunk Among Nations by Les de Villiers (International Books, London, 1975)
South Africa Belongs to Us by Francis Meli (Zimbabwe Publishing House, Harare, 1988)
Speeches of Managaliso Sobukwe (Pan-Africanist Congress, New York, 1989)
Steve Biko – I Write What I Like by Aelred Stubbs (The Bowerdean Press, London, 1979)
A Survey of Race Relations in South Africa (South African Institute of Race Relations, Johannesburg: Annual issues for years from 1952 to 1988)
Time Longer than Rope by Edward Roux (Victor Gollancz, London, 1948)
What Did Sobukwe Say? (University of Fort Hare and Steve Biko Foundation, 2003)
Year of Fire, Year of Ash by Baruch Hirson (Zed Books, London, 1979)

Index

Acts
  Civil Defence Act 254
  Criminal Law Amendment Act 150
  General Law Amendment Act 185
  Group Areas Act 51, 72
  Immorality Act 51, 78, 285
  Industrial Conciliation Act 110
  Mixed Marriages Act 51, 285
  Native Land and Trust Act 19
  Official Secrets Act 333
  Physical Planning Act 256-257
  Population Registration Act 51, 212
  Prohibition of Disguises Act 333
  Prohibition of Political Interference Act 285
  Promotion of Bantu Self-Government Act 81
  Public Safety Act 254
  Representation of Natives Act 19
  Separate Representation of Voters Act 52
  Suppression of Communism Act 51, 254
  Terrorism Act 258-259
Adlai Stevenson Institute, Chicago 343
African Claims in South Africa (ANC charter) 23
Africanist, The 66
Africanists 82, 84-97, 100
  attitude to whites 101-103
  first national conference 90-97
  see also African Nationalists; Pan-Africanist Congress
African National Congress (ANC) 22-23, 50, 52-53, 212, 403, 410, 412
  anti-pass law campaign 113-114, 118, 121, 140-141, 391
  banned 146, 384
  bill introduced to ban 142
  and conflict over Transvaal in late 1950s 82-88
  Defiance Campaign 52-53, 117
  in exile 161
  and Freedom Charter 59-61
  inception 22
  membership 121
  and multi-racialism 100-101
  national conference, December 1949 46
  provincial conference, June 1949 46
  trials in 1967 257-258
  unbanning of 384
  Youth League, *see* Congress Youth League (CYL)

African Nationalists 59, 61-62, 66, 85, 100
  see also Africanists; Pan-Africanist Congress
African Renaissance 391, 411
African Resistance Movement (ARM) 213
Africa Special Report 334
African Union 392
Alexander, Neville 381
Alexandra 83
All-African Convention (AAC) 19, 29
All-Africa Trade Union Federation 160
Anglo American Corporation 306-307, 323
Angola 335
Anti-Apartheid Movement 161
Ashe, Arthur 325
Ashford, Nicholas 335
Asians 93, 105 (*see also* South African Indian Congress)
Azanian People's Liberation Army (Apla) 386
Azania, Malaika wa 411-412
Azapo (Azanian People's Organisation) 350
Azikiwe, Nnamdi 21, 218, 252

baasskap 80
Balzac, Honoré de 232
Banda, Hastings 91, 334
Bantustans 80-81
Bantu World, The 56
Barnard, Christiaan 358, 361-363, 371
Barnard, Marius 368, 371
Basson, Japie 298
Basutoland 182-183, 219
Basutoland Congress Party 33
Belgian Congo 115
Benson, Ivor 101
Berman, Monty 154-155
Berry, Ian 132-133
Beware 28
Biko, Khaya 400
Biko, Steve 349-351, 370, 397-400, 402, 405
Billheimer, Robert S. 221, 231, 243
Bills
  Extension of University Education Bill 76
  General Laws Amendment Bill 211
  Improper Interference Bill 255
Birley, Robert 322
Black Consciousness 349-350, 392, 396, 400, 410

Black Economic Empowerment 308
Black People's Convention 350
Black Sash 115, 144-145, 196
Bloemfontein 46, 358
Bodley, Bob 109
Boipatong 132
Boksburg 166
Bonhoeffer, Dietrich 234, 269, 272-273
Bophelong 132
Boraine, Alex 362, 364
Botha, Elize 401
Botha, M.C. 256
Botha, P.W. 334, 384, 401
Botha, Robert 328
Bowdler, William 375-376
Boy Scouts of South Africa 387
Britain 160-161
Brockway, Lord 260
Brookes, Edgar 20
Browde, Jules 391-392
Brown, Peter 381, 405
Bunting, Brian 145
Bureau of African Nationalism 50
Bureau for State Security (BOSS) 197, 333
Burger, Die 203
Burnett, B.B. 319
Business Day 386
Buthelezi, Mangosuthu 230, 331-332, 336, 345-346, 374-376, 393

Caley, George 13-14, 16, 40-43
Caley, Helen 13-14, 16, 40, 42-43
Calvinism 75
Cape Argus 195, 223, 291
Cape Law Society 339-340
Cape Times 195, 223, 291
Cato Manor 116, 146
censorship 185, 212
Central Population Register 79
Champion, W.R.G. 25
'children's revolt' 351, 372, 384, 397
China 217
Chirwa, Orton 29
Chitepo, Herbert 29
Christian National Education 75
churches 160, 221, 269-270, 290, 319
  apartheid practised by 160
Cinderella prison 222
Ciskei 230
Coaker, John 297
Coalbrook mining disaster 116
Coetsee, Kobie 239, 354-355
Collins, L. John 341
communism 65, 68, 233, 282-283
  legislation against 184
Communist Party of South Africa (CPSA) 25-26, 51, 85, 106, 154, 158-159, 212, 384
Congress of Democrats (COD) 53, 104, 181
  and Freedom Charter 59-61
Congress of the People (25-26 June, 1955) 60

Congress Youth League (CYL) 23-29, 50, 52-53
  at ANC provincial conference, June 1949 46
  Fort Hare branch 45-46
Constitutional Court 396
Consultative Committee 115
Contact 64-65, 69, 84, 104, 124, 133, 138, 143, 145, 205, 276
Cook, P.A.W. 9
Cooper, Saths 350
Cottesloe Consultation 160

Dadoo, Yusuf 24
Dagbladet 338
Dagbreek en Sondagnuus 179
Dagutt, Merton 62
Daily Dispatch 21
Daily Maverick 402, 411
Dayan, Moshe 294-295
De Beers 323, 329
De Blank, Joost 160
Defence and Aid Fund 209, 212, 254
Defiance Campaign 52-53, 117
De Klerk, F.W. 384, 410
De Lille, Patricia 388, 410
Democratic Alliance (DA) 410, 412
Dent, Clifford P. 43
detention 259
  deaths in 342
  periods of 159
  without trial 212, 227
De Villiers, Les 347
De Wet, Carel 135
Diamond Fields Advertiser 395
Drum 41, 132
Dubois, David 118, 175
Duncan, Patrick 64, 104, 145, 175, 205, 276
Dunne, Laurence 161
Du Plessis, J. du K. 50, 52-53
Du Plessis, T.G. 317-318, 370
Duquesne University 411
Durban 116, 142, 146, 156-157

Economica 241, 250
Economic Freedom Fighters 409, 411
education system 75-76, 94, 257
elections, general'
  1958 71
  1966 254
  1994 386
English Digest 195
Erasmus, Frans 140, 143
Evaton 132, 137

Fast, Howard 246
Federation of Free African Trade Unions (Fofatusa) 96, 111, 120, 126
ffrench-Beytagh, G.A. 290, 327-328
Foreign Affairs 346
Fort Beaufort 11
Fort Hare, *see* South African Native College, Fort hare

419

Fort, The 148, 163
Freedom Charter 59-61, 412
Friedman, Mrs. Bernard 277
Froneman, G.F. van L. 233-234, 283

Gaitskell, Baroness 260
Galeshewe 307, 388, 393
Galsworthy, John 21, 117-118
Gandar, Laurence 69, 222, 297, 308, 310, 320, 353, 405
Gandhi, Mohandas 384
Ghana 78
Golden City Post 156
Gomas, John 106
Graaff-Reinet 5-6, 369, 389, 392, 396, 400
Grahamstown 90
Grant, C.W. 40-41
Groote Schuur Hospital 358, 360-363
Guardian, The (South African) 328
Guma, Samson 29

Hailey, Lord 20
Hani, Chris 405
Healdtown 9-14
Hellman, Ellen 352
Henderson, Moira 202, 243, 322, 360, 362, 365-367, 372, 375
Herbstein, Philip 340
Hertzog, Albert 284
Hertzog, J.B.M. 19
Hewitson, Rodney 361
Hirson, Baruch 213
HIV/AIDS 400, 404, 408
Hjul, Peter 145, 209, 220-221
Hleli, Temba 33
Hoek, Jan 132
homelands 285-286, 333-334
homosexuality 400
Hook, Derek 410-411
Horatius 1, 191
Horrell, Muriel 60, 155
Huddleston, Trevor 104
Hughes, T. Gray 218-219

Illicit Diamond Buying 313-314
Independent Democratic Party 388, 410
Independent, The 369
India 77-78
Inkatha Freedom Party 393
Inkundla 125
Inkundla ya Bantu (Bantu Forum) 27, 46
International Confederation of Free Trade Unions 111
Isaacs, Henry 385
Israel 274-275

Jabavu 56
Jandrell, J.D. 49
Jandrell Secondary School, Standerton 44, 49
Johannesburg 56, 83, 102, 142, 257
Johannesburg Stock Exchange 407

John O'London's 195
Johnson, Lyndon B. 216-217, 231, 253-254, 296
Jolobe, William 140-141
Jonathan, Leabua 33
Jordan, A.C. 45
Judaism 233, 291-292

Kaunda, Kenneth 91
Keke, Hamilton Zolile 183, 191, 349
Kennedy, Robert 253-254, 296
Kentridge, Sydney 297, 308
Kgosana, Philip 138-139, 156, 180, 387-388
Kgosana, William 143-145
Kgware, W. 43
Khama, Seretse 15
Kimberley 305-307, 388-389, 394-396, 400
Kitson, Norma 320
Kloppenberg, Theo 299
Koch, Bodo 352-353, 355-359, 368
Koestler, Arthur 247, 269
Kotze, Theo 270-271
Kruger, Jimmy 353, 355, 358-360, 363-364, 370, 402
Kruger, Susan 402, 403, 413
Kuper, Leo 23

labour, black 73-75 (*see* also trade unions)
labour bureaux 73-74, 211-212
Laher, Achmat 330, 345
Laher, Fatima 330
Langa 138, 142-144, 180, 196
Lapinsky, Sheila 340
Laurence, Patrick 319, 370
Lawyers for Human Rights 391
Leballo, P.K. 61, 67, 83, 85-88, 95, 101-102, 108, 136, 152, 166, 175, 177-178, 180-184, 349
Leftwich, Adrian 213
legislation (*see* Acts; Bills)
Lembede, Anton 23, 30, 66, 108
Leon, Sonny 377
Lethala, Patricia Thabisa 182
Letlaka, Tsepo 43, 377
Lewis, Anthony 337-338
Lewis, Michael 369
Liberal Association 53
Liberal Party 53, 68, 71, 97, 114-115, 122, 144-145, 204, 215, 285, 350, 381
Lichaba, Cynthia 182
Lincoln University (Pennsylvania) 218, 242, 343
London, University of 276, 298
Louw, Eric 157
Louw, Raymond 353
Lowell, James Russell 229
Luthuli, Albert 85-86, 122, 139-141, 370, 405

Maake, Nhlanhla 392
Mabieskraal 179
MacCreath, Francis 271
Mackenzie, Kenneth 185
Marikana massacre 411
McKenzie, Precious 161
Macmillan, Harold 115-116

Madzunya, Josias 83-88, 95, 125, 148-149, 255
Mahomo, Nana 122, 197, 242-243
Mail & Guardian 387, 408
Makaud, Alice 394
Makhele, Joyce 395
Makwetu, Clarence 386
Malan, D.F. 22, 52
Malema, Julius 409
Mandela, Nelson 15, 23, 85, 158, 175-176, 212, 239, 270, 354-355, 384, 390, 392, 400, 402, 405
Manong, Gabriel 395-396
Marquard, Nell 197, 252, 269, 298
Marshall, Margaret 250
Mashatile, Paul 404
Mathe, Veronica Zodwa 33, 50, 55 (*see* also Sobukwe, Veronica)
Mathiane, Nomavenda 386
Matolengwe, Patrick 362, 365-366, 372, 374-375
Matthews, Anthony 185
Matthews, Frieda 39
Matthews, Joe 29
Matthews, Z.K. 25, 28-29, 39, 44, 46, 56, 209
Maud, John 322
Maxwell Institut of Utrecht 299
Mayakovsky, Vladimir 288
Mbeki, Thabo 408
McDonald, Steve 327
McKay, Vernon 234
M'Cwabeni, W.S. 44, 49-50, 54, 56
Mda, A.P. 23, 28, 30-31, 45-46, 50, 66, 120
Mdunga, Solomon 151-152
Medical Foundation for the Care and Treatment of Victims of Torture 302
Medical University of South Africa 387
Methodist Church 270-271
Mgomezulu, Sipho 172
Mgxashe, Mxolisi 119, 192
Mhlaba, Raymond 386
Middle East War (1967) 274-276
Minority Rights Group 353
Mitchell, Mike 178-179, 283-284
Mlambo, Johnson 214, 393
Mlonzi, Lennox 120, 129, 136, 172, 349, 377
Moabi, Joe 165-166, 171
Modder B Prison 155-156
Moeng, Mary 244
Mofolo 57
Mogoba, Mmutlanyane Stanley 386-388, 390
Mokgoro, Yvonne 395-397
Mokhehle, Ntsu 29, 33
Mokitimi, Seth 10, 30
Mokoape, Aubrey 156, 163, 169
Mokoena, Matthew 191
Mokonyane, Nomvula 409
Molete, Z.B. 62, 102 119, 140, 142, 168-169, 183
Moolman, Jan 404-405
Molotsi, Peter 88, 368
Moroka, James 46
Moshoeshoe I 275
Mosley, Oswald 101

Mothopeng, Zephaniah 67, 84, 86, 102, 106, 140, 175, 332, 349, 369, 385
Motjuwadi, Stanley 137
Motlana, Nthato 27, 29, 32, 53-54, 85, 370
Motlana, Sally 370
Movement for Colonial Freedom 260
Mozambique 335
Mpethi, Alton 388
Mphahlele, Letlapa 388
Mqhayi, S.E.K. 230
Mugabe, Robert 15
Musi, Obed 156
Msamane, G.I. 56

Naidoo, Shantavothie 343-344
Namibia 254, 258
Nation, The 375
National Action Council 158
National Association for the Advancement of Coloured People 211
National Heroes' Day 108-109
National Party 21, 27, 71
'outward policy' 284
National Union of South African Students (NUSAS) 250
Natives' Representative Council (NRC) 19-20, 24-25, 29
Native Trust Fund 16
Naudé, Beyers 405
Ndungane, Njongonkulu 400-401, 404, 407
New African, The 192
New Age 96
New Partnership for Africa's Development (NEPAD) 392
New York Times, The 337
Ngcobo, A.B. 102, 176, 186, 374
Ngendane, Selby 87, 89, 136-137, 171
Ngubane, Jordan 23, 125
Nigeria 115, 252
Njisane, M. 377
Nkoana, Matthew 40, 167
Nkrumah, Kwame 78, 91, 112, 149, 213, 218
Noble, Hamish 13, 40, 42-43
Nobrega, Joe 361, 363-367
Nobrega, Nita 361, 363-367
Nodada, Butana Eleazor 49
Nokwe, Duma 83
Nossiter, Bernard D. 339
Ntloko, Cecil 18-21, 39
Nursing Council 77
Nyanga 138, 144, 180
Nyaose, Jacob Dumdum 95-96, 102, 111, 136, 175
Nziba, Rosett 29, 136
Nzimande, H.Z.M. 309, 339, 395

Observer, The 214, 223, 241
Ogilvie Thomson, Julian 322-323
'One settler, one bullet' slogan of PAC 386-387
Oppenheimer, Harry 313, 323, 326
Oxford University Press 59

Paarl 180
Padmore, George 252
Pakistan 77-78
Pan-Africanist Congress (PAC) 94-96, 212, 276, 349
   Afrikaner attitudes to 107-108
   attitude to coloureds 106-107
   banned 146
   Bill introduced to ban 142
   claims concerning Sobukwe's death 368-369
   conference, December 1959 112-113
   in exile 161, 385
   formed 94-96
   membership figures in 1960 120-121
   and multi-racialism 204-205
   Orlando meeting (31 May 1959) 106-107
   and Poqo 180-185
   Security Police action against 108, 393
   status campaign 109
   unbanning of 384
propaganda at ceremony on Robben Island, 2009 403
Parker, Aida 222-223
pass laws 2, 78, 81, 286, 407
   ANC campaign against 113-114
   PAC campaign against 113-114, 118-147
   suspension of 140
Paton, Alan 251, 381, 405
Peddie 179
Pelser, P.C. 255, 259-261, 264, 266, 272, 281-283, 298, 300, 313, 343
'People of Africa Pledge Courtesy' campaign 109
Peres, Shimon 294-295
Pheko, Motsoko 388
Pitje, Godfrey 28-29, 33, 43, 45, 50, 377, 391
Pitout, Hendrik Cornelius Jacobus 5
Pitts, Stanley 9, 14
Pityana, Barney 399
Pokela, John 257, 368-369
Population Registration 78-80
Poqo 159, 180-184, 257, 349, 386
Port Elizabeth 118, 142, 179
Portugal 335
Poverty Datum Level 75
Pratt, David 146
Pretoria Central Prison 164
Prevention of Violence Abroad Proclamation 219
Prisons Trial 297-299, 308, 320
Programme of Action 46-47, 52-53, 59, 61, 84, 412
Progressive Federal Party 82, 362
Progressive Party 81-82, 115, 210
Purves, Jack 346, 367

Rabinowitz, Bennie 221
Raboroko, Peter 67, 97
race classification 285
   boards 78-80
Rademeyer, C.I. 123, 139
Ramaphosa, Cyril 413
Rand Daily Mail 67-71, 97, 101, 108, 115, 130,
132-133, 195, 197, 218, 221-222, 226, 241, 292-293, 297, 310, 346-347, 353-354, 370, 381, 395
Reader's Digest 195-196, 291
Reality 350, 377, 381
Rees, John 397-398
Reeves, Ambrose 104, 114, 136
Reilly, Gerald 366
religion
   Sobukwe's attitude to 291-293
   see also churches
Resha, Robert 23, 96-97
Rhodes, Cecil John 306
Rhodesia 258
Rhodes University 90
Ribeiro, Fabian 268
Ribeiro, Florence 268
Robb, Noel 202, 243
Robben Island 186 *et seq.*
Robert Mangaliso Sobukwe Trust 390
Robespierre, Maximilien de 295
Robinson, John 273-274
Rogers, Howard 20
Roosevelt University 343
Rotberg, Robert I. 323
Roux, Edward 20

Sacks, Harold 132
St Jorre, John 346
Sandburg, Carl 267
Sassoon, Anne 320-321
Sassoon, Hazel 357
Sauer, Paul 157
Schlapobersky, John 302
Schwarz-Bart, André 295
Sekhukhuneland 73, 179
Selope Thema, R.V. 25
Senghjor, Leopold 233
Shakespeare, William 62
Sharpeville massacre 132-137, 157, 384, 410
Sheridan, Richard 295
Sikhululekile ferry 404
Sisulu, Walter 23, 46, 405
Sisulu, Zwelakhe 375
Siwisa, Denis 10, 12, 17, 20, 28, 44, 392
Slovo, Joe 154-155, 169, 391
Smuts, Jan 22
Snow, C.P. 232, 294-295
Snyman, Lammie 391
Sobukwe, Angelina 6-8, 351
Sobukwe, Charles 6-7
Sobukwe, Dalindyebo 58, 370, 390, 402, 405
Sobukwe, Dedanizizwe 58, 390, 402, 405
Sobukwe, Dinilesizwe 325-326, 370, 376-377, 390, 395, 402-403, 405-407
Sobukwe, Ernest 6-8, 11, 39, 190, 272, 321, 374
Sobukwe, Herbert 6-8, 55
Sobukwe, Miliswa 58, 244, 248, 325-326, 370, 390, 402-403, 405-407
Sobukwe, Robert Mangaliso
   birth 5-6, 389

childhood 6-8
primary education 8
tribal initiation 8-9
at Healdtown school 9-14
contracts TB 13
at South African Native College, Fort Hare 14-44
and Fort Hare Congress Youth League 29
becomes President of Student's Representative Council at Fort Hare 32
speech at Completers Social, Fort Hare 33-39
teaching at Jandrell Secondary School, Standerton 47-50
and ANC Defiance Campaign 53-54
marriage 55
teaching at University of the Witwatersrand 55-66
and ANC Freedom Charter 59-61, 65
and Transvaal conference 85-86
offered post at Rhodes University 89-90
at first Africanist conference 91-96
attacks white liberals 103-104
speech to PAC on coloureds 106-107
and anti-pass law campaign 110, 113, 118-137
at PAC conference, December 1959 112-113
arrest 136-137
attacks ANC 141
imprisoned in The Fort 148, 163-164
resigns from University of the Witwatersrand 149
trial 150-154
in Pretoria Central Prison 164-166
in Stoneyard prison 167-170
in Cinderella prison 170
in Stofberg prison 170-172
in Witbank prison 172-173
testifies at trial of PAC members 173
in Pretoria local prison 173
and Poqo 183
on Robben Island 186 *et seq.*
registers for Bachelor of Economics degree with University of London 195
applies to emigrate 199-200
sits first University of London exams 219-220
in hospital 238-239
discussions on religion 269-274
views on Middle East War 274-276
writing activities on Robben Island 277-278
further detention confirmed 281
sits final University of London exams 287
obtains Bachelor of Economics degree 288
applies to take MA in English at London University 288
release from Robben Island 300-304, 308, 402
at Kimberley 305-306
begins law studies 339-341
qualifies as attorney 341
practicing as attorney 395-397
  application to leave South Africa refused 342-343
meeting with Buthelezi in John Orr's department store 345-347
attends mother's funeral 351, 397
meeting with Biko 351
illness and hospital treatment 352-366
returns to Kimberley following operation 366-367
final illness 367-368
death 368, 384
funeral 369-377, 393-394
memorial unveiled 392-393
posthumous Doctor of Laws *honoris cause* from Wits 392
remembered in Robert Sobukwe Wing, Graaff-Reinet library 401
Sobukwe, Veronica (née Mathe) 174-175, 178, 190, 193, 196, 211, 215, 220, 236, 239-243, 248, 256, 259, 261, 266, 272, 279-280, 296, 299, 301, 362-363, 365-366, 369, 372, 389, 393-6, 400
(*see also* Mathe, Veronica Zodwa)
'Sobukwe Clause' 184, 186, 210, 237, 259, 261
solitary confinement 302-303
Sono, Themba 410
Soper, Lord 260
Sophiatown 72-73
South African Bureau for Racial Affairs (Sabra) 80, 107-108
South African Coloured People's Organisation (SACPO) 53, 59-61
South African Congress of Trade Unions (Sactu) 111
South African Council of Churches 221, 319, 397-398
South African Indian Congress (SAIC) 24, 53, 59-61, 99
South African Institute of Race Relations 114, 221, 228, 257, 352, 386
South African Native College, Fort Hare 14-15, 17-21, 27, 33-34, 389, 399
South African Students' Association (SASO) 349-350, 399
South West Africa 78
Soviet Union (U.S.S.R.) 384
Soweto 56-57, 72, 384
Soweto student uprising 384
Sparks, Allister 370
Spear of the Nation (*Umkhonto weSizwe*) 159, 179, 212, 384
Spectator, The 185
Spector, J. Brooks 411
Stampa, Galaza 20, 28
Standerton 47-49
Star, The 98, 134-135, 160, 283, 319
State of Emergency
  detentions under, in 1960 154-155
  lifted 157
Stellenbosch, University of 238
Steyn, J.J. de Wet 131
Steve Biko Foundation 399
Stofberg prison 170-173

Storey, Peter 397
Stott, Eulalie 196, 202, 242-243, 268, 281, 289, 322, 375
Strachan, Harold 225-226, 241
Strijdom, J.G. 80
Struggles Within the Struggle 385
Stuart, Kelsey 297, 310
Stubbs, Aelred 398-399
Sunday Express 223
Sunday Independent 408
Sunday Times 223, 291, 297
Sunday Tribune 222
Susan Kruger 402-403
Suzman, Helen 210-211, 237-238, 261-262, 282, 308, 313, 372, 373, 381
Swapo (South West Africa People's Organisation) 258
Swartz, Derrick 399
Swaziland 207, 391

Tambo, Oliver 15, 23, 85-87, 142, 405
Tanzania 347
Taylor, Charlotte 221, 243-244, 298
Taylor, Thomas 243
Tembuland 73
Terblanche, Ignatius 143-144
Thamm, Marianne 403-404
Thomson, Diana 324-325
Thomson, Jim 324-325
Times, The 335
torture 159, 259, 302
Toure, Sekou 91, 112
Trade Union Council of South Africa (Tucsa) 111
trade unions 73-74, 96, 110-111
Transkei 43, 179-180, 285
Treurnicht, Andries 350
trials
 after disturbance of March 1960 156-157
 of ANC members in 1967 257-258
 of Poqo members in 1967 257
 Prisons Trial 244-246, 297-299, 308, 320
 of Sobukwe in 1960 150-154
Tribune 178
Tsafendas, Demetrio 254
Tsele, Peter 29, 65
Tshabalala, Raphael 102
Tshaka, Present N. 43
Tucker, Raymond 317, 340, 344, 398
Tutu, Desmond 368, 373, 376, 398, 405
Tyler, Humphrey 132-133
Tystad, Jan 338

Umkhonto weSizwe (Spear of the Nation) 159, 179, 212, 384
Unesco 402
Union Exposition 146
United Democratic Front 384
United Nations 77-78, 160
 Development Fund (Unicef) 387
 Special Committee on Apartheid 393

United Party 81, 185, 211, 218, 237, 260, 283, 298
United States of America 78, 231
United States Information Service (USIS) 118
Unterhalter, Jack 173, 341, 342

Vaderland, Die 135
Van den Bergh, Hendrik 197-198, 333
Vanderbijlpark 132
Van der Byl, P. 230
Van Rensburg, Patrick 104
Van Schalkwyk, G. 224
Van Wyk, Fred 216
Vereeniging 132
Verster, L.B. 201-202
Verwoerd, Hendrik 73, 80, 108, 116, 135, 146, 157-158, 228
 assassination of 254
Victoria Hospital, Alice
 nurses strike at 32-33
Vietnam War 231, 253-254
Vigne, Randolph 138, 145, 341, 347, 369
Visser, J.G. 201-202
Volksblad, Die 97
Vorster, John 179, 181, 186, 196-197, 210, 218-219, 221-222, 237-241, 255, 260, 266, 293, 332-333
Wachman, Marvin 242, 343
Wallace, Irving 297
Walston, Lord 293
Walters, Tom 225
Warmbaths 179
Washington Post 339
Webber, Reg 177, 197, 269
Wellington, Professor 196
Wentzel, Ernie 33, 197, 213, 215, 260, 269, 301-302
Wentzel, Jill 197, 269
Wessels, C.A. 199
Western Cape, University of 410
West African Pilot 21, 252
Whyte, Quintin 221
Wilson, Harold 186, 216-217
Wilson, Monica 39
Wisconsin, University of 343
Witbank prison 172-173
Witwatersrand, University of 55, 149, 288, 299, 390-391
World Council of Churches 160, 221
World Federation of Trade Unions 111
Wynberg, David 312

Xuma, A.B. 22-26, 46, 53

Young, Andrew 325-327, 371
Yu Chi Chan Club 212-213
Yutar, Percy 224-225, 262

Zackon, Barney 215-216, 221
Zuma, Jacob 407, 412
Zwelonke, D.M. 192

www.ingramcontent.com/pod-product-compliance
Lightning Source LLC
Chambersburg PA
CBHW070833160426
43192CB00012B/2186